Immortal Remains

The Evidence for Life after Death

STEPHEN E. BRAUDE

ROWMAN & LITTLEFIELD PUBLISHERS, INC.
Lanham • Boulder • New York • Oxford

ROWMAN & LITTLEFIELD PUBLISHERS, INC.

Published in the United States of America
by Rowman & Littlefield Publishers, Inc.
A Member of the Rowman & Littlefield Publishing Group
4720 Boston Way, Lanham, Maryland 20706
www.rowmanlittlefield.com

PO Box 317
Oxford
OX2 9RU, UK

British Library Cataloguing in Publication Information Available

Library of Congress Cataloging-in-Publication Data

Braude, Stephen E., 1945–
    Immortal remains: the evidence for life after death / Stephen E. Braude.
        p. cm.
    Includes bibliographical references and index.
    ISBN 0-7425-1471-4 (alk. paper) – ISBN 0-7425-1472-2 (pbk: alk. paper)
    1.   Future life. 2. Spiritualism. I. Title.

    BF1311.F8 73 2003
    133.9'01'3—dc21   2002036944

Printed in the United States of America

♾™ The paper used in this publication meets the minimum requirements of American
National Standard for Information Sciences—Permanence of Paper for Printed Library
Materials, ANSI/NISO Z39.48-1992.

Immortal Remains

For Djurdjina

Contents

Preface

My initiation into the world of psychic phenomena occurred in graduate school, during an impromptu séance with two friends in my home. I'd never dabbled in anything psychic before. In fact, I'd never given psychic phenomena much thought.[1] And in those days I fancied myself to be a hard-nosed materialist, although (I have to admit) I hadn't thought that through very carefully either. Materialism—in fact, reductionistic materialism—was merely one of several intellectual conceits I was cultivating at the time. At any rate, in my arrogant ignorance I believed that psychic phenomena made no sense and shouldn't occur. But it was a typically slow day in Northampton, Massachusetts; my friends and I had seen the only movie in town; and so my friends suggested trying a game they called "table up." What they meant was: let's have a séance. They said they'd played this game a few times before, and they assured me that when it worked it was loads of fun. Now I won't mince words. What happened that afternoon scared the hell out of me. For three hours I observed my own table tilt up and down, without visible assistance.

That was enough to rattle my complacency. But it wasn't all that happened. By means of a cumbersome code adopted by my friends,[2] the table spelled out messages, ostensibly from three communicating entities. But only the last of those communicators provided any verifiable information. That entity said his name was Horace T. Jecum (our awkward code may have garbled the spelling), and he claimed to have built my slightly spooky eighteenth-century house. Unlike the assertions made by the previous two communicators (especially the one claiming to be the River Styx), this assertion seemed easy enough to confirm. I simply needed to locate the appropriate records at City Hall. Unfortunately, my house was so old that it antedated city records. So I never learned who built the house, much less whether the person's name was anything like that of Horace T. Jecum. I also recall trying unsuccessfully to discover whether someone with a name like Horace T. Jecum had lived in or near the area. But I'm certain that my additional inquiries (such as they were) were no more than perfunctory. I made no intensive effort to pursue the matter further and seriously challenge my philosophical complacency. I ended my inquiry at that point.

But despite my resistance and lingering skepticism, I was convinced that the observed table movements were genuine. And that conviction hasn't wavered. However, I also know there's no way to describe the occasion so as to allay all skeptical concerns. I can only note the following. First, the phenomena occurred in daylight, with ample opportunity to examine them closely as they occurred. Second, I was strongly motivated to discover that the table movements resulted from a hoax. I would have been much more comfortable believing my friends were having some fun at my expense. Third, the phenomena occurred in my home and with my table. The table wasn't somebody's prop, and my friends had no opportunity to plant and conceal an apparatus capable of producing the phenomena. Also, I'm convinced for several other reasons that my friends weren't pulling a trick on me. I knew them well, and I knew that practical jokes weren't their style. I'm certain that only our fingers touched the top of the table and that they rested lightly on the table's surface. Moreover, if one of my friends left the table to go to another room, the table continued its movements, and it moved in directions opposed to whatever pressure the remaining two sitters applied to the tabletop. The table rose *under* our fingers, all fingers were visible atop the table, and I could see clearly that the table made no contact with our legs or knees. In fact, sometimes we rose and stood next to the table, keeping our fingers in contact with the tabletop, and still the table moved up and down under our fingers. I should also add (and I suppose this is important) that we weren't stoned.

My introduction to "table up" turned out to be a pivotal experience in my life, although I had enough sense to put it aside until I completed my Ph.D., landed a teaching job, did some respectable mainstream philosophy, and earned tenure. (I may be crazy, but I'm not stupid.) I made no effort for at least seven years to think about the event or to learn any more about parapsychology. I remained an ignoramus about psychic stuff, and I really put my impressive experience "out of mind." So I had no idea how closely my experience resembled what many had reported and documented carefully during the previous century. And I was unaware how clearly it illustrated classic problems concerning evidence for postmortem survival.

I've since tried to reconstruct why this incident frightened me, and I don't believe it's because the phenomena seemed, at least on the surface, to indicate postmortem influence. Rather, I think it's because I realized, however dimly, that one or more of us seated around the table might have caused the table to move, but not by any normal means. Why, exactly, that should be so scary is itself a complex story, and I've dealt with it elsewhere (see, e.g., Braude, 1987, 1997). What matters here is the curious link between one of the ostensible communicators and one of my two friends. That friend was another philosophy graduate student (the other was his wife), and one of his interests was classical mythology. Although I knew vaguely that the River Styx figured somehow or other in Greek mythology, that was all I knew. But the mythical river, I now realize, was probably far more familiar to my friend, and quite possibly something that would have been particularly meaningful to him in the context of a séance. I now know that the River Styx was a kind of moat of the underworld. It prevented the living from entering and the dead from leaving, and Charon would ferry souls across the river into Hades. I lost touch with my friend many years ago, and I have no idea where he is now. So I can't confirm whether he drew any connections at the time between this classical conception of the River Styx and the activity of communicating with the dead. But this is just the sort of connection that I now find very interesting, and for which we need to be alert when evaluating evidence suggesting survival.

Let me lay my cards on the table. For much of the survival evidence, it's not clear what to say. It's not clear to what extent it can be explained away in terms of normal or abnormal processes, or even in terms of paranormal processes among the living. And some of the evidence scarcely makes sense even if we accept postmortem survival. These are matters I'll examine at length in the course of the book. But overall, I'd say that the evidence most strongly supports the view that some aspects of our personality and personal consciousness, some significant chunk of our distinctive psychology, can survive the death of our bodies, at least for a time.

I've written this book to document why it's so difficult to reach that conclusion, and why it's especially difficult to rule out counter-explanations in terms of psychic or at least highly unusual capacities of the living. What we need to examine, and what I believe others have considered only very superficially, is why we're *ever* entitled to rule out such things as my friend unconsciously (and perhaps psychically) simulating evidence for survival, perhaps by drawing on associations that were particularly meaningful to him.

I've found writing this book to be both a luxury and a duty. It's a duty because this research is the next obvious step in an intellectual odyssey that began more than twenty-five years ago, when I became tenured and took my first serious look at the evidence in parapsychology. As I noted once before (and far more truculently—Braude, 1997), I realized that I needed to examine that evidence carefully, or else my avowed philosophical commitment to the truth was a sham. That was three books and many articles ago, and I'm at last able to deal with issues for which (I hope) those earlier works have prepared me.

But why is writing this book also a luxury? The older I become, and the older my friends and acquaintances become, the more people try to reassure me about the benefits of aging. Of course, I'd like to believe them, and I'm still hoping to find that I've grown wiser with age. In the meantime, though, I suppose I'm just lingering here in the vestibule of enlightenment. Nevertheless, I'm able to take comfort in a more modest privilege, one that comes with my job, and also with my grudging membership in the ranks of the chronologically challenged. I find I can spend many hours wondering about death and the possibility of postmortem existence without appearing to suffer from a morbid preoccupation.

Actually, I've wanted to tackle this particular topic for some time. But I knew I had to deal first with some substantial preliminaries, and I felt that writing the book any sooner would have been presumptuous and premature. First, I needed to acquaint myself thoroughly with both the experimental and nonexperimental evidence for psychic capacities of the living. Only then would I be able to evaluate properly the hypothesis that apparent evidence for survival is actually evidence for psychic functioning among the living. Moreover, for reasons noted in chapter 1, I've found most of the literature on personal survival either conceptually naive or empirically myopic. I knew I couldn't conscientiously write a book on survival without a comprehensive grounding in the literature on dissociation. Similarly, I knew I needed to survey the scattered, diverse, and frustratingly incomplete studies of savants, prodigies, and exceptional human abilities.

In the following chapters we'll study several different types of evidence for survival. But most of the cases I discuss fall into two classes. The first is mediumship (or channeling), in which individuals apparently act as intermediaries between this world and a world of discarnate or surviving entities. The second is reincarnation and possession, in which a person seems to be (or seems to reimbody, or be overtaken by) a formerly living person. These two sets of cases, likewise, assume different forms, some of which raise interesting and distinctive clusters of issues. I'll also examine out-of-body and near-death experiences, ostensible hauntings, and transplant cases, some of which are perhaps more important than others, but all of which are fascinating. As we proceed, it should be clear why I focus primarily on mediumship and reincarnation/possession. But in a nutshell it's because the best of these cases are especially impressive and particularly difficult to explain away.

The outline of the book is as follows. Chapter 1 sets the stage conceptually for the rest of the book. In addition to making several crucial distinctions, it situates this work within the larger literature on postmortem survival. Although (like many other authors) I survey some of the best evidence suggesting survival, my primary goal is to remedy what I see as serious and pervasive shortcomings in previous works on the subject. So in this introductory chapter I explain what those shortcomings are, clarify some of my working presuppositions, and thereby indicate the novel perspective of this book.

Chapters 2 and 3 consider issues in connection with mediumship.

Chapter 2 introduces the reader to the general features of mediumship and then examines a particular type of case called "drop-in" mediumship, in which deceased communicators appear uninvited and usually unwanted. At their best, these cases pose interesting explanatory challenges and seem to make sense psychologically only from the communicator's point of view. Chapter 3 surveys the spectacular mediumistic careers of Mrs. Piper and Mrs. Leonard. Because both women were remarkably successful, for long periods, in providing evidence suggesting postmortem survival, these cases seem particularly difficult to explain away along non-survivalist lines. This chapter examines the relevant theoretical issues in detail. It turns out (probably not surprisingly) that those issues are more complex than most have appreciated. I conclude this chapter with remarks on a collection of mediumistic communications called the "cross correspondences."

Chapter 4 considers another complex set of issues, this time in connection with a case of apparent reincarnation. Many believe that ostensible xenoglossy (speaking an unlearned language) provides unusually compelling evidence for survival. That view may be correct, at least in principle. But once again it turns out that most who adopt it are guilty of several confusions and a failure to consider relevant issues and bodies of evidence (concerning, for example, the nature and limits of human abilities, and also second-language acquisition). Moreover, the case in question raises another important set of issues, about the role of psychopathology in cases suggesting survival. In fact, previous studies of the case exemplify one of my recurring complaints throughout the book: how most writing on survival is inexcusably superficial psychologically.

Chapter 5 considers one of the most puzzling and interesting cases in the history of psychical research, the case of Patience Worth. On the surface it looks like a case of mediumship, but it provides no verifiable evidence for anyone's former existence. What makes it remarkable is the mind-bogglingly creative, and apparently unprecedented, literary, linguistic, and improvisational fluency demonstrated by the medium. So this case is important for what it suggests about latent human creative capacities, an issue I pursue also in connection with several somewhat less impressive cases.

Chapters 6 and 7 survey specific bodies of evidence and consider whether they can be explained away along even exotic non-survivalist lines. Chapter 6 considers several interesting and impressive reincarnation and possession cases, and chapter 7 examines haunting cases and also recent cases emerging from heart-lung transplantation. These various bodies of evidence are not all equally compelling, but the reincarnation and possession cases seem especially difficult to explain away, and for reasons I discuss, we should perhaps interpret the transplant cases as a subset of possession cases.

Chapter 8 considers two related bodies of evidence, out-of-body experiences and near-death experiences, which many incorrectly take to be strongly suggestive of survival. So this chapter inspects a smattering of cases and looks closely and critically at the reasoning and questionable assumptions underlying that point of view.

Chapter 9 sums things up and offers my admittedly tentative assessment of the evidence for survival. It looks first at what would constitute ideal cases suggesting survival, to remind us how evidence could, in principle, point compellingly to survival, even in the face of ingrained philosophical prejudices to the contrary. Then it considers how survivalists might account for physiological data that many find incompatible with a belief in survival. Finally, after deflecting some remaining skeptical concerns, and after brief remarks about the "stuff" that might survive, I offer my reasons for concluding that the evidence, when viewed as a whole, provides more reason for believing in some form of personal postmortem survival than for believing in any alternative view.

Of course, it's philosophically momentous to conclude that there's satisfactory evidence for some sort of postmortem survival. That inference, if sound, poses clear-cut challenges to much of received science and to a common (if not the prevailing) materialist worldview. But apart from a few provocative suggestions here and there, I'll make no effort to meet those challenges in this work. Tracing the ontological implications of survival cases is another, and quite different, project. And it's a task that shouldn't be undertaken until we work through the issues addressed in this book and determine whether the ontological project is anything more than a philosophical exercise. My aim, here, is to examine carefully the best types of evidence for survival, and to see how successfully they resist explanation in terms of unusual (and possibly paranormal) capacities of the living. Others have attempted to engage this side of the debate over survival, but for reasons I explore in the following chapters, those efforts have been unsatisfactory. As I hope this book makes clear, the issues are more far-reaching, complex, and subtle, and I believe more interesting, than most commentators have realized.

In fact, that's one big reason why I'm not offering a comprehensive survey of the evidence for survival. Others have done that nicely, and I'll provide references throughout this book to bodies of material I can't take time to discuss. I prefer to focus on some big, unjustifiably ignored issues, and to do that I'm forced to pick and choose from a very large body of cases. In fact, I've had to omit discussion of certain *kinds* of evidence which some may consider important. These include, for example, so-called *electronic voice phenomena* (EVP) and combination-lock tests. The former concern ostensible manifestations of survival heard in electronic noise, and frankly, I regard these as little more than a type of Rorschach test. The latter, which to my knowledge have yet to succeed, concern efforts to obtain the keys to locks which only the deceased supposedly know. At any rate, I apologize to those readers who'd like to see more or different cases discussed. But *for this project* I felt something else was needed: namely, to present at least some important cases in relevant detail and demonstrate the sorts of considerations that can then be applied to additional cases.

My case selection was guided by my primary objective in this book: to determine whether there's any reason for preferring a survivalist explanation of the evidence over explanations positing exotic (including paranormal) activities among the living. That guiding objective has also influenced my decision to present many of my cases in what some might consider excessive detail. For example, I know that some readers would prefer a more cursory survey of a larger number of cases. But once we decide (as I think we must) that there are plenty of good cases to consider—cases that can't easily be explained away in terms of what I call The Usual Suspects (see chapter 1), it becomes increasingly important to focus on minutiae. We need to examine good cases *very* carefully to decide whether the survival hypothesis succeeds where its rivals fail. Moreover, I know that some readers would simply prefer less detail and maybe also fewer cases. But you can't please everybody. So my advice to readers is this: If you feel overwhelmed by the case details, I suggest you skip or skim over them. You might later agree with me that the details really do matter and that the issues I address about them are crucial.

A few words about terminology before diving headlong into our inquiry. In speaking about psychic abilities or psychic functioning (not necessarily the same thing; see Braude, 2002), I'll frequently use the now-familiar term "psi" as a replacement for the adjective "psychic." I'll also follow standard practice in using it sometimes as a noun, in which case "psi" is roughly synonymous with the phrases "psychic phenomena," "psychic functioning," and "psychic abilities." I'm not sure the term "psi" offers any theoretical benefits (see Braude, 2002, for a discussion of that issue), but it definitely saves a few syllables.

I'll also use the familiar abbreviation "PK" for "psychokinesis" (roughly, "mind over matter"—see Braude, 1997, for a more thorough analysis). And I'll rely on the traditional distinction between two forms of ESP: *telepathy* and *clairvoyance*. To oversimplify considerably, "telepathy" picks out the direct causal influence of one mind on another, whereas "clairvoyance" picks out the direct influence of a remote physical state of affairs on a mind. So an example of telepathy would be one person's thought about fire directly causing another person to think about fire. An example of clairvoyance would be a house on fire causing a sensorily remote individual to think about fire (see Braude, 2002, for a detailed discussion of these concepts).

Finally, many people have aided me as I've worked through the issues in this book. For helpful comments on earlier versions of various chapters, I'd like to thank Carlos Alvarado, Mary Rose Barrington, Richard Broughton, Frank Dilley, James Hall, Peter Mulacz, John Palmer,

Joyanna Silberg, Donald West, and my colleague Steven Yalowitz. Thanks, too, to Robert Almeder, for many long and stimulating discussions of the issues, to Richard Gale for invaluable suggestions on both style and content, and to Joanne D. S. McMahon and Carolyn Steinberg for their help in obtaining some of my research materials. I'm especially grateful to Lisa Roulston, whose resourcefulness and ingenuity were put to good use as my research assistant, and most of all to Alan Gauld, from whose insightful criticisms, suggestions, and breathtaking command of the literature I've learned more than I know how to express. I'm also indebted to the Bial Foundation in Porto, Portugal, whose generous research grant provided me with free time to work on this project.

Parts of this book have appeared, in one form or another, in previous publications. Material from Braude, 1996 is scattered through chapter 1; some of the material in chapter 2 appeared in Braude, 2001b; an ancestor of parts of chapter 4 is my paper Braude, 1993; much of chapter 5 appeared as Braude, 2000; and a version of chapter 8 was published as Braude, 2001a. My thanks to the editors of these various books and journals for the permission to use that material here.

Researching and writing this book has taken nearly a decade, and I'm afraid I may have neglected to thank people who've helped me along the way. If so, I apologize; perhaps those folks can take comfort in the thought of retribution, certainly in this life, possibly in the next.

NOTES

1. In fact, while pursuing my undergraduate studies in London, I lived very near the Society for Psychical Research in Kensington, and I would pass its headquarters at 1 Adam & Eve Mews (yes, that's right) every day on the way to the Underground. But I didn't even know the SPR was there. I'm not even sure I knew the society existed. Of course, in the clarity of hindsight, I now regard this as just one of many life opportunities missed.

2. My friends suggested having the table tilt once for "A," twice for "B," and so on. No wonder we had only three communicators in three hours. Had we known more about the history of table tilting, we could have adopted the more customary spiritualist procedure of asking "yes/no" questions and having the table tilt (say) once for "yes" and twice for "no."

Chapter 1
Preliminaries

I have gazed into the Abyss, and
the Abyss has gazed into me, and
neither of us liked what we saw.
—Brother Theodore

1. Introduction

Many people wonder whether they will somehow survive the death and dissolution of their bodies, and the scenario that interests them is a very personal one, engaging their deepest hopes and interests. It's not the future scenario promised by some Eastern religions, in which we lose our individuality and merge with the infinite, or being-in-general (a grand soup of consciousness). No doubt that would count as a kind of *life after death*, but it wouldn't be personally interesting, and it's certainly not the *survival of death* that has intrigued humankind for centuries and which many either anticipate or desire. Unlike merging with the infinite, personal postmortem survival would be a condition that *preserves* (rather than obliterates) who we are—or at least something we consider essential to who we are (many say it's our mind or soul).

So when people look for *evidence* of survival, they turn to cases of apparent mediumship (or "channeling"), or cases of apparent reincarnation, or familiar ghost stories. They look for evidence that someone's distinctive personality continues to manifest, even though that person's body may no longer exist. Clearly, then, people who wonder about surviving bodily death have something specific in mind. They wonder whether they will continue to exist after death as a future *individual*, the same individual as their present self—though perhaps without a physical body. Usually, they hope that this future individual will have a fairly rich palette of experiences, thoughts, and feelings, and that it will retain at least some of their memories and personality traits. In fact, many hope that, after they die, they will retain their idiosyncratic preferences, attachments, antipathies, concerns, and interests. They wonder whether *they* will be able to continue communicating with loved ones on earth,

1

consoling them if necessary, guiding or at least monitoring their lives, sharing memories, and (for the more vindictive among them) tormenting their former earthly enemies. And, of course, many wonder whether they will be able to reunite with those who died before them.

But although many wonder (and have strong opinions) about postmortem existence, few appreciate how difficult it is to determine whether a belief in personal survival is justified. They don't realize that many complex issues need to be confronted first. In fact, even so-called "experts" underestimate the complexity of the issues.

The systematic study of survival began with the founding of the Society for Psychical Research (SPR) in 1882, and two questions have dominated its proceedings ever since. The first is: "Do human beings have psychic (psi) abilities (ESP or PK)?" The second is: "Does human consciousness survive bodily death?" In my opinion, we can confidently answer "yes" to the first question.[1] What remains unclear is how pervasive, extensive, and refined psychic abilities might be. That's not to say that answering the first question was easy. In fact, researchers faced imposing and interesting problems concerning the nature and reliability of human testimony, and subtle and technical puzzles about randomness and probability. They've also had to confront a recalcitrant and incredibly annoying problem: namely, that if psychic abilities exist, then by their very nature they could elude all conventional experimental controls. But no matter how troublesome those matters have been, even greater obstacles stand in the way of answering the question about survival, and they are the subject of this book. In fact, if we decide that psychic abilities exist, then that greatly complicates our efforts to determine whether we survive death. We must then consider whether evidence suggesting postmortem survival is actually disguised psychic functioning among the living.

Of course, theorizing about survival began long before the founding of the SPR. Philosophers have been at it for more than two thousand years, and they (at least) have recognized that the study of survival can't be purely empirical. In fact, there's no such thing as a purely empirical inquiry. Even the most apparently straightforward or innocent empirical claims rest on underlying abstract presuppositions, both metaphysical and methodological. So to that (limited) extent, the study of survival resembles any scientific investigation. However, in at least one crucial respect, so-called survival research differs from other scientific inquiries. In most areas of science, fundamental philosophical assumptions form part of the working scientist's conceptual background. But in the case of survival research, abstract and deep philosophical issues often dominate the foreground.

2. Survival and Personal Identity

For example, some have argued that the very *concept* of postmortem survival is unintelligible. They claim, therefore, that we should reject the survival hypothesis *a priori*. Now I believe it's legitimate to argue *a priori* against ostensibly empirical claims. Nevertheless some arguments are bound to be more persuasive and profound than others. And in fact, some arguments against the possibility of survival have been disappointingly shallow.

For example, Antony Flew has claimed that the sentence "we all of us survive death" is contradictory, because (he says) the meaning of the term "survive" in this context is the same as when we classify victims of a shipwreck as having died or survived (Flew, 1976; 1987). But clearly, words can have multiple meanings, and those who say we survive death don't use the words "survive" and "death" in the sense noted by Flew (see Almeder's discussion in 1992, pp. 261–262). Equally disappointing is Flew's objection to what we might call the *conceivability argument*: roughly, that survival is possible because bodiless existence is conceivable.[2] Flew contends that no form of bodiless existence is conceivable, and specifically he argues that I can't imagine (i.e., form a mental image of) *my* witnessing my own funeral. But clearly, the inability to imagine something doesn't show that the thing is impossible. For that matter (and what Flew should have said instead), the ability to imagine something doesn't show that it's possible. There are many things I can't imagine (much less produce a mental image of), some of which are impossible (e.g., square circles) and others of which are not (38-million-sided polygons). Similarly, of the many things that seem easy to imagine, some are possible and others appear not to be (e.g., time travel, singing swords, cartoon characters existing offscreen).

Although Flew's skeptical arguments are relatively easy to rebut, they represent a more refractory and deeper concern about a cluster of related concepts—in particular, *identity* and *person*. The worry is that we simply can't use those concepts intelligibly when we talk about postmortem survival. For example, some wonder whether *anything deserving to be called "Stephen Braude"* could survive my bodily death. That's because they doubt that we can make sense of the claim that a postmortem individual is *the same as* some formerly living individual. And the customary basis for that worry is a certain metaphysical thesis: the claim that personhood and personal identity are intimately and essentially tied to our physical embodiment.

But that concern may be misplaced, or at least premature. Of course, in everyday life we often identify and reidentify people on the basis of characteristic (if evolving) physical features. But at other times, we decide who someone is on the basis of what they say and how they behave—more specifically, their memory claims and continuity of charac-

ter. Not surprisingly, philosophers dispute which approach to identifying persons (the physical or the psychological) is *metaphysically* fundamental, and that debate is complex and very interesting (readers wishing
to survey the issues should consult Corcoran, 2001b; Martin and
Barresi, 2003; Perry, 1975, 1978; Rorty, 1976). But the strictly philosophical concern about identity differs from our more familiar practical
concern. Metaphysicians are dealing with an *ontological* problem: they
want to know *what it is* for one individual to be the same as a previous
individual. By contrast, our familiar focus is on a more down-to-earth
epistemological problem: namely, *deciding* if an individual is the same as
someone else.[3] In daily life we *need* to decide whom we're dealing with,
and we simply work with whatever evidence we have at hand. And for
the most part, we do pretty well. In fact, most of us make these practical
decisions without the aid (or hindrance) of a reasoned or articulated
underlying metaphysics, much less proposed abstract criteria of identity.
And quite probably, any of several different metaphysical theories will
be compatible with our everyday, preanalytic criteria for identifying persons.

Like most of our concepts, our ordinary and usually unproblematic
concept of personal identity is loose and elastic. It relies on both physical and psychological continuity, and under optimal conditions we're
able to identify people on the basis of both sorts of continuity. However,
in many cases we have only one sort at our disposal. We might see
somebody but not observe any psychologically significant behavior, or
we might interact verbally with a person (say, via telephone or computer) but not see the person's body. So although we ordinarily conceive
of and identify persons on the basis of both physical and psychological
criteria, we weight those criteria differently in different cases.

Moreover, our ordinary concept of a person is largely *normative*
(what Locke called a "forensic" concept). When we use the term "person" in ordinary life, we're not picking out a *natural kind*—that is,
something whose nature scientific inquiry will decide (for example,
something that inevitably links persons to the biological species *homo
sapiens*). Ordinarily, we take persons to be (among other things) entities
who presumably have an inner life relevantly similar to our own, who
have various rights and perhaps obligations, and who deserve our
respect, consideration, etc. And we embrace the normativity of this conception of personhood irrespective of our views (if any) about how persons might (or must) be configured biologically or otherwise (e.g.,
whether dolphins, computers, or brains in a vat could be persons). So
our ordinary concept of a person fundamentally carries ethical obligations or imperatives along with it. It concerns things we value about
ourselves and each other, and it rests on various presuppositions about
the ways people should be treated. In fact, what we value most about
persons are their psychological traits. No doubt that's why we're often

content, in real-life situations, to make judgments about identity on the basis of psychological criteria alone. (I'll return to this point shortly.)

Now, philosophers often try to clarify our thinking about personal identity by considering puzzle cases—extreme versions of situations in which judging identity is a problem. Usually these are sci-fi thought experiments or other exotic scenarios concerning brain transplants and other types of fission or fusion (sometimes, we're asked to imagine that God, rather than a future scientist, splits or otherwise reconstructs us). Of course, postmortem survival cases seem to fall into this general category. They tease us with the apparent persistence of identity, not just in the absence of familiar sorts of bodily continuity, but sometimes in the absence of *any* bodily continuity.

Typically, we don't know what to say (at least initially) when confronted with puzzle cases, and so we must *decide* how to describe and interpret them. Although many believe that's a useful conceptual challenge, opinions divide over why it's useful, at least in connection with our ordinary ways of thinking about persons. The three leading positions on the matter seem to be as follows. (1) Some think these far-fetched scenarios test our intuitions concerning personhood and identity and thereby help us determine which of our customary (but shifting) criteria of personal identity matter most. (2) Others believe that consideration of puzzle cases helps with important conceptual housecleaning. They believe that our concept of personal identity (like many ordinary concepts) is confused and needs to be replaced with a more adequate instrument, arrived at after careful conceptual analysis and with the aid of puzzle cases (real or imagined). (3) Still others (more modest conceptual reformers) maintain that puzzle cases show how we can *extend* our ordinary concept of personal identity to cover exotic scenarios.

Arguably, many of the now-familiar hypothetical cases are conceptually incoherent. That would be the unfortunate state of affairs if (as I and others have argued) memories and other mental states can't literally be stored or encoded into bits of matter—for example, parts of brains. But even if those concerns were unfounded, puzzle cases may not be as useful to this inquiry as many believe. Actually, I'm willing to grant that they might help clarify our usual intuitions about persons. But it's doubtful that they are distinctively useful in that respect. After all, our ordinary concept of personal identity applies to ordinary cases, cases in which we take persons to be familiar, unitary, psychophysical entities. As a result, our intuitions seem to be tested just as well in the face of some *real-life* cases—most notably, multiple personality (or dissociative identity) disorder (MPD/DID)(Braude, 1995).

But what about the remaining two alleged virtues of puzzle cases? Perhaps they can lead to valuable conceptual reform, or perhaps they can help us extend our ordinary concepts in useful ways. However, that also seems doubtful. First, even if puzzle cases reveal limitations in our familiar concepts (or, for that matter, in our underlying metaphysical commitments), they needn't *undermine* our ordinary concept of personal identity. No matter what we ordinarily take personal identity to be, there's no reason to think that our usual standards or criteria must apply to every hypothetical case, or even to unusual real-life cases like MPD/DID. In fact, "some hypothetical cases of personal identity may not be decidable by any means at all, let alone by some 'criterion'" (Aune, 1985, p. 91). So even if puzzle cases strain the ordinary concept of personal identity, that needn't reveal a defect in the concept. Our ordinary concept may be just fine for ordinary cases.

In fact, puzzle cases—or at least postmortem cases—seem to require little (if any) conceptual shift or stretch. That's because even when we're unsure what to conclude about who survives, it's still clear what matters to us most about people, and (when push comes to shove) what concerns us most about their survival—either day-to-day or in an after-life. Anthony Quinton got this point right. He wrote,

> Why, after all, do we bother to identify people so carefully? What is unique about individual people that it is important enough for us to call them by individual proper names? In our general relations with other human beings their bodies are for the most part intrinsically unimportant. We use them as convenient recognition devices enabling us to locate without difficulty the persisting character and memory complexes in which we are interested, which we love or like. It would be upsetting if a complex with which we were emotionally involved came to have a monstrous or repulsive physical appearance, it would be socially embarrassing if it kept shifting from body to body while most such complexes stayed put, and it would be confusing and tiresome if such shifting around were generally widespread, for it would be a laborious business finding out where one's friends and family were. But that our concern and affection would follow the character and memory complex and not its original bodily associate is surely clear. (Quinton, 1975, pp. 64-65)

Whether we call it a soul (as Quinton proposes), a mind, or possibly even a person, what in everyday life we care about in people is "the essential constituent of personality" (Quinton, 1975, p. 65), and we understand that to be "a series of mental states connected by continuity of character and memory" (p. 65). It's that psychological complex whose persistence is often sufficient for everyday acts of personal identification. And it's that psychological complex whose persistence after death many desire or expect, and which survival cases seem to indicate.

Revealingly (as Ducasse observed), the evidence for postmortem survival presents us with a situation similar to a far more familiar scenario (Ducasse, 1961). Suppose I received a phone call over a noisy connection from an individual purporting to be my friend George, whom I thought had died in a plane crash. Although I can't establish the speaker's identity by confirming his bodily continuity to the George I knew, nevertheless my conversation can provide a solid practical basis for concluding that George is really speaking to me. The speaker could demonstrate that he had certain memories that no one but George should have, and he could exhibit characteristically George-ish personality traits, verbal mannerisms, as well as idiosyncratic motives and interests. Whether or not the persistence of these traits satisfies a metaphysician's criteria of identity, they will often suffice for real-life cases. Moreover,

> evidence of just these kinds is at least evidence *without which* one would have *no grounds at all* for supposing that some human beings may in some sense survive the dissolution of their bodies. (Gauld, 1982, p. 31)

Similarly, if my phone conversation was with a person who claimed to be speaking to George and relaying his words to me (and vice versa), this situation would be analogous to cases where a medium conveys messages from communicator to sitters. Obviously, it's more difficult to discern the communicator's personality traits under these conditions, and that clearly deprives us of one type of evidence of survival. Nevertheless, if the content of the conveyed information is highly specific and intimate, it might justify concluding that George lives and is communicating directly to the person on the phone.

Apparently, then, we should be able to apply to postmortem cases the same psychological criteria of identity that we apply, usually unproblematically, in everyday cases. Granted, many of us are at least closet or casual metaphysicians. So we might still feel puzzled by the postmortem cases, and we may be unable to explain (or say anything interesting about) how survival could occur following bodily death. We may simply be at a loss philosophically and scientifically. But that's hardly unique to postmortem cases. We're often at a loss theoretically to explain antemortem instances of survival. For example, in everyday acts of identification we're not usually stymied by our ignorance of biology, medicine, or the metaphysics of personal identity. In fact, higher-level theoretical concerns seem irrelevant. After all, it's likely that our generally workable strategies for identifying people have been relatively stable for millennia, despite profound changes in prevailing philosophies and scientific background theories. So if our ignorance or theoretical naivete is no barrier to judging identity in everyday cases, it's not clear why it should matter in connection with apparent postmortem survival.

Of course, as we've seen, some want to dismiss the evidence suggesting survival by appealing to their (presumably physicalist) views on what is or is not possible. But that's a suspicious strategy in many areas of inquiry, and it certainly is in this one, which after all seems to test various assumptions currently fashionable in academic circles. I suggest we heed the words of Trenton Merricks, who, despite his commitment to a physicalist conception of persons, warns sagely (in a slightly different context) against placing too much faith in our intuitions concerning the limits of the possible. He writes,

> The dogmatic insistence on...outright impossibility...betrays...an exaggerated and overweening confidence in one's modal intuition, in one's ability to peer into the space of possibility with a clear and unfaltering gaze and to see that what seems to be possible, in some sense and to at least some of us, is not really so. Modesty is more becoming. (Merricks, 2001, p. 197)

So as we proceed in this inquiry, we should probably aim for at least a temporary metaphysical agnosticism. After all, we have here some dandy, *real-life*, puzzle cases to consider, which (if advocates of puzzle cases are right) should offer a golden opportunity to sharpen our thinking and deepen our metaphysics.

Besides, it's easy to construct hypothetically ideal cases in which a person's distinctive psychology manifests in various ways after the person's bodily death and dissolution (see chapter 9). And these cases can be so coercive that, if they were actual, we would feel compelled to describe them as indicating apparent personal survival. Granted (as I've noted), we might be unsure how to articulate what we meant by that, or at least how to do it in a way philosophers would find satisfying. (In chapter 9 we'll consider briefly the impact of survival cases on our metaphysics.) But for now what matters is how, in a state of comparative metaphysical innocence, we would assess apparently good evidence for survival. And presumably, what we'd want to say depends largely on the same thing that concerns us most in everyday cases: *how we value persons*.

So it seems that survival cases don't force us to abandon our familiar and normative concept of a person, because that concept easily tolerates what those cases require: namely, relying on psychological continuity alone as a basis for judgments about identity. In any case it's pretty much irrelevant—although it may still be annoying—that hypothetically ideal cases challenge us conceptually and even violate some people's abstract metaphysical assumptions. Practical considerations trump abstract philosophy every time, and if we really encountered a case as good as those we can construct, and especially if the case mattered to us personally, our reflective metaphysical scruples would count for nothing.[4]

In the meantime, we should take seriously the way both actual and hypothetically ideal survival cases conform to our everyday norms and practices with regard to identifying persons. These cases show that the evidence can't be rejected for the sorts of facile reasons provided by Flew, and more generally that the inquiry into survival can't be carried out as if data were irrelevant.[5] Indeed, because interesting real-life cases present *prima facie* evidence of survival, one obvious challenge for any serious study of the topic will be to determine how good the actual cases are and how closely they approach the theoretical ideal.

3. Survival and Anomalous Knowledge

But before we can tackle that and other important issues, we must make some additional preliminary observations. And let's begin with a useful distinction, between different types of knowledge exhibited in survival cases. Generally speaking, a case suggests survival because (a) some living person demonstrates knowledge closely (if not uniquely) associated with a deceased person, and (b) we have good reason to believe that this knowledge wasn't obtained by ordinary means. These anomalous displays of knowledge tend to fall into two broad categories: the articulation of facts or items of information (often called "knowledge-*that*") and the manifestation of abilities or skills (usually considered a type of knowledge-*how*[6]). In cases of the first sort, subjects provide pieces of information which couldn't have been obtained normally, but which would have been known to a deceased person apparently communicating that information. Suppose, for instance, that a medium purporting to convey messages from my late Uncle Harry tells me the location of a secret document known (normally, at any rate) to no living person, and known previously only to Uncle Harry. Or suppose that this information is provided by a child purporting to be the reincarnation of my Uncle Harry. In cases suggesting knowledge-how, a living person exhibits an ability or skill never displayed by that person before, and perhaps one that was idiosyncratic to a deceased person. For example, suppose that a medium or child suddenly manifests an unlearned ability associated with Uncle Harry—say, the ability to write music or speak Swedish. These cases become even more impressive when the anomalous abilities also display certain idiosyncratic characteristics distinctive of Uncle Harry (e.g., a particular style of humor or musical composition). And they become more impressive still when the abilities in question (a) are rare or probably can't be learned at all (e.g., exquisite musical or artistic gifts, which only a few enjoy), or (b) can be learned normally only after a period of practice which we're reasonably certain never occurred. Finally, it's icing on the cake if the abilities in question are radically discontinuous with the subject's other abilities—for example, if a formerly tone-deaf, uneducated medium began to demonstrate the refined musical abilities of a deceased composer.

I should add that knowledge-that can also be radically discontinuous with what a person presumably knows already. And in certain cases that discontinuity might likewise furnish *prima facie* evidence for survival. For example, suppose that a three-year-old child appears to be the reincarnation of Bertrand Russell, and suppose that in conversation the child demonstrates a detailed command of Russell's philosophical writings and an intimate understanding of Russell's views (e.g., his theory of definite descriptions). Actually, a case like this is probably a hybrid of knowledge-*that* and knowledge-*how*, because the ability to converse on technical subjects seems to be a *skill* that presupposes a substantial body of propositional knowledge.

I should also note that, like many superficially plausible distinctions, the distinction between knowledge-that and knowledge-how may not be as straightforward as many have believed. In fact, some philosophers argue that knowledge-how is really a *species* of knowledge-that (e.g., Brown, 1970; Ginet, 1975; Stanley & Williamson, 2001). But for present purposes, we needn't take a stand on that issue. Nothing in this book hinges on the general viability of the distinction between knowledge-that and knowledge-how. All that matters is that the survival evidence falls into two roughly but easily delineated groups of anomalous behavior.

Beginning with the next chapter, we'll take a close look at various types of evidence for survival, and we'll examine some of the better and more interesting cases in detail. But we still need to do some more stage setting. As the reader probably knows, there's not exactly a shortage of books and articles on the topic of survival. In fact, there's not even a paucity of philosophical works on the topic. In many respects, this body of work is exciting and worthy of close study. The empirical literature abounds with provocative and impressive cases, and the theoretical literature, too, is frequently thoughtful, insightful, and very careful. Nevertheless, the literature on survival is consistently disappointing in some crucial respects. In particular, it's plagued by several nagging problems which not even the best works address successfully. These are the problems I want to confront in this book, and it's this relatively late stage in the survival debate that I'm selecting as an entry point.

4. The "Super-Psi" Hypothesis

Of course, real cases suggest postmortem survival to varying degrees, and they deservedly command our attention when we can't plausibly or easily explain them away in more ordinary terms. As a first requirement, a good survival case should resist explanation in terms of a few obvious skeptical counter-hypotheses: namely, fraud, misreporting, malobservation, or hidden memories (cryptomnesia). Let's dub these "The Usual Suspects." Not surprisingly, it's often difficult to determine whether appeals to the Usual Suspects succeed. And in fact, proponents of the survival hypothesis (hereafter, *survivalists*)[7] have been reasonably successful in deflecting these sorts of counter-explanations. That's undoubtedly one reason for the continued interest in the topic of postmortem survival.

However, appealing to the Usual Suspects is merely the first wave of skepticism about postmortem survival, and it posits nothing more than relatively normal (or possibly abnormal) processes as alternatives to survival. But some anti-survivalists resort to more exotic counter-explanations. These explanations are much more difficult to undermine, and they fall into two classes. The first class posits decidedly abnormal or rare processes, such as dissociative pathologies, rare mnemonic gifts, extreme or unprecedented forms of savantism, or equally rare latent creative capacities. We could call these alternatives "The Unusual Suspects," and although we can often rule them out, survivalists have done a relatively poor job of countering them in general.

But before we confront that issue (which I'll do in the next section), we need to consider the second, and even more recalcitrant, set of exotic counter-explanations, positing *psychic functioning among the living*. These are often called "super-psi" explanations, because they apparently require more refined and extensive psychic functioning than we discover in controlled laboratory studies. However, parapsychologists disagree on what super psi is and what super-psi explanations should look like, and two distinct views emerge from this dispute. The first of these, the *multiple-process* hypothesis, treats super psi as an organized collection of refined psychic tasks. For example, apparent mediumistic communications could be explained in terms of the medium's exquisitely timed and detailed ESP, either of the sitter's thoughts, the thoughts of other relevant individuals, or of various pertinent physical states of affairs (e.g., the location of hidden documents). Or, it could be explained in terms of the *sitter's* ESP of some of these items, followed by telepathic influence on the medium. The second view of super psi avoids the task-complexity posited by the multiple-process hypothesis, and (following Eisenbud) we could dub it the *magic wand* hypothesis. According to the magic wand hypothesis, even the most extensive or refined psi requires nothing more than an efficacious wish or desire, as if the subject simply waved a magic wand to achieve a desired effect. So this hypothesis treats psychic functioning as analogous to other human achievements that seem comparably oblivious to apparent underlying complexity. For example, in biofeedback studies, subjects have been able to do remarkable things (e.g., fire a single muscle cell in the arm, but none of the surrounding cells) simply by wishing or willing for them to happen. In fact, subjects often do best in biofeedback tasks when they don't actively try to achieve the desired result. Typically, they succeed under a condition of *passive volition* (in which they don't actively strive for a result) or after a *release of effort*. And perhaps most important, they succeed at biofeedback tasks without having to monitor the underlying physiological processes, and usually in total ignorance of what those processes are (see, e.g., Basmajian, 1963, 1972).

Not surprisingly, many find both views of super psi to be antecedently incredible, and they consider the magic-wand view to be the most incredible of all. Consequently, many dismiss super-psi explanations without much thought, often with a contemptuous flourish. I understand and sympathize with those reactions; initially they were my reactions as well. Nevertheless, the reactions are hasty, and the issues are more interesting than most people realize.

In fact, the problems here are remarkably complex, and they begin with the term "super psi." This unfortunate expression is the offspring of several major confusions, and it's undoubtedly the source of at least some of the difficulties plaguing the survival literature. For one thing, it's questionable whether, in order to counter survivalist explanations, we need to posit a higher level of psychic functioning than what's already been well documented in living people *outside* the lab (Braude, 1997). (We'll examine this topic as the book progresses.) For another, the term "super" is unclear and inappropriately evaluative. Obviously, there's no standardized scale for determining when something, much less a psychic event, counts as super. What's super for one person may not be for another. Moreover, many treat the word "super" in "super psi" as being more closely related to its use in "super hero" than in "super glue." As a result, many feel, right from the start, that super-psi explanations posit an implausible degree of psychic functioning and shouldn't be taken seriously. Nevertheless, at this relatively late stage in the game, we have little to gain from overturning such a well-entrenched terminological tradition. So I propose that we continue to call this alternative to survivalism the "super-psi" hypothesis, and I recommend simply that we remain alert to the controversial assumptions surrounding it.

My major complaint about the treatment of the super-psi hypothesis is that most discussions underestimate its subtlety and force. All too often, critics set up a straw man by considering the hypothesis in an unacceptably weak or implausible form. The most common form of this error is to adopt the indefensible assumption that if super psi occurred, we'd know it if we saw it. Elsewhere, I called this the *sore thumb* assumption, because it takes super psi to be the sort of thing that always stands out like a sore thumb (Braude, 1997). For example, some argue that we can reject the super-psi hypothesis because there's no evidence for psychic functioning of that magnitude or degree of refinement. And when critics say this, they're not asserting simply that we lack evidence for *flagrant* super psi. Their claim is that we have no evidence *at all* for super psi.

But that claim is hardly obvious. First of all, we have to grant—simply as a matter of principle—that if super psi occurs, it might blend in with or be masked by an extensive network of surrounding normal events. Consider: there needn't be an *observable* difference between paranormally produced events and normal events (for example, a plane

crash caused psychokinetically and one caused by normal engine failure). Those events may differ only in their unobservable causal histories. Of course, some PK effects, such as object levitations, don't occur
under normal circumstances. So those phenomena *would* inevitably
stand out like a sore thumb. But other sorts of PK effects could occur
inconspicuously—for example, if we were unconsciously affecting the
cycle of traffic lights, foiling radar traps on the highway, aggravating a
despised coworker's migraine, or crashing her computer. Now it might
be that even these subtle forms of super psi would attract attention if
they persisted for any length of time. But it's also difficult to know how
quickly we'd distinguish persistent psychic functioning from, say, runs
of (good or bad) luck. Unless we were disposed already to look for the
operation of psi in everyday life, it might be all too easy to see its recurrent manifestations as something else. Analogously, some people don't
recognize that their spouse suffers from MPD/DID, and they all too easily interpret the signs of multiplicity as, say, moodiness or eccentricity.
Furthermore, there are good reasons for thinking that even if super psi
occurs surreptitiously, it might be unlikely to occur with enough regularity to attract attention. We'll examine that issue in chapter 3.6 (and
see also Braude, 1997).

In fact, we have no reason to expect *any* kind of everyday psychic
functioning to be conspicuous. The observations above about PK apply
also to ESP. Telepathic experiences are likely to be noticed only among
people who know and communicate with each other. And even then,
they have to be experiences that command our attention—for example,
crises or other unpleasant or unexpected occurrences. Similarly, we probably won't notice instances of clairvoyance and apparent precognition
unless they, too, concern events that grab our attention. But in that
case, we probably won't know when (or how often) we interact telepathically with the minds of strangers or acquire information clairvoyantly
about distant but uninteresting events. If our psychic impressions rise to
the level of conscious awareness (and there's no reason to insist that
they must), it might be easy to dismiss them as common types of incongruous thoughts.

Furthermore, we must be careful not to suppose that psychic functioning occurs in total isolation from the full range of ordinary human
needs and organic capacities. Assuming that psychic functioning occurs,
it's more reasonable to believe that it plays a role in life, that it may be
driven by our deepest needs and fears (rather than those of which we're
immediately or consciously aware), and that it doesn't occur only when
parapsychologists set out to look for it. For that reason, the super-psi
hypothesis in its strongest form is really a *motivated*-psi hypothesis. That
is, it posits the operation of psychic abilities in the services of some a-
gent's genuine or perceived needs and interests. But in that case, our
psychological interests might be served most effectively when our para-

normal activities remain covert.

Generally speaking, people in Western industrialized cultures are uncomfortable with the idea that we might have extensive psychic influence over (or awareness of) distant events. Actually, most find it easier to contemplate beneficial uses of psychic abilities (as in healing) than malevolent uses of psi (as in hexing). And that attitude is revealing. When even the mere possibility of exercising psychic abilities raises intimidating issues of responsibility, we might simply prefer not to know. In fact, the fear of psi may have played a significant role in shaping the data of parapsychology (see Eisenbud, 1992; Braude, 1997). So in order to take the super-psi hypothesis seriously, we must accept (whether we like it or not) that deeply motivated psychic functioning might be sneaky and naughty, and that its manifestations might range from the dramatic and conspicuous to the mundane and inconspicuous. (See Braude, 1997, chapter 7, for a more thorough discussion of this topic.)

The sore thumb assumption, or at least a close relative of it, emerges in the form of a familiar argument, which we may call the *Sore Thumb Argument*. When writers reject super-psi explanations in survival cases, they often reason along the following lines:

> (1) The evidence for ESP and PK suggests that these phenomena occur only to a modest degree.
>
> (2) But super-psi explanations of the better survival cases require prodigious psychic abilities.
>
> (3) *Therefore*, super-psi explanations posit degrees of psychic functioning for which we have no other evidence.

The problems with this argument begin with the first premise. Of course, it seems to rest on the questionable assumption that super psi must be conspicuous. But the problems don't end there. Often, when people assert premise (1), they're expressing an indefensibly parochial attitude toward parapsychology generally, according to which only controlled laboratory experiments are potentially credible sources of data. Now this is not the place to fight that battle again. As I noted earlier in this chapter and in the preface, this book is engaging the debate over survival at a somewhat advanced stage in the argument. So to move things along, we need to assume that there's decent evidence for psychic functioning from both inside and outside the lab (but see Braude, 1997 and Broad, 1962 for discussions of nonlaboratory evidence). Still, it takes more than an appreciation of spontaneous cases to undermine allegiance to the sore thumb assumption. Even informed commentators balk at the apparent gulf between the degree of psi reported in the better spontaneous cases and the super psi needed to explain away the evidence for survival. So perhaps we can sympathize with Robert Almeder's claim that "we need to have some independent empirical evidence...for the existence of super-psi in other contexts before we can appeal to it as a way of explaining...features of...alleged cases of reincarnation [or survival generally] (Almeder, 1992, p. 53). Nevertheless, several considerations help to downgrade Almeder's concern, even if they don't mitigate it entirely.

First, it's true that we may not have direct evidence for the exact form of super psi needed to explain away good survival cases. But there *is* a substantial body of direct evidence, from outside the lab, for at least pretty *dandy* psi. The most astonishing examples may be cases of physical mediumship. But a decent argument could be made that the ESP reported in some spontaneous cases is mightily impressive as well (see, e.g., Gurney, Myers, & Podmore, 1886; Rhine, 1981; Sidgwick, 1922; Society for Psychical Research, 1894; Tyrrell, 1942/1961). These bodies of evidence show, at the very least, that psychic functioning can operate on a level of magnitude and refinement far exceeding anything demonstrated unambiguously in laboratory experiments. That has to weaken the argument that psychic functioning is unlikely to operate at a higher level still. Besides, as I noted earlier, it's not as if there's a clear standard by which we measure how "super" a psi phenomenon is.

But no matter whether we regard the phenomena reported in these cases as super or merely dandy, they're arguably as super as anything posited to explain away the evidence for survival. As we'll see when we begin examining some of the best survival cases in detail, it's questionable whether we need psi of unprecedented levels of magnitude or refinement to accommodate the survival evidence. So premise (2) likewise turns out to be contentious. To appreciate why, we do need to examine specific cases. But one general point is worth making now. No matter whether we're concerned with paranormal or normal causation, we needn't suppose that effects must be proportional to their causes. In particular, a massive event can be produced by a small event. For example, to collapse a mine or blow up an airplane psychokinetically, all that's needed is a nudge in the right place, not an event on a comparably grand scale.

Furthermore, in addition to the direct evidence for large-scale or refined psychic functioning, we have an interesting body of *indirect* evidence for super psi. This comes from cases of apparent precognition and also PK experiments with prerecorded targets. The reason these cases suggest the operation of super psi is that the next most plausible explanation posits a phenomenon even more deeply controversial: namely, backwards causation (Braude, 1997, chapter 6). At any rate, we'll ultimately have to determine on a case-by-case basis whether super-psi explanations are viable alternatives to survivalist explanations. So we'll confront this topic squarely in later chapters, as we consider compelling pieces of evidence.

The next point is more abstract. It addresses more directly Almeder's claim that we need independent evidence for super psi before we can accept super-psi explanations in survival cases. The problem is this. Even if we accept the existence of psychic functioning, we know almost nothing about its *nature*. We don't know how it operates, and we don't know its natural history—that is, what general role (if any) it plays in life. But considering the magnitude of our ignorance concerning the nature of psi, we must (at the very least) entertain the possibility of extensive psi once we grant that it can assume more moderate forms. Richet once noted, in connection with the evidence for materialization,

> it is as difficult to understand the materialization of a living hand, warm, articulated, and mobile, or even of a single finger, as to understand the materialization of an entire personality which comes and goes, speaks, and moves the veil that covers him. (Richet, 1923/1975, p. 491)

We can generalize this point. At our present, impoverished, level of understanding, large-scale or refined psychic phenomena are no more incredible or puzzling than more modest phenomena. For example, in the case of PK, since we have no idea how agents affect remote physical systems, we have no grounds for assuming that PK effects are inherently limited in scope or refinement. Despite the theoretical posturing of some parapsychologists, we don't understand how even the smallest-scale PK violates or circumvents the usual constraints on influencing other physical systems.[8] So we're in no position to set limits in advance on how far those apparent violations may go. In fact, not only might we have to entertain the possibility of extensive psi, we might have to entertain the possibility of *unlimited* psi (at least in principle).

Granted, if we had a thoroughly developed and well-supported psi theory, one that embraces *all* the available evidence for psi (not just the laboratory evidence) and explains how or why psi functions both in and out of the lab, we might be able to insist that psi effects have inherent limits. But at present, no decent theory forbids large-scale or super psi. Most simply ignore it and deal instead only with laboratory evidence. And no scientific theory renders any form of psi improbable (Braude, 1997, chapter 1). Whether we like it or not, at our current level of understanding, super psi is as viable as puny psi. And quite apart from our having evidence for phenomena that are at least close to being super, the lack of direct or unambiguous evidence for anything grander is simply an annoyance we have no choice but to accept.

This line of reasoning has led some to complain that "nothing could count for the nonexistence of super-psi" (Almeder, 1992, p. 53), and therefore that the hypothesis is empirically meaningless. That concern is understandable, but I believe we can dispose of it fairly easily. I would concede only that super-psi explanations fail strict Popperian tests of falsifiability. But that's not the same as saying that nothing can count against those explanations. Super-psi explanations are less like hypotheses in the physical sciences and more like humdrum (but perfectly acceptable) explanations of people's behavior in terms of needs, interests, motivations, etc. We can't strictly falsify those latter hypotheses either. But some are more viable than others, and that viability rests both on what the evidence is and on a variety of pragmatic considerations. For example, when we explain Jones's behavior as an expression of his insecurity rather than his unfriendliness or arrogance, there's no evidence that conclusively falsifies *any* of the proposed explanations. In principle, we can always formulate a (possibly convoluted) conjecture to explain how, despite appearances, Jones's behavior is really an example of *veiled* insecurity (unfriendliness, arrogance, etc.). Similarly, apparent evidence for a person's lack of anger can always be reinterpreted as evidence for veiled anger. Nevertheless, we can have good reasons for preferring one explanation over the other.

Perhaps we can make this a bit clearer by distinguishing two respects in which a hypothesis can be unfalsifiable. Let's call these *strong* and *weak unfalsifiability*.

> "Hypothesis H is *strongly unfalsifiable*" =df "nothing *whatsoever* can count against H"

> "Hypothesis H is *weakly unfalsifiable*" =df "(a) both H and not-H are compatible with the data, but (b) some evidence can reasonably be taken as rendering H less plausible than not-H"

I'd say that the super-psi hypothesis is unfalsifiable in only the weak sense. So when I say that any ostensible evidence for survival will be compatible with an alternative super-psi explanation, I don't mean that nothing can count against the super-psi explanation.

Almeder has taken issue with this (Almeder, 1996a; 1996b). He's argued that if we had something close to an ideal case suggesting survival, no super-psi explanation would even be compatible with the facts. For example, if a person claimed to be a reincarnation of Napoleon, spoke Napoleonic French, and had a wealth of information and behavioral traits that could only have come from or been associated with Napoleon, this would not be consistent with *any* motivated super-psi explanation. And the reason for that, he says, is that never in the history of parapsychology or psychology has there been evidence that a person could have such abilities simply in virtue of deeply needing to have them.

Now for reasons we'll examine closely in later chapters, I think Almeder underestimates what we can learn, both from abnormal psychology and from parapsychology, about the range of human abilities. For example, I think he takes the evidence for xenoglossy (speaking an unlearned language) more seriously than it deserves; there are interesting data and issues about second-language acquisition which Almeder and others simply never address (see chapter 4).

But quite apart from that, even a good Napoleon case would be *com-*

patible with a super-psi alternative. The lack of independent or unambiguous evidence for the requisite degree of psi (if indeed there is such a lack) doesn't make the super-psi hypothesis incompatible with the facts. It simply makes it less plausible than it would be otherwise. I actually agree with Almeder that if we were confronted with a good Napoleon case, or any case closely approaching an ideal, we'd have good reason to accept the survival hypothesis. I even agree that it would be irrational (in some suitably robust sense) not to (see chapter 9 for more on ideal cases).

But as we'll see, no case comes close to the ideal ones we can construct. That's the problem. The best cases all approach an ideal to varying degrees and from different angles. And often, those cases remind us primarily of how little we know about various aspects of human nature.

James Wheatley (in a review of Braude, 1997) raised what, to me, is a more interesting question regarding the position I've just expressed (Wheatley, 1998). He wondered whether, when I declare a statement to be nonfalsifiable, I mean something different from merely saying we can't know *for certain* whether the statement is false. That *is* what I seem to be saying, for example, about the super-psi hypothesis, and also about statements concerning others' mental states. But in that case, would I say that *any* scientific hypothesis counts as falsifiable? After all, on any sort of reasonable, non-aprioristic view of science, the claims of science are always fallible and open to revision or abandonment. In that sense, they're never certain.

I won't pretend to have a fully worked out view on this. But I do have a position. First, I would agree that scientific hypotheses generally are, in a sense, uncertain. The data will always be compatible with an indefinite number of rival hypotheses, and our choice from that set invariably depends on very general theoretical and pragmatic criteria (e.g., systematicity, conceptual cost, predictive fecundity, and maybe aesthetic preferences such as explanatory simplicity). Moreover (being a good pragmatist), I have to add that certainty, like physical strength, is a matter of degree. And the same can be said for truth. As William James once remarked, these are ideal vanishing points that give us something to aim for and "towards which we imagine that all our temporary truths will some day converge" (James, 1978, pp. 106–107). They aren't goals we ever attain, or ever *could* attain. As James vividly put it, they're on a par "with the perfectly wise man, and with the absolutely complete experience" (James, 1978, p. 107).

Nevertheless, unlike the super-psi hypothesis, and perhaps to a lesser extent unlike everyday conjectures about others' mental states, most scientific hypotheses are *not* compatible with *all* the data. Typically, scientific hypotheses allow us to generate quite specific predictions, and these enable us to falsify the hypotheses. But neither the super-psi hypothesis *nor the survival hypothesis* enjoy that advantage. In fact, one of the most frustrating features of the topic of survival—at least at the point where I take up the issues—is that we must choose between two weakly unfalsifiable hypotheses: survival and super psi. We know so little, not only about psi generally, but also about the plausible features of an afterlife, that we're unable to predict with any confidence at all what the data *should* look like. Generating testable hypotheses about the survival evidence is simply not feasible.

Some might find this claim surprising, and they might protest as follows. "Granted, if super psi can be both sneaky and naughty, then we can make no specific, falsifiable predictions about what the evidence for super psi would look like. But the evidence for survival isn't like that; it *does* allow us to make 'certain testable predictions' (Almeder, 2001, p. 347)—for example, that the subject would have particular memories that only the deceased person could have, or abilities idiosyncratically possessed by that person."

But that's simply false. First, it's hardly a *specific* prediction to say that subjects will have certain memories or abilities. In fact, we haven't a clue *which* particular memories or abilities, or which particular kinds of memories or abilities a subject is likely to have, especially in the absence of questionable and presumably arbitrary assumptions about how the trauma of bodily death would affect us cognitively. We can only guess what sorts of impairments or enhancements, or what changes in personal attitudes, that transition might produce. We'll see, as this book progresses, how both survivalists and anti-survivalists rely on highly controversial nonempirical assumptions as they speculate about the nature of the evidence. In fact, we'll see in chapter 9 how this undermines the common skeptical prediction that reincarnation is incompatible with population growth. In the meantime, an interesting episode from the history of parapsychology illustrates nicely the tenuous nature of our predictions about an afterlife.

F. W. H. Myers, the distinguished Cambridge scholar and one of the founders of the SPR, distinguished *telepathy* from *telergy* (Myers, 1890, p. 320; 1903, vol. 2, pp. 197, 526; also, Barrett, 1918). The former was direct mind-to-mind interaction, but the latter process was a form of *possession*, or psychokinesis directed onto another person's organism. During telergy, one mind (embodied or discarnate) controls the brain and nervous system of a person so as to produce, say, a mediumistic trance-impersonation. Myers theorized that surviving minds would not all be equally adept at communicating, and he conjectured that the most skilled or evolved communicators would use telergy to produce the dramatic and seemingly robust simulation of the surviving personality. By comparison, presumably, mere telepathic communication seemed bland or limited in the range of data it could provide. After Myers's death, various mediums (not surprisingly) purported to channel postmortem Myers communications. And interestingly, in his ostensible postmortem theoretical speculations (conveyed through Mrs. Willett), Myers changed his mind and claimed that telepathy was the superior form of communication. Telergy, he now said, was a "clumsy, creaking process."

This shift in position prompted C. D. Broad to quip, "It seems that we die and learn" (Broad, 1962, p. 299). The moral for us is that we can only guess, with virtually nothing to go on, what postmortem existence—and thus, the evidence for survival—should be like. (And of course the same is true, given our current level of ignorance, about the range and refinement of psi in life.) This point will be driven home repeatedly throughout this book, and it's why choosing between the super-psi and survival hypotheses inevitably requires appealing to tentative arguments about plausibility. As with our conjectures about the mental lives of others, we might be able to draw conclusions with a reasonable degree of confidence. But as I hope we'll see by the end of this book, we're kidding ourselves if we think we can decide for or against survival with a high degree of confidence. So I must disagree with Almeder, who claims that belief in survival "is certainly as well established as (if not better than), say, the belief in the past existence of dinosaurs" (Almeder, 1992, p. 2).

My position, then, is this. We can (at least in principle) have good reasons for rejecting either the super-psi or the survival hypothesis, even if they remain (as they now seem) compatible with all the data. However, the question we need to confront is whether (or to what extent) any actual evidence takes us to that point, at least in a compelling way. And we need to consider whether theoretical or pragmatic considerations help us tip the scales toward the survival hypothesis. That's the primary goal of this book.

Before surveying the remaining major problems with the survival literature, we should look briefly at another point concerning super-psi explanations. We'll return to this point occasionally in later chapters, but it's best to address it now and keep it in the back of our minds. Ironically, survivalists are in a uniquely bad position to object to super-psi counter-explanations. That's because survivalist and non-survivalist explanations seem to require the same degree and kind of psychic functioning. So survivalists may not be able to claim that super-psi explanations require an antecedently implausible amount of psychic functioning.

For example, in cases of mental mediumship, survivalists clearly require what would be considered super psi if it happened between living persons. That is, survivalist and typical super-psi explanations don't differ over the *amount* or *type* of psychic functioning required to produce the evidence. The main difference is that super-psi explanations posit psi only among the living. Consider: In typical cases of mediumship, the medium ostensibly conveys messages imparted to her by a communicator, or else she acts as a vehicle for communication—for example, by relinquishing bodily control to the communicator (in cases of so-called "trance impersonation"). Later, we'll look at mediumship in greater detail, but for now we can afford to oversimplify slightly. What matters here is that, from the survivalist's perspective, mediumship suggests two primary types of paranormal causal influence. Either (1) the medium is "reading" the surviving mind of a now-deceased communicator, or (2) the communicator's surviving mind is influencing or controlling the mind or body of the medium. But clearly, these forms of mental → mental or mental → physical causation must be as successful, refined, and accurate as what super-psi counter-explanations require. In fact, survivalists must posit interactions looking exactly like the maligned forms of super psi—except (of course) that one of the agents is deceased. For example, instead of saying that the medium reads the thoughts of sitters at a séance (or those of more remote individuals), survivalists propose that the medium reads a discarnate individual's thoughts. And instead of saying that the medium is influenced by the thoughts of living persons, survivalists say that the medium is influenced by a surviving individual's thoughts.

Obviously, we need to keep this in mind as we evaluate the evidence later on. In chapter 3, we'll return to this issue and consider one possibly important respect in which survivalists and anti-survivalists seem to require different levels of psychic achievement. But in the respects already noted, survivalists and anti-survivalists may find themselves at a standoff. We can't balk at what strikes us as too much (or implausibly refined) psi among the living *in favor of* survivalist explanations requiring the same degree of psychic functioning between the living and the previously living.

Unfortunately, that happens all too frequently. Consider the case reported by Zorab (Zorab, 1962), concerning a Dutch bookkeeping clerk who died unable to explain a large deficit in the accounts he kept for his employer. The bookkeeper denied any wrongdoing, and so the ledgers were checked carefully. But it still looked as if the bookkeeper had embezzled money. The poor man died protesting his innocence and imploring his children to clear his name. Later, one of his sons experienced an apparition, a white figure telling him repeatedly to look in the ledger at the dates. The son did this the next day, and he found that a date at the top of a column had been added into the sums below. That error increased the total by the exact amount allegedly embezzled.

Zorab, to his credit, suggested clairvoyance as a likely explanation. He saw the white figure as a typical symbol of good tidings, and the apparition more generally as a "special scene enacted by the dramatizing dream consciousness" (p. 416). However, others have seen the case as one that strains the super-psi hypothesis to the breaking point (see, e.g., Keen, 1999). But consider this. The father hadn't figured out the problem with the ledgers when he died. If he had, he would have pointed out the error. But then if psi is involved at all, we need to posit clairvoyance no matter what, either on the son's part, or on the father's. Of course, another possibility is that the son solved the problem subconsciously, drawing on memories of his earlier, normal, perception of the ledger. (The dream figure would then have dramatized this revelation.) But if we rule that out and opt for a paranormal explanation, then presumably either the deceased father or the son found some nonsensory way of acquiring the relevant information about the ledger.

A related objection to super-psi explanations concerns, not simply the *amount* of psi required, but the apparently incredible *complexity* of the task. For example, mediums sometimes provide detailed and intimate information concerning a communicator, and often that information is not known to the sitter(s) or to any living person. In these cases, apparently, we need to suppose that the medium can access multiple sources of information, almost instantaneously, in order to respond appropriately to sitters' questions and comments. And when the medium delivers that information by means of a convincing impersonation of the communicator, the task apparently becomes even more daunting. Presumably, the medium would also need to access additional information about the communicator's mannerisms, tone of voice, etc., and somehow synthesize it all, without benefit of practice (and in the absence, usually, of any previously displayed talent for mimicry), into an accurate simulation of the communicator's behavior (see, e.g., Ducasse, 1961, p. 196).

But this objection, too, may be overrated. There are good reasons for thinking that task complexity may not matter, at least not in the way (or to the extent) that many suppose. But to appreciate why, we need to examine several different issues, which I think are best treated separately in connection with actual case material. In the next chapter, we'll consider the problem of accessing multiple sources of information, and in chapters 3 and 6 we'll consider problems in connection with dramatic impersonations by mediums and children in reincarnation cases.

Before moving to our next topic, I should try to ward off a potential misunderstanding. I've been surprised at reactions to some of my previously published remarks on survival. Apparently, and despite explicit statements to the contrary, they've created the impression that I'm opposed in principle to the survival hypothesis and that I believe the evidence can all be accommodated by positing some form of super psi. So let me try again to make my position clear.

I can imagine nothing more exciting than indisputable evidence for survival. In fact, if I have any bias in the matter, it would be that I *hope* we survive the death of our bodies in some sort of interestingly robust way. It certainly seems to be better than the alternatives. The famous hypnotherapist Milton Erikson once quipped to his wife, "Don't worry.

Dying is the last thing I'm going to do."[9] And I can assure you that I hope that dying is *not* the last thing I do. But mere hope doesn't sustain me in this matter, and fortunately there's actual evidence we can examine. However, to base a case for survival on the evidence, we can't be content to reject alternate explanations (especially super-psi explanations) in the anemic or simplistic forms in which they've been considered. So my concern, all along, has been to show just how daunting a task it is to rule out super-psi explanations. And the primary reason for that has been not to mount a case against survival, but to help raise the literature on survival to a more advanced level of analysis.

One last point. The topic of super psi connects with the distinction noted in the previous section, between knowledge-that and knowledge-how. Many believe that a decent case for survival can be made on the basis of evidence for knowledge of either sort. But the prevailing view is that good evidence for knowledge-how makes for a stronger case. Although I tend to agree, I think we need to question the assumption on which that view usually rests. The assumption is that no matter how outlandish we feel super psi might be, it's more plausible to think that a medium could psychically access the confirmable information conveyed in a séance than to think that she could manifest an unlearned ability closely resembling that of a deceased communicator. For reasons I discuss briefly below and which we examine more closely (and from different perspectives) later (especially in chapters 2 through 6), the situation seems to be considerably more complicated than this. It may be surprisingly difficult to provide credible ESP explanations for the obscure information revealed in the best cases. And the skills or abilities actually manifested in the best cases may not be so difficult to explain along non-survivalist lines.

5. What Else Is Wrong with the Literature on Survival

A second problem with the survival literature concerns its superficial treatment of dissociation. Beginning at least as far back as the Delphic Oracle, and continuing through the more recent and rich history of hypnosis, we find many indications that dissociative phenomena elicit (or at least accompany) psychic functioning. And of course, it takes only a casual acquaintance with hypnosis and multiple personality to see striking similarities between their manifestations and the behavior of many mediums. We have to wonder, then, whether the entities apparently communicating through a medium are nothing more than dissociative parts of the medium's mind, parts that simply claim and otherwise appear to be deceased communicators. But all too often, writers on survival have only a casual acquaintance with the literature on dissociation generally and multiple personality in particular. As a result, they frequently offer naive opinions about the nature of mediumship and the likelihood of dissociation both in those cases and in reincarnation cases. This deficiency in the survival literature is both astonishing and disappointing. It seems obviously premature to settle on an explanation of the best evidence for survival without a firm grounding in the experimental and clinical literature on dissociation. That seems to be a clear prerequisite for deciding whether (or in what respect) the behavior of mediums or subjects in reincarnation cases differs from dramatic forms of dissociative behavior.[10]

The third problem with the literature on survival is that it fails to address central issues concerning the nature and limits of human abilities, especially those arising from (a) the vast literature on dissociation, (b) the study of savants and prodigies, and (c) the growing literature on intelligent or gifted "underachievers." The relevance of (a) is that in hypnosis, multiple personality, and certain forms of automatism, dissociation seems to liberate or permit the development of abilities that presumably wouldn't have manifested otherwise. The relevance of (b) is that prodigies and savants (and even ordinary people) can display abilities without undergoing a normal process of learning and practice, and (perhaps more important) in the absence of other skills and capacities that we would normally expect to occur alongside them. This is demonstrated most dramatically in the case of savants, whose anomalous abilities may be strikingly discontinuous with their other capacities. Consider, for example, a calculating savant who can factor any number presented to him but who can't add the coins in his pocket, or the musical savant who is spastic unless playing the piano. Furthermore, both (a) and (c) strongly suggest that we might all be reservoirs of latent intelligence and creativity. It may simply be a kind of historical accident whether or not we develop and express all or most of our capacities, or whether we develop them to their fullest. Clearly, then, we need to pay close attention to these different bodies of evidence as we evaluate survival cases suggesting the persistence of skills or abilities (i.e., knowledge-how)—for example, the evidence for communicating in unlearned languages (responsive xenoglossy). (See chapters 4 and 5 for a discussion of those issues.)

So when we consider together these last two defects in the survival literature, we see that several issues haven't yet been confronted satisfactorily. Perhaps the most urgent are (i) the extent to which normal learning and practice are prerequisites for the manifestation of abilities, (ii) the extent to which humans generally might possess impressive but latent creative, artistic, and linguistic capacities, whose expression or development are ordinarily hampered by interfering psychological and social pressures, and (iii) the extent to which physical, cognitive, and emotional obstacles to optimal performance might be overcome in dissociative and other types of altered states—including the unusual states of subjects in survival cases. In later chapters, we'll consider these and related matters in more detail.

The fourth weakness in the literature on survival, which connects clearly to the others, is that investigators of survival cases seldom probe beneath the psychological surface. This shortcoming afflicts discussions of both the Usual and the Unusual Suspects, but it's probably most acute in deliberations about motivated super psi. In those contexts, we try to determine whether people surreptitiously use their psychic abilities to obtain evidence or influence events in ways suggesting survival. So in those contexts the important question to consider is: Whose conscious or unconscious needs would be served by the appearance of evidence for survival? Unfortunately, however, investigators usually make only perfunctory efforts to answer that question. And as a result, the people involved in survival cases come off looking like psychological stick figures. We need to recognize that these people are typical human beings, despite the oddness of their experiences. Like the rest of us, they're teeming cauldrons of needs and interests, grappling with grubby real-life demands and concerns. And (of course) they're also saddled with a profound interest or investment in the phenomena swirling around them. But instead of recognizing and trying to penetrate the depth and complexity of their subjects, investigators often treat these individuals as if they're little more than potential emitters of (or vehicles for) psychic functioning.

Granted, sometimes investigators do speculate about the possible causal role of subjects' motivations, etc. But when they do, their efforts tend to be woefully inadequate. To put it bluntly, if their conjectures count as attempts to understand subject's motivations, it's only in the naive way we expect questionnaires or casual conversations to reveal the deepest secrets of one's soul, or else it's in the halfhearted or superficial way searches are usually conducted by the lazy or frightened.[11] We get no sense of who the subjects are, what really moved them, and what were the profound personal issues that shaped their lives and actions. But since it's antecedently plausible that psychic functioning is largely interest-relative and need-determined, this failure to probe beneath the psychological surface is clearly unacceptable. Here too, after we examine some of the better cases in detail, we'll be in a position to assess the severity of this problem.

But before we evaluate the psychological superficiality of particular case reports, we need to consider a different and more generic manifestation of the problem. Understandably, survival researchers want to examine the evidence, not simply on a case-by-case basis, but from a more global perspective. They want, naturally enough, to be able to generalize about the cases and look for revealing patterns in the data. So far, so good. But surveys have their limitations, and it's important to know what the crucial questions are and which ones can be asked profitably.

Virtually all case studies and surveys in survival research are modeled after the pioneering efforts of Ian Stevenson (see, e.g., Stevenson, 1974a, 1974b, 1975, 1977, 1980, 1983, 1984, 1990, 1997a, 1997b, 2000a, 2000b; Stevenson & Keil, 2000; Stevenson, Pasricha, & McLean-Rice, 1989; Stevenson & Samararatne, 1988). Although in many ways I regard that as unfortunate, it would also be a great mistake to underestimate the value of Stevenson's massive body of work. For one thing, from a public relations or political point of view, Stevenson has probably done more than any other investigator to make survival research respectable within the academic community. That's not to say that he's silenced all objections to the legitimacy of survival research. But Stevenson's work has seemed so meticulous, thorough, and level-headed (or perhaps merely conservative) that many open-minded readers have been willing to take seriously what they might otherwise have dismissed both uncritically and disdainfully. Moreover, Stevenson has done much to help rule out the Usual Suspects: the counter-hypotheses of fraud, misreporting, malobservation, and cryptomnesia. And also to his credit, Stevenson recognizes that the Unusual Suspects, and motivated super-psi explanations (positing various subconscious or unconscious motivations along with psi among the living) are more refractory.

It's not surprising, then, that other survival researchers have emulated Stevenson's methods and embraced his (usually tacit) assumptions about which issues matter (see, e.g., Haraldsson, 1991, 1995, 1997, 2000a, 2000b; Haraldsson & Samararatne, 1999; Keil, 1991, 1996; Mills, 1989, 1990a, 1990b, 1994; Pasricha, 1990a, 1990b, 1992, 1998). In the chapters that follow, I'll explain in detail why I've found some of Stevenson's work to be psychologically superficial, even when he attempts to address the topic of his subjects' motivations, and elsewhere I've very briefly lodged a similar complaint against his protégé and occasional collaborator, Satwant Pasricha (Braude, 1992b). To illustrate further how profoundly unilluminating this general body of work tends to be, I would like to consider a recent paper by Pasricha, which is characteristic of much of the literature on survival, and which at least appears to address a subtle psychological issue (Pasricha, 1992).

Pasricha considers and then rejects the *hypothesis of parental influence*, according to which "parents may assign to, and even impose on a child the personality of a deceased person" (p. 168), or (in other words) that "cases of the reincarnation type occur due to parental guidance of a child to speak or behave like a particular deceased person" (p. 177). This hypothesis is a close relative of the Usual Suspects. It's a sociopsychological alternative to a survivalist interpretation of reincarnation cases. Moreover, although it's a perfectly reasonable hypothesis that raises important issues about the evidence, I think Pasricha is justified in rejecting it. The problem, however, is that her arguments are unconvincing and miss the central issues.

Ostensibly, Pasricha's discussion is an effort to dig beneath the psychological surface, to deal with important questions regarding motivation. After all, if the hypothesis of parental influence is on the right track, the influence in question concerns the parents engaging in very subtle forms of manipulation and suggestion, presumably unconsciously. Otherwise (that is, if the parents consciously trained their child to act the part of a previous personality), the issue becomes one of fraud. So to counter the hypothesis of parental influence, it's important to look closely at the parents' motivation, and also the intricate and covert processes by which they might convey their desires to their children. But Pasricha never addresses these topics. She claims that the hypothesis of parental influence "presumes a detailed knowledge of such [reincarnation] cases and the deceased person on the part of the parents who are providing a model for the child" (p. 168). For her, the two crucial issues to consider are (a) whether the subject's parents "know, or at least know about, the presumed previous personality and/or his family" and (b) whether they "know the details of the features of other cases" (p. 177).

There are several problems with this position. First, even if the proposed parental influence requires knowledge of the deceased person, it seems false that it requires detailed knowledge of other reincarnation cases. In fact, those details may be largely irrelevant to what really matters in such cases: namely, the personal meaning *behind* the detail. To put the point another way, there needn't be a lawlike connection between (on the one hand) the importance to the parents of a reincarnation case in the family and (on the other) the actual details of the case. In fact, in the absence of two critical pieces of information, we simply have no idea what particular features of a given case are likely to be important. These are (i) *why* the parents might want their child to behave as if he/she is the reincarnation of *some* previous personality or other, and (ii) why it would be important for the parents to single out the specific previous personality whom their child appears to be. But Pasricha and Stevenson apparently seldom (if ever) ask the sorts of questions that would elicit this information. Or if they do, they apparently don't pursue those matters with the tenacity or attention to detail that characterizes their treatment of peripheral features of the cases. Certainly, these deeper issues fall outside the scope of their surveys.

Revealingly, what Pasricha finds relevant and potentially important about the cases are features the parents would probably consider trivial. These include (a) the interval between the previous personality's death and the subject's birth, (b) whether the previous personality died violently or naturally, and (c) the age at which the subject started (or stopped) speaking about a previous life. Another feature, the difference in caste level, is obviously more likely to matter. But not even that needs to be important to the parent. Granted, membership in a higher socioeconomic class provides "at least a motive for linking the subjects' family to that of the previous personality" (p. 177). But we can't subvert the hypothesis of parental influence by showing that there is no evidence for—or that there is evidence against—the existence of any such link. There may simply be other details about a previous personality that matter more than socioeconomic status. Actually, it may be the mere *fact* of reincarnation, rather than any particular details, that matters to the parents. In general, what matters most in evaluating the hypothesis of parental influence is the personal significance the subject's parents attach to their child's claims of a former life. Clearly, that kind of personal meaning or psychological investment may be wildly idiosyncratic from one case to the next, and of course it can't be detected with general and relatively impersonal surveys.

A further example of the psychological superficiality (or naivete) of Pasricha's study is the following remark. "Another reason why it is unlikely that parents shape and guide the child's statements or behavior, is that in many cases...the previous life presented by a child is uncongenial and even annoying to the parents" (p. 178). Apparently, Pasricha is assuming that parents in those cases wouldn't consciously or unconsciously encourage annoying behavior in their children. Now perhaps some parents would never do such a thing. But you don't have to be a mental health professional to recognize that this assumption isn't true of parents generally, or (more generally still) to recognize that people often act contrary to their avowed or surface interests. So for Pasricha's argument to carry any weight, she'd have to show why specific parents in specific reincarnation cases were not doing what most parents probably do at some time or another. And once again, no survey can elicit that information.

Along the same lines, Pasricha counters the hypothesis of parental influence by arguing that "although Hindu parents of northern India almost all believe in reincarnation, most of them believe that a child who remembers a previous life will become ill and even die prematurely" (p. 178). Here, her assumption is that Hindu parents who have that belief want no harm to befall their children; thus, they wouldn't (unconsciously) encourage their children to act as if they were a previous personality. But once again, you don't need to be a mental health professional to see what's wrong with Pasricha's assumption. People's wishes and actions often run contrary to their conscious desires, and parents *do* sometimes harbor death wishes against their offspring (just as children sometimes harbor death wishes against their parents). Moreover, these are truths about people generally, not rare or unusual individuals.

I should emphasize that I'm not interested in singling out Pasricha, or anyone in particular, for criticism (at least not here). Pasricha's paper is characteristic of much of the empirical literature on survival in its psychological superficiality and attention to peripheral or irrelevant detail. But it's important to grasp what sorts of insignificant details most authors focus on, how they frequently display an astonishing degree of psychological naivete (especially disappointing in cases when the authors are psychologists or psychiatrists), and how they either ignore or simply don't understand the importance of examining the *meaning* of the phenomena suggesting survival. Later chapters will reinforce this point in connection with specific cases.

I should also emphasize that I direct these criticisms toward the literature on survival generally, not simply studies of apparent reincarnation. Most case studies of mediumship likewise have only skimmed the psychological surface. At any rate, now that we're fortified by (or saddled with) these various admonitions and other preliminaries, we can dive fearlessly into the messy particulars of actual cases. Only then can we determine how successfully the survival and super-psi hypotheses handle the evidence.

NOTES

1. The literature surveying the evidence is now so vast that providing a comprehensive reference list at this point is out of the question. To readers unfamiliar with the data, I (not-so-humbly) recommend Braude, 1997 and 2002 for philosophical appraisals, and also Broughton, 1991 and Radin, 1997 for accessible and level-headed surveys.

2. Perhaps surprisingly, this argument has been advanced by several prominent philosophers. See, e.g., Schlick, 1936; Wisdom, 1952; and more generally on the concept of bodiless existence, Ayer, 1973; Mackie, 1982.

3. That's one reason why Fred Feldman's discussion of survival is disappointingly superficial (Feldman, 1992, chapter 6). Although his discussion is both interesting and clever, he treats the topic as if it can be settled merely by paying attention to the careful use of terms and the framing of crisp definitions. One could also object that this approach was doomed anyway, quite apart from its obliviousness to case material, because concepts or terms are always more vague than Feldman's approach can tolerate.

4. Among recent writers on the subject, Trenton Merricks has been especially careful to draw this distinction. See, e.g., Merricks, 1998, 2001. Also, Paterson, 1995, pp. 21–22.

5. To that extent I sympathize with the "Minimalism" advocated by Mark Johnston (see, e.g., Johnston, 1992). Johnston writes,

> The Minimalist has it that although ordinary practitioners may naturally be led to adopt metaphysical pictures as a result of their practices, and perhaps a little philosophical prompting, the practices are typically not dependent on the truth of the pictures. Practices that endure and spread are typically justifiable in nonmetaphysical terms. To this the Minimalist adds that we can do better in holding out against various sorts of skepticism and unwarranted revision when we correctly represent ordinary practice as having given no hostages to metaphysical fortune.
>
> In the particular case of personal identity, Minimalism will imply that any metaphysical view of persons that we might have is not indispensable to the justification of our practice of making judgments about personal identity and organizing our

Chapter 1

practical concerns around those judgments. (Johnston, 1992, p. 590)

A related position (which we can't examine here) is Paterson's rejection of the purely philosophical worries about identity on the basis of their intractability. He writes,

> From our failure to discover the *fons et origo* of the continuing and unique identity we ascribe to living persons it follows that we have no special, imperative, inescapable intellectual obligation to discover it and set it forth in the case of deceased persons. (Paterson, 1995, p. 23)

6. Some writers on survival suggest that knowledge-how entails (or can be defined in terms of) possessing certain abilities or skills. But it's clear that a person can have knowledge-how without possessing any corresponding ability. For example, a now disabled tennis pro (or simply a moderately skilled instructor) may know how to hit effective passing shots without being able to do so.

7. Clearly, in this book I'm not using the term "survivalist" in the now somewhat familiar sense in which it denotes members of certain paramilitary groups.

8. I participate in an insider's parapsychology discussion group on the internet. Members of the group engage regularly in interesting, sophisticated, and thoughtful debates over the best ways to explain the data. What these discussions illustrate dramatically is how little even the people who study psi most closely understand about it. Often, debates center precisely on the issue of whether competing theoretical approaches accommodate the more extreme or refined phenomena for which we seem to have evidence. The bottom line: nobody has a clue. And I'd say that the problem we face as a result is that we're not in a position to rule anything out.

9. I thank Adam Crabtree for reminding me of this remark, mentioned in one of his recent lectures (Crabtree, 1998).

10. C. D. Broad, to his credit, was not guilty of this oversight, and his discussion of survival remains one of the most valuable in the philosophical literature (Broad, 1962). Unfortunately, although Broad had more than a passing acquaintance with the literature on multiple personality, we've learned a great deal in the interim about the variety and subtlety of its manifestations. So Broad's discussion of those issues, regrettably, now seems rather quaint. Contemporary authors, of course, have no such excuse, and as we'll see in later chapters, their evaluations of the evidence suffer accordingly.

11. The attempts in the survival literature to understand subjects' psychologies often remind me of the way my stepson used to look for a lost item he preferred someone else to spend time locating. He would open his closet door (say), look around quickly, and announce, "I can't find it."

Chapter 2
Drop-In Communicators

1. Introduction

Although many survival cases are impressive, some are particularly useful in helping us get a feel for the issues. Accordingly, we begin with a type of case that illustrates clearly not only the challenges facing super-psi explanations, but also the reasons why those explanations are difficult to dismiss. First, however, we should survey quickly some general features of mediumship.

Mediumship, like humor, comes in different styles. One way to distinguish the varieties of mediumship is with respect to the medium's degree of altered state or "trance." Some mediums relay messages from (or describe) communicators without significantly modifying their normal waking state. They claim that their mediumistic activities are as routine, clear, and natural as reporting statements of (or describing) people standing next to them. Other mediums experience a light trance, in which they are slightly "spacy" or distracted but are nevertheless able to go about their usual business (e.g., washing dishes in the kitchen). Still other mediums experience a much deeper alteration of consciousness, similar (at least on the surface) to what occurs in cases of multiple personality (or dissociative identity) disorder (MPD/DID). Like multiples, these mediums "lose time," and their normal waking state is replaced by another state of consciousness (that of the ostensible communicator). Usually, the medium has no knowledge of what transpired during the communication and apparent possession of her body.

In addition to these variations in the mediumistic *state*, we can also discern variations in the mediumistic *process*. Some mediums seem almost to be taking dictation, as if they were listening to someone and then simply repeating or interpreting what they were told. For example, the medium might say, "Your Uncle Harry is speaking to me now, and he wants you to know that..." Other mediums, rather than "hearing" communicators, experience mental images which they then describe or interpret. For example, the medium might say, "I see an older, bearded man, fairly short, and wearing a dark suit of the kind worn in the late

31

1800s. The suit is torn, and the man is pointing to a large bruise on his forehead. I feel as if he has had an accident involving heavy machinery."

But the most dramatic cases are those in which mediums seem to be physically controlled by a communicator. Some relinquish command only of parts of their bodies, as in automatic writing or drawing. Others apparently have their entire body possessed or controlled by a so-called *trance-personality* (or persona), who speaks in a different voice from that of the medium and whose behavior (in the best cases) resembles that of a formerly living person. In the most evidential cases, these similarities extend to subtle verbal mannerisms, voice quality, and characteristic facial expressions. Although trance personalities often supplant a medium's waking consciousness, others leave the medium moderately functional. For example, some mediums can do housework and even write letters while communicators speak or write through them. But not all heavy-trance mediums deliver their messages through trance-personalities. For example, Mrs. Piper would sometimes swoon and drop her head onto pillows arranged in front of her on the table, after which she would produce automatic writing. The sitters then had to move the paper to prevent her words from running off or piling up.

Mediumship can also be a group experience—for example, when sitters gather around a ouija or planchette board, or when they assemble around a séance table for table-tilting. In the case of ouija board communications, the pointer spells out messages one letter at a time (sometimes at a very rapid pace) as it moves around the board. When the planchette is used, sitters lightly touch a pointer attached to a pencil, which writes messages on an underlying piece of paper. And in the case of table-tilting, sitters rest their hands on top of a table. Messages can then be spelled out according to a simple code, or the table can indicate "yes" or "no" to questions posed by the sitters. Generally speaking, participants in these forms of group mediumship feel that some power other than their own moves the objects beneath their fingers. And as with other forms of mediumship, the most interesting cases are when the received messages convey information known normally to no one present at the séance.

Of course, in some instances it seems clear that the material originated from the deep strata of a sitter's mind. The following example from Gauld is too good not to be repeated.

> I was once a sitter in a circle which received pungent communications from Goering and Goebbels and other deceased Nazi leaders. They favoured us with such interesting pieces of information as that Hitler was alive and well and operating a petrol pump in the town of Clifton, Arkansas, and that Martin Bormann was in Gothenburg disguised as a priest by the name of Father Odo. They favoured us also with various apologias for Nazism. After several sessions it became apparent that this little band of unrepentant sinners only communicated when the finger of one particular

person was on the glass. Very reluctantly he admitted that many years before he had gone through a phase of admiration for certain features of Hitler's Germany, and he had joined an extreme right-wing political organization. Now he repudiated, even abhorred, his former paltering with Nazism. None the less these views were clearly still alive in him somewhere, and slipped out when his conscious censorship was circumvented by the ouija board. I am absolutely certain that he was not deliberately manipulating the glass—his embarrassment was too great, and he refused to participate further. (Gauld, 1982, pp. 26–27)

Granted, the material here was initially implausible and relatively easy to trace to a sitter's mind. And Gauld assures me that nobody at the time took these communications to be evidence of survival. Still, the case illustrates nicely how unconscious needs and interests of the living can manifest in mediumistic contexts. Clearly, what we need to consider is whether similar unconscious processes are at work when the ostensible communications are less obviously bogus.

Mediums often work through so-called *controls* or *control-personalities*. These are recurrent and self-consistent characters who act as interpreters or intermediaries (or masters-of-ceremony) between sitters and communicators. Typically, they also look after the medium's interests, but some controls belligerently assert their own self-interest (e.g., by throwing tantrums and refusing to cooperate with sitters unless appeased). Most controls are flagrantly artificial personalities, often claiming to be from locales that would be exotic to the medium, and often claiming to be and acting like children. Eileen Garrett's control, Uvani, claimed to be the spirit of a deceased Arab. Mrs. Garrett would speak in a low, masculine tone, and Uvani would usually introduce himself by saying "It is I, Uvani. I bring you greetings, friends." Mrs. Leonard's principal control, Feda, was childlike and unpredictable, but often charming. During Feda's periods of control, Mrs. Leonard was very animated, gesturing frequently and broadly, and she spoke in a childlike, girlish voice, in a foreign accent and with unusual pronunciation of many words. But Uvani and Feda were merely colorful. Other controls are more comical and bizarre. Often, controls of English mediums have claimed to be Native Americans, Black Africans, Arabs, or Chinese, and their opinions, behavior, and diction had the "stilted and stylized" appearance of a caricature or cinematic stereotype (Gauld, 1982, p. 115). Moreover, some controls exhibit extreme ethnological confusions. One, claiming to be a Black African child, asked C. D. Broad for the *key to his wigwam*. Another, who claimed to be a Native American chief, requested the sitters to encourage him by singing "Swanee River" (Broad, 1962, p. 254).

Control personalities provide ammunition for those opposed to survivalist interpretations of mediumship. Given their obvious artificiality, there can be little doubt that the medium constructed them subconsciously. In fact, as Gauld observed in connection with Mrs. Piper,

> Even the most life-like and realistic controls, such as GP, show signs of
> being impersonations (not deliberate ones). They break down at just the
> point where Mrs. Piper's own stock of knowledge runs out, viz. when they
> are required to talk coherently of science, philosophy and literature (which
> the living GP could readily have done). (Gauld, 1982, p. 114)

Some of Mrs. Piper's controls offered a familiar but unsatisfactory explanation of these deficiencies. They claimed to be confused and disori-
ented by coming into the medium's "light." But, as Gauld recognized,

> The confusion which obliterates the controls' grasp of science and philoso-
> phy does not prevent them from spouting reams of pompous nonsense
> upon religious and philosophical topics and presenting it as the profound-
> est truth...; so that we have to attribute to them not just confusion but
> downright tale-spinning, which was certainly not a habit of the purported
> communicators in life, nor yet of the normal Mrs. Piper. (Gauld, 1982, p.
> 115)

Gauld continues,

> Similar tale-spinning tendencies are manifested in the way in which con-
> trols cover up their mistakes. Controls will, generally speaking, not admit
> their blunders. They will rationalize, explain away, concoct any excuse,
> however tenuous and childish. All other considerations seem subordinated
> to an overwhelming urge to keep the drama flowing without pause or hic-
> cup. (Gauld, 1982, p. 115)

Granted, some controls are compellingly lifelike. But as Gauld also
notes, it doesn't help that the most convincing communicators adamantly vouch for the authenticity of the least plausible controls. That
makes it seem as if "the authenticity of the former is inextricably and
disadvantageously tied up with the authenticity of the latter" (p. 115).
So it doesn't require much of a leap to suspect that realistic communicators are likewise creative constructs, possibly based on information
the medium acquired psychically.

I should add that the communicators themselves are also sometimes
clearly fictional, although seldom as extravagantly contrived as the controls who apparently transmit their messages. For example, in 1909
Stanley Hall deceived Mrs. Piper's Hodgson control by asking for, and
then receiving, messages from a niece, Bessie Beals, who never existed.
When confronted by Hall, the Hodgson-control could only offer lame
explanations. The interesting exchange between investigator and spirit-
control was as follows (Tanner, 1910, p. 254; Sidgwick, 1915, pp.
177–178) (The expression "Hodgson$_p$" refers, not to Hodgson himself,
who was dead, but to the mediumistic Hodgson-*persona*).

> Dr. Hall: Well, what do you say to this, Hodgson. I asked you to call Bessie
> Beals, and there is no such person. How do you explain that?

Hodgson$_p$: Bessie Beals is here, and not the —
(Note by Miss Tanner)
[At this point we laughed and I made some remark to the effect that that was just what we had said Hodgson would do, and the hand continued thus,]
Hodgson$_p$: I know a Bessie Beals. Her mother asked about her before. Mother asked about her before.
Dr. Hall: I don't know about that, Hodgson. Bessie Beals is a pure fiction.
Hodgson$_p$: I refer to a lady who asked me the same thing and the same name.
Dr. Hall: Guess you are wrong about that, Hodgson.
Hodgson$_p$: Yes, I am mistaken in her. I am mistaken. Her name was not Bessie, but Jessie Beals.

Mrs. Sidgwick's comment on this exchange was understated, to say the least. She wrote, "We can only say about this explanation that it is not plausible" (Sidgwick, 1915, p. 178). Nevertheless, it's difficult to know what, exactly, was going on. For example, we may need to account for the role played by the investigators' skeptically contemptuous and deceptive attitude. It's possible, if not likely, that the results Tanner and Hall obtained with Mrs. Piper represent a kind of experimenter effect found throughout the history of parapsychology and elsewhere in the behavioral sciences. In fact, these investigators seemed clearly to have a chilling effect on Mrs. Piper's mediumistic abilities. In the next chapter I'll return to that episode and discuss other sorts of outside influences on mediumistic performance.

Of course, not all mediumistic communicators are dramatically ludicrous or otherwise easily dismissed. One reason mediumship is interesting is that some cases provide compelling evidence suggesting survival, and very clear evidence that *something* paranormal was going on. Obviously, then, the crucial issue is whether this residue of mediumistic phenomena favors a survivalist explanation even more than a super-psi explanation.

2. Outline of the Issues

In the previous chapter I noted that subjects in good mediumistic and reincarnation cases demonstrate anomalous sorts of knowledge—either in the form of information (knowledge-that) or as embodied in skills and capacities (knowledge-how). In many of the mediumistic cases, this knowledge is supplied by what Ian Stevenson has termed "drop-in" communicators. As the name suggests, drop-in communicators arrive uninvited, and often neither medium nor sitters know who they are. Of course, in the most intriguing cases, drop-ins make statements about themselves which are later verified and which nobody present at the séance knew to be true. And occasionally, the drop-in's behavior (as expressed through the medium) resembles that of the communicator when alive.

Although drop-in communications are fairly common in mediumistic settings, only a small number seem to have been verified (e.g., Gauld, 1971, 1993; Gibbes, 1937; Haraldsson & Stevenson, 1975a; Myers, 1903, vol. 2, pp. 471–477; Stevenson, 1970, 1973; Tyrrell, 1939; Zorab, 1940). Presumably, that's because verifying a drop-in case is a complex and laborious business. Typically, it demands careful note taking at the outset, and then the painstaking processes of conducting detailed interviews, and locating and inspecting public records. Probably, most sitters at casual séances would rather avoid such a time-consuming investigation. Moreover, sitters may be more interested in apparent personal communications from deceased friends and relatives, and of course they may be convinced already about the reality of survival. So they would probably find it either irrelevant or unnecessary to gather careful evidence of survival.

As Gauld noted, good drop-in cases discourage super-psi explanations for two main reasons (Gauld, 1982, pp. 58ff). The first concerns the identity and apparent purpose of the communicator. We need to explain why the medium (or someone else present at the sitting) would use ESP to obtain information about an individual who was unknown to those present at the séance. Generally speaking, those attending séances are interested primarily in "contacting" individuals they knew. Why, then, would a medium apparently waste time providing information about a total stranger, one whose story can't be verified without further (and probably tedious) investigation? If the medium is using psi or normal sleuthing to obtain information about purported communicators, why not just gather information about those likely to be targeted by the sitters? We also need to explain why the communicator supplies information of no apparent interest to the sitters but of understandably serious concern to the communicator. (A good example is the case of Runki's leg, which we examine below.) By contrast, the survival hypothesis seems appealingly straightforward. To put it simply, the séance provides a forum for communication which the drop-in exploits for urgent personal reasons (e.g., to console a grieving relative or to take care of important unfinished business).

The second obstacle facing super-psi explanations concerns the obscurity and diffuseness of the information provided by the drop-in. According to the super-psi version of events, sitters at the séance use ESP to obtain this information themselves. However, in the best cases that information is hidden and also seemingly irrelevant to any living person's concerns. So in addition to considering why a living person would have been motivated to dig up that obscure information, advocates of super psi must explain how the medium or sitters were able to *locate* it in the first place. Since the information was apparently personally meaningless, what pointed them in the right direction? Moreover, although in most cases the information would need to come from only a single source (e.g., a written record, or one living person's memory), in others it would have to be assembled from separate and equally obscure sources (e.g., different written records and memories). To many, that attributes an implausible degree of accurate psychic functioning to those at the séance. By contrast, on the survival hypothesis the necessary information may all be reasonably and conveniently attributed to a single, conspicuous source: the drop-in communicator.

Certainly, we can agree with Gauld that the first of these problems is substantial. At least on the surface, the psychodynamics of drop-in cases are most prominent and straightforward from the communicator's point of view. The second problem, however, may be overrated. One reason (noted in chapter 1) is that we presently have no grounds for imposing any limits on the scope or refinement of psychic functioning. But another problem concerns the notion of *obscure information*. Ordinarily, we understand (roughly at least) what it means to say that some information is obscure. But that conception of obscurity applies only to *normal* methods of acquiring information. For example, we consider information to be obscure when it's outside our perceptual field or otherwise difficult to access physically (e.g., if it's behind layers of security or other barriers, or if it's remote geographically and not accessible electronically). By contrast, we don't understand how any physically or perceptually remote information might be acquired by ESP, whether it's the carefully sealed picture on the table before us or an object thousands of miles away. But then we're in no position to insist that normally obscure information is also psychically obscure. And in fact, most targets identified by ESP satisfy our ordinary criteria of obscurity. So right from the start, it's implausible to insist that normal forms of obscurity are barriers to the operation of ESP. Similarly, we're in no position to insist that the diffuseness of information is a barrier to successful ESP. As far as we know, psychically accessing multiple sources of normally obscure information is no more imposing than accessing one.

Furthermore, as we evaluate the possibility of super psi, we should be careful not to assume that super psi is merely a collection of really good psi, of the kind we apparently see in limited forms in some lab experiments. When we do that, it's all too easy to think that psychic functioning involves an *effort* of some kind, so that if one psi performance is difficult, several ought to be out of the question. Instead (as I noted in the last chapter), we need to consider the super-psi hypothesis in all its intimidating richness. In fact, we need to look beyond multiple-process forms of super psi and consider seriously a kind of *magic wand* hypothesis. According to that hypothesis, (a) psi agency requires nothing more than an efficacious need or wish (under favorable conditions), and (b) given such an efficacious need or wish, virtually *anything at all* can happen. But in that case, we needn't suppose that fine-grained ESP requires complex search procedures—for example, of the sort used in looking up references in a library, acquiring information over the internet, or foraging for clues in a police investigation. And we needn't suppose that refined PK demands constant ESP monitoring of the results of one's activities—for example, as steering a car and brain surgery require sensory feedback. It may be enough merely to wish for something to happen, and then it does. Task complexity may simply not be an issue.[1]

I also noted in the last chapter that from this perspective, successful psychic functioning would resemble placebo effects or success in biofeedback studies, where subjects produce remarkable physiological changes without conscious effort and without knowing how they accomplished the task. In fact, several converging lines of parapsychological research suggest an intriguing parallel with biofeedback studies. In both cases it appears that subjects do best under conditions of *passive volition*—that is, when (instead of actively trying to succeed) they simply wish, want, or expect, a result to occur (e.g., Palmer, 1978, pp. 90–92; Schmeidler, 1994, pp. 175–176).[2] Furthermore, it's not just in connection with the super-psi hypothesis that the apparent irrelevance of task complexity is an issue. Conventional experiments with random number generators also suggest that task complexity has little if any effect on the success of psi tasks (e.g., Braude, 2002; Schmidt, 1975, 1976.) So it's hardly unprecedented to suggest, in this context, that successful psychic functioning may be insensitive to task complexity, or at least more so than is commonly supposed.

The first problem, that of explaining the identity and apparent purpose of the communicator, raises more vexing (if less bizarre) issues. In fact, the survival hypothesis has obvious advantages when it comes to explaining why the medium "connects with" one unknown deceased person rather than another. Whereas advocates of super psi need to explain why a living person *selects* an unknown deceased person out of an unlimited pool, survivalists tell an apparently simple story. The communicator self-selects (Gauld, 1982, p. 61). Indeed, as Stevenson once remarked, "Some 'drop-in' communicators have explained their presence very well" (Stevenson, 1970, p. 63). But according to Gauld, on the super-psi hypothesis "we seem reduced...to supposing that selection of communicator depends upon the random operation of wholly unknown factors" (p. 59). Stevenson concurs, and his way of stating the point brings its weakness squarely into the open. He writes,

> Since the [super-psi] theory assumes that discarnate personalities do *not* exist, it has to attribute motive for a particular mediumistic communication or apparitional experience to the subject. But evidence of such a motive is not always available, and we should not assume that one exists in the absence of such evidence. (Stevenson, 1984, p. 159)

The proper reply to this has two parts: First, we shouldn't assume that the evidence of motive is *absent* unless we look for it; and second, hardly anyone looks for it, except in the casual or relatively superficial way mentioned in the last chapter. If the motives in question exist, they're unlikely to reveal themselves to the sorts of investigations Stevenson and others conduct. Without an extensive and penetrating examination into the lives of clearly relevant (and perhaps even seemingly peripheral) personnel, we have no basis for rejecting explanations in terms of motivated super psi.

Some might feel that this criticism is unfair. First, sometimes a cigar is just a cigar. That is, sometimes sitters' motives seem quite clear, and additional competent questioning turns up nothing worth pursuing (the sitter group described by Gauld, 1971, 1993, may well belong in that category). Moreover, our goals and interests are often unconscious and difficult to discern, and in actual case investigations we may have no real prospect of ferreting out subjects' deepest needs and concerns. That's especially true for older cases, where we can no longer interrogate medium and sitters.

Now I grant that some cases seem psychologically straightforward. And I grant that in many (if not most) cases we may never get a handle on the potentially relevant underlying psychodynamics, no matter how hard we try. Still, that's no reason for not trying, even in cases that seem clear. And often we don't have to probe very far to glimpse some of the significant psychological activity simmering beneath the surface. Indeed, a few case studies reveal clearly how much we stand to learn from psychological detective work, and they show why even sensitive questioning of the sitters may not reveal relevant dispositions and behavioral patterns.

3. The Cagliostro Case

Possibly the best example is Eisenbud's intriguing and brilliant analysis of Mrs. Chenoweth's Cagliostro persona (Eisenbud, 1992, chapter 14). The case is complex and deserves to be read in its entirety. As in all the best cases, it's the details that count, and no summary can do justice to the subtlety and shrewdness of Eisenbud's review. Unfortunately, however, we have no choice but to summarize.

James Hyslop was Professor of logic and ethics at Columbia University from 1889 to 1902 and also one of the founders of the American Society for Psychical Research. A staunch advocate of the survival hypothesis, Hyslop wrote extensively on psychical research and conducted many detailed investigations of mediums. In 1914, he held a series of sittings with one of his favorite mediums, Mrs. Minnie M. Soule, whose pseudonym was "Mrs. Chenoweth." Another sitter was Doris Fischer, the subject of W. F. Prince's monumental study of multiple personality (Prince, 1915/16). Hyslop, too, had a professional interest in Doris, because he suspected that multiple personality was a disguised form of mediumship (Hyslop, 1917).

Over the series of sittings, several trance personalities manifested through Mrs. Chenoweth. One of the most interesting was a drop-in who claimed to be Count Alessandro Cagliostro, the notorious eighteenth-century mystic, healer, and (as some have alleged) con artist. The behavior of this trance personality was vivid and flamboyantly salacious, but nevertheless rather one-dimensional. Cagliostro came through as a vigorous defender of sexual freedom, including that of women, and as a severe critic of Christianity. In fact, the Cagliostro persona behaved like "a reckless blasphemer who wouldn't have lasted forty-eight hours in the Church-dominated Europe of the time" (Eisenbud, p. 230). More important, however, the behavior of the Cagliostro persona was probably quite different from that of the actual Cagliostro.

The real Cagliostro was arrested in Rome in 1789 and brought to trial by the Holy Inquisition. Charged with freemasonry, heresy, and promulgating magic and superstition, he was condemned to death, although that sentence was later reduced to life imprisonment. But Mrs. Chenoweth's Cagliostro-persona gave no indication of that history. Nor did it match the personality of Cagliostro emerging from available biographies. Instead, it corresponded more closely to a very different portrayal of the Count, one that apparently originated with the Vatican. Eisenbud claimed that the Vatican's description of Cagliostro remained buried in its archives and that the Cagliostro-persona's behavior matched none of the accounts of Cagliostro's life published up to the time of the sittings. According to Eisenbud, it wasn't until 1972 that an account of Cagliostro appeared which presented the Vatican's version of the trial, and that account wasn't translated into English until 1974.

So this case presents a surprising puzzle. The Cagliostro trance persona failed to match the picture of Cagliostro painted by all the reliable sources available, not only at the time of the sittings, but until the present time as well. Outside of the Vatican's version of the facts, not even critical accounts of Cagliostro accused him of being lascivious or religiously cynical. Indeed, there is reason to think that Cagliostro's trial was rigged and that it was simply expedient for the Vatican to charge him with blasphemy and rampaging licentiousness.

It seems clear, then, that Mrs. Chenoweth's trance impersonation presented no evidence for the survival of Cagliostro. But in that case, what was the function, psychodynamically speaking, of the Cagliostro-persona? Why should a colorful but historically inaccurate trance personality emerge who was so flagrantly sexual and religiously cynical? Whose needs might that have satisfied? Eisenbud recognized that these were the appropriate questions to ask, and he offered intriguing reasons for thinking that the Cagliostro-persona had a great deal to do with, among other things, the sitters' sexual repressions and religious upbringing. Here, of course, is where details count most; but we'll have to settle for a tasteful selection.

For example, Hyslop, who "apparently devoted much of his life to spiritual and moral development" (Eisenbud, pp. 233–234), predictably found the Count to be a deplorable figure. So it seems particularly interesting and significant that Hyslop—by his own admission—repeatedly encountered nonspiritual, immoral, and "sensuous" characters in sittings he conducted. As Eisenbud nicely put it, "Hyslop seemed to find himself locked into some sort of epic Manichean struggle against the forces of evil" (p. 234). And as Eisenbud also recognized, in those days few took seriously as a "psychological possibility" that there might be "an internal dynamic connection between the spiritually inclined professor and the low 'sensuous' characters who kept turning up at the séances he attended" (p. 234). In fact, in those days few appreciated the possibility of experimenter effects in case investigations. But as many now recognize, investigators can't be viewed simply as passive outside observers and note takers, playing no role in the production of the phenomena. Of course, this problem is especially serious in the behavioral sciences, where there are many opportunities for subtle and uncontrollable forms of experimenter influence and subject-experimenter interactions. But in that case, experimenter effects, both normal and paranormal, are presumably as likely in the study of mediums as in more conventional laboratory tests.

But Hyslop wasn't the only séance participant who may have had a deep investment in the Cagliostro-persona. Doris (like Hyslop) was a model of moral propriety. In fact, she seemed almost to be a caricature of naive virtue. According to W. F. Prince, "A purer, more guileless soul it was never the writer's good fortune to know." Prince also notes that Doris had a "notable lack of sex-instinct." Now it apparently never occurred to Prince (or, for that matter, Hyslop) that Doris's lack of sexuality may have indicated an inhibition of powerful sexual desires. And as I noted above, in 1914 few considered seriously the possibility of experimenter-influence, and in particular the possibility that persons other than the medium might play an active role in shaping the material presented by a medium.

Furthermore, Mrs. Chenoweth betrayed a surprisingly intense attachment to the Count when it looked as if other communicators might banish him from the scene. (To appreciate the powerful emotions behind her words, I suggest reading her comments aloud.) Crying to the other ostensible communicators who tried to exorcise him, Mrs. Chenoweth said, "You give him back [Pause] You give him back...Give the Count back to me." Hyslop asked who wanted the Count, and Mrs. Chenoweth replied, "We all do. We are lost. We are lost, we are lost, we are lost [Pause] Oh, Devils, to take him away from us. [Distress and crying]...I won't stand it [Pause] I don't want your old God. I want the Count."

For these and other reasons, Eisenbud proposes that the Cagliostro-persona might have been a composite "dream figure omnibus for the repressed unconscious hankerings of all the principals at the sittings" (pp. 237–238). And considering some of the startlingly close correspondences between the trance personality and the behavior attributed to Cagliostro by the Church, it appears as if one or more of Mrs. Chenoweth, Hyslop, and Doris Fischer psychically raided an extremely obscure portrayal of Count Cagliostro to provide some material for the sitting.

Alan Gauld, whose mastery of both contemporary and historical sources is nothing short of breathtaking, has expressed some doubt about Eisenbud's conjectures. He informs me that the Vatican view of Cagliostro was initially published, at least in part, in a book printed in Rome in 1790. That book was then translated into French the following year. According to Gauld, the book "appears to contain quite enough about [Cagliostro's] licentiousness and heresy to have supplied the source for much subsequent scuttlebut about him" (personal communication, May 15, 1999). Gauld adds that "in addition to historical works about Cagliostro...he appeared in quite a lot of novels and plays, some by well-known authors (including one who had known him, Catherine II of Russia). (He was also a communicator through at least one other medium!) So the scope for medium or sitters to have heard all kinds of things about him, good and bad, was very large even at that date."

Now Gauld may be right. There may have been several sources, besides the apparently spurious and obscure Vatican version, from which members of Mrs. Chenoweth's circle could have constructed the Cagliostro persona. And it may be that no psi was required to provide the relevant information. But for present purposes, it doesn't matter particularly whether Eisenbud's psychoanalytic conjectures are correct. And it doesn't even matter whether the correspondences between the Cagliostro-persona and the Vatican account are accidental, attributable to a familiar pool of information, or arranged through psychic sleuthing. What matters is the level at which Eisenbud attempted to evaluate the data.

In psi research, it's always something of a mystery how best to trace the putative psychic causal lines. The value of Eisenbud's speculations is the match he seems to have uncovered between (on the one hand) the sitters' "unconscious hankerings" and life issues and (on the other) the character of the vivid but one-dimensional trance persona. The Cagliostro-persona offers nothing convincing in the way of evidence of survival, and it may well be historically inaccurate even if Gauld's concerns are justified. But it was at least as dramatically satisfying as most mediumistic trance-personalities, and for that reason it's precisely the kind of mediumistic performance that makes a strong *prima facie* case for survival. So despite Gauld's reservations, Eisenbud's essay illustrates the level of psychological probing required for illuminating survival research. By understanding how compelling, but non-evidential, mediumistic evidence is produced, we can be more alert for the operation of similar processes in more evidential cases. Still, Eisenbud's proposals do make good sense of the evidence, including peculiar and otherwise unexplained bits of behavior on the part of the sitters. So even if we reject Eisenbud's view concerning the origin of the trance-persona's characteristics, it's still plausible that the Cagliostro-persona makes most sense as a dramatic creation by one or more of the sitters.[3]

I suppose some might think that psychological archeology is especially critical in cases such as this, which are emotionally and dramatically potent but also non-evidential. However, I'd argue that they matter most in cases that are apparently evidential, where it's all too easy to overlook underlying and relatively pedestrian human concerns. After all, both evidential and non-evidential cases may be emotionally charged, and participants may care deeply about the form and content of the phenomena. The Cagliostro case seems to demonstrate both a high level of dramatic creativity and possibly also a kind of psychic collaboration among some of the sitters. But with that sort of evidence staring us in the face, it's both presumptuous and naive to rule out super-psi conjectures in cases where no comparable depth-psychological study has been conducted. Regrettably, however, by comparison to Eisenbud's standard of analysis, most other case investigations are unacceptably superficial.

4. Runki's Leg: The Case

As I noted earlier, there are several related respects in which drop-in communicators are particularly intriguing, and in virtue of which super-psi explanations may seem less plausible than survivalist alternatives. First, the communicators are unknown to the sitters at the time of the sitting. Therefore (and second), it's hard to see why that particular communicator came to be dramatized or represented during the séance. What pointed the medium's (or sitters') psi in that direction? And third, in the best cases the communicator's motive for communicating seems both greater and clearer than any living person's motive to receive those communications. That is, the communicator in these cases has a much clearer agenda than any we might reasonably attribute to medium, sitter, or anyone else. So a viable super-psi explanation of a good drop-in case faces several challenges. Naturally, it must account for the verifiable information provided in the sittings and (if necessary) the accurate dramatic representation of the previous personality's behavior. But more important, it must also explain away the drop-in's apparent motivations. And for the super-psi explanation to be *preferable* to the straightforward survivalist explanation, it must specify which living person(s) had needs, even stronger than those of the drop-in, for the séance to unfold as it did. That's a tall order.

Probably the best drop-in case of all time comes from Iceland, a nation with a rich and distinguished tradition of mysticism, spiritism, and mediumship. The medium in this case, Hafsteinn Bjornsson (1914-1977), is arguably Iceland's most famous medium (his main competitor would be the physical medium Indridi Indridsson). Hafsteinn's psychic abilities first surfaced in childhood, and apparently they remained strong thereafter. He began holding regular séances in 1937, and although he didn't earn a living from these activities, he did accept fees for his services. Hafsteinn was a trance medium, and communicators as well as regular controls spoke through him. (For additional information on Hafsteinn, see Haraldsson, Pratt, & Kristjansson, 1978; Haraldsson & Stevenson, 1974; 1975a; 1975b.)

The case we're now considering began in the autumn of 1937, during a series of séances held at the home of E. H. Kvaran in Reykjavik. A drop-in appeared at one of the séances, and when asked to give his name, he responded by identifying himself with a stereotypically Icelandic male name intended clearly to be fictitious. He then added, "What the hell does it matter to you what my name is?" One of the sitters asked what he wanted, and the drop-in replied, "I am looking for my leg. I want to have my leg." His leg, he then said, was in the sea.

For the next year this communicator continued to appear at the séances in Kvaran's home, continuing to ask for his leg and still withholding his identity. In the autumn of 1938 the séances moved to the home of Lilja Kristjansdottir (with a few changes in personnel), and again the communicator manifested, still demanding his leg and still refusing to give his name. On January 1, 1939, a new sitter joined the circle. He was Ludvik Gudmundsson, a fish merchant and owner of a fish processing factory in Sandgerdi, a village about thirty-six miles from Reykjavik. Although Ludvik and his wife owned a house in Sandgerdi, they lived in Reykjavik. Apparently, Ludvik was introduced to the sittings through a relative and one of the recent additions to the circle, Niels Carlsson. Ludvik had never met Hafsteinn, and the medium apparently knew nothing about Ludvik or his family.

When Ludvik joined the circle, the drop-in said he was glad to meet him. Ludvik didn't know what to make of this, and he asked the communicator to reveal his identity. Although the communicator continued to refuse, he mentioned that Ludvik knew about his missing leg, which he said was in Ludvik's house in Sandgerdi.

The drop-in's behavior during this period differed considerably from that of Hafsteinn. Unlike the medium, he was brusque and rude, and in addition to demanding coffee and alcohol, he often asked for snuff (which Hafsteinn never used). Frequently, he would go through the motions of lifting his hand to his (i.e., the medium's) nose and sniffing. Moreover, whereas Hafsteinn drank only one or two glasses of wine a year, the communicator's demand for alcohol corresponds to his later intimation (and some independent evidence) that, in life, he had been a heavy drinker.

After additional sittings in which the drop-in continued to conceal his identity, Ludvik and Niels presented an ultimatum. They said they would do nothing to help him so long as he refused to say who he was. Apparently, that annoyed the drop-in, who then made no appearance for a while. Finally, he returned, probably during the late winter or early spring of 1939 (for some reason the date of that event was not recorded), and he did so by abruptly and aggressively ousting another communicator from the scene. The drop-in then told the following story.

He said that his name was Runolfur Runolfsson (nickname, Runki) and that he was fifty-two years old when he died. Runki lived with his wife at Kolga or Klappakot, near Sandgerdi, and he had been walking home, drunk, from Keflavik (about six miles from Sandgerdi) in the latter part of the day. When he reached Sandgerdi he stopped at a friend's house and had some more to drink. When he was ready to continue his journey home, his friends protested. Because Runki was inebriated and because the weather was so bad, they said Runki shouldn't leave unless someone went along with him. But that offer of a designated walker angered Runki, who said he wouldn't go at all if he couldn't go alone. So, since Runki's house was only about fifteen minutes' walk away, he left by himself. (Evidently, Runki's friends were ready for him to leave.) At one point, wet and tired, Runki sat on a rock near the sea for a rest, and for another drink from the flask he carried with him. He then fell asleep, was carried away by the tide, and drowned. Runki said this happened in October 1879. The following January, his body washed ashore, and dogs and ravens then tore it to pieces. The remnants of Runki's body were recovered and buried in the graveyard in Utskalar, about four miles from Sandgerdi and six miles from Keflavik. But a thigh bone was missing from Runki's remains. It was carried out again to sea, and later washed onshore at Sandgerdi. Then, after being passed around for a while, it ended up in Ludvik's house. Runki also mentioned that he had been very tall, but it's not clear from the records whether he mentioned that detail at this sitting or at an earlier time.

Runki claimed that his story could be confirmed by checking the church book at Utskalar Church. So the sitters located the church book and found the record of someone named Runolfur Runolfsson, whose date of death and age at the time of death matched the story told by the drop-in. Runki's claim about his height was confirmed by Runki's grandson, who said his grandfather had been more than six feet tall. In the meantime, Ludvik asked elderly residents of Sandgerdi if they knew anything about an unclaimed leg bone in the vicinity. Some recalled vaguely that during the early 1920s a thigh bone (femur) had been "going around" and that it had been washed up by the sea. But they didn't know whose bone it was or what had become of it. However, one person said he seemed to remember that a bone, not associated with any particular person, had been placed in the wall of Ludvik's house by a carpenter who had built one of the inner walls downstairs. After an unsuccessful search in one of Ludvik's walls, an employee of the fish factory helped identify the correct wall. At one point he had lived in a room in Ludvik's house, and he said he knew of the carpenter placing a femur between two walls. Ludvik tore down the wall he indicated and found what was clearly the femur of a tall person. So, a bone that seemed to be Runki's was found more than forty years after Runki's death and approximately three years after Runki's first appearance.

I imagine that many readers will be puzzled by the manner in which the residents of Sandgerdi handled the unclaimed femur. But according to Haraldsson (a native of Iceland), in that culture and community "it would be considered disrespectful, if not sacrilegious...simply to throw a bone away. At the same time, it would be infeasible to bury a bone in the consecrated ground of a cemetery without knowing the identity of its owner" (Haraldsson & Stevenson, 1975b, p. 40, n.13).

Examination of records from Utskalar parish and elsewhere confirmed various details of Runki's story (see Haraldsson & Stevenson, 1975b for specifics). One of the most interesting documents is the following, from the Utskalar clergyman's record book.

> On October 16, 1879, Runolfur Runolfsson, living in Klappakot, was missing on account of some accidental or unnatural occurrence on his way home from Keflavik during a storm with rain near his farm, in the middle of the night. He is believed to have been carried along by the storm down to the beach south of the farm boundary at Flankastadir from where the sea carried him away, because his bones were found dismembered much later and his clothes were also washed up separated [i.e., apart from his bones]. (Haraldsson & Stevenson, 1975b, p. 42)

The clergyman also noted that Runki's remains were buried on January 8, 1880, and that Runki was fifty-two years old when he died.

A second record of Runki's death, also written by the clergyman at Utskalar, appeared later in a book, *Annals of Sudurnes*. This book was unpublished and virtually unknown at the time of the sittings. The manuscript was held in Reykjavik's National Library and was finally published in 1953. Both accounts claim that Runki's body was dismembered, and neither states that a leg bone was missing from the remains recovered near the shore and buried the following January. But the account in *Annals* differs in some respects from that found in the church record book. For example, it notes that Runki had been drinking alcohol around the time of his death. Moreover, the *Annals* account fails to mention Runki's last name, or the fact that his remains were buried at Utskalar. So if the mediumistic communication was derived psychically (or normally) from existing accounts, it couldn't have come from just one of those written by the clergyman. Runki's grandson also couldn't have been the sole source of the confirmed information. Although he knew that his grandfather had been tall, he had never known his grandfather and apparently was ignorant about the bone and other relevant facts of the case.

Unfortunately, the femur found in Ludvik's house was never conclusively linked with Runki. However, several considerations lend credibility to that connection. We know that Runki's body was described as "dismembered," and although no one claimed that bones were missing from the remains found onshore, the femur was clearly the bone of a tall person. Moreover, it's rare for bones to be washed ashore in that part of Iceland (or anywhere in Iceland, as far as I know). So it's plausible to associate recovered bones with the few people known to have died along the coast. Haraldsson and Stevenson were prepared to have Runki's body disinterred, and they even obtained the consent of his grandchildren. But the graves in Utskalar are unmarked, crowded together, and perhaps also layered atop each other at the same plot of ground. So there seemed no way of determining where to look.

After recovering the bone from his wall, Ludvik had a coffin built for it. He kept the bone for a year and then had it buried during a ceremony conducted at Utskalar. Those present at the ceremony believed they were burying Runki's final remains. The clergyman eulogized Runki, the choir sang, and afterwards the clergyman held a reception with refreshments at his home. That reception was attended by several of Hafsteinn's regular sitters. At the next séance held by Hafsteinn, Runki came and expressed gratitude for the proper disposal of his leg. He claimed he had been present at the ceremony and reception, and he described those events in detail. Although Runki didn't disappear after his business was settled, as many drop-ins do, he did mellow and continued to serve as Hafsteinn's principal control.

5. Runki's Leg: Theoretical Considerations and Nagging Concerns

Haraldsson and Stevenson investigated this case carefully and considered whether Hafsteinn might have obtained the relevant information by normal means, either by visiting the National Archives in Reykjavik where the Utskalar parish records were kept, or the National Library where the *Annals* were located. It turns out that Hafsteinn had visited the National Archives during the sittings, but about six months after

Runki had provided the account of his demise. Originally, Hafsteinn claimed not to have visited the Archives at all, but after Haraldsson told him that his signature had been found in the guest book for November 24, 1939, he recalled that he had gone there to examine the records which sitters told him they had verified. Haraldsson and Stevenson also determined that the guest book at the National Archives is not an entirely reliable record of visitors, and that some visitors' signatures are never recorded. Still, for reasons Haraldsson and Stevenson discuss in detail, I'm inclined to agree either (a) that we should interpret Hafsteinn's initial testimony as an honest memory lapse for an event that took place thirty-two years before he was interrogated, or (b) that Hafsteinn suppressed the information of his visit out of fear that his trip to the Archives would look suspicious. Besides, the documents in the National Archives and Library don't deal with the matter of the leg found in Ludvik's home. So at best they cover only part of what makes the case so interesting.

Of course, no case is ideal. There are always vast numbers of details to examine, and omissions may loom larger in the clarity of hindsight. So presumably there will inevitably be annoying respects in which even the best cases could be stronger. Not surprisingly, then, some puzzling features of this case merit attention. Some cast doubt on the survivalist interpretation of the evidence, and others simply deepen the mystery of the case.

First, when Runki gave details about his life, he said he was fifty-two years old when he died. But if the church records are correct, Runki was in fact about two months shy of fifty-one at the time. Curiously, though, the Utskalar parish notebook entry also says that Runki was fifty-two when he died. Haraldsson and Stevenson mention this discrepancy in a footnote, and they offer a reasonable (but not compelling) explanation. They suggest that the clergyman who made the note might have meant to say that, at the time Runki's remains were recovered and Runki's death was confirmed (in January 1880), Runki was in his fifty-second year. However, this detail may be more revealing than Haraldsson and Stevenson realized. Consider: If Runki wasn't actually communicating, and if someone at the séance had, either normally or paranormally, scoured existing records for information, this is the sort of error we could expect to see. To figure out Runki's actual age at the time of death, one would have to locate the appropriate records and do some calculating. But to identify Runki as fifty-two years old at his death, one would only have to read it off the false or misleading record in the parish notebook.

Now let's play devil's advocate and be as sympathetic as we can to the survivalist. From that point of view, we have to concede that Runki might have been confused (both before and after bodily death), either from the ravages of alcoholism or from the possible strain of communicating mediumistically. Even if it opens the door for reckless survivalist speculation, we must admit that, if postmortem communication is possible, we have no idea how difficult or easy it might be. For example, we don't know what sort of toll it might take on mental acuity, whether we might remain stuck with the cognitive impairments we had at death, or how "noisy" the mediumistic channel might be. And certainly there's no reason to assume that survival increases (or even preserves) the clarity and accuracy of our memories. After all, the banality and fallibility of most ostensible communications is notorious. So for all we know, the error communicated about Runki's age when he died may be a typical (if not predictable) lapse and therefore no grounds for suspicion, especially if there are no other lingering doubts about the evidence.

But there are some additional nagging concerns. Originally, Runki said his leg was in the sea. Only after Ludvik joined the circle did Runki say it was in Ludvik's house and not the sea. How do we make sense of that shift in position? Survivalists have several explanatory options, none of which strike me as compelling or attractive, but none of which we can conclusively rule out. First, survivalists might argue that, before Ludvik joined the circle, nobody at the séance would have been in a position to help Runki find his leg. So perhaps Runki was merely seizing the opportunity to vent his frustration over his missing leg. Then, after Ludvik joined the group, that might have helped Runki focus on the location of his leg, or perhaps it finally gave him reason to direct the sitters to Ludvik's house. However, I don't see why Ludvik's absence from the sitter group would have prevented or discouraged Runki from directing the sitters to the appropriate house in Sandgerdi. Survivalists might also argue (again) that Runki was confused, or that in the struggle to communicate he might not have conveyed clearly that his leg *had* been in the sea. As we've noted, we have no reason to insist that mediumistic communications are easy or noise free.

On the other hand, suppose that living persons were (normally or paranormally) assembling the Runki story as the case progressed. In that case, Ludvik's arrival and the existence of somebody's (not necessarily Runki's) femur in his house, made it viable *at that time* to construct a more compelling case. It's possible, but highly unlikely, that once Ludvik had been invited to join the circle, the medium did some quick research and incorporated into the séance the information about the hidden femur. But considering the obscurity of that information and the lengths to which Ludvik had to go in order to learn about and locate the leg, I think we can rule this out. But, on the super-psi hypothesis, the information could have been acquired psychically, once Ludvik joined the circle.

Moreover, although this is not the only case in which a crucial sitter joins the circle after the drop-in's first appearance,[4] it certainly seems to be a striking bit of serendipity that Ludvik arrived on the scene. How is that to be explained on either the survivalist *or* super-psi reading of the case? As just a piece of good luck, or as a sequence of events orchestrated somehow in order to make the case more convincing? And if the latter, who would have been able to pull it off? Let's grant, plausibly (but at least for the sake of argument), that the medium is innocent of any normal shenanigans in determining the sequence of events. And in fact, there's no evidence of any conspiracy involving medium or sitters, and no basis for sustaining a general suspicion about Hafsteinn's integrity. So could we plausibly regard Runki as the director behind the scenes? I don't pretend to know how to answer these questions. I consider them simply to be lingering puzzles about the case.

We might also wonder why Runki disappeared for several months after Ludvik and Niels presented their ultimatum. Haraldsson and Stevenson claimed that Runki seemed annoyed, but since they mention no other behavioral signs of annoyance, that conjecture seems charitable at best. We need to be both fair-minded and circumspect with matters of this sort, and it's not outrageous to interpret Runki's disappearance with more suspicion. Since the details of Runki's story were provided only after Runki returned from his hiatus, we might wonder, reasonably, whether that period was needed for some normal or paranormal information gathering. But before we get carried away with skeptical musings, we should also remember that Hafsteinn's confirmed visit to the National Archives was six months *after* Runki told his story, and (as I noted) that account tells only part of the story. So although I see no solid reasons for worrying about Runki's absence during this period, the case would be even more convincing if that absence had not occurred.

Finally, why didn't the communicator help identify Runki's unmarked grave? It would have been a powerful addition to the evidence to have found those remains missing a femur of the appropriate size. Haraldsson and Stevenson's observations about the configuration of unmarked graves, although legitimate, do little to allay concerns. After all, if Runki could identify where his missing leg was located, why couldn't he also direct investigators to the rest of his bones? Or (to put a super-psi spin on this), if Hafsteinn could paranormally locate the leg, why not also the site of Runki's other remains? There may well be reasonable answers to these questions, although I don't know what they are. And although I don't consider our inability to answer them reason to dismiss an otherwise very provocative case, they remain sources of concern, and they illustrate again how far from ideal this case is.

But despite its weaknesses, the case of Runki's leg illustrates clearly how drop-in communications lend support to the survival hypothesis. Haraldsson and Stevenson nicely summarize the issues concerning the correct information provided during the séances.

It does not seem feasible to attribute all of this information to any single person or any single written source. And this would be true, we believe, whether the medium acquired the information normally or by extrasensory perception. We think, therefore, that some process of integration of details derived from different persons or other sources must be supposed in the interpretation of the case. It may be simplest to explain this integration as due to Runki's survival after his physical death with retention of many memories and their subsequent communication through the mediumship of Hafsteinn. On the other hand, sensitives have been known to accomplish remarkable feats of deriving and integrating information without the participation of any purported discarnate personality. (Haraldsson & Stevenson, 1975b, p. 57)

So, as far as the case's behavioral details and underlying psychology are concerned, there's both good news and bad news for the survivalist. The bad news is that we have no idea what Runki's character was like, except for the evidence that he drank heavily. Therefore, we don't know what to make of Hafsteinn's Runki trance-persona. Besides, the Cagliostro case reminds us that vivid behavior different from that of the medium needn't be evidential. The good news is that the drop-in's motivations to communicate are much clearer and more straightforward than those we would need to ascribe to the sitters, and even to Hafsteinn, who at this early stage in his mediumistic career already had a solid reputation as a psychic. Even if he might have benefitted somewhat from additional good publicity, he didn't need this case either to establish or cement his reputation. Furthermore, the drop-in's behavior, after the burial of the femur, adds credibility to the survivalist interpretation. Runki seemed satisfied that his bones were now all properly disposed of, and although it would have been appropriate for him (and typical behavior for a drop-in) to depart once his affairs were settled, his mellower and helpful participation at subsequent séances was no less appropriate.[5]

6. Concluding Remarks

Although the best cases are by no means coercive, the evidence for drop-ins, overall, seems to strengthen the case for survival. Granted, we can't conclusively rule out explanations in terms of motivated psi among the living. But as the challenges facing super-psi explanations mount, their antecedent plausibility decreases. Even if we grant that task complexity may be overrated as an obstacle to psi success, and even if we grant that what really motivates people may not be the concerns lying closest to the surface, drop-in cases make particularly good sense in terms of the ostensible communicator's expressed motives for communicating. As a result, survivalist interpretations of those cases seem more parsimonious than their super-psi alternatives. As we observed earlier, anti-survivalists need to explain why a séance participant used ESP to gather information about a person known to nobody present. They also need to explain why the communicator's needs or interests are so much more clear-cut than those we could reasonably attribute to medium or sitter, even after reasonable probing. And of course, whereas communicators supply information they would be likely to know, living persons would have to derive that information from different and often (normally) obscure sources.

Moreover, the very fact *that* there are drop-in cases seems to strengthen the case for survival. As Gauld correctly observes,

> if there were no verified cases of "drop in" communicators the survivalist case would be considerably weakened. For if people do survive death with some at least of their former interests and affections, and if communication is a possibility, we should expect that not a few deceased persons would try to contact living persons for exactly the sorts of plausible-sounding reasons that "drop in" communicators quite often give. (Gauld, 1971, pp. 276–277)

NOTES

1. I'm aware of the intense and deep resistance this conjecture arouses in most people, and I realize that it usually survives even a painstaking appraisal of the issues and examination of the relevant evidence (e.g., of the kind provided in Braude, 1997). But although that resistance is understandable emotionally, it may be indefensible intellectually. Like so much else in this area, this issue is much more interesting and complex than it might seem initially. Still, I don't expect the reader to take this on faith, and we can't review all the relevant material here. So I simply urge readers to keep an open mind on the subject and tentatively accept the possibility of unlimited psychic functioning, if only as a thought experiment, just to see where it leads in the context of this discussion.

2. For information on placebos and biofeedback, see, e.g., Basmajian, 1963, 1972; Frank & Frank, 1991; Rossi & Cheek, 1988; White, Tursky, & Schwartz, 1985).

3. In fact, a contemporary case lends indirect support to Eisenbud's conjecture. In the early 1970s, members of the Toronto Society for Psychical Research received ostensible spirit messages (primarily through table rapping) from a communicator they invented ("Philip"), and in whose fictitious history and personality they immersed themselves in preparation for the séances. Sitter-group members realized that the raps in the table seemed to be, as one member put it, "psychokinesis by committee" (Owen & Sparrow, 1976). Although the invention of Philip was an overt project, the sittings nevertheless support the view that something similar could occur surreptitiously.

4. In the drop-in case of Edward Druce (Gauld, 1971, pp. 301–302), sitter R. W. (who knew Druce) joined the circle after Druce's initial appearance.

5. Colleagues and students have made very helpful comments and suggestions to me about this case. In particular, I'd like to thank Christian Perring and my student, Pratima Thotakura.

Chapter 3
Trance Mediumship

1. Introduction

Although mediumship takes various interesting forms, probably the most impressive cases are those in which mediums adopt *trance personalities* and apparently behave as the communicator did when alive. It's clear enough why investigators attach great importance to these cases. If (as it seems) a communicator controls the medium's body and vocal organs, evidential material isn't confined simply to *what* the communicator says but also to *how* the communicator says it. The medium might replicate the communicator's distinctive phraseology, inflection, and even vocal timbre, and the accompanying bodily movements or gestures might also resemble those displayed by the communicator when alive. Of course, when communications are produced through automatic writing (rather than trance impersonations), it's still possible to replicate some of the communicator's distinctive modes of expression. But trance impersonations can exhibit evidential behavioral and personality traits which other forms of mediumship don't reveal at all, or reveal less clearly.

Fortunately, since the founding of the British SPR in 1882, researchers have uncovered a decent supply of first-rate mediums, many of whose careers they documented in painstaking detail. In this chapter, we'll examine two justifiably classic cases (Mrs. Piper and Mrs. Leonard), and we'll look more briefly at other notable mediums throughout the book. But we should keep in mind that this is not a general review of the evidence for survival (or the evidence from mediumship in particular). For a well-rounded and thoughtful review of mediumship generally, I recommend Gauld, 1982. And see Broad, 1962, for a probing discussion of Mrs. Leonard and Mrs. Willett.

A good case of mediumship has at least two obvious requirements. First, there should be no doubt as to the medium's honesty. Researchers must be able to rule out, among other things, the possibility of confederates surreptitiously gathering data on sitters, or the medium exploiting other covert sources of information. Second, the mediums must provide information that is too copious, wide-ranging, intimate, and specific to be attributed to chance or explained away in terms of normally accessible channels of information.

But even when these requirements have been met, the best cases are difficult to interpret as unambiguous evidence of survival. Without exception, they present a frustrating mixture of (a) material suggesting survival, (b) material suggesting psi among the living, and (c) apparent rubbish. At their best, of course, mediums furnish detailed information for which no normal explanation will suffice. In the cases most strongly suggesting survival, that information concerns the past lives of the deceased. But sometimes mediums also provide information on the present actions, thoughts, and feelings of the living, and that's one reason why some cases suggest psi among the living. Moreover, to complicate matters further,

> gems of correct, detailed, and relevant information are nearly always imbedded in an immense matrix of twaddle, vagueness, irrelevance, ignorance, pretension, positive error, and occasional prevarication. (Broad, 1962, p. 259)

This mediumistic debris is difficult to interpret, and it's also difficult to ignore. But it's also important not to make too much of it. For one thing, it's easy to imagine why mediums might sometimes (or often) produce communications that are clearly irrelevant, ignorant, vague, etc., and later we'll consider some of those possibilities. And for another, there's a large residue of impressive material that can't be explained away in terms of the Usual Suspects and which can't simply be brushed aside. In fact, assuming that something paranormal is going on, the rubbish might even furnish valuable clues as to the underlying process. Needless to say, any such clues will be welcome; even after more than a century of careful investigation, the nature of mediumship remains largely mysterious. As Broad recognized,

> although instructed opinion is almost unanimous in holding that trance-mediumship supplies data which require a paranormal explanation of *some* kind, there is no consensus of experts in favour of any one suggested paranormal explanation. (Broad, 1962, p. 259)

Of course, there's no reason to suppose that the best cases of mediumship demand only one kind of paranormal explanation. In principle at least, they might exhibit a subtle mixture of psi among the living with manifestations of survival. And as James observed, when we consider the entire spectrum of mediumistic productions from the sublime to the absurd, it's tempting to think that the medium's organism

> not only transmits with great difficulty the influences it receives from beyond the curtain, but mixes its own automatic tendencies most disturbingly therewith. (James, 1909/1986, p. 277)

Later, James suggests

> Extraneous "wills to communicate" may contribute to the results as well as a "will to personate," and the two kinds of will may be distinct in entity, though capable of helping each other out...The two wills might thus strike up a sort of partnership and stir each other up. It might even be that the "will to personate" would be inert unless it were aroused to activity by the other will. (p. 356)

Gauld dubbed this the theory of "overshadowing." As he described it, behind the medium's

> dramatic rendering of communication from the dead, overshadowing it and somehow directing its course, there might sometimes lie those same deceased persons who figure as characters in the drama. The medium writes many of the speeches, and ensures continuity in the plot; but some of the lines (perhaps the most important ones) are filled in by outside authors. (Gauld, 1982, pp. 117–118)[1]

Moreover, as James argued, it may be antecedently incredible that the entire mass of mediumistic communications is *nothing* but humbug, as it would be if we could explain mediumship away in terms of the Usual Suspects, or even in terms of super psi. All non-survivalist explanations of mediumship contend that "communications" from the deceased are really constructs *by the living* designed merely to appear as evidence of survival. The super-psi versions of those explanations hold that mediums (and maybe other living persons) *subconsciously* use their psychic abilities to generate these illusions. Of course, explanations in terms of subconscious deception avoid charging mediums with criminal or blatant dishonesty. But according to James, as a general explanatory strategy that gambit seems to posit an implausible degree of duplicity. He wrote,

> The notion that so many men and women, in all other respects honest enough, should have this preposterous monkeying [subliminal] self annexed to their personality seems to me so weird that the spirit-theory immediately takes on a more probable appearance. The spirits, if spirits there be, must indeed work under incredible complications and falsifications, but at least if they are present, some honesty is left in a whole department of the universe which otherwise is run by pure deception. The more I realize the quantitative massiveness of the phenomenon and its complexity, the more incredible it seems to me that in a world all of whose vaster features we are in the habit of considering to be *sincere* at least, however brutal, this feature should be wholly constituted of insincerity. (James, 1909/1986, pp. 284–285)

If nothing else, James's appeal to cosmic aesthetics is an interesting defense of the survival hypothesis. But it's unlikely to sway those with different sensibilities. So let's look at some case material and see whether we can find a more forceful basis for accepting a survivalist explanation.

2. Outline of Mrs. Piper's Mediumship

Probably no case of mediumship is stronger or more thoroughly documented than that of Mrs. Leonora E. Piper (1857-1950). Apparently Mrs. Piper's first mediumistic stirrings occurred in childhood. At the age of eight, she had a veridical vision concerning the demise of her Aunt Sara, who (it was later discovered) had died at that time. According to Mrs. Piper's daughter, similar incidents occurred occasionally throughout her mother's childhood, but otherwise that period of her life was normal (Piper, 1929, p. 13). Mrs. Piper's mediumistic career began in 1884, shortly after she married William Piper, who worked in a large store in Boston. In the hope of relieving the lingering effects of an accident years earlier (a collision with an ice sled), she paid a visit to a blind medium and healer named J. R. Cocke. On her first visit, Mrs. Piper fell into a short trance. And after falling into a trance again on her second visit, she rose from her chair, picked up a pencil and paper, and wrote down a short message for another of the persons present, Judge Frost from Cambridge, Massachusetts. The message purportedly came from the judge's deceased son, and although Frost had been investigating spiritualism for more than thirty years, it impressed him more than any he had previously received. After that, word of Mrs. Piper spread quickly, and before long she came to the attention of William James.

After her experiences with Mr. Cocke, Mrs. Piper began holding regular séances in her home. In those early days, several different controls or spirit-guides took charge of the séances, and all were somewhat incredible as actual surviving personalities. The first to appear was a Native American girl called "Chlorine," and other frequent controls were J. S. Bach, Longfellow, and Commodore Vanderbilt. Eventually, Mrs. Piper's early controls yielded to a vivid personality called Dr. Phinuit, who claimed to be a French physician, and who in most respects was no more believable than his predecessors. No records of him existed at the medical schools where he claimed to study, and his knowledge of the French language was minimal at best. In fact, both the Bach and Phinuit controls may have been borrowed from Cocke, presumably unconsciously. Bach was also one of Cocke's controls, and another was a French doctor called "Finny" (Hodgson, 1892, pp. 46–50; Sidgwick, 1915, p. 9). At any rate, as we noted in the previous chapter, control personalities tend to be flagrantly artificial. Phinuit's importance, like that of most controls, concerned the information he provided about other ostensible communicators.

In the early days of her mediumship, with Phinuit as principal control, Mrs. Piper communicated by voice rather than by writing. Most of the time, Phinuit spoke through Mrs. Piper on behalf of other communicators, but sometimes other communicators appeared to use the medium's organism on their own. And during these days, the onset of Mrs.

Piper's trance was accompanied by unpleasant convulsive movements. Moreover, it was clear that her trance state was similar to those observed in many hypnotic subjects. Like them, the entranced Mrs. Piper was undisturbed by ammonia held under her nose, and she was insensitive to the pain of having a needle suddenly pushed into her hand. When Phinuit finally appeared, he spoke in a gruff, male voice, in what Oliver Lodge called a "Frenchified" manner (Myers, Lodge, Leaf, & James, 1889-90, p. 448), and he relied frequently on slang and profanity quite uncharacteristic of Mrs. Piper. Toward the end of Phinuit's reign as principal control, Mrs. Piper communicated increasingly through automatic writing rather than through speech. The reason given for this change was that communication by voice was considerably more fatiguing to the medium. During that transition period, Phinuit would sometimes communicate by voice while another personality communicated through writing. Interestingly, by the time Mrs. Piper's controls communicated mostly by writing, the medium's onset of trance had become more placid.

In 1892, a new communicator appeared and gradually displaced Phinuit as Mrs. Piper's primary control (for the full story, see Hodgson, 1898, pp. 295ff). This personality, "G. P.," purported to be George Pellew (usually referred to under the pseudonym "Pelham"), an acquaintance of Hodgson who was keenly interested in literature and philosophy and who had died accidently several weeks earlier. The real G. P. had attended one of Mrs. Piper's séances five years before, but he had been introduced under a pseudonym, and it's virtually certain that Mrs. Piper never knew who he was. G. P. manifested in automatic writing, and Phinuit occasionally (and sometimes simultaneously) continued to communicate by speech until his manifestations ended almost completely.

The period marked by G. P.'s reign as principal control lasted until 1897, at which time Mrs. Piper came under the regular control of a band of "high spirits," who assumed imposing names such as "Rector" and "Doctor" to disguise their real identities, and whose leader was a personality called "Imperator." Under their direction, the content of séances shifted away somewhat from evidential communications to lofty and often pretentious teachings, as well as occasional forays into pseudo-scientific speculation. But when Hodgson died in 1905, a Hodgson communicator manifested frequently as one of Mrs. Piper's controls, and sittings once again provided large amounts of ostensibly evidential material. Mrs. Piper also played a role in the complex communications called the "cross-correspondences," which we will consider later (section 7). Beginning around 1909, the medium's ability to enter into trance declined noticeably, and it ceased altogether in 1911. This end to Mrs. Piper's trance mediumship may have been hastened by some apparently insensitive experiments conducted by Prof. G. Stanley Hall and

Dr. Amy Tanner (see Tanner, 1910, and the review of this book in Sidgwick, 1911. Also, Mrs. Sidgwick's subsequent comments in Sidgwick,
1915, pp. 12–15). Nevertheless, Mrs. Piper continued to do automatic
writing after 1911.

It was William James who first brought Mrs. Piper to the attention of
the parapsychological community. After a dozen sittings with her, he
was sufficiently impressed to conduct a follow-up investigation in which
he sent twenty-five sitters to Mrs. Piper under pseudonyms. Although
this investigation didn't convince James of the reality of survival, he
concluded that Mrs. Piper at least possessed an unexplained power
(James, 1886/1986; 1890/1986). She "showed a most startling intimacy" with sitters' family affairs, "talking of many matters known to no
one outside, and which *gossip* could not possibly have conveyed to her
ears" (James, 1886/1986, pp. 15–16).

James reported the results of his investigations to the leaders of the
SPR, and as a result, Richard Hodgson moved to Boston in 1887 and
took charge of the case. Hodgson had earned a reputation as a careful
and skeptical investigator of psychic phenomena and as an expert in the
detection of fraud. He scheduled séances without revealing the identity
of the prospective sitters, and then he introduced them to Mrs. Piper
either anonymously or under the pseudonym "Smith." He also paid particular attention to first sittings, when the medium's knowledge of her
clients would be at a minimum. Hodgson realized that with each successive séance, Mrs. Piper would have additional opportunities to learn
about her clients and their lives—for example, from the sitters' inadvertent revelations. Moreover, to insure that Mrs. Piper wasn't surreptitiously acquiring information about her sitters through outside sources,
Hodgson employed detectives for several weeks to shadow the medium
and her husband. That investigation confirmed that Mrs. Piper wasn't
gathering data normally about current or prospective sitters. Despite
these and other precautions, Mrs. Piper's séances continued to be very
impressive. Hodgson concluded,

> after allowing the widest possible margin for information obtainable...by
> ordinary means, for chance coincidence and remarkable guessing, aided by
> clues given consciously and unconsciously by the sitters, and helped out by
> supposed hyperaesthesia on the part of Mrs. Piper,—there remained a large
> residuum of knowledge displayed in her trance state, which could not be
> accounted for except on the hypothesis that she had some supernormal
> power. (Hodgson, 1898, p. 285)

Mrs. Piper was then brought to England, because she had only "a
very slender knowledge of English affairs and English people" (Myers *et
al.*, 1889-90, p. 438), and because other members of the S.P.R. could
then supervise séances and examine her trance-phenomena for themselves. In many cases, sitters just happened to be passing through Cambridge at the time and were certainly unknown to Mrs. Piper. As usual,

investigators introduced most sitters under false names and kept detailed records. And as before, Mrs. Piper produced a great deal of impressive material.

Although sittings with Mrs. Piper convinced James about the reality of ESP, and although he was impressed by many of the apparent communications from his friend Hodgson, he remained uncertain about the reality of survival. Hodgson, however, had been so impressed by Mrs. Piper that he came to accept the reality of survival. Initially, he seemed to be predisposed against that position, but the G. P. communications changed his mind. Even the skeptical Frank Podmore conceded that

> the impersonation, if it were an impersonation and not the actual G.P. manifesting through Mrs. Piper's organism, was consistently and dramatically sustained. (Podmore, 1910/1975, p. 180)

Moreover, the G. P. communicator seemed to have a very detailed knowledge of Pellew's life. Thirty of the 150 sitters introduced to G. P. were people known to the living Pellew, and G. P. recognized twenty-nine of them. The thirtieth, whom he failed to identify at first, was someone who had grown from a girl to a woman since the last time she saw the real G. P. The G. P. communicator interacted appropriately with these sitters, and he seemed to know a great deal about their lives and relationships with Pellew. Nearly all these sitters were struck by the realism of the G. P. persona, and some of those who knew Pellew most intimately came to believe that they were really communicating with their deceased friend.

Gradually, it became clear to many that Mrs. Piper's phenomena could not all be explained away in terms of the Usual Suspects. Fraud seemed easy to rule out, and it was also easy to reject some other initially credible hypotheses. For example, some communications seemed explicable, at least in principle, in terms of a prodigious trance-memory, and some seemed potentially explicable in terms of a "grapevine" theory, according to which Mrs. Piper gained information on her clients through an ever-growing network of connected families throughout Boston. (See Gauld, 1982, pp. 35–37, for a good discussion of these hypotheses.) But even when these proposals are taken together, too much remains unexplained. That was also clear to Podmore, despite his generally high level of skepticism over mediumistic phenomena. He concluded that Mrs. Piper's accurate trance statements

> are so numerous and so precise, and the possibility of leakage to Mrs. Piper through normal channels in many cases so effectually excluded, that it is impossible to doubt that we have here proof of a supernormal agency of some kind—either telepathy by the trance intelligence from the sitter or some kind of communication from the dead. (Podmore, 1910/1975, p. 222)

3. Examples of Mrs. Piper's Mediumship

Podmore was right about this. He also recognized how difficult it was to decide whether just one or both types of supernormal agency were at work in Mrs. Piper's mediumship. In many cases, telepathy with the living seemed clearly to play a role. The following examples are representative. (a) One day Hodgson had been reading Sir Walter Scott's *Life and Letters*, after which he spent some additional time reflecting on Scott, who interested him greatly. The next day, at a sitting with Mrs. Piper, an outlandish Walter Scott purported to communicate (Sidgwick, 1915, pp. 85, 297ff, 437–448). Similarly, (b) the day after Hodgson read an account by Stainton Moses of his meeting with the medium D. D. Home, an unconvincing Home communicator appeared and commented on having met with Moses when they were both alive (Sidgwick, 1915, p. 85). (c) On November 24, 1888, a Mrs. A. was introduced under a pseudonym to Mrs. Piper, who told her that her brother had a paralyzed arm. Mrs. Piper then pointed to a spot above the elbow where the problem was supposed to have originated. As it happened, Mrs. A.'s eldest brother suffered from writer's cramp, which seriously interfered with his work, and in fact there was a painful lump on his arm near the elbow. However, that lump was below the elbow, not above it. But *at the time of the sitting* Mrs. A. believed it to be above the elbow, in the region Mrs. Piper had indicated (Myers *et al.*, 1889-90, pp. 581–583; Podmore, 1910/1975, pp. 165–166). (d) During a sitting on April 28, 1892, the G. P. control was asked to look in on Mrs. Howard and report what she was doing. G. P. then produced a detailed description of Mrs. Howard's activities. But that description closely matched things Mrs. Howard had done during the previous two days, and it seems that knowledge of those activities could only have come from Mrs. Howard's memory (Hodgson, 1898, pp. 304–307; Podmore, 1910/1975, pp. 178–180). (e) In 1889, Phinuit correctly told Mr. J. T. Clarke that he was in financial trouble. But then he produced a string of claims—for example, about individuals who hadn't dealt honorably with Clarke, all of which turned out to be false. However, those claims corresponded to what Clarke believed at the time (Myers *et al.*, 1889-90, pp. 568–571).

Moreover, many of Mrs. Piper's séances combined statements about the living with statements about the dead, and (as Podmore recognized) the two sets of statements were often otherwise indistinguishable. For example, on January 22, 1889, Mr. Harlow Gale sat with Mrs. Piper in England. He was a stranger to Mrs. Piper and was introduced to her anonymously and unexpectedly. During the séance, Mrs. Piper rattled off a long string of descriptions of Gale's relatives and friends. All the statements were presented by Phinuit as if he had direct knowledge of the individuals he mentioned, and although neither set of statements was free of inaccuracy, the information provided about the living tended to be as accurate and vivid as that provided about the dead. So there was "no means, as a rule, of discriminating between them either as regards substance or source" (Podmore, 1910/1975, p. 171; also Myers *et al.*, 1889-90, pp. 642–643).

By contrast, however, many incidents suggest survival rather than telepathy, even if psi among the living remains a serious option. Two are often cited in summaries of the Piper case: the so-called Pecuniary Messages and the Fist-Shaking Incident (see James, 1909/1986, pp. 276–277, 348–349). Of course, in the best cases the information received was unknown to anyone present at the séances. Regrettably, most of those cases are difficult to present in a compact form, but the following is an exception. It's taken from Mrs. H. Verrall's long paper analyzing apparent messages from a recently deceased young man, Bennie Junot, to the surviving members of his family.

On February 11, 1902, Hodgson supervised a sitting for Mr. N. B. Junot (Bennie's father). At that sitting, N.B.J. tried to send a message through his son to Hugh Irving, who had worked for him as a coachman and who had died two months earlier. Mr. Irving had left N.B.J.'s service about two months before his death and had taken Mr. Junot's dog Rounder with him. Accordingly, N.B.J. wanted to know from Irving where Rounder was. The answer came during a séance on April 2. As Mrs. Piper was emerging from trance, the Bennie communicator said "John Welsh has Rounder." Afterwards, according to Mrs. Verrall,

> Mr. Junot succeeded after some difficulty in tracing "John Welsh," but unfortunately it proved impossible to discover whether he had ever had the dog in his possession. It is certain, however, that he was closely associated with the coachman, who took the dog away, and it was through his attempts to find John Welsh that Mr. Junot recovered the dog. (Verrall, 1910, p. 354)

It turned out that Rounder was in the hands of a person named James M., who had been entering the dog in lucrative rat-killing matches. James M. had also been a coachman in N.B.J.'s neighborhood, and he claimed that Hugh Irving had given him the dog (Verrall, 1910, p. 516). The local deputy sheriff, Walter W., interrogated Welsh on a few occasions about Rounder. Although Welsh was reluctant to communicate about the matter, he eventually claimed that Hugh Irving had given the dog to "a colored man, whom he knows by sight, but not by name" (Verrall, 1910, p. 518). So even though Bennie's statement that Welsh had Rounder in his possession seems to have been false, it's still significant that he gave the name of someone closely associated with Hugh Irving and also likely to know of the dog's whereabouts.

Mrs. Verrall recognized clearly what was important about this incident, and also how the super-psi hypothesis lurks annoyingly in the background.

Neither Mr. Junot [senior] nor any of his family had ever to their knowledge heard of John Welsh (at any rate under that name)[he also went by the name of John Walsh, and many knew him as "Old Happy"—S.B.], still less his connexion with the dog. Doubtless people could have been found to whom all these facts were known, but they were not people with whom Mrs. Piper had ever been brought into contact. Until we know to what limitations, if any, telepathy between living minds is subject, we cannot determine whether it is a sufficient explanation of such phenomena as this. (Verrall, 1910, p. 354)

Before moving on to the case of Mrs. Leonard and eventually to some theoretical considerations, I want to examine another, earlier episode from the Piper case, from the period when Hodgson was investigator rather than ostensible communicator. The séances in question are undoubtedly first-rate. Even so, they still present a curious mixture of statements strongly suggesting survival, statements suggesting telepathy from the living, and a certain amount of rubbish.

In December 1893, Hodgson booked two sittings with Mrs. Piper for the Reverend and Mrs. Sutton. The Suttons were introduced under a pseudonym, and a veteran note taker (Mrs. Howard) recorded the proceedings. Although a great deal of veridical material came through Mrs. Piper, the majority of it concerned the Sutton's recently deceased daughter Katherine (nicknamed "Kakie"). The report of the sittings was later written by Mrs. Sutton. I quote from this report at length, for several reasons. In order to assess a super-psi explanation of Mrs. Piper's mediumship, it's not enough to focus on specific "hits" or isolated segments of her sittings. It's also important to appreciate the character of entire séances—for example, the overall conversational "flow," and the way in which the density and frequency of veridical material varies even in the best séances. Moreover, I want the reader to see how communicators come and go and how topics shifted in the course of Mrs. Piper's sittings. Here, we'll concentrate on the first of the two séances and on the pivotal communications dealing with Kakie. And to help the reader focus on those parts of the séance, I reproduce the relevant passages of the transcripts in bold print. The annotations in square brackets were supplied afterwards by Mrs. Sutton, and those followed by an asterisk were added in 1897. Although a child communicator's voice (presumably that of Kakie, or of Phinuit simulating her voice) occasionally issued from Mrs. Piper, most of the time Phinuit either spoke or gestured on Kakie's behalf.

First sitting, Dec. 8, 1893.

Mrs. Howard held Mrs. Piper's hands. She became immediately entranced under the control of Dr. Phinuit. After a brief communication to Mrs. Howard I took Mrs. Piper's hands and Phinuit said: This is a lovely lady,—she has done much good,— has helped so many poor souls. **A little child is coming to you. This is the dearest lady I have met for a long** time—the most light I have seen while in Mrs. Piper's body. He reaches out his hands as to a child, and says coaxingly: Come here, dear. Don't be afraid. Come, darling, here is your mother. He describes the child and her "lovely curls." Where is papa? Want papa. [He takes from the table a silver medal.] I want this—want to bite it. [She used to bite it.*] [Reaches for a string of buttons.] Quick! I want to put them in my mouth. [The buttons also. To bite the buttons was forbidden. He exactly imitated her arch manner.*] I will get her to talk to you in a minute. Who is Frank in the body? [We do not know.] [My uncle Frank had died a few years before. We were much attached. Possibly Phinuit was confused and my uncle was trying to communicate.*] A lady is here who passed out of the body with tumour in the bowels. [My friend, Mrs. C., died of ovarian tumour.*] She has the child—she is bringing her to me. [He takes some keys.] These bring her to me—these and the buttons. Now she will speak to me. Who is Dodo? [Her name for her brother George.] Speak to me quickly. I want you to call Dodo. Tell Dodo I am happy. Cry for me no more. [Puts hand to throat.] No sore throat any more. [She had pain and distress of the throat and tongue.*] Papa, speak to me. Can not you see me? I am not dead, I am living. I am happy with Grandma. [My mother had been dead many years.*] Phinuit says: Here are two more. One, two, three here,—one older and one younger than Kakie. [Correct.*] That is a boy, the one that came first. [Both were boys.*]

The lady has a friend, Elizabeth,—Lizzie. Mary wants to send love to Elizabeth. [This last is not intelligible to us.]

The little one calls the lady, Auntie. [Not her aunt.*] I wish you could see these children. Phinuit turns to Mr. Sutton and says: You do a great deal of good in the body. [To me.] He is a *dear* man! Was this little one's tongue very dry? She keeps showing me her tongue. [Her tongue was paralysed, and she suffered much with it to the end.] Her name is Katherine. [Correct.*] She calls herself Kakie. She passed out last. [Correct.*] Tell Dodo Kakie is in a spiritual body. Where is horsey? [I gave him a little horse.] Big horsey, not this little one. [Probably refers to a toy cart-horse she used to like.] Dear Papa, take me wide. [To ride.] Do you miss your Kakie? Do you see Kakie? The pretty white flowers you put on me, I have here. I took their little souls out and kept them with me. Phinuit describes lilies of the valley, which were the flowers we placed in her casket.

Papa, want to go wide horsey. [She plead this all through her illness.] Every day I go to see horsey. I like that horsey. I go to ride. I am with you every day...[I asked if she remembered anything after she was brought down stairs.] I was so hot, my head was so hot. [Correct.*] [I asked if she knew who was caring for her, if it was any comfort to her to have us with her.] Oh, yes,—oh, yes. [I asked if she suffered in dying.] I saw the light and followed it to this pretty lady. You will love me always? You will let me come to you at home. I will come to you every day, and I will put my hand on you, when you go to sleep. Do not cry for me,—that makes me sad. Eleanor. I want Eleanor. [Her little sister. She called her much during her last illness.*] I want my buttons. Row,

Row,—my song,—sing it now. I sing with you. [We sing, and a soft child voice sings with us.]
Lightly row, lightly row,
O'er the merry waves we go,
Smoothly glide, smoothly glide
With the ebbing tide.
[Phinuit hushes us, and Kakie finishes alone.]
Let the winds and waters be
Mingled with out melody,
Sing and float, sing and float,
In our little boat.
Papa sing. I hear your voice, but it is so heavy. [Papa and Kakie sing. Phinuit exclaims: See her little curls fly!] [Her curls were not long enough to fly at death, six weeks before.*] Kakie sings: Bye, bye, ba bye, bye, bye, O baby bye. Sing that with me, papa. [Papa and Kakie sing. These two songs were the ones she used to sing.] [She sang slight snatches of others in life—not at the sitting.*] Where is Dinah? I want Dinah. [Dinah was an old black rag-doll, not with us.] I want Bagie [her name for her sister Margaret.] I want Bagie to bring me my Dinah. I want to go to Bagie. I want Bagie. I see Bagie all the time. Tell Dodo when you see him that I love him. Dear Dodo. He used to march with me.—he put me way up. [Correct.*] Dodo did sing to me. That was a horrid body. I have a pretty body now. Tell Grandma I love her. I want her to know I live. Grandma does know it, Marmie—Great–grandma, Marmie. [We called her Great Grandmother *Marmie* but *she* always called her *Grammie*. Both Grandmother and Great Grandmother were then living.*]

Here is Hattie. Speak to her. I am so happy. [Button string broke—Phinuit is distressed. We gather them up and propose to re-string them.] Hattie says that is a pretty picture there. [Hattie was the name of a dear friend who died several years ago. She was very fond of my copy of the Sistine Madonna, and in her last illness asked to have it hung over her bed, where it remained till after she passed away. This did not occur to me when Phinuit gave her words, nor for some weeks after the sitting.]

I want the tic-tic. Take the buttons and give me the pretty tic-tic. Open the tic-tic. Mamma, do you love me so? Don't cry for me. I want to see the mooley-cow,—where is the mooley-cow? [R.H.: Did she so call it? A: Yes.*] Take me to see the mooley-cow. [She used to be taken almost daily to see the cow.] Phinuit says: I cannot quite hear what it is she calls the tic-tic. She calls it "the clock," and holds it to her ear. [That was what she called it.] I want you to talk to me before I go away from this pretty place.

Phinuit asks: What was the matter with her tongue? She shows it to me. All well now. She has the most beautiful, great, dark violet eyes. [Correct.*] She is very full of life—very independent, but very sweet in disposition. She is very fond of Bagie and Dodo, and so very glad to see you.

Here is Eddie—little thing passed out quite small—she knows him. [Correct.*]

Phinuit tries to get a new name—Louie—Louie—Alonzo. He is here with Kakie and he is a dear fellow. He says: Don't think it wrong to call me back,—I am so glad to come. Did not you dream about him after he passed away? Some time ago? A few years since? [Not that he remembers.] Here is a little one Kakie calls your brother. Alonzo, Kakie wants you to speak to her uncle Alonzo. [Mr. Sutton had a brother Alonzo, also Eddie, who died young, and his mother lost a still-born child.] [Boy.*] Mr. Sutton asked: Can he hear and speak in that life? [He was a mute.] He can hear. We talk by thought here. [Phinuit, for Alonzo.] How strange your voice is! I went up, up, up, and came into the light. I suffered a great deal more than you realised, and was depressed. I will take the best care of your little ones. [He had dreaded death, thinking of it as going down into the dark.*]

Phinuit tries to give the full name—says it has two t's, ends in *ton*—tries to pronounce it Csutton. Mr. Sutton said the middle initial in his name was C. "That is it," cried Phinuit. Alonzo C. Sutton. He is very happy. He can look back and see you and your work. Adeline—little Addie—he remembers her. [His sister's baby at the time of his death.*]

[Kakie again.] I will be with you when you do not see me. I want you to tell Eleanor [her little sister.*]. I send her my love, and my love to Bagie. I don't forget Bagie. Do not worry for us, we are so happy. Where is Grandma Sutton? I want her to know that I love her and come round her, and sing "Bye, bye," when I am in heaven. I am so happy with all these little girls. What was the pretty white thing, with the pretty flowers hanging over it, that you put in the little mound? [The little casket of our dead, new born baby.] Phinuit says: Three little mounds, but only their bodies there; their spirits are happy here.

Phinuit says the lady who has Kakie wants to speak to me. He tries to give her name—Mary—where is the school? C___—who is Mary C___? [That is the name of the lady.] [The surname correctly given but omitted at request of sitters.—R.H.] She wants you to always remember that your brothers and I are always with those children. [I had one brother only, but Mr. Sutton may have been meant, or both.*] I will be with them as you would wish me to be. [I asked about her death.] The thread connected me with the body for a time, till at last I passed up and saw the body. Phinuit says: A___ in the body, daughter to Mary? Mary says so, and sends her love. A great change in her life since she passed out. She is pleased—it was not right that A___ should be so much alone. [Name and statement correct.*]

There will be more harmony by-and-bye. She likes him very well. [This to my question if she likes him.] A___ will understand him better later on. There is opportunity for him to grow spiritually. They will be happy together.

[Kakie again.] I will put my hand on papa's head when he goes to sleep. Want the babee. [Her characteristic pronunciation.*] Phinuit takes the doll and says: She wants it to cuddle up to her, so. She wants to sing to it, Bye baby, bye bye. God knew best, so do not worry. The little book. Kakie wants the little book. [She liked a linen picture book.*]

The séance continued with extended and (in the first case) veridical messages from two more communicators. The séance ended as follows.

We thought the sitting over, and Mr. Sutton had gone across the room, when **Kakie's voice piped up. Want papa—want papa. Dear papa. [Phinuit pats his face.] Do you love me, papa? Want babee. Sings, Bye, bye—papa, sing—mama sing. Cuddles doll up in neck and sings. [An exact imitation marvellously animated and real.*]**

Katharine Paine Sutton
(Hodgson, 1898, pp. 485–489)

Whether or not we take this sitting to demonstrate survival or telepathy among the living, I think we must agree with Gauld that the flow of paranormally acquired information here is unusually quick, bountiful, and free from error (Gauld, 1982, p. 41). And in fact, the transcript would seem even more impressive if it had been reproduced in its entirety. Granted, the flow of veridical material isn't constant. For example, there are periods during the séance where Phinuit (or the communicators) repeat earlier material or make predictable comments or assurances about the communicators' postmortem existence. But those moments are appropriate to the context, and there's nothing that looks suspiciously either like "padding" or fishing for information.

Besides, although it's important not to overlook the potential significance of Mrs. Piper's false statements, inaccurate personations, surprising examples of ignorance, periods of rambling, etc., it's also crucial not to inflate their importance. Granted, Mrs. Piper sometimes had quite poor séances, or periods during a sitting that were clearly non-evidential. But to be as fair as possible to the survival hypothesis, we must consider the sorts of things that might reasonably disrupt or impede communication with the deceased. For example, it's not difficult or preposterous to suppose that communicators might face great obstacles in getting their messages across. For example, the process itself (or channel of communication) might be imperfect at best—perhaps like an irremediably noisy telephone connection. Moreover, the communicator might be impaired in any number of ways. If survival is a fact, then the process of transition, or the postmortem state itself, might simply not be optimal for producing clear communications. As William James noted, much of the non-evidential material "is more suggestive...of dreaminess and mind-wandering than it is of humbug" (James, 1909/1986, p. 355). But then, we must be open to the possibility that "at the time of communicating, the communicating spirits are themselves in a dreamy or somnambulic state, and not in full possession of their faculties" (James, 1909/1986, p. 322). Furthermore, the medium might add another set of obstacles to the mix, either all the time or just part of the time. She might have her own varying degrees of resistance, or she might allow her own thoughts to crowd onto those passing through her.

We should also be charitable with regard to the tendency of mediumistic utterances to become stereotyped and repeated. As James remarked in connection with comments made by Mrs. Piper's Hodgson-control,

Whatever they may have been at the outset, they soon fall into what may be called the trance-memory's "stock," and are then repeated automatically...This habitual use of stock-remarks by Mrs. Piper may tempt one to be unjust to the total significance of her mediumship. If the supernormal element in it, whatever it is, be essentially discontinuous and flash-like, an utterance that to-day belongs to the regular trance-stock may have *got into* that stock as a former moment of supernormal receptivity. (James, 1909/1986, p. 286)

Furthermore, we can't ignore the possible role of sporadic or recurrent investigator (or sitter)-influence (normal or paranormal) in cases of mediumship. These types of experimenter effects might account for inconsistencies in a medium's performance or for outright experimental failures (perhaps just for some investigators). Sir William Barrett made the point nicely.

It is doubtless a peculiar *psychical* state that confers mediumistic powers, but we know nothing of its nature, and we often ruin our experiments and lose our results by our ignorance. Certainly it is very probable that the psychical state of those present at a séance will be found to re-act on the medium. We should get no results if our photographic plates were exposed to the light of the room simultaneously with the luminous image formed by the lens. In every physical process we have to guard against disturbing causes. (Barrett, 1917, p. 120).[2]

With these observations in mind, then, let's return to the séance excerpted above. As Gauld correctly noted, certain features of this séance and its successor are particularly interesting and perhaps difficult to explain in terms of psi among the living. In particular, on both occasions Kakie requested some items from her parents. Ostensibly, these objects were meaningful to Kakie, but the Suttons failed to recognize what Kakie had in mind until she helped them out. So Mrs. Piper communicated what were apparently strong associations only in Kakie's mind, not in the minds of her parents. (For Hodgson's discussion of these incidents, see Hodgson, 1898, pp. 386–389.)

For example, toward the beginning of the first séance, Kakie asked for "horsey." But when she was given a little toy horse, she replied, "Big horsey, not this little one." At that point, Mrs. Sutton concluded that Kakie was referring to a toy cart-horse she used to like. A few moments later, Kakie said she wanted to ride a horse that she sees every day. Mrs. Sutton noted that Kakie made this request throughout her illness, but again she didn't identify the horse in question. And it's unclear whether the toy cart-horse mentioned by Mrs. Sutton is something Kakie could have ridden. Then, at the second séance, Kakie again requested the horse, and again Mrs. Sutton seemed not to realize which horse Kakie had in mind. The relevant passage from the second séance is as follows. Phinuit is speaking.

> Kakie wants the horse. [I gave him the little horse she played with during
> her illness.] No, that is not the one. The big horse—so big—[Phinuit shows
> how large]. Eleanor's horse. Eleanor used to put it in Kakie's lap. She loved
> that horsey. [This horse was packed, in Trenton, and had not occurred to
> me in connection with Kakie. What she said of it was true.] (Hodgson,
> 1898, p. 491)

Now this horse, presumably, is not one Kakie used to ride, because it
was something that fit in Kakie's lap. So it remains unclear which horse
Kakie wanted to ride. Nevertheless, the important point here is that
Mrs. Sutton was not clear about this either. Apparently, Mrs. Piper was
communicating desires and associations appropriate to Kakie but outside of Mrs. Sutton's conscious awareness.

Also in the first séance, Kakie requested "the little book," and Mrs.
Sutton surmised that she meant a linen picture book. But at the second
sitting Kakie twice asked for books. Initially, she requested "the book
with red letters and pictures of animals" (Hodgson, 1898, p. 492). Mrs.
Sutton then commented that this was a "correct description of a book
she was fond of," and it may have been the linen picture book Mrs. Sutton mentioned in the previous sitting. If so, this might indicate nothing
more than telepathy between Mrs. Piper and Mrs. Sutton. But later in
the second séance, Kakie once again requested a "little" book. Phinuit
says,

> Kakie wants the little bit of a book mamma read by her bedside, with the
> pretty, bright things hanging from it—mamma put it in her hands—the last
> thing she remembers. [This is curious. It was a little prayer-book, with
> cross, anchor, and other symbols, in silver, attached to ribbons for marking
> the places. It was sent to me by a dear friend, after Kakie had ceased to
> know anyone, except, perhaps, for a passing moment. I read it, and so did
> our physician, in the night watches, when she seemed unconscious, and
> *after her death* I placed it in her hands to prevent the settling in the nails.
> The last thing she remembered was my placing it in her hands! What does
> this signify?] [Mrs. Piper held her hands in just that position when she
> asked for it.*] (Hodgson, 1898, p. 493)

This last example will not impress partisans of the super-psi hypothesis. After all, the prayer-book had played an important role in Kakie's
final hours and had undoubtedly meant a great deal to Mrs. Sutton. So
even if Mrs. Sutton had not been thinking about the book during the
séance, memories and feelings about it were presumably easily retriev-
able or accessible (especially in the context of apparent communication
with Kakie). So (one might argue) those memories and feelings might
be relatively easy targets for mediumistic ESP.

Nevertheless, these examples raise serious questions about the super-
psi hypothesis. As Gauld notes,

> If we are to say that Mrs. Piper could select from the sitters' minds associa-

tions conflicting with the ones consciously present and utilize them in order to create the impression that the communicator's thoughts moved along lines distinctively different from the sitter's, we are beginning to attribute to her not just super-ESP but super-artistry as well. (Gauld, 1982, p. 42)

Gauld's concern in understandable. After all, in order to explain the episodes just related in terms of Mrs. Piper's ESP, we would need to posit more than the already impressive ability to extract *unconscious* memories and dispositions from the minds of the living. In addition, we might need to suppose (a) that Mrs. Piper could extract this material at the appropriate times in the course of a séance,[3] and then (b) present it so that it appeared to represent the perspective of the communicator. Now this might justifiably strain credulity, even for partisans of super psi (and I'll return to that issue more fully in section 5). But before we consider whether Mrs. Piper's achievement goes beyond any plausible application of the super-psi hypothesis, we should scrutinize Gauld's claim that Mrs. Piper's performance here required exceptional artistry.

Granted, it would have taken some creativity for Mrs. Piper to transform psychically received information so that it could be presented from Kakie's point of view. But if that's what Mrs. Piper was doing, presumably she was doing it unconsciously, in order to avoid personal responsibility for her mediumistic messages. And clearly, if Mrs. Piper's pseudo-communications resulted simply from subconscious ESP, there are several obvious reasons why she—or any medium—would have presented them in the dramatic form of messages from the deceased. First, it's in a medium's psychological best interest to view herself as a mere recipient of information, rather than a psychic sleuth with potentially terrifying abilities to dig into the recesses of living minds.[4] Second, a medium needn't feel personally responsible when the communicators' behavior takes provocative forms. In fact, by attributing risky behavior, thoughts, or feelings to discarnate entities, a medium can deflect responsibility more thoroughly than she could if she assigned them instead to a subliminal self. Third, when communicators offer advice or nuggets of philosophy, these will obviously seem more impressive if they appear to originate, not from the medium, but from entities who possess the wisdom gained from higher plains (or the experience of a former life). Moreover, when the communications are indirect and funneled through a control personality,

> less is demanded from a spirit friend limited to communicating through another spirit, who may misunderstand what he is supposed to repeat, than from one purporting to talk with the sitter directly. As a matter of fact, the difficulty of this indirect communication is constantly adduced as an excuse for failure or confusion. (Sidgwick, 1915, p. 77)

But then, it's not clear whether the mediumistic transformation of psychically acquired material is unusually impressive. It may be no more extraordinary than the creativity displayed by many hypnotic subjects—for example, during clearly spurious "regressions" (see chapter 4). Moreover (and perhaps more to the point), it seems no more impressive than many familiar—and presumably subconscious or unconscious—human activities, especially those in which we try to escape responsibility for our actions. Consider, for example, the cunning and often extraordinary ways in which people act self-destructively—for example, by repeatedly entangling themselves in lethal romantic relationships, or by orchestrating conflicts in friendships or at work, and doing so in a way that allows them to assume the role of hapless victim. In short, we shouldn't underestimate our potential for unconscious creativity and resourcefulness, either in mediumistic or hypnotic settings, or in more humdrum everyday contexts.

Now Gauld may still be right. It may be that the artistry required by Mrs. Piper is exceptional and that it transcends not only what highly hypnotizable subjects can do, but also what most people exhibit as they proceed through the dramas of their lives. However, that claim will be very difficult to establish. For one thing, just as it's unclear how to determine which psi counts as "super," it's not clear what the standard of measurement should be for unconscious artistry and creativity. And for another, Gauld's assessment can only be justified by comparing processes and abilities of which we are largely ignorant and which *by hypothesis* are covert.

William James, too, was both impressed by, but wary of overestimating, the creativity which super-psi explanations must attribute to Mrs. Piper. In discussing the Hodgson-control in sittings with Prof. Newbold, James remarked,

> If the R.H. who appeared therein be only a figment of Mrs. Piper's play-acting subconscious self...,we must credit that self with real genius for accumulating the appropriate in the way of items, and not getting out of the right personal key. (James, 1909/1986, p. 321)

On the other hand, James conceded,

> the notion that Mrs. Piper's subliminal self should keep her sitters apart as expertly as she does, remembering its past dealings with each of them so well, not mixing their communications more, and all the while humbugging them so profusely, is quite compatible with what we know of the dream-life of hypnotized subjects. Their consciousness, narrowed to one suggested kind of operation, shows remarkable skill in that operation. If we suppose Mrs. Piper's dream-life once for all to have had the notion suggested to it that it must personate spirits to sitters, the fair degree of virtuosity it shows need not, I think, surprise us. Nor need the exceptional memory shown surprise us, for memory usually seems extraordinarily strong in the subconscious life. (James, 1909/1986, p. 284)

We'll return to these considerations shortly. But first, we need to broaden our view of the empirical landscape and examine another impressive case of mediumship.

4. Mrs. Leonard's Mediumship

Like many other mediums, Mrs. Gladys Osborne Leonard (1882-1968) experienced childhood visions. However, her parents disapproved of these experiences, and so Gladys managed to suppress them. Nevertheless, a significant psychic episode occurred when she was a young adult, working and touring as an actress. That experience was a veridical vision of her mother at the time of her death. But Mrs. Leonard became fully aware of her mediumistic gifts only after she married, in the course of conducting table-tipping experiments with some of her actress friends in their dressing room. On that occasion she became entranced, and a communicator calling herself Feda spoke through her. Feda claimed to be the spirit of an Indian girl who had married one of the medium's ancestors in the nineteenth century, and eventually she became Mrs. Leonard's primary control. Although Feda's claimed origin was never verified, Mrs. Leonard recalled her mother mentioning a Hindu ancestress who died at a young age during childbirth. Toward the beginning of the First World War, Mrs. Leonard took up mediumship professionally in order to help the bereaved. Soon after, she became famous when Sir Oliver Lodge published his book *Raymond,* an account of ostensible communications from a son killed in the war (Lodge, 1916).

The control-persona Feda spoke in a high, squeaky voice, with occasional errors in grammar, misunderstandings of words, and consistent eccentricities of pronunciation (e.g., substituting the letter "l" for the letter "r"). Her personality was distinctively childlike (if not childish), and her relationship with Mrs. Leonard was less than cordial. Feda could be capricious and petulant, and although her attitude toward Mrs. Leonard was occasionally protective and appreciative of the medium's indispensability, more frequently it was mildly antagonistic and disdainful. Moreover, Feda had the annoying and (to Mrs. Leonard) embarrassing habit of soliciting gifts from sitters, which she adamantly insisted were hers and not the medium's.

Mrs. Leonard's mediumship resembled that of Mrs. Piper in several important respects. Both mediums permitted members of the SPR to study them extensively and closely, and investigators had both women shadowed by detectives to ensure that they weren't learning about their sitters on the sly. Moreover, both mediums produced communications through writing as well as speech. However, whereas Mrs. Piper eventually relied exclusively on the former, Mrs. Leonard engaged primarily in the latter. In most cases a control personality (usually Feda) acted as

intermediary, although occasionally other communicators would apparently control Mrs. Leonard's vocal organs and body.

Furthermore, Mrs. Leonard seemed to demonstrate telepathy with
the sitter in forms similar to those occurring with Mrs. Piper. For example, when Mrs. Beadon one day encountered a woman she hadn't seen
for twenty-four years, she was reminded of that woman's brother who
died twenty-five years earlier. A few days later, at a sitting with Mrs.
Leonard, Feda mentioned that man by name and provided identifying
details. Mrs. Beadon claimed that Mrs. Leonard had on many occasions
provided ostensible communications connected with people she had
met shortly before the sitting (Salter, 1921, pp. 69–72).

In fact, the case of Mrs. Leonard raises the problem of super psi in
an especially potent form. For one thing, Mrs. Leonard, like Mrs. Piper,
often provided accurate information about the living as well as about
the dead (I give an example of this below). Although I'm aware of no
detailed and general studies on the topic, this seems to be rather common among good mediums. However, it's worth noting that H. F. Saltmarsh analyzed 142 sittings with the medium Mrs. Warren Elliott. He
found that there were more veridical statements about events occurring
after the communicators' death than there were about events prior to
death. Moreover, he found that there was a higher *percentage* of
veridicality in the statements about events subsequent to death (Saltmarsh, 1929, p. 91). None of this is clearly incompatible with the survival hypothesis, but as Dodds noted, it "is hardly what [one] should
expect if the source of the communications were [a] surviving personality" (Dodds, 1934, p. 155). After all, information about the living is not
something uniquely possessed by the ostensible communicators. And
since the communicators are deprived of a physical body, their access to
this information would presumably count as an example of ESP. But if
communicators can exercise their ESP to learn about the living, why
not the medium? For these cases at least, the survival hypothesis seems
gratuitous and unparsimonious. Obviously, then, survivalists require
cases in which communicators provide information which they alone
should know.

But not even the best of Mrs. Leonard's sittings provide unambiguous evidence of survival. Probably the most impressive features of Mrs.
Leonard's mediumship are her numerous *book-tests* and *proxy sittings*,
the best of which seem to require an appeal either to survival or to a
nearly omniscient form of ESP. Of these, the book-tests are perhaps the
most intriguing; Mrs. Leonard was not the first medium to attempt
proxy sittings. Apparently, the idea for the book tests was proposed by
Feda, rather than by any of Mrs. Leonard's investigators. But it's easy to
see why investigators found them provocative and potentially valuable.
The general format for a book-test is as follows. The communicator,
through Feda, tries

to indicate the contents of a particular page of a particular book which Mrs. Leonard has not seen with her bodily eyes, and which is not, at the time of the sitting, known to the sitter. For example, Feda might tell the sitter that the communicator wants him to go to the book-case between the fireplace and the window in his study, and in the third shelf from the bottom to take the seventh book from the left and open it at the 48th page, where about one-third of the way down he will find a passage which may be regarded as an appropriate message from the communicator to him. In most typical cases the interior of the sitter's residence, and sometimes even the sitter's name, is unknown to Mrs. Leonard. The sitter himself is unlikely consciously to remember what book occupies the exact place indicated, and even if he has read the book, which he often has not, it is practically certain that he does not know what is on the specified page. (Sidgwick, 1921, p. 242)

Clearly, then, a successful book-test would seem to rule out telepathy between medium and sitter. But it doesn't rule out telepathy with others; and it doesn't rule out clairvoyance. Now the first of these options might seem far-fetched even to partisans of super psi; it seems to postulate "a very omniscient kind if telepathy...by means of which the information can be gained from the mind of any person who has read the book in question" (Tyrrell, 1938/1961, p. 221). In fact, as Tyrrell also noted, "This would have to extend to the reading of another copy of the same edition, as sometimes the particular volume indicated has been unread and the pages are still uncut" (p. 222).

Mrs. Sidgwick noted, further,

There is...no instance I think of the communicator calling attention to the fact that a page referred to was uncut. And the impressions, right or wrong, alleged to be derived from pages which prove to be uncut are described with as much fulness and detail as others. (Sidgwick, 1921, p. 359)

Granted, a *magic wand* super-psi hypothesis can accommodate a psychic achievement of this magnitude (see chapter 2). It requires no more than a causally efficacious psychological state; it needn't posit an intervening process between that state and the effect—for example, an underlying telepathic search-procedure. But for those unwilling to adopt that explanatory strategy, it remains unclear how Feda or Mrs. Leonard would be able to pick out the relevant person with the relevant knowledge of the book. These issues don't arise for the second super-psi option, clairvoyance, because book-tests specify target-locations. But other problems of psychic selectivity take their place. If the medium uses clairvoyance to identify the book contents, it's still unclear how she knows which passages would pertain to the communicator and which of those would be recognized by (or be meaningful to) the sitter or others. That knowledge seems to require intimate and detailed telepathic access to other living minds, and possibly also clairvoyant access to physical records providing information about the communicator. But if we eschew a magic-wand explanation of that accomplishment, we need to explain how the medium could home in on the right details, in the right minds or records, and at the appropriate time during a séance. We'll return to these issues in section 5. First, however, let's consider the results of some book-tests.

One very striking case from Mrs. Sidgwick's collection (Sidgwick, 1921, pp. 253–260) has been summarized nicely by Gauld.

> An anonymous sitter (Mrs. Talbot) received through Feda a message from her late husband advising her to look for a relevant message on page twelve or thirteen of a book on her bookcase at home. Feda said the book was not printed, but had writing in it; was dark in colour; and contained a table of Indo-European, Aryan, Semitic and Arabian languages, whose relationships were shown by a diagram of radiating lines. Mrs. Talbot knew of no such book, and ridiculed the message. However, when she eventually looked, she found at the back of a top shelf a shabby black leather notebook of her husband's. Pasted into this book was a folded table of all the languages mentioned; whilst on p. 13 was an extract from a book entitled *Post Mortem*. In this case the message related to a book unknown to medium and sitter (indeed, so far as could be told, to any living person), but undoubtedly known to the communicator. (Gauld, 1982, p. 48)

I should add that the extract from *Post Mortem* seemed particularly apt. It described the author's blissful experiences following bodily death.

Regrettably, few cases are as clear as this. One problem is that Feda often said merely that on a specified part of a page the sitter would find a "message" that would be meaningful or appropriate to the communicator. Obviously, without further indication of what, exactly, that message is, we can't tell if the passage was simply fortuitously meaningful. Moreover, specifying the precise page of a book turned out to be somewhat problematic. For one thing, it wasn't always clear whether the page number mentioned by Feda was supposed to identify the page with that number printed on it, or the page identified by counting both numbered and unnumbered pages from the beginning of the book. In many, but not all, cases, Feda seemed to mean the latter. Moreover, the page with the items mentioned by Feda was sometimes the page immediately before or after the one she named. That happened often, and in ways that seemed to promise insights into the nature of clairvoyance itself, or at least Mrs. Leonard's version of it. The following case illustrates the problem.

On August 28, 1918, Feda (as intermediary for the communicator A.V.B.) clearly identified a specific shelf and then picked out the fifth book from the left. Then she said,

> On page what is called one four of this book, fourteen, wait a minute, something made her feel, gave her a feeling of heat, something hot, heat, about half way down that page. But she'd better explain, it might come from two sources, it might come from a mention of heat, like a hot sun, or

a hot fire, or it might come from a mention of great anger, but spoken of as heat; in fact, she'd be obliged if you'd tell which it is next time you come. (Sidgwick, 1921, pp. 281–282)

The book referred to was M. Pickthall's *Larkmeadow*, which hadn't been read or opened by the sitters. The pages have thirty-three lines, and on the sixteenth line of p. 14 were the words "ardent patriot." Although those words don't refer directly to heat or fire, they could easily be taken to do so metaphorically. But on the facing p. 15 was the word "bonfire," and when the book was closed (as it had been on the shelf), the words "ardent" and "bonfire" almost touched each other. Mrs. Sidgwick also noted that the chapter containing pages 14 and 15 refers to a great deal of anger in connection with the bonfire.

It's reasonable to wonder whether Mrs. Leonard's successes in book-tests could be attributed to chance. Because of the inherent vagueness and ambiguity of Feda's instructions and the subjective nature of many of the apparent correspondences, it's difficult to decide this matter with any precision. Nevertheless, some investigators addressed the problem, and all determined that the successes were unlikely to occur by chance. For example, in her long paper on Mrs. Leonard, Mrs. Sidgwick examined the results of verified sittings with thirty-four sitters. Book-tests were given at 146 sittings with these individuals, and from those sittings

> 532 separate book-test items occurred, not including statements about titles or other outside things. The number of items at a sitting varied from 1 to 15. These 532 items may be classed as 92 [17%] successful; 100 [19%] approximately successful; 204 complete failures; 40 nearly complete failures; 96 dubious. (Sidgwick, 1921, pp. 245–246n)

Control experiments were conducted as well. In one, 1800 "sham" book-tests were evaluated. Sixty people participated in the experiment. They were instructed to choose ten books at random, and then to open an envelope containing three "messages," along with indications of page and position on the page. These were compared to the corresponding parts of the ten selected books, and then ranked as either "success," "partial," or "nil." The three "tests" for each book were:

(1) A passage which is particularly relevant to your father. *Top quarter of page 60 in each book.*
(2) An allusion to circles of some kind. *Bottom half of page 35 in each book.*
(3) Frost and snow, or a passage conveying that idea. *The top ten lines of page 84 in each book.*

Of the 1800 resulting tests, only 34 (2%) of them were rated as successful and 51 (<3%) as partially successful (see Society for Psychical Research, 1923).

Theodore Besterman pursued a slightly different strategy (Besterman, 1931-32). He numbered the 26 full shelves of books in his study and sent a list of the numbers 1 through 26 to three members of the

SPR. Without explaining why, he asked them to match each of those numbers with a figure no higher than 20, followed by an "R" or an "L." That procedure yielded references to 78 books selected at random. For example, if the number 17 was matched with 5R, that would indicate the fifth book from the right on shelf 17. In the meantime, another S.P.R. member selected three actual book-tests with Mrs. Leonard, and the page-references given by Feda were matched to the books chosen by Besterman's method. That yielded a total of 234 entries. For reasons discussed by Besterman, the results of this test were difficult to summarize. But it's clear that the results were consistent with the earlier control experiments. As Besterman put it, "chance produces far worse results than does Feda" (p. 97).

Besterman also attempted another sort of control experiment. He invited "individuals (other than mediums) who are thought to have supernormal faculty or who are successful in sittings with mediums" (p. 60) to try a book-test on the books in his flat and then to mail their tests to the Secretary of the SPR. For various reasons, only a small number of replies (18) were received, but the results were, again, consistent with the other control experiments. Besterman estimated that the 18 replies contained a total of 113 separate confirmable statements, only 5 of which were evidential hits. Of those, he concluded that only one was "comparable with a good Leonard booktest" (p. 67).

As investigators realized at the time, these control experiments only reinforced the conclusion that something paranormal was going on, not necessarily communication from the dead. The possibility of first-rate ESP was still a live option. And to complicate matters further, some of Mrs. Leonard's tests seemed clearly to suggest ESP on the part of the medium. On some occasions, ostensible communicators were able to give information about books even though (a) the books had no special significance for the communicator, and (b) experimenters placed them on shelves in locations the communicator had never visited. But in that case, attributing this knowledge to deceased communicators seems gratuitous. As Gauld recognized,

> if these communicators can exercise clairvoyance of such remarkable degree, why should not Feda? Why should not Mrs. Leonard herself? The information given is no longer such as the alleged communicators are specially qualified to supply. (Gauld, 1982, p. 49)

In fact, in a few cases Feda gave correct information about books written in classical Greek (Sidgwick, 1921, pp. 300–313). But that language was unknown to Mrs. Leonard, the sitters, and also the alleged communicator. In these cases the person who lent the books, Mrs. Salter, knew Greek; but

> she had never regularly used the copies of Thucydides and Demosthenes in question. She may have occasionally used them to refer to, but in reading

those authors she had used other annotated editions. (Sidgwick, 1921, p. 309)

So it appears that even telepathy with Mrs. Salter leaves crucial matters unexplained. If Mrs. Salter hadn't used those books for careful study or hadn't used them at all, it's unlikely she possessed even subconscious knowledge of the location of the specific passages mentioned in the sittings.

The following incident illustrates further how Mrs. Leonard's mediumship is both impressive and difficult to interpret. We might think of it as a somewhat spontaneous and unstructured variant of a classic book-test, and it demonstrates nicely why, with Mrs. Leonard at least, the super-psi hypothesis remains a viable option. The séance occurred on October 4, 1921, and the sitter was Mrs. Salter, who acted as her own note taker. Mrs. Leonard produced a long stream of fairly impressive ostensible communications from Mrs. Salter's father, the classical scholar Dr. A. W. Verrall, who died in 1912. The specific incident I want to examine occurred during the course of these communications. (See Salter, 1930.)

As she traveled that day to Mrs. Leonard's house, Mrs. Salter purchased the October issue of the *Strand Magazine* to read on the train. She purchased the magazine sometime between 9:30 and 10:00 a.m., and the relevant portion of the séance took place shortly after 11:00 a.m. When she arrived at Mrs. Leonard's house, Mrs. Salter placed the magazine closed on a chair. Mrs. Leonard made no attempt to examine the magazine, and she was never left alone with it. After two or three minutes of conversation, Mrs. Leonard passed into trance. Eventually, the following exchange occurred.

> FEDA. Over on the chair, the book over on the chair. Your book on the chair over there (indicates *Strand Magazine*).
> H.S. In this room?
> F. Yes. Will you look about page fourteen? Something there should remind you of Mr. Arthur's old haunts, old pursuits. He's just thought of that and was afraid of losing it. (Salter, 1930, p. 324)

Like many magazines, the *Strand Magazine* numbered its pages consecutively from the beginning of the year. So Mrs. Salter assumed that Feda was referring to page fourteen of the current issue (which was numbered 302). Although that page seemed to contain no mention of her father's old haunts, there were clear connections to his old pursuits as a classical scholar. Mrs. Salter also noted that the passage in question connected nicely with references throughout the séance to her father's friend and fellow classical scholar, Henry Jackson.

> Near the bottom of the left-hand column (the *Strand* is printed in double columns) the following passage occurred: "It is all very well to excite pity and terror, as Aristotle recommends, but there are limits. In the ancient

Greek tragedies it was an ironclad rule that all the real rough stuff should take place off-stage, and I shall follow this admirable principle." To my father's life-long preoccupation with Greek tragedy, his many published works on Aeschylus and Euripides abundantly testify, and it may be noted that this allusion is very aptly interpolated in the midst of references to an old friend with whom my father's classical interests were closely associated, the friend to whom, as I have already mentioned, he dedicated the first of his three volumes of Euripidean studies, *Euripides the Rationalist*. The reference in the *Strand* to Aristotle constitutes a further link with Henry Jackson, whose lectures on Aristotle were a familiar institution at Cambridge for many years. (Salter, 1930, pp. 324–325)

Could Mrs. Leonard have known about that passage through normal channels of information, or through telepathy with the sitter? Mrs. Salter addressed those issues.

I had not myself at the time of the sitting read the story in which the quoted passage occurs, but I cannot of course be certain that my eye had not fallen on it in turning the pages. It seems, however, unlikely that I should have made the mental calculation involved in referring to page 302 as the fourteenth page. Mrs. Leonard, when I questioned her after the sitting, without giving a reason for the question, said she had not read the October *Strand*, which on the 4th of October had only been out a few days, and the argument in regard to calculating the page applies to Mrs. Leonard as well as to myself. She could, of course, have no motive for deliberately preparing the test beforehand, for she could not possibly know that I should buy the *Strand* that day and bring it with me to the sitting. So far as my recollection goes, I had never done such a thing before. (p. 325)

Investigators realized that it was important to find cases that ruled out telepathy between medium and sitter, and they documented many apparent cases of that type throughout Mrs. Leonard's career (see, e.g., Radclyffe-Hall & Troubridge, 1920, pp. 487–546; Salter, 1926). However, these tended to concern incidents that occurred unexpectedly in the course of a séance. So, in an effort to eliminate more systematically the possibility, however remote, of unconscious telepathy between medium and sitter, experimenters conducted frequent proxy tests with Mrs. Leonard. In these tests, the sitter represents a third party—ideally, one about whom sitter and medium know as little as possible (see, e.g., Allison, 1934; C. D. Thomas, 1932-33, 1935, 1938-39, 1939). Unfortunately, it's difficult to summarize Mrs. Leonard's proxy tests both adequately and briefly, because most extended over a series of sittings.

However, the following example illustrates the kind of evidence investigators sought. In a sitting on July 20, 1937, with Lydia Allison as sitter/recorder and proxy for Mr. Francis Blair (pseudonym) of Boston, Feda described the death of Mr. Blair's wife. She correctly noted that in the last few days before her death, Mrs. Blair had experienced difficulty breathing, and she remarked, "I do not think it was an accident that took her over. I feel rather a quick exhausted feeling" (Allison, 1941, p.

202). Feda had other "hits" as well, but these are particularly significant. That's because at the time of the séance Mrs. Allison believed, *incorrectly*, that Mrs. Blair had died in an accident. So, although we can't rule out telepathy from Mr. Blair, telepathy between medium and sitter seems out of the question.

But to complicate matters, some of Mrs. Leonard's proxy tests served only to fuel speculation about telepathy with persons other than the sitter, and clairvoyance as well. For example, in a sitting taking place in England on June 3, 1929, with Lydia Allison as sitter/recorder and proxy for J. F. Thomas, Mrs. Leonard accurately described the area around Thomas's cottage on Orchard Lake in Michigan, some of his recent activities there, and his feelings and thoughts at the time (J. F. Thomas, 1937, pp. 87ff). Thomas previously had sat only twice (anonymously) with Mrs. Leonard (two years earlier), and the matters Feda described were certainly unknown to Mrs. Allison.

Although the cases of Mrs. Piper and Mrs. Leonard provide compelling evidence of some sort of paranormal process, it's difficult to rank them, either as cases suggesting survival, or as cases demonstrating super psi. That merely illustrates, again, a point I've made repeatedly: namely, that there are no clear standards of psychic achievement to which we may appeal. Nevertheless, it's not futile to speculate about the strength of the evidence, and there are several important issues to address.

5. Mediumship and Super-ESP

We're now in a position to consider whether (or to what extent) successful trance mediumship can be explained in terms of super psi. Although (as we'll see) super-psi explanations face daunting and perhaps insurmountable obstacles, some attempts to reject super psi clearly don't work. For example, some seem to think that if mediumistic super psi existed, it would work in an implausibly straightforward and relatively unobstructed way. Then, when the evidence can't be explained away in terms of psychic functioning *as they erroneously construe it*, they conclude that the survival hypothesis is a viable alternative. For example, Drayton Thomas considered the possibility that Mrs. Leonard might have psychically "reached out" to search for appropriate information, and he claimed that this hypothesis was difficult to square with the facts—specifically that Mrs. Leonard's results varied widely from complete failures to striking successes. He wrote,

> If the medium's own activity obtained the information, it should have been more uniformly successful. There were some complete failures just where success should, on this hypothesis, have been most likely, namely in those instances where I had interviewed the applicant shortly before the sitting.

Such personal intercourse showed no superiority over the cases where no interview had taken place. (C. D. Thomas, 1932-33, p. 156)

In a similar vein, he continued,

the medium's own faculty is not the factor to which we can attribute these proxy results. If my richly stored memory yielded so little when I was sitting in the medium's presence, is it likely that the minds of distant and unknown persons would yield as much? And yet one or two of the proxy cases have not only equalled, but have surpassed in evidential richness the majority of communications received from my own deceased acquaintances. (pp. 157–158)

These passages contain several errors and confusions. First, Thomas seems to confuse physical (and perhaps temporal) proximity with psychic closeness or intimacy, or at least he supposes that the two must be closely correlated. But that's no more plausible than supposing that people are most likely to succeed in telepathy experiments when their heads are touching. Moreover, Thomas seems to ignore the complex interpersonal and other contextual variables that presumably affect psychic functioning. It's no more plausible to think that a medium will automatically respond telepathically to a psychically primed sitter than it is to think that people will respond sexually just because their partner is "in the mood." The history of psi research suggests strongly that psychic functioning, like most other cognitive capacities, is highly situation-sensitive, context-dependent, and susceptible to an enormous range of positive and negative influences, including mood, belief system, interpersonal relations, and even geophysical and celestial variables (such as, respectively, earth's geomagnetic field and local sidereal time). (For intriguing studies of the latter two possibilities, see, e.g., Berger & Persinger, 1991; Gearhart & Persinger, 1986; Lewicki, Schaut, & Persinger, 1987; Persinger, 1985; Spottiswoode, 1997. The former set of variables should be too obvious to mention.)

A less naive, but possibly more familiar objection to the super-psi hypothesis was expressed by Ducasse. Like many others, he resorted to a form of the Sore Thumb Argument, protesting that the super-ESP required to explain the best survival cases "vastly exceeds any that is independently known to occur" (Ducasse, 1961, p. 198). In chapter 1 we considered several reasons for believing that this argument is problematic. So we can now deal with it rather quickly. First, even when a good medium provides accurate and specific information it's questionable whether the ESP needed to explain that away exceeds, much less vastly, detailed ESP documented in other contexts. The U.S. government-sponsored remote viewing trials offer perhaps the most recent examples of highly accurate and richly detailed psychic hitting, although the information obtained was not of a personal nature (see, e.g., May, 1995; 1996; Puthoff, 1996; Targ, 1996). Moreover, here too it's unclear how we even measure psychic achievement—that is, how "super" a given instance of psychic functioning is.

But quite apart from the problem of assessing the amount or quality of the material, Ducasse's objection must be used with caution. If applied too liberally, we could forever avoid acknowledging either the first detected instance of a rare ability, or the existence of one that, as it happens, manifests only in the context under consideration. There's no reason to insist, *a priori*, that an ability manifesting in mediumistic contexts must occur in other situations. Analogously, certain behaviors, aptitudes, or abilities, emerge only in sexually intimate settings, or when one is feeling frightened or intimidated (e.g., when one's life is in danger), or in unusually supportive environments (e.g., in front of an adoring audience). Moreover, as far as we know, ESP might resemble certain athletic abilities that manifest in their most exquisite forms, and also break down dramatically, only during actual contests, when the athlete's motivation and anxiety are unusually strong and the stakes are unusually high.

However, Ducasse raised another point against super-ESP that I find more compelling. Actually, Ducasse didn't quite get the point right. But rather than digress by discussing the fine details of Ducasse's argument, here's the point I believe he was trying (or should have been trying) to make. It brings us back to the issue about mediumistic artistry we considered first in section 3.

To simplify discussion, let's focus on the phenomenon of trance impersonation in an anonymous (but not proxy) sitting. With suitable changes, the same issues arise (sometimes in even more extreme forms) in connection with proxy sittings. So, suppose a medium presents a credible trance persona of the sitter's friend Tom. By what psychic process could the medium make the Tom-persona into a convincingly lifelike impersonation? More specifically, consider what the medium needs to do if the Tom-persona is merely a dramatic artifice, constructed telepathically from thoughts and memories in the sitter's mind.

First, we need to explain how the medium can respond to comments and questions in ways the sitter finds believably Tom-like. That seems to require either

(a) telepathic access to the sitter's memories and beliefs about Tom *throughout* the conversation with the sitter,

or perhaps even less plausibly

(b1) telepathic access to a great many of the sitter's beliefs and memories in advance (or at the beginning) of the séance,

along with

(b2) reliable memory throughout the séance of the information previously extracted.

But how plausible is that? Option (a) requires, not just sporadically highly accurate ESP, but an unusually and perhaps implausibly long string of successes. Option (b) seems to demand extracting nearly *everything* the sitter remembers or believes about Tom, in order to be able to retrieve the appropriate elements throughout the séance. Moreover, option (b) may still require incredibly successful, ongoing, and refined telepathy with the sitter during the séance. Otherwise, it's unclear how the medium could be sure which particular bits of previously extracted information the sitter would regard as appropriate.

The problems for the super-ESP hypothesis don't end here. We're supposing that a medium constructs the Tom-persona psychically from the *sitter's* memories, etc. So consider what's needed for that persona to be convincing to people *other than* the sitter—for example, those who knew Tom and who later examine the transcript of the séance. At least two important conditions must be fulfilled. First, the sitter's memories must be accurate, or at least shared by many people; and second, the medium's access to them must also be largely successful and accurate. Now that may be asking too much, especially when we consider the highly idiosyncratic views and memories different people often have of the same person.

To see why, suppose a medium presented a postmortem communication from me, fashioned telepathically from my ex-wife's memories and opinions. I'll bet the communicating persona would differ greatly from one based on ESP with people whose relationships with me were not so acrimonious. So if a trance-persona is to be *generally* convincing, the medium might need to synthesize a composite picture of the communicator from several (or many) minds, written records, etc. But in that case, the problem of avoiding hopelessly idiosyncratic associations, memories, etc., only increases. After all, idiosyncratic and possibly false beliefs, memories, and associations about me won't be limited to my ex-wife. In addition to those beleaguered souls who've known me as spouse, there will be those who knew me primarily as sibling, cousin, student, teacher, friend, or fellow-musician, to name just a few. So there might be as many idiosyncratic sets of beliefs, etc., about me as there are people who knew me in different situations or life-roles. In fact, we've already considered a precedent for this sort of problem in our examination of Mrs. Piper's mediumship. We considered instances in which she apparently picked up a living person's distinctively false beliefs about a communicator.

Granted (as Mrs. Piper sometimes demonstrated), a medium's trance persona might on one occasion exhibit behaviors or knowledge meaningfully appropriate to sitter *A*, and then on other occasions the trance persona might display different behaviors or knowledge appropriate (respectively) to sitters *B* and *C*. In that sense, a Tom-persona could be generally convincing in virtue of being individually convincing, in different ways, to different sitters. In cases of that sort, what makes the Tom-persona convincing is precisely the idiosyncratically appropriate nature of its interactions with different sitters. But of course, that hardly lessens the challenge for super-psi explanations. Not only would the medium's ESP need to be accurate and reliable over a series of sittings, it would also need to target those idiosyncratic memories and beliefs which individual sitters would find personally compelling.

Apparently, then, for an ESP-constructed Tom-persona to be generally convincing, the medium must focus largely and selectively, either on specific but generally shared information about Tom, or else distinctive but true bits of information culled from different sources. (Remember, if the Tom-persona is based on idiosyncratically *false* beliefs of sitters, or false documents, that only lends weight to super-psi explanations.) So in either case a successful simulation of Tom requires consistent ESP success and (perhaps more important) success of just the right sort. Not just any telepathically or clairvoyantly extracted information will do. It must be true, not too general, and of a sort that makes the Tom-persona credible to several individuals.

Advocates of super psi might insist that we can't rule out psychic achievements of this magnitude, at least in principle. And they're right. But at what point are we entitled to protest, "This degree of success is simply too incredible"? We can (and should) remain open-minded about the magic wand super-psi hypothesis and grant that task complexity may be overrated as an obstacle to psi success. But we needn't agree that task complexity *never* matters, or that no degree of complexity can be dismissed as *prima facie* implausible. So how should we evaluate a trance persona that convinces many people in specific, intimate, and subtle detail, and not simply general features which, with perhaps a little charity, we could agree were features of the communicator during life? In that case, continued, highly accurate clairvoyance and telepathic interaction from *many* sources seems necessary but also quite unlikely.

But maybe this is more of a problem in theory than in practice. Granted, such a full-bodied mediumistic achievement would strain all but magic-wand type super-psi hypotheses. But how many actual cases attain the required degree of generality, accuracy, and sitter-intimacy? Certainly, the best drop-in cases fall far short of it. For example, in the case of Runki's leg (probably, the best of the lot) the medium provided interesting pieces of information which—if they were derived through ESP—could only have come from different sources. But those bits of information concern relatively general and impersonal aspects of Runki's career, many of which are mentioned in public records. We have little if any basis for saying that Hafsteinn successfully simulated Runki's behavior. Moreover, most of the evidence provided about Runki's life was produced in a great burst, more than a year after Runki's first appearance, rather than in a steady stream over a long period. As we noted in chapter 2, if anything tips the scales in favor of a survivalist interpretation of the Runki case, it would be that the case makes good or clear sense *psychologically* only from the point of view of the communicator.

Moreover, it seems that not even Mrs. Piper produced a trance persona (or relayed one through Phinuit) that, *for any extended period of time*, closely simulated the communicator's behavior during life. Her most convincing trance personalities produced sporadic and relatively brief surges of behavior that sitters found compellingly lifelike. Now those achievements are impressive even if they fail to strain the super-psi hypothesis to an obvious breaking point. Actually, the best of those incidents may lead us to *favor* a super-psi explanation. I'm claiming only that those cases are far enough from the ideal not to do so coercively.

We should also bear in mind some points expressed nicely by E. R. Dodds in his classic paper, "Why I Do Not Believe in Survival" (Dodds, 1934). First, Dodds noted that we should be cautious about accepting sitters' testimony that a trance persona was convincingly lifelike. He wrote,

> When the tones of the trance speech are recognized by the sitter as those of a familiar voice, or when certain mannerisms or *façons de parler* are felt by him to be characteristic of a certain person, it is very rarely possible to check the objectivity of the recognition, as can usually be done when a name, a date or an event is in question. The door is commonly left wide open to the insidious temptations of the will-to-believe. (Dodds, 1934, p. 162)

Dodds's point is well taken; we shouldn't assume that a trance persona is accurate enough to strain the super-psi hypothesis simply because sitters find the persona to be lifelike. A strong survival case needs impartial (or at least clearheaded) judgments that the persona's behavior is unusually characteristic of the communicator. And of course the similarities, ideally, should be specific and distinctive of the communicator, not as indefinite or common as (say) a deep, male voice, a hearty laugh, or a child's reference to a clock as a "tic toc." But it's unclear how many mediumistic performances pass that stringent test of verisimilitude. Probably, if any succeed, they do so only to a degree. For example, some of Mrs. Piper's communications from G. P. might fall into this exalted class. But if so, it's only in virtue of approaching (rather than reaching) the ideal. So at the very least, Dodds's caveat reminds us how good a trance persona must be to strain the super-psi hypothesis and how few actual cases pass muster. Nevertheless, it remains true that the more continuously and minutely lifelike a trance persona is, the more implausible the super-psi hypothesis becomes.

Dodds also claimed that "certain mediums can on occasion 'reproduce' the personalities of the unknown living with as much success as those of the unknown dead" (Dodds, 1934, p. 162). But he noted that the evidence for that is not overwhelming, and indeed, the relevant cases are considerably less impressive than the best of those suggesting communication from the dead (see, e.g., Salter, 1921, pp. 133ff; J. F. Thomas, 1937, pp. 206–207). In fact, one case Dodds mentions—the Gordon Davis case—has now fallen under a cloud of suspicion (see Soal, 1925). For at least fifty years this seemed to be the strongest case of apparent postmortem communication from the living. But the investigator (S. G. Soal) was subsequently found to have doctored the records of some ESP tests, and that obviously tainted his research generally (Markwick, 1978). Moreover, some have found grounds for suspicion in the Gordon Davis case itself (e.g., Gauld, 1982, pp. 137–138; Harris, 1986; and see West, 2000, for a partial rebuttal).

But whatever the merits of the Gordon Davis case may be, this general class of cases may not pose much of a problem for the survivalist. Granted, a lifelike trance persona of the living *would* seem to demand a paranormal, but not a survivalist, explanation. So long as we rule out the Usual Suspects, it would seem to demonstrate that the medium needs only ESP and human creativity to acquire the relevant information about the "communicator" and transform it into a convincing trance impersonation. And that would, indeed, be a significant strike against the survival hypothesis. It would show that—for a large collection of good cases—the survival hypothesis is gratuitous. But we must heed Dodds's own warning when deciding how successfully a medium reproduces a living personality. After all, if sitters' judgments about the accuracy of trance personalities are imprecise and vulnerable to biases and wishful thinking, they're suspect *generally*, not just when the ostensible communicators are nonliving. Moreover (and perhaps more important), I'm aware of no case in which a living person's character was presented nearly as thoroughly as in the best cases of apparent communication from the dead, such as that of G. P., Mrs. Piper's Hodgson-control, or even Kakie. So it's still reasonable to claim that an unusually lifelike trance persona of the dead would strain the super-psi hypothesis, possibly to the breaking point. In those cases it still looks compellingly like there is a direct, although possibly intermittent, connection between the living and the deceased. Nevertheless, the challenge actually (not just theoretically) posed by veridical impersonations of the living is minimal, at best.

So far, then, we've seen that the super-psi and survival hypotheses face analogous problems. In both cases we can specify potential weaknesses in the evidence, but in both cases it's doubtful that the evidence poses as much of a challenge *in fact* as it does in principle. Certainly, Dodds's considerations don't rule out survival, even if his caveats are sensible and he's correctly pinpointed how the evidence *could* be unfavorable to the survival hypothesis. Similarly, we've seen that the super-psi hypothesis can be strained by a sufficiently strong case. But here, too, actual cases always seem to fall somewhat short of the appropriate threshold. Granted, some people who understand the issues and who know the evidence well have come to believe in survival on the basis of certain spectacular cases. But we can't ignore the fact that there are also reasonable, intelligent, well-informed, and open-minded people who haven't been persuaded by those cases, or by the evidence generally. So we might wonder: Do any considerations regarding the mediumistic evidence more clearly *support* the survival hypothesis? Must we resign ourselves to a stalemate? Or can we move beyond the apparently intractable problem of deciding whether a given case is impressive enough?

6. Survival and the Causal Nexus

I now suspect that we can take at least a small step in that direction. And ironically, we can do that by first making a major concession to advocates of super psi and granting the possibility of highly refined and extensive psychic functioning among the living. As we've seen, on the super-psi hypothesis we'll need to interpret the most outstanding examples of mediumship, not simply as dandy psychic functioning, but as astonishingly *consistent* high-quality psychic functioning. After all, in the best cases mediums provide accurate but obscure information frequently, and over extended periods of time. So let's provisionally accept the super-psi interpretation of mediumship, at least for the sake of argument, and let's assume therefore that a kind of psychic omniscience is possible, even if only temporarily. That is, let's assume that at least some people—perhaps only sporadically and for brief periods—but nevertheless repeatedly, can psychically access a great deal of highly specific information from multiple sources, virtually on demand.

It's at this point that a surprising problem arises for the super-psi hypothesis. For reasons I'll explain, it seems that not even great psychic virtuosity should be able to manifest consistently enough to account for the best actual trance personalities. And apparently, the more virtuosic or super we allow psi to be, the less likely it becomes that a super-psi hypothesis will handle the evidence. Or so I'll try to argue. The argument that follows is fairly complex, and to simplify later discussion we should give it a name. So let's call it the *Argument from Crippling Complexity*.

First, we need to consider a parallel with psychic omnipotence. We need to consider why, even if thoughts can kill or maim, so many of us are still alive and intact. As I've noted elsewhere (Braude, 1997), even if psychic functioning is theoretically unlimited in refinement or magnitude, it might be severely curtailed in practice. For one thing, most (if not all) of our abilities or capacities are situation-sensitive; how and to what degree we express them depends on many contextual factors. Consider, for example, our capacity to circulate blood, focus our eyes, digest food, discuss intimate details of our lives, show compassion, display our wit or patience, or remember what we've read. These capacities, and probably all others, are neither constant nor uniform. They vary with our mood, health, age, time of day, level of stress, etc., and in general they can be diminished or enhanced in many ways. Even virtuosic abilities are vulnerable to numerous influences. For example, the performance of a great athlete can be impaired by injury, illness, temporary loss of confidence, preoccupation with personal problems, great opponents, or even weak opponents having a great day. Similarly, a great comedian's ability to be funny (or an exceptional musician's ability to perform) can be undermined, countered, or neutralized in various ways and to varying degrees. Now it's reasonable to think that psychic capacities would also exhibit these vulnerabilities. And in any case, the evidence suggests strongly that psychic functioning is, in fact, highly situation-sensitive and susceptible to various forms of interference. So it seems reasonable to suppose that no matter how extensive, refined, or virtuosic our psychic capacities might be, like our other capacities they will also be subject to actual case-by-case limitations.

So even if hostile psi is unlimited in scope or refinement, it's unlimited only in principle. It would still be subject to numerous actual constraints, just like normal forms of hostility. It would be embedded within an enormously complex web of interactions, psi and nonpsi, overt and covert, local and global, and it would be vulnerable to equally potent interferences or checks and balances (including psychic defenses) within that network. This conjecture strikes me as uncontroversial and (in fact) commonsensical. Once we assume or grant that psychic interactions occur, then we must take a very broad view of how our attempted psychic efforts might be thwarted, even during periods of maximum fluency or potency. We must admit the possibility of an expanded range of obstacles or checks and balances, a range that now includes psychic phenomena—and more specifically, psychic counterparts to more normal forms of interference. Of course, we might still be defeated by guilt, incompetence, and carelessness, just as we are in everyday cases. We might also be defeated by our intended victim's adequate defenses (which now must include psychic defenses). But perhaps most important, we might also get "caught in the crossfire" (so to speak) of processes otherwise unrelated to our interests—for example, outside distractions and interference.

The following example should make this clear. Suppose I hire the world's greatest assassin to eliminate my contemptible colleague, Jones. No matter how skilled this assassin is, his attempted "hit" could be frustrated in a number of ways, *none of which detract from his expertise*. Of course, Jones could go into hiding, hire bodyguards, or make other se-

curity arrangements that make the assassin's task more difficult. But
more relevantly, other people will all the while be going about their own
business, oblivious to the assassin's mission, and some of their actions
may inadvertently get in the way. The attempted hit could be thwarted,
fortuitously, by a vast range of countervailing factors and ongoing processes. And notice, these needn't reflect negatively on the assassin's virtuosity, and they may have nothing to do with the assassin's particular
assignment. Consider, for example, the potential impact of traffic jams,
a flat tire, faulty telephone, airport weather delays, lost luggage, icy
roads, elevator malfunction, a migraine headache, upset stomach, aller-
gic reaction, an attack of the flu, pedestrians getting in the line of fire,
or a mugger. Although the greatest assassin might cope successfully
with at least some of these unexpected developments, it's not a weakness that he's still vulnerable to unforeseeable and uncontrollable outside influences and interferences. No matter how skillful the assassin
might be, he can't anticipate or prevent every potential source of interference. So these remaining vulnerabilities don't indicate a lapse in the
assassin's skill or level of deadliness. They're simply vulnerabilities to
obstacles which *anyone* might have to confront.

Now the difference between this relatively normal case and that of
hostile psi is that in the latter the opportunities for causal preemption
seem to increase dramatically. We need to entertain a much broader
range of potentially countervailing factors—in particular, the full range
of under-the-surface psychic interactions. After all, both experimental
and anecdotal evidence—not to mention common sense—suggest that
psychic processes can be triggered unconsciously. But in that case, presumably *every person* would be making multiple attempts to influence
the world psychically, to serve a variety of genuinely motivating needs or
interests. Unless we think in these terms, we won't be taking the possibility of hostile psi (or super psi generally) seriously. But once we do
allow for this vast reservoir of potentially interfering factors, we might
reasonably expect few (if any) of our psychic "efforts" to succeed, no
matter how unlimited or powerful psi might be in principle. It may not
be miraculous when one of those efforts successfully navigates the
dense web of hindrances confronting it. But it might be more remarkable for it to succeed than for it to fail.

The prospect of mediumistic omniscience raises a parallel set of issues. According to the super-psi hypothesis, a medium must rely on ongoing or repeated ESP, not only to sustain a trance persona, but to be
consistently successful from one sitter to the next, especially over the
course of an entire career. Presumably, then, that degree of success requires circumventing, for an unusually long period, all the obstacles
that could conceivably interfere with psychic information-gathering.
Now a super-psi explanation of mediumship posits the operation of unconscious psychic sleuthing on the part of the medium. But presumably

it's not only mediums who, on that hypothesis, can engage in unconscious ESP. Presumably *anybody* (or at least a great many people) can
do it. Even if mediumistic abilities, like musical and athletic abilities,
are unevenly distributed throughout the human population, at the very
least the evidence from parapsychology suggests that ESP experiences
occur widely. The great mediums, according to the super-psi hypothesis,
would simply be people whose ESP works unusually well. But just as
countless lesser musicians and athletes can exercise their unimpressive
abilities while the superstars ply their trade, presumably there will be
many lower-level psychics scanning more or less successfully for information while the mediums carry out their own searches. So, since a
super-psi explanation of mediumship forces us to be quite generous and
open-minded about the range and refinement of ESP, and also liberal in
our assumptions about the ubiquity of undetected psi, it seems also to
require a formidably complex network of under-the-surface psychic activity, of which the mediums' psychic efforts are only a very small part.

But that's the problem. The more complex and extensive we allow
the underlying network of psychic activities to be, the more obstacles
there will be for any particular psychic inquiry or effort to navigate. And
just as potential PKers, like the assassin, can be caught in the crossfire
of others' psychic efforts, potential ESPers can be thwarted by others'
psychic activities, even when those activities are unrelated to their own
interests. Analogies are easy to come by—for example, slow searches on
clogged internet channels, trying to hear someone speaking from across
a busy and very noisy street, and threading one's way through an oppres-
sive crowd of shoppers to find a salesperson. As the sets of competing
activities in these scenarios become more dense or chaotic, the probability that any given effort will succeed decreases.

If these considerations are on the right track, they can even be extended to magic-wand versions of the super-psi hypothesis, according to
which needs or wishes alone can be causally efficacious and task complexity is irrelevant to psi-success. Inevitably, successful ESP or PK will
have to navigate the dense underlying causal nexus, whether or not
those psychic efforts are themselves causally simple or complex. So even
if psychic functioning works like a magic wand, that means only that the
causal relation between a mental state and its psychic effect is primitive.
According to the magic-wand hypothesis, individual psychic activities
are causally streamlined. They will not be analyzable in terms of a finer-
grained, underlying sequence of events between cause and effect. But
that sort of causal simplicity doesn't rule out causal preemption. Even
primitive causal processes are vulnerable to the surrounding network of
potentially countervailing influences and crisscrossing causal chains. So
even if we grant that magic wands can work, it doesn't follow that they
work *no matter what*. Spinners of legends and fairy tales understood
this. Wizards can duel and lose a fight; they can be caught in the cross-

fire; and magic wands can sputter or fail.

Perhaps we can now see why a standard objection to the super-psi hypothesis carries little weight. Consider, for example, H. F. Saltmarsh's comments on the possibility of "unlimited mind-reading" in connection with trance mediumship. He wrote,

> For a being endowed with potential omniscience, and having at her disposal all the contents of the mind she is reading, the medium exhibits an extraordinary lack of intelligence in selecting the items of information which she retails. The ordinary person would do far better: surely potential omniscience should not fall behind our ordinary everyday intelligence. (Saltmarsh, 1929, p. 112)

But as we've seen, even if mind reading can be unlimited, that doesn't mean "constrained by nothing." If ESP is unlimited in its range or refinement, it's unlimited only in theory, not in fact. In this respect, our psychic abilities would be continuous with our other, more familiar, capacities. Psi may have vast (and even unlimited) potential, and it may exhibit occasional bursts of breathtaking efficacy. But realizing our full psychic potential is presumably an unattainable ideal, just as it is for all the mundane activities in which we routinely perform below—in fact, considerably below—our theoretical best. After all, we usually fall far short of perfection. But that's neither a disgrace nor a surprise. We're imperfect, limited, and erratic, and life is complex, difficult, and brimming with obstacles. We have no problem grasping our failures and limitations for nonpsi achievements, and I can't see why this should be any harder to comprehend in connection with psychic functioning. And of course, if psychic information-gathering can be impeded by under-the-surface psychic "traffic" created by the entire community of minds, the possibility of failure seems considerable. In fact, that's why, even on a sympathetic and maximally open-minded or liberal approach to the super-psi hypothesis, mediumistic failures become not only intelligible, but perhaps almost mandatory. So apparently (and ironically), the super-psi hypothesis suggests that ESP faces too many natural obstacles to be consistently successful, at least to the degree required by the best cases of mediumship.

Notice that this way of repudiating super-psi explanations of mediumship differs in an important respect from the usual strategy. The usual strategy, which I decried in chapter 1, is to set up a straw man by arguing against an eviscerated or unsubtle form of the super-psi hypothesis. But the irony of the approach just taken is that the greater the scope and refinement we allow psychic functioning to enjoy, the less likely it becomes that any given effort will succeed. And presumably, it's less likely still that a series of such efforts will be successful. Therefore, the more super we allow psychic functioning to be, the less likely it becomes that a medium's ESP could produce an extended and accurate trance persona.

I should emphasize that what makes the best mediumistic cases so impressive is not simply the *amount* of veridical material revealed during sittings. After all, a medium may impart a great deal of correct information over a long period. But it may only be a very small percentage of the total material she provides, the rest of which is false or typical mediumistic twaddle. So what makes the best cases so impressive is both the amount of correct material and the *consistency* with which subjects provide it.

I don't want to overestimate the importance of this line of reasoning. It's hardly novel to suggest that super-psi explanations have trouble handling both multiple sources of obscure information and also the consistency of mediumistic achievements. But what's usually missing is an explanation of why, exactly, these pose problems for the super-psi hypothesis. So I see the *Argument from Crippling Complexity* as a very modest contribution to the survival debate. Its principal virtue is that it gives us more to go on than the mere intuition that super-psi explanations have their limitations. By exposing at least one set of underlying assumptions and issues, it provides a basis for evaluating the tenability and limitations of super-psi explanations.

Now I believe that the *Argument from Crippling Complexity* has considerable merit. But it also raises a number of serious questions. Notice, first of all, that some ways of acquiring information seem relatively impervious to interference by others' activities. For example, if I'm looking at an object in front of me, others can look at it also and not get in my way. And it doesn't matter whether the other observers are nearsighted or using special vision-enhancing goggles (analogously, whether the other persons are psi-incompetents or psi-virtuosi). So perhaps I've overestimated the degree to which extensive or refined psychic activity increases the obstacles to psi success. Perhaps I've simply chosen misleading analogies in presenting the *Argument from Crippling Complexity*. Perhaps psychic interference is no more inevitable in the case of ESP than ordinary perceptual interference is inevitable in the case of vision.

However, I suspect that the proper analogy *is* trying to look at an object in a crowded, bustling room, where somebody could (among other things) walk in front of me, turn off the light, move the object, or place another object in front of it. (Similarly, sounds and smells can be obscured in a variety of familiar ways.) Granted, most of our ordinary perceptions are relatively unimpeded, even when other perceivers are in the vicinity. But according to the super-psi alternative to survival, something akin to observation, some form of information acquisition, takes place in an arena (the world at large) where an unimaginably vast amount of psychic activity is also occurring, and where the prospects for interference are considerable and (perhaps most important) not subject to the usual spatial constraints. After all, ordinary perception can occur in situations where we can be shielded from the interference of others. I can be alone in a room, behind a screen, wearing headphones, etc. But it's unclear whether there's an analogue to these kinds of perceptual isolation in the case of ESP. For example, ESP experiments have been successful over great distances and with subjects shielded in Faraday cages. And the more potent and potentially invasive we allow ESP to be, the more apt the crowded room analogy becomes.

A more serious problem may be the following. I've been arguing that medium-sitter psychic interaction can be stymied by the crippling complexity of the underlying causal nexus. And because I treated this line of reasoning as a kind of indirect support for the survival hypothesis, I've been suggesting that medium-*communicator* psychic interaction would be relatively immune to the ravages of causal complexity. Apparently, then, I've been assuming that causal interaction between medium and deceased communicator is more direct than that between medium and sitter, as if the deceased in some sense stand apart from the causal web or rise above it. But why should that be? If survival is a fact and we can interact with the deceased, then deceased communicators should be included among those operating within the causal nexus. So if the extensive network of under-the-surface causality can interfere with medium-sitter interaction, it should also frustrate either mediumistic efforts to "read" communicators' minds, or communicators' attempts to influence mediums. But in that case, causal complexity seems to be a problem no matter what.[5] It's no longer clear why medium-sitter psychic interaction is more difficult to explain than medium-communicator interaction. If the difficulties facing medium-sitter psi increase with the complexity of the underlying psychic causal nexus, that should also be true of medium-communicator psi. Presumably, both sorts of interaction face a huge variety of potential obstacles. So if both the living and the deceased contribute to the vast web of underlying causality, then presumably both mediums and deceased communicators could be caught in the crossfire of underlying psychic activities.

In fact, actual cases seem to bear this out. Mediums often seem to encounter normal interference from their own ongoing thought processes, and occasionally psychic interference from other living sources (e.g., sitters). And some cases suggest another type of interference: competition among aspiring communicators, each vying for control of the medium, or for the mediumistic analogue of a telephone or microphone.

This reservation about the *Argument from Crippling Complexity* strikes me as legitimate and serious. It seems arbitrary to suppose that discarnate communicators stand apart from the causal nexus, once we grant the possibility of their existence and their interaction with the living. But in that case, it's unclear why there should be less difficulty interacting with disembodied minds than with embodied minds. Presumably, it should be as difficult for communicator and medium to create (say) a consistent, long-term trance impersonation as it would be for the medium to accomplish the same thing through clairvoyance and telepathy with the living. Both tasks would encounter inevitable obstacles from the bustling underlying nexus of psychic activity, and that underlying causal network would have to include attempts by the deceased to gather information and influence the living. Now as I noted, the mediumistic data is at least compatible with this picture. Real cases suggest interference from both living and deceased sources. Moreover, no case is as consistently good as it presumably would be if communication between the deceased and the medium were direct and unimpeded. But similarly, no case is as good as it would be if psi among the living were unimpeded and subject to no actual constraints. So once again, we seem to face a standoff between the super-psi and survival hypotheses.

Or do we? There still seems to be a disanalogy between the super-psi and survival hypotheses, and I think this one works in favor of survival. For the survivalist, a convincingly Tom-like trance-persona requires no more than successful interaction between the medium and the deceased Tom. Even if activity within the causal nexus interferes with medium-communicator interaction, the integrity of that single link (however sporadic) is all that matters. So long as medium and communicator make decent contact from time to time, they stand a chance of producing a credible trance impersonation, even if it's not dazzling in its accuracy and consistency. So even if that causal link is frequently broken due to inevitable clutter or traffic within the nexus, survivalists need only posit *one* reliable source of information.

However (as we've seen), the situation is different for partisans of the super-psi hypothesis. The most daunting cases for super-psi are those requiring access to *multiple* obscure sources of reliable information, all of which are potentially vulnerable to interference from within the causal nexus. So in principle, it looks like we might have to give an explanatory edge to the survivalist, at least on grounds of parsimony.

Interestingly, these considerations have brought us back to a topic we considered in connection with drop-in communications. As we noted in the last chapter, good drop-in cases seem to challenge the super-psi hypothesis because the information they provide about ostensible communicators can be obtained normally—or by ESP—only from multiple and recondite sources. However, we also noted that what's normally obscure may not be paranormally obscure. So this feature of good drop-in cases didn't clearly favor the survivalist. Now our discussion of crippling complexity has led us back to the potential importance of multiple sources of information. But I think we may have learned something in the process. Perhaps we can now appreciate more clearly why multiple sources might be problematic for the super-psi hypothesis. If my speculations above are on the right track, it's not because the information obtained is obscure. The problem concerns the unimaginably complex network of psi interactions in which every particular psychic effort is embedded. And if that's right, we can evaluate the importance of multiple sources while avoiding the apparently hopeless task of deciding whether psychically derived information counts as obscure. Furthermore, we don't have to rely merely on a vague intuition that it's easier for a medium to do one thing (i.e., interact with a communicator) than to do many (i.e., psychically raid multiple minds or records). We can now say something credible about the background conditions that make consistent psychic interaction more challenging with multiple sources than with only one.

But this enlightened perspective shouldn't obscure a valuable lesson we can learn from the *Argument from Crippling Complexity*. That argument still highlights a serious limitation of *both* the super-psi and survival hypotheses. Partisans of the super-psi hypothesis can't glibly assume that super psi in its most potent form *could* explain outstandingly consistent mediumship. Even if no actual cases are as good as we could wish, the super-psi hypothesis still seems self-defeating in the way explained above. It still seems true, and ironic, that the more super we allow psychic functioning to be, the less likely it becomes that a medium's ESP could produce an extended and accurate trance persona. So it seems that the super-psi hypothesis has a serious, and apparently unheralded, problem. It seems either too weak or too strong to do its job. If psi can't overcome the problems of task complexity and multiple sources of information, then it will be too weak to account for the best actual cases. But if we allow psi to work more like a magic wand, it seems that it would be defeated by its own power and ubiquity.

But equally ironically, it now seems that this insight works, perhaps to a lesser extent, against the survival hypothesis. If deceased communicators exist and interact with the living, then presumably both they and the living contribute to the total underlying causal nexus. In that case, one would expect the deceased to confront the same sort of interferences that frustrate psychic activities among the living. But then, an extended, consistently and specifically accurate, and nonsporadic trance persona seems mysterious from *any* point of view. And regularly producing a string of such personae over an entire mediumistic career seems more mysterious still. Granted, no actual case comes close to that ideal. Nevertheless, if there were such a case, it's still worth noting that neither the survival nor the super-psi hypothesis seems able to explain it satisfactorily.

Of course, since no actual case *is* close to the ideal, and since even the best cases exhibit the frustrating mixture of veridical material and rubbish we noted earlier, the evidence may provide no firm basis for deciding in favor of survival over super psi. Assuming that psychic functioning can be obstructed by an unimaginably complex mass of underlying psychic activity, actual cases of mediumship look pretty much as we'd expect—on both the survival and super-psi hypotheses.

7. The Cross-Correspondences

We should now take a quick look at an interesting body of mediumistic evidence, considered by some to be the strongest of all. However, I don't share that assessment, and the considerations just raised about crippling complexity help to explain why. Nevertheless, this body of material is undoubtedly intriguing.

The cross-correspondences are a vast collection of apparently linked mediumistic messages that began in 1901 and lasted for thirty-one years. All the mediums were women, and they were scattered widely around the globe (the United States, England, and India). The main participants, on "this side," were (a) Mrs. M. de G. Verrall, wife of the well-known classical scholar A. W. Verrall, (b) her daughter Helen (later Mrs. W. H. Salter), (c) Mrs. "Willett" (a.k.a. Mrs. Winifred Coombe-Tennant, (d) Mrs. "Holland" (Mrs. Fleming, the sister of Rudyard Kipling), and (e) Mrs. Piper (the only professional medium in this group). The initial and principal participants on "the other side" were prominent founders of the SPR: Edmund Gurney, Henry Sidgwick, and F. W. H. Myers, who had died (respectively) in 1888, 1900, and 1901. And the principal investigators of the scripts were several leading members of the SPR: Alice Johnson, J. G. Piddington, G. W. Balfour, Sir Oliver Lodge, and Mrs. E. M. Sidgwick. The idea for these communications apparently originated with the communicators. In fact, the cross-correspondence material appeared for a while in mediumistic messages before anyone realized it.

The communications in question were fragmentary and sprinkled liberally with Greek and Latin phrases, as well as many classical and literary allusions. Ordinarily, that would seem to detract from their value, but in fact the disjointed nature of the communications was a vital part of the alleged underlying plan. The messages were *supposed* to be apparently meaningless when considered by themselves, and also of no personal significance to the medium. But they were supposed to show *design* and hang together when deciphered by investigators familiar with the personalities and interests of the ostensible communicators. Podmore stated nicely why the design of these messages seemed significant.

> How are we to get behind the secondary personality of the medium? We cannot...base our faith on the relation of intimate details known to no one but ourselves and the dead, for we can place no certain limits on the mysterious agency of telepathy. The only evidence that can satisfy us of the sur-

vival of an active and individual intelligence is evidence of the present activity of such an intelligence. (Podmore, 1910/1975, p. 225)

Of course, even if the cross-correspondences suggest a guiding active
intelligence, that intelligence might (at least in principle) be one or
more living persons. So it's not surprising that as with other forms of
mediumistic evidence, the cross-correspondences raise two crucial issues: (1) whether *anything* paranormal is going on, and (2) whether the
apparently evidential material can be linked causally to the ostensible
postmortem communicators.

Naturally, some wondered whether the links between scripts could
be due merely to chance, along with a reader's decent ability to draw (or
stipulate) connections between things (concepts, terms, symbols). If so,
then perhaps the alleged coherence of the fragmentary scripts reveals
little more than the imagination and educational breadth of the observer.[6] Moreover, it could also reflect the fact that similarly educated
mediums, and telepathically active or accessible sitters, are likely to
share a broad background of knowledge and reservoir of allusions. Mrs.
Verrall stated the problem nicely.

> It is sometimes contended that too much ingenuity has been exercised in
> the discovery of supposed cross-correspondences, and that by an exercise of
> similar ingenuity similar connexions could be found in any group of such
> rambling and disjointed writings as those with which these reports are con-
> cerned. In that case chance alone might be sufficient to account for the
> resemblances between the scripts. (Verrall, 1911, p. 153)

One way to address that issue would be to try simulating cross-correspondences by comparing pseudo-scripts written by outsiders. Mrs.
Verrall carried out a study of this sort, using six subjects, each producing six spurious scripts, and each following instructions designed to replicate what she called the "literary trend" of the cross-correspondences.
Nevertheless, the resulting matches (such as they were) differed in several obvious ways from those of the best cross-correspondences, and
they seemed clearly to lack evidence of design or a guiding intelligence
behind the scenes (Verrall, 1911).

I think it's fair to say that the best examples of cross-correspondences
resist explanations in terms of normal or abnormal processes. And I encourage readers (especially those with plenty of time and patience) to
inspect the evidence for themselves. In any case, let's assume (if only
for the sake of argument) that the best cases demand some kind of paranormal explanation. Predictably, the biggest (or perhaps just the most
interesting) problems concern the need for survivalist explanations of
those cases.

Of course, some cases are clearly more impressive than others, and
the question we need to consider is whether the super-psi hypothesis
can handle them gracefully. Regrettably, most of the good cases are

both very complex and difficult to summarize briefly. (They also require a familiarity with classical languages and literary sources beyond that of most educated contemporary readers—and also of this author.) However, one good case can be presented fairly easily, and probably for that reason it's the case most often cited in brief summaries of the material. This is the so-called *Hope, Star, and Browning* case (see Johnson, 1914-15, pp. 28–49; Piddington, 1908, pp. 59–77).

On January 16, 1907, Piddington had a sitting with Mrs. Piper, through whom Myers was purporting to communicate. Piddington proposed that "Myers" indicate when a cross-correspondence was being attempted by drawing a circle with a triangle inside. Later that month, Mrs. Verrall produced automatic scripts, purportedly from Myers, in which the words "star" and "hope" were given repeatedly, along with anagrams of "star" (e.g., "rats," "tars," and "arts"). Investigators considered the anagrams significant because "Myers was in life greatly addicted to anagrams" (Gauld, 1982, p. 81). In fact, one of Mrs. Verrall's scripts contained the word "aster" (Latin for "star") and "teras," an anagram of "aster" (occasionally used in Greek to mean "wonder" or "sign"). After that, Miss Verrall's "Myers" gave a number of quotations from Robert Browning's poetry (beginning with "The world's wonder") along with related Greek phrases. They were followed by drawings of a triangle inside a circle and also of a triangle inside a semicircle. The next month, Myers purported to come through Miss Verrall, drawing a monogram, a star, and a crescent, and writing "A monogram, the crescent moon, remember that, and the star." Some believed this showed knowledge of the content of Mrs. Verrall's earlier Myers-communications, as well as Piddington's proposal to Mrs. Piper's "Myers."

Then later in February, Mrs. Piper's "Myers" asked if Mrs. Verrall had received the word "Evelyn Hope" (the title of a Browning poem), adding, "I referred also to Browning again. I referred to Hope and Browning...I also said star...look out for Hope, Star and Browning." About a week after that, Miss Verrall's "Myers" drew a star and then wrote, "That was the sign she will understand when she sees it...No arts avail...and a star above it all *rats* everywhere in Hamelin town" (a clear reference to Browning's poem on the Pied Piper of Hamelin).

Finally, three scripts from Mrs. Piper's "Myers" ended this cross-correspondence. On March 6 "Myers" told Piddington that "he" had given Mrs. Verrall a circle and a triangle. On March 13, the Piper-Myers again claimed to have drawn a circle and a triangle for Mrs. Verrall, and then "he" said, "But it suggested a poem to my mind, hence BHS" (i.e., Browning, Hope, Star). Then on April 8, the Piper-Myers said he had drawn a circle, a star, and a crescent moon. (For a helpful chart of the course of events in this series of correspondences, see Gauld, 1977, pp. 596–597.)

It seems clear enough that some sort of paranormal explanation is

required for this case, even if the correspondences aren't impressive
enough to appease all skeptical doubt. In any event, let's assume that we
can't account for the correspondences in terms of chance, or normal or
abnormal processes. Nevertheless, the best cross-correspondence cases
don't seem to demand survivalist explanations. In fact, they seem to
pose less of a challenge to the super-psi hypothesis than do individual
outstanding mediumistic careers (such as those of Mrs. Piper and Mrs.
Leonard), and perhaps even specific extended episodes within those
careers (e.g., Mrs. Piper's G. P. control). By comparison to these exceptional examples of mediumship, the cross-correspondences don't exhibit
or require the same degree of consistent success, and so the threat of
crippling complexity seems greatly reduced. Even in the best cases,
there was no need for the mediums to respond on the spot to questions,
or compress a lot of information about a person into a short period. The
cross-correspondences can be put together by means of sporadic snip-
pets of material over an indefinitely long period. So even if we waive
concerns about assessing the significance of the apparent correspondences, or about investigator ingenuity, a kind of super-telepathic collaboration remains a serious option.

Moreover, we can't underestimate the obscure nature of the references and allusions allegedly orchestrated by Myers and friends. Of
course, it's interesting that Myers, Gurney, and Sidgwick (but especially
Myers) were classical scholars, and also that both Mrs. and Miss Verrall
had known Myers and Sidgwick and were themselves classical scholars.
In fact (as I noted above), Mrs. Verrall was married to a renowned classical scholar. So the frequent classical phrases and allusions in the
Verralls's and the other automatists' scripts *prima facie* suggest psi
among the living as much as they do postmortem communication. But
we can set that issue aside for the moment. After all, the best cross-correspondences contain many sorts of interesting and obscure connections between scripts, and if we rule out magic wand super-psi accounts
(which we may not be entitled to do), super-psi explanations can become quite tortuous (see Gauld, 1982 for a good summary; also Podmore, 1910/1975).

Even so, a prominent feature of the cross-correspondences remains
troubling. Much of the voluminous cross-correspondence material is
devoted to detailed and seemingly inconclusive debates over the proper
translation, interpretation, and significance of its obscure allusions and
quotations. And it seems obvious that material is evidentially weak if it
consistently provokes these sorts of apparently unresolvable debates,
even among readers sympathetic to parapsychological data.[7] Of course,
all the survival material is controversial to some extent, even within
parapsychology. But the debates over the cross-correspondences seem
particularly pervasive and fundamental. Unlike the cases of Mrs. Piper
and Mrs. Leonard, and unlike good reincarnation and possession cases,

even the best cross-correspondences generate substantive concerns about their *prima facie* evidentiality, and sometimes even their paranormality. No wonder Thouless commented,

> The cross-correspondence technique was too elaborate. It seems to be the products of minds who realized the necessity for evidence but not the equal necessity for the value of evidence being easily assessed. (Thouless, 1959)

Moreover, I have another, and related, nagging concern about the cross-correspondences. I have to wonder: By what rational standard of evidence would anyone ever suppose that a cross-correspondence is evidentially superior to (say) a good mediumistic trance-impersonation, or even just a good series of mediumistic messages providing *direct* indications of survival? In chapter 1 I warned against prejudging the relative difficulty of different forms of postmortem communications. Nevertheless, one feature of the cross-correspondences seems especially difficult to swallow. According to the survivalist interpretation, discarnate individuals orchestrate an intricate and obscure cross-correspondence among different mediums over an extended period, drawing on obscure but allegedly idiosyncratic classical and literary references and allusions. But if they could pull that off, couldn't they more easily (or just as easily) have provided a single medium with evidence that's not so perplexingly indirect—for example, incontrovertibly convincing and detailed straightforward manifestations of their surviving memories, personalities, interests, and activities? A cross-correspondence simply multiplies obscurities and adds an interpretive challenge thankfully missing from (say) Mrs. Piper's G. P. or Hodgson manifestations. And I find it hard to believe that Sidgwick, Gurney, and Myers, who were so consistently perspicacious in life, would in the next life fail to grasp this relatively simple point about evidential strength—especially if they were still cognitively sophisticated enough to assemble the more elaborate and sophisticated cross-correspondences.

So perhaps we need to look elsewhere in order to decide conclusively between survival and super psi. At this point we may have grounds for doubting the viability of the super-psi hypothesis. But the usual, good mediumistic evidence doesn't decisively tip the scales one way or the other, even if concerns about crippling complexity suggest that survivalists have a slight explanatory advantage. Because even the best cases have significant shortcomings, reasonable minds can still disagree over how best to interpret them. Of course, the evidence for survival takes other forms, and we'll have to revisit the *Argument from Crippling Complexity* to see whether the super-psi hypothesis can handle these, and eventually to see how well it accounts for the data as a whole. In the following chapters, we'll examine bodies of evidence that allow us to reexamine the issues from several different angles.

NOTES

1. This view has also been suggested by Hick, 1976, pp. 136–137; Richmond, 1936, p. 22; Tyrrell, 1938/1961, p. 216.

2. Barrett continues, in a somewhat more curmudgeonly vein, reflecting his irritation over the arrogance, stupidity, and (often) dishonesty of many scientists who study the paranormal.

> If, for example, the late Prof. S.P. Langley, of Washington, in the delicate experiments he conducted...exploring the ultra red radiation of the sun—had allowed the thermal radiation of himself or his assistants to fall on his sensitive thermoscope, his results would have been confused and unintelligible. We know that similar confused results are obtained in psychical research, especially by those who fancy the sole function of a scientific investigator is to play the part of an amateur detective; and accordingly what they detect is merely their own incompetency to deal with problems the very elements of which they do not understand and seem incapable of learning. (Barrett, 1917, pp. 120–121)

For even angrier comments, see Braude, 1997.

3. An alternative to this seems even more outlandish: namely, that Mrs. Piper extracted all the information she *might* need earlier (either at the beginning of the séance or—even worse—before she met the sitters for the first time) and then remembered it, so that she could bring up appropriate bits later at an opportune time. See section 5 for further comments on this sort of conjecture.

4. Of course, it's not only the medium who recoils at this possibility. The fear of psychic snooping is more general than that, affecting snooper and snoopee alike. As H. F. Saltmarsh remarked,

> There is...an extremely strong instinctive repugnance to the idea that the privacy of one's thoughts can be invaded by an inquisitive intruder, and that one's memories, both conscious and subconscious, can be ransacked. (Saltmarsh, 1929, p. 151)

5. I'm grateful to John Palmer for reminding me of this.

6. There may be a contemporary counterpart to the sort of knowledge, creativity, and skill at issue here. A few years ago many people played a game called "Six Degrees of Kevin Bacon." The game was to begin with a reference—usually from show business, and often quite obscure—and to see who could draw a connection, in the fewest steps, from that reference to the actor Kevin Bacon. Some people were particularly good at this game, presumably because they had a deep familiarity with show business minutiae and also a gift for making the required sorts of associations. They were able to draw a link to Kevin Bacon when others failed, or else they could make the connection in an astonishingly small number of steps. So a serious concern about the cross-correspondences is that the allegedly meaningful links between scripts are similar sorts of associative constructs imposed on the scripts by their interpreters.

7. Sadly, some current prominent members of the SPR have not learned this lesson, as they've demonstrated by their dogged advocacy of the transparently questionable "Scole" mediumistic material. See *Proceedings of the Society for Psychical Research* 58 (part 220), November 1999, pp. 155–452.

Chapter 4

The Case of Sharada: Psychopathology and Xenoglossy

1. Introduction

I noted in chapter 1 what I consider to be the most serious common defects in even the best works on survival. One of those, I argued, is that writers on survival seldom probe beneath the psychological surface of their cases. As a result, they don't consider adequately whether the needs and interests of the living support a plausible super-psi explanation of the evidence. To help decide between survivalist and super-psi accounts, we need to ask: Whose interests might be served by the appearance of evidence for survival? Often, it's clear enough what the communicator's interests might be, and in many cases it's also obvious what sitters at a séance stand to gain. But human beings are too complex for us to be content with identifying their most blatant motives and needs, much less those that they consciously avow. And it seems obvious that survival cases are at least as likely as everyday situations to conceal a rich tapestry of underlying conflicts and concerns. Unless investigators try to discover what these might be, their recommended explanations carry little weight.

I also observed in chapter 1 that writers on survival tend to have only a surface familiarity with research on dissociation. As a result, they tend to underestimate the force of counter-explanations in terms of dissociative phenomena and dissociative pathology. The case we examine in this chapter illustrates this deficiency in the literature.

Regrettably, few (if any) of the good survival cases have been treated to careful psychological probing, and it's unlikely now that they will yield up any secrets. Fortunately, however, one well-known reincarnation case has been described in sufficient detail to permit retrospective clinical speculation. This is the case of Sharada, unquestionably one of the most interesting (and potentially one of the most valuable) cases in the survival literature. Actually, it's probably too late even in this case to reach a definitive interpretation of the evidence. But at least we have a reasonable amount of detail to work with, and it's enough to illustrate the psychological superficiality that, sadly, is the rule rather than the exception in survival research. The case also demonstrates why we should be wary of deciding too quickly in favor of apparently obvious survivalist explanations, and it provides valuable clues about things to look for in other cases. Moreover, as we'll see, it raises important issues about super psi, knowledge-how, and the apparent postmortem persistence of skills that will trouble us repeatedly throughout this book.

The rival hypothesis I want to consider in the Sharada case, and which I submit has been seriously underestimated, is a type of motivated super-psi hypothesis. We could perhaps call it a *dissociation + psi* hypothesis, although that doesn't really do it justice. The hypothesis is (a) that the puzzling aspects of the Sharada case can be understood partially in terms of dissociative processes similar to those found in multiple personality (MPD/DID), (b) that dissociation facilitates the use of rather refined psychic functioning at critical points along the way, and (c) that latent and impressive abilities or capacities may be developed or liberated in dissociative or other sorts of unusual states.

One final comment before getting down to details. As we examine the Sharada case, I'll be addressing certain matters of depth psychology. Now I don't pretend to be a mental health professional. But I do know something about dissociative phenomena, and I feel I have a reasonable (though hardly prodigious) grasp of at least some sorts of real-life human needs and dilemmas, as well as various coping strategies and hidden agendas. So if it's easy for *me* to detect the psychological shortcomings in the discussions of the Sharada case, I would imagine that persons more cunning and penetrating than I can find additional and perhaps more persuasive reasons for challenging (or possibly for accepting) the reincarnationist or survivalist interpretation of the case. And I should emphasize, as I did in chapter 1, that my aim is not to lobby for a non-survivalist position that I antecedently believe is correct. Rather, I want to raise the discussion of the evidence to the level of sophistication (both psychological and parapsychological) at which it should have been conducted from the start.

Similarly, although I'll focus my initial criticisms on two authors in particular (Stevenson and Akolkar), I'm not interested in "picking on them" or in singling them out for attack. Rather, I want to illustrate how analyses of even allegedly strong cases have been psychologically superficial and therefore weak in a crucial respect. The case for survival and against motivated super psi simply can't be made on the basis of the sorts of considerations offered by Stevenson, or with the quality of the supplementary analysis provided by Akolkar.

2. Outline of the Case

The Sharada case isn't merely a case of ostensible reincarnation. It's also a case of apparent responsive xenoglossy. And one reason this case is so important is that, unlike most cases of responsive xenoglossy, the subject spoke an apparently unlearned language quite fluently. Another reason is that the previous personality (Sharada) made several verified statements about a family that lived at the appropriate time and location. However, I would say that the case's most compelling features are linguistic. Other examples of ostensible reincarnation have offered more impressive (that is, finer-grained and more specific) evidence for the knowledge of a former life. We'll examine some of those in chapter 6.

The subject in this case is a Marathi-speaking woman named Uttara Huddar, born in 1941, who lived and worked part-time as a lecturer in public administration in Nagpur, India. At the age of 32 she began to manifest a personality named Sharada, who spoke fluent and somewhat archaic Bengali, and who claimed to be and acted as if she were a Bengali woman of the early nineteenth century. Sharada claimed to have died at age 22, after a cobra bit her on the toe. When she "awoke" in 1974 she didn't recognize Uttara's family and friends, and she apparently didn't understand them when they spoke in Marathi, Hindi, or English. (However, she did eventually learn a few words and phrases in Marathi.) Uttara never married, and as we'll see, she appears to have been profoundly disappointed and frustrated in affairs of the heart. But Sharada dressed and behaved like a married Bengali woman. She spent much of her time in (sometimes old-fashioned) Bengali religious practices, and she appeared perplexed by modern ways and somewhat repelled by Marathi customs.

When Uttara's mother was pregnant with Uttara, she often dreamed of being bitten on the toe by a snake. Those dreams ceased when Uttara was born, and her mother claims to have forgotten them until Sharada appeared and mentioned that she had died of a snakebite on the toe. However, the mother's claim to have forgotten the dream may not be entirely credible. Both parents report that Uttara had a severe phobia of snakes throughout much of her childhood, and that after the age of sixteen her attitude toward snakes changed to one of attraction. So there's reason to believe that the topics of snakes and Uttara's fear of snakes would have been fairly common in the household, at least until Uttara's phobia disappeared.

As previous investigators have recognized, it's important to determine the extent of Uttara's normal exposure to the Bengali language and to Bengali customs. And initially at least, it looks as if we should be skeptical, because there's no doubt that Uttara had studied Bengali and that she had at least a modest ability to read the language. On the other hand, certain features of the case lend support to a survivalist interpretation of the evidence. For one thing, it's not clear whether Uttara had demonstrated the somewhat independent ability to *speak* Bengali. And for another, Sharada's spoken Bengali differed in various ways from the modern Bengali Uttara presumably learned while in school.

Nevertheless, a survivalist explanation of Sharada's proficiency in Bengali faces serious obstacles. Since Uttara had learned some modern Bengali, it's reasonable to think that it provided a foundation for Sharada's proficiency. Moreover, it's probable that learning a second language is a distinct process from learning a language for the first time. And when the second language isn't radically different from one's native tongue (or from a second language one has already learned), the process may be relatively easy, especially for someone proficient in language. (In section 5, I examine these matters in more detail.) But we know that Uttara *was* reasonably sophisticated linguistically and that she had the ability to learn new languages. She spoke English, and she had also studied Sanskrit in high school. In fact, since Sanskrit is the language from which North Indian dialects evolved (just as Spanish, French, and Italian evolved from Latin), Uttara's proficiency in Bengali doesn't seem particularly mysterious, *if* we allow that additional exposure to Bengali could have occurred normally (but unconsciously) and also possibly through ESP. It might also be relevant that approximately ten thousand Bengalis live in Nagpur. So although the city in which Sharada claimed to live was 500 kilometers from Nagpur, there may well have been numerous opportunities closer to home for exposure to crucial information about the Bengali language and customs.

It's also worth noting that Uttara seemed to be deeply interested in Bengal and the Bengalis, and she even "claims that she had a strong desire to learn Bengali" (Akolkar, 1992, p. 214). Beginning in her teens, Uttara became quite attached to her father, who was "a great admirer of Bengali revolutionaries and leaders" (Akolkar, 1992, p. 214), at least one of whom had stayed with him in his home. Moreover, some of Uttara's relatives spoke Bengali, and Uttara had read Bengali novels translated into Marathi. According to Stevenson, Uttara "complained that Marathi literature displayed no real heroines; in contrast, she thought that Bengali women were more courageous and also more feminine than other Indian women" (Stevenson, 1984, p. 81). Furthermore, as Anderson properly observes, both Akolkar and Stevenson "include information on the linguistic features of Sharada's Bengali suggesting that her command of the language, while impressive, is not that of a native" (Anderson, 1992, p. 252).

Sharada first appeared in 1974. It was a period in Uttara's life during which she experienced a variety of emotional and physical problems. In the early 1970s Uttara had developed a deep attraction to a former childhood friend, F, with whom she had recently restored contact after a lapse of several years. (Stevenson refers to F as "Priyadarshan Dinanath Pandit.") But F didn't reciprocate Uttara's feelings; in fact, he was interested in another woman. Uttara felt so exhausted and shaken by F's rejection that she decided to devote herself to a life of spiritual development and meditation (which she had practiced regularly since 1965).

While all this was going on, Uttara was also contending with various physical maladies, including asthma, menstrual problems, and a skin disease that seems to have been eczema. In 1970 she was examined by a homeopathic physician, Dr. Z (referred to by Stevenson as Dr. J. R. Joshi), described by Akolkar as "an elderly man in his fifties" (Akolkar, 1992, p. 217). Dr. Z had established a combination ashram/hospital in Dabha, 7 kilometers from Nagpur, and for several years he treated Uttara as an outpatient.

Uttara's relationship with Dr. Z is puzzling, and it deserves close scrutiny. The mysteries begin with their first meeting, which Uttara found to be a very intense experience. She reports that when Dr. Z first touched her, it felt "familiar" and she felt herself irresistibly drawn to him. She also felt that there was a connection between Dr. Z and a recurring vision she had experienced during meditation and in dreams. The vision was of a fair, tall, slim man on horseback, and it may be related to a recurring childhood dream reported by Stevenson (and in less detail by Akolkar). In that dream, which Uttara reported to her parents until the age of eight, "she saw her husband (as she said) coming to her riding a pony; he caressed her pleasantly" (Stevenson, 1984, p. 81).

Uttara claimed that her interest in Dr. Z differed from her attraction to F. Presumably, what Uttara meant by this was that her interest in the doctor wasn't romantic. Now whether or not that's true, Uttara's interest in Dr. Z (whatever it may have been) was apparently expressed differently from her interest in F. In fact, it bordered on the obsessive.[1] In 1973 Uttara went to stay at Dr. Z's ashram with the intention of never returning home. She acknowledged that she was having strong maternal feelings and that she considered adopting an infant and marrying Dr. Z. Uttara claimed that she didn't really care to be Dr. Z's wife, but she wanted their relationship to take a socially acceptable form. She also maintained that by marrying Dr. Z her friend F might feel free to marry the woman of his choice. Moreover, although Uttara insisted that she wanted only a spiritual relationship with Dr. Z, her behavior often suggested otherwise. Dr. Z told Uttara's father that she claimed they had a relationship in a previous life (Akolkar, 1992, p. 221). And in fact, Uttara sometimes behaved as if she were a jealous spouse or lover. On one particularly notable occasion, Uttara "suddenly burst into the room" (Stevenson, 1984, p. 74) where Dr. Z was dining with one of his female assistants, and began berating him in what appeared to be the Bengali language. According to Stevenson, this is one of several incidents that contributed to Dr. Z's decision to send Uttara away from the ashram.

One further interesting hint emerges from Akolkar's report, although

Akolkar himself apparently fails to notice it (along with other hints discussed later). Uttara's physical ailments may have been linked to emotional problems, and possibly even to problems of a psychosexual nature that had begun to develop before her frustrating rejection by F. In fact, Akolkar cites Uttara's own accounts of how menstrual difficulties followed the reading of certain evocative pieces of literature. For example, after reading T. S. Eliot's "The Waste Land," Uttara felt "as though woman's womanhood had come to an end; only lust remained" (Akolkar, 1992, p. 216). This was followed by profuse menstrual bleeding described by Uttara as "like abortional bleeding." Uttara continues, "the next day as I taught the poem 'The Boy Stood on the Burning Deck' to my class, I experienced great mental restlessness at the thought that I should have such a son, and once again there was profuse bleeding" (p. 216).[2]

3. Objections to Stevenson's Report

Initially, the principal source of information concerning the Sharada case was Stevenson (Stevenson & Pasricha, 1979, Stevenson & Pasricha, 1980; and most fully in Stevenson, 1984). But those reports either glossed over or omitted altogether the sorts of interesting details contained in a revealing and independent account by Akolkar (Akolkar, 1992), published eight years later. Akolkar's report deals primarily with psychological and sexual issues mentioned earlier, and although his handling of the material is flawed as well, I'll discuss those problems more fully in the next section. In this section we'll consider the shortcomings of Stevenson's analysis—in particular, his failure to probe more deeply into the psychology of the case. Because the sorts of issues and tensions noted by Akolkar seemed clearly to figure into the overall scheme of things, Stevenson's account leaves the reader in no position to settle on a plausible explanation of the case. Fortunately, Akolkar recognized the relevance of deep psychological issues, and despite problems with his own analysis, he succeeded in filling in some missing details.

To their credit, Stevenson and his associates did a great deal of valuable and careful investigative work to rule out the Usual Suspects—that is, explanations in terms of normal processes. Most of that investigation was devoted to uncovering the extent to which Uttara might have learned normally about Bengali history and customs, and whether she was ever exposed to the Bengali language in a way that would explain her apparent facility in speaking it. But despite all the detail Stevenson provides, the reader gets no feel whatever for Uttara and other relevant individuals as persons. We have no idea what moved them, what their needs and desires were, and what were the profound personal issues that shaped their lives and actions. This is all the more remarkable considering how many aspects of the case seem to cry out for penetrating psychological investigation.

For example, Stevenson has surprisingly little to say about the apparently pivotal relationship between Uttara and Dr. Z. Regarding Dr. Z's first touch, which Uttara said felt surprisingly "familiar" and as the result of which she felt drawn to the doctor "like an iron particle to a magnet" (Akolkar, 1992, p. 217), Stevenson says only that Uttara felt "strangely moved" (p. 105). Not only is that far too little to help one examine the relationship between Dr. Z and Uttara, but Stevenson offers no reason for thinking that Uttara's intense reaction to Dr. Z's touch was particularly strange, or different from a rather common phenomenon. Probably most adults have at some time experienced a sudden, intense, and apparently inexplicable—but seemingly cosmically significant—attraction to another person, only to discover later that the intensity of the original experience made good sense in terms of rather pedestrian hidden needs and agendas. Akolkar, by contrast, seems more sensitive to that possibility.

More important, however, Stevenson fails to explain what seems, on the surface at least, to be puzzling behavior on the part of Dr. Z. Stevenson notes that Dr. Z visited Uttara at home "a few times" (Stevenson, 1984, p. 105) after her discharge (or banishment) from the hospital. That's at least initially perplexing, because Dr. Z had apparently been feeling beleaguered by Uttara's annoying displays of interest and affection. So one might think that if Dr. Z had found Uttara's behavior objectionable enough to send her away from the ashram, he wouldn't have wanted to risk deeper or additional entanglements by visiting her at home. Stevenson explains Dr. Z's actions in terms of his "interest and perhaps compassion," but he says the doctor "indicated no deeper attachment to either Uttara or Sharada" (p. 105). Evidently, Stevenson attempted to figure out whether there had, in fact, been a deeper attachment, but according to Stevenson Dr. Z was evasive and unrevealing during his interviews. The only explanation Stevenson offers for that evasiveness was that the doctor found Sharada's attentions embarrassing.

But that explanation is difficult to accept, especially in the face of rather obvious doubts that Stevenson makes no effort to dispel. For example, it's not clear why Dr. Z would have felt embarrassed by Uttara's attention and affection. Patients often fall in love with their doctors. So it's reasonable to think that a doctor in his fifties would have encountered that phenomenon before. But in that case, we might have expected Dr. Z simply to take Uttara's interest in stride. Moreover, if Uttara's behavior was so embarrassing and her attention "discomfiting and potentially compromising" (p. 105), why did the doctor visit her several times at home? That couldn't have helped to quell any affection Uttara might have felt for him, and it could only have offered further opportunity for embarrassing confrontations. If Dr. Z was moved only by interest or compassion, as Stevenson claims, then probably his embarrassment wasn't all *that* acute, or else the doctor's interest and compassion were strong enough to overcome it. But in either case it's unclear why Dr. Z would have been evasive in an interview. If he felt no (or only a little) embarrassment, it's difficult to understand what he might have wanted to conceal, especially in conversation with a psychiatrist who presumably understands the concepts of transference, countertransference, and other aspects of the patient/doctor relationship. And if Dr. Z was feeling ordinary human compassion and a strong (but merely professional) interest in the case, one would have expected him to be more cooperative and forthcoming in his interview, even if he felt embarrassed by Uttara's behavior. After all, he was talking to a medical colleague, not (say) a tabloid reporter.

There may, in fact, be nothing worth fussing over here. But given the sketchiness of Stevenson's discussion, there's no way to know. For one thing, it's simply not enough to be told *what* subjects said. For example, it's not particularly helpful to learn simply *that* Dr. Z. denied feeling attracted toward Uttara (or Sharada). It's important also to know *how* he denied those feelings—that is, what his tone and manner were. Might they have shown that he had something to hide? Stevenson tells us only that the doctor "practiced masterly evasion" during their interview (p. 106). And that comment only reinforces the suspicion that Stevenson omitted crucial details of their discussion.

Stevenson sheds equally little light on the subject of Uttara's feelings for men. He recognizes the potential significance of the fact that Uttara never married and that Sharada claimed to be married. In fact, he concedes that "frustrated aspirations for an independent domestic life may have found fantasied satisfaction in the role of Sharada" (p. 144). But after noting that Sharada "hardly satisfies all the criteria of the idealized, fulfilled, married woman" (p. 144), Stevenson dismisses that possibility with the rhetorical question, "why did she not complete the fantasy with a happy ending?"

I find it curious that Stevenson abandons the topic at this point. Apparently, he made no effort to understand Uttara's fantasy life in all its richness and subtlety (and Akolkar's report shows that Uttara's fantasy life was decidedly robust). Or, if he did look more deeply into Uttara's psychology, he doesn't share his results with his readers so that they could answer his rhetorical question. But perhaps more important, Stevenson seems to think that if Uttara *had* used another persona to act out her fantasies, that persona would have been an idealized model for her aspirations. But it's quite incredible (especially for a psychiatrist) to think that people generally express their fantasies in such a straightforward and flagrant way. For one thing, living out a fantasy in too obvious a manner often robs the fantasy of its psychological utility; it may be best for us *not* to realize what we're up to and how we're trying to deceive ourselves and others. Moreover, fantasies may simultaneously represent feelings on many different issues. Inquiring minds need to know, exactly, how Uttara felt about men, children, and marriage generally, and perhaps also her parents' marriage in particular and the major male figures in her life (her father, Dr. Z, and F). And they need to know how that entire *constellation* of feelings might have expressed itself in fantasy.

Fortunately, Akolkar's report deals more thoroughly than Stevenson's with underlying psychological issues. So let's now turn our attention to his efforts.

4. Akolkar's Report

One reason Akolkar's report is so striking is that he shows, much more clearly than Stevenson and apparently more clearly than Akolkar himself realizes, why it's plausible to interpret the Sharada case in terms of dissociative pathology with a little psychic functioning thrown in for good measure. However, Akolkar's view of the evidence differs from the one I'm suggesting here, and it differs also from that of Stevenson, who sees the case as supporting a relatively conventional reincarnationist thesis. To Akolkar, the case suggests either possession (presumably by the surviving Sharada) or the persistence of a previously existing Sharada residue deep in Uttara's mind. Perhaps Akolkar's conclusion is correct. But I submit that he has unwittingly presented an even stronger case *against* his own position. The root of the problem may be his unfamiliarity with the literature on dissociation and perhaps also with the more general literature on psychopathology. Akolkar may also be somewhat credulous and naive about parapsychology generally and the reports of Indian mystical phenomena in particular. For now, though, we need to consider only the first of these problems.

Before launching into specific criticisms of Akolkar's report, we must examine a related, but more general, issue. One of the principal concerns of this book is to evaluate how successfully a motivated psi hypothesis can explain the evidence for survival. And that means we must consider seriously whether subjects in survival cases are displaying phenomena similar to those described in the literature on dissociation generally and dissociative psychopathology in particular. Previous discussions of this issue have tended to consider whether subjects (usually, only mediums) are manifesting something akin to MPD/DID. And typically, the problem afflicting those discussions (even very good ones) is that by focusing only on MPD/DID and also by relying on a somewhat outdated picture of that disorder, they underestimate the scope and variety of dissociative phenomena that might occur in survival cases (see, e.g., Broad, 1962; Gauld, 1982).

Interestingly, an analogous problem threatens discussions of survival even when the author is familiar with the current state of research into dissociation. For example, in a recent paper, D. J. Hughes examined similarities between MPD/DID and trance channeling, and she concluded that the two activities differ in many respects (Hughes, 1992). But Hughes didn't address the crucial underlying issue. What matters is not whether we can explain the evidence for survival as a form of multiple personality (or dissociative identity) *disorder*. In principle, there may be various, and relatively functional, forms of multiple personality that don't qualify as types of psychopathology (or instances of MPD/DID). What matters is whether mediums and subjects in reincarnation cases display possibly *non-pathological* forms of multiple personality, or else other dramatic dissociative phenomena closely related to MPD/DID.[3]

Returning now to Akolkar's report, consider, first, that Uttara's dramatic personality shift began at age 32. That's late for a typical reincarnation case, and late also for MPD/DID, which typically begins in childhood. But it's not at all surprising for someone suffering from a dissociative disorder other than MPD/DID. Moreover, the Sharada personality appeared after Uttara entered Dr. Z's ashram and while Uttara was apparently preoccupied with "emotionally charged thoughts regarding her friend F as well as Dr. Z" (Akolkar, 1992, p. 223). Let's assume (as we have good reason to do) that Uttara is reasonably gifted hypnotically. Then it's not at all difficult to imagine how her painfully thwarted relationship with F might have led to the creation of Sharada as a dissociative defense, a defense that would accomplish at least two important goals. First, by developing an alter-like entity (Sharada), Uttara could express and experience emotional and physical urges she could not reasonably expect to satisfy as Uttara. And second, that alter identity (or ego state) would allow Uttara to feel as if she (that is, Uttara) had become "spiritual" in the sense of transcending the physical and emotional needs manifested by Sharada. Unfortunately, however, Akolkar accepts Uttara's description of her spiritual quest at face value. In fact, according to Akolkar, we have no reason to think Uttara suffered from *any* emotional or psychological disorder. He writes, "There is no evidence of mental illness or behavioral abnormality" (p. 241).

But that claim is preposterous. Quite apart from the evidence suggesting that Sharada was created as a dissociative defense, Akolkar notes (p. 220) that at the onset of the Sharada phenomena, Uttara "experienced spells of blankness and an inability to recall." In Uttara's own words, "there was a veritable tug of war" that would make her weep. "She would gaze at the moon for hours and would sometimes stay awake for four or five consecutive nights" (p. 220). Sometimes she would "feel frightened, hear strange sounds, see luminous columns of air infused with consciousness, and occasionally have sensations of soft, cool, fragrance." More interesting still, Uttara suffered "repeated occurrences" (p. 221) of visions, including (Uttara reports) "somebody beating me," which "would interrupt her meditations and prayers" (p. 221). "Sometimes, in a frightened state of mind, she would feel like running, shouting, rolling at someone's feet, and she would long for somebody to console her" (p. 221).

Akolkar's report contains several other puzzling comments, which suggest that Uttara had intense relationships and feelings that required further exploration. And some of these additional hints are disquietingly reminiscent of patterns emerging from the literature on dissociation and abuse. For example, the curious reader can only want to know more about Uttara's relationship with F's father, Bhau, which seems to have been rather intimate. Uttara dreamed "of becoming the daughter-in-law of Bhau's renowned family" (p. 216). She also apparently confided to him her feelings for F and her frustrations with their relationship. In fact, she "implored" Bhau to intervene and convince F to marry either her or the woman he claimed to love. But Bhau took no action. In itself, that reticence is not peculiar; Bhau might simply have felt it was not his place to interfere. But Akolkar quotes Uttara as saying something that suggests a rather different sort of motive on the part of Bhau. Uttara claims that Bhau told her "Like a straw to a drowning man, your support is like that of a little goddess" (p. 216). But Akolkar provides no context for that remark. Not only does he fail to note and explain its sexual overtones, he never even explains what sort of support Bhau might have been referring to.

And as if all this were not enough, Akolkar gives many examples of the overlapping of Uttara and Sharada. Stevenson had noted this as well, remarking at one point that "the boundary between the two personalities was not...impermeable....Uttara was not totally unaware of events occurring during the Sharada phases, and Sharada sometimes behaved as if she vaguely remembered persons Uttara had met" (Stevenson & Pasricha, 1980, p. 336). Akolkar believes this counts in favor of his interpretation of the case and against one treating Sharada as a dissociative defense. That's because he thinks that Sharada would be more independent of Uttara if the former were merely a dissociative construct. But researchers into dissociation have known for a long time that dissociative processes seem never to be totally independent (see, e.g., Messerschmidt, 1927-28; Hilgard, 1986; Eich, Macaulay, Loewenstein, & Dihle, 1997), and in fact, the overlap of Sharada and Uttara looks very much like several forms of co-consciousness observed in cases of MPD/DID (for an inventory of these, see Braude, 1995, pp. 88–89). So, contrary to what Akolkar believes, the overlap of Uttara with Sharada strengthens the anti-survivalist hypothesis we're considering.

An additional fact supporting that hypothesis is that Uttara engaged in automatic writing, which relatively few people can do, but which some dissociators and other hypnotically gifted individuals do quite well. Also, when Professor Kini (a consultant on yoga) touched Uttara's forehead with his index finger, Uttara went immediately into Sharada (Akolkar, 1992, p. 220). That, too, looks like the behavior of a highly hypnotizable individual. And again, Akolkar reports that Uttara would "sort of see" another image behind her own in the mirror (p. 223). That, too, is similar to a phenomenon reported by many multiples, who tend not only to be gifted hallucinators, but who even hallucinate their alters at distinct locations in a room.

Apparently to support his easy acceptance of Uttara's interpretation of the facts, Akolkar claims that "Uttara had the capacity for honest, self-searching introspection" (p. 241). Now it may well be that Uttara's accounts of her emotional life are honest. But contrary to what Akolkar apparently thinks, that doesn't rule out the possibility of self-ignorance and self-deception. In fact, Akolkar offers several clues suggesting that Uttara's capacity for self-searching introspection had definite limitations, especially when it came to her sexual and emotional needs. We've already considered how Uttara seems to have suppressed or repressed her sexuality and need for a male partner and retreated to a form of sexless spirituality. In addition, however, Uttara was "enraged" when her responses to a Rorschach test were interpreted as indicating sexual abnormality (p. 212). And she refused to reveal a dream with possibly erotic imagery to a psychologist "for fear of its being interpreted according to Freudian analysis" (p. 220).

In light of these clues, as well as Akolkar's admission of Uttara's "important biopsychological needs" (p. 241) and frustrations, it's astounding to find Akolkar claiming that Uttara "did not derive any gain through the representation of Sharada" (p. 243). Quite apart from Sharada's obvious utility as a dissociative defense against Uttara's emotional and sexual frustrations, there are even further clues, provided by both Stevenson and Akolkar, as to what Uttara could accomplish by creating a kind of alter identity. Sharada's behavior allowed Uttara to do many things that would otherwise have been unacceptable. For example, her jealous and intrusive behavior toward Dr. Z could be disowned, so to speak, and ascribed instead to a previous personality who claimed that Dr. Z had been her husband in a former life. Moreover, as I suggested earlier, Sharada provided a way for Uttara to behave, dress, and feel like a married, childbearing woman, while avoiding the condemnation she would almost certainly incur by acting out those feelings as Uttara. So perhaps it's not surprising that the Sharada manifestations declined as Uttara reached her forties, at which time the prospects of marriage and childbearing would no doubt have seemed more remote. Moreover, Sharada, but perhaps not Uttara, could successfully criticize both the lifestyle and home of Uttara's parents, and also adopt conde-scending attitudes toward them and toward Marathi culture. In fact, as Sharada, she could even avoid helping Uttara's mother with chores. These sorts of conjectures are commonplace and plausible both in ev-eryday contexts and in the clinical literature on dissociation. And in this case they seem particularly obvious and compelling, so much so that the burden of proof shifts to those who want to reject them.

It also seems as if Akolkar errs when he claims that Sharada displays a "full range of...personality" (p. 242). Granted, Sharada isn't an obvi-ous or crude personality caricature; she doesn't seem to be as flat a character as some personality fragments in cases of MPD/DID, which may have no more than a single identifiable function (Braude, 1992, 1995). And of course, it would be hasty to conclude that Sharada was a dissociative construct simply because her personality was limited in cer-tain ways. After all, many non-multiples have severe personality limita-tions. But neither Stevenson nor Akolkar provide evidence that the Sharada personality was more robust than what we find in most highly developed cases of alter identities.

Akolkar's report disappoints on other counts as well. But the forego-ing considerations demonstrate clearly that the case of Sharada is more interesting as a human drama than investigators have realized or ac-knowledged. In fact, it's likely that *most* cases are more interesting psy-chologically than their case reports would suggest. We can only wonder, then, how plausible motivated psi hypotheses might seem in other ap-parently strong survival cases if only investigators had looked more care-fully under the psychological surface.

Still, even if it's plausible to think that the Sharada persona is a dissociative defense, that doesn't rule out survival as an important fea-ture of the case. For example, some will say that we can't tip the scales in favor of motivated psi among the living simply by demonstrating how neatly and thoroughly Sharada satisfies Uttara's apparent needs and interests. For all we know, Uttara's psychology might have led her to be "drawn to, and 'connect with', a kindred but discarnate personality named Sharada who had similar needs and inclinations" (Cook, 1997, p. 161). Cook is right, of course; that remains a possibility. But we must remember that this case is weak evidentially; Uttara provided little (if any) evidence for the previous existence of a person corresponding to the Sharada persona. Apart from Uttara's xenoglossy, the case very strongly resembles many relatively humdrum cases of dissociative pa-thology for which survivalist conjectures aren't even tempting. Were it not for the xenoglossy, I doubt we would seriously consider this case as providing anything but superficial evidence for survival. We would take it no more literally than we do cases of MPD/DID in which psychologi-cally useful alter personalities are clearly modeled after childhood icons or images (e.g., Snow White), or Turkish cases in which alters claim to be the jinns (or genies) of Turkish folklore (see, e.g., Sar, Yargic, & Tutkun, 1996; Zoroglu, Yargic, Tutkun, Ozturk, & Sar, 1996).

Nevertheless, we still need to account for Uttara/Sharada's proficiency in Bengali. And since we're taking the possibility of survival seriously, we have to allow for the possibility of dissociative defenses utilizing both ante- and postmortem sources of information. Therefore, we need to consider carefully whether the missing elements of Uttara's knowledge of Bengali could have been acquired without postmortem assistance (possibly with the help of antemortem ESP). So let's focus now on the ability highlighted in the Sharada case: responsive xenoglossy—the ability to converse in an unlearned language.

5. Super Psi and Knowledge-How

Some writers on survival (including Stevenson) recognize that we can't rule out, *a priori*, explanations in terms of super-ESP. Even so (they would say), super-psi explanations can only handle cases of apparent knowledge-*that*; they can't explain the types of knowledge-*how* demonstrated in survival cases. That is, even if we grant that people can paranormally "perceive" or acquire remote bits of information, it's implausible to suppose they can paranormally acquire someone's abilities or skills, especially in forms that are as idiosyncratic as the person's fingerprints.

This position might seem reasonable enough, at least initially. But in fact, it's enormously complex and not at all obvious once the relevant issues are exposed. I want to examine only some of those issues now and consider the rest in later chapters. We'll be returning to this general topic frequently as the book progresses. For now, let's ignore the questions arising in connection with the persistence of a deceased person's *idiosyncratic* abilities, such as a distinctively quirky sense of humor or highly specialized technical expertise. Let's focus now on more general abilities, such as the ability to write or speak in a foreign language, play a musical instrument, compose music, discuss theoretical physics, or solve mathematical problems, never mind the singular forms the abilities might take. If a non-survivalist hypothesis can't account for these general competencies, we needn't worry about more highly specialized forms.

So let's restrict our attention to the widespread, non-idiosyncratic, sorts of skills or abilities demonstrated by subjects in survival cases, and let's consider why some think we need a survival hypothesis to account for their manifestation. The general line of reasoning behind this position is as follows. Mere information or propositional knowledge is the sort of thing we can acquire simply through a process of communication (normal or paranormal). But skills, such as playing a musical instrument or speaking a language, can't be accounted for in this way. Granted, obtaining information is often a necessary part of skill development, but it's hardly sufficient. That's because skills are things people develop only after a period of *practice*. But since the subjects in survival cases who display anomalous skills have had no opportunity to practice them first, it's reasonable to reject explanations in terms of super-ESP and resort to survivalist explanations instead.

This argument is not outlandish. Nevertheless, it's seriously flawed, and to see why, we must approach the matter from several different angles. In one of his discussions, Stevenson claimed that the reasoning rests on the usually tacit principle that "if skills are incommunicable normally..., they are also incommunicable paranormally" (1984, p. 160). According to Stevenson, it was Ducasse who first applied this principle to the evidence for survival (Ducasse, 1962), and Stevenson apparently considered it to be self-evident, or at least not worthy of a defense. Now first of all, it's not clear that the argument above does rest on this principle, because it's not clear that *communicating* skills is at issue. All we know is that some individuals *manifest* anomalous abilities. *How* they got them remains a mystery, and (as we'll see) non-survivalist explanations needn't appeal to a process of transmission or communication. In any case, Ducasse's principle isn't nearly as obvious as Stevenson suggests,[4] and if it's really an essential step in the survivalist argument, it may be more a liability than a virtue.

Consider: if Ducasse's principle is true, that's not because it's an instance of the more general principle,

(K): If any bit of knowledge x is incommunicable normally, then x is incommunicable paranormally.

I'm not sure if anyone has defended this principle, or what the status of the principle is supposed to be—for example, whether it's supposed to be a conceptual truth or an empirical generalization. In any case, principle K will have to be judged false by anyone who accepts the evidence for ESP. In ESP people can have access to data which at that time is inaccessible through all known channels of information. So if we accepted principle K, we'd have to conclude that ESP is impossible. Therefore, it's reasonable to assume that Stevenson and others don't accept this more general principle.

But then if Ducasse's principle is true, presumably it's true only of skills, not propositional knowledge or knowledge-that. But why think it's true even of skills? There are at least four crucial topics to consider here: (1) the extent to which we can express and develop skills by sidestepping our customary resistance-laden modes of cognition; (2) whether it's question-begging (in this context) to talk of *acquiring* skills; (3) the relationship between skills and practice; and (4) the difficulty in generalizing about skills or abilities, including the ability to speak a language. These different issues overlap considerably, but I'll try to keep them distinct.

Consider, first, the sorts of things that can interfere with skill development, even when we have opportunities to practice. For one thing, when we learn a new skill we usually do a certain amount of unlearning, if only of acquired motor and cognitive habits which would interfere with manifesting that skill. For example, in learning how to lecture more effectively, a teacher might have to overcome tendencies to mumble, giggle nervously, revert to obscure technical jargon, sneer disdainfully at stupid questions, or conclude assertions with the phrase "You dig?" Similarly, a piano student might have to unlearn long-ingrained habits of fingering and pedaling in order to advance to the higher level of expertise required by a difficult new piece. Moreover, learning of any kind (whether of skills or information) is often highly resistance-laden; it can be hampered by an endless number of interfering beliefs, insecurities, and other fears.

Now you might think that these barriers to learning a new skill only strengthen the survivalist position. After all, they only increase the number of challenges facing a medium (say) who manifests a communicator's skills without benefit of practice. However, these physical, cognitive, and emotional obstacles can be overcome relatively easily in hypnotic or other profoundly altered states. For example, under the influence of stage hypnotists, good hypnotic subjects do things they've never done before—for example, dance the tango, accurately imitate their boss (or various farm animals), behave in an overtly seductive manner, and more generally display dramatic and creative abilities they might otherwise be too inhibited to express.

Interestingly, Stanford psychiatrist David Spiegel made a fascinating film of a subject who, under hypnosis, started behaving and spouting New-Age platitudes like a typical contemporary channel or medium. Granted, his apparent trance mediumship lacked the fluency of some seasoned (or well-rehearsed) New-Age channels. Instead, it more closely resembled equally familiar but ostensibly more impeded mediumistic communications. Nevertheless, Spiegel's subject adopted novel speech patterns, tone of voice, and the awkward body language presumably appropriate to one who finds himself in a strange body and unexpected surroundings. To my knowledge, this subject hadn't previously displayed the capacity to produce spontaneously consistent dramatic impersonations. And it's reasonable to think that hypnosis enabled him to accomplish what his normal fears and inhibitions might otherwise have prevented. More generally, it's plausible that manifesting a skill might be *facilitated* if the process bypasses the normal states in which our inhibitions and other constraints are strongest. We *know* that people can exhibit unexpected abilities or perform at unexpectedly high levels under certain unusual conditions. What's at issue is whether subjects in survival cases fall into this class—that is, whether they find themselves in situations that are conducive to surprising levels of performance or the manifestation of surprising skills.

In order to resolve that issue, we need to examine not simply sporadic instances of dramatic dissociation such as the performances elicited from good hypnotic subjects by experimenters or stage hypnotists. We need also to consider recurrent or chronic forms of dissociation, especially MPD/DID. It seems clear that dissociation facilitates the emergence and development of personality traits and skills which might never be cultivated or displayed under normal conditions. For example, alternate personalities/identities exhibit behavioral and cognitive styles which are not explainable simply in terms of propositional knowledge, and which we would have judged highly unlikely in light of the multiple's previously observed repertoire of skills and level of achievement (Braude, 1995; Putnam, 1989; 1997; Ross, 1997). In addition to changes in handedness and handwriting, an alter's cognitive style may encompass, for example, artistic and literary ability, mechanical aptitude, and the skills of drawing, sculpting, and writing poetry. But because alters appear suddenly and sometimes evolve quickly, their distinctive skills apparently emerge without any practice. So it seems clear that good dissociators, at the very least, can develop or manifest novel abilities and skills without benefit of practice or a normal process of learning. But then, since children and entranced mediums generally—not simply Uttara—probably experience periods of dissociation, we're hardly in a position to assert the improbability (much less the impossibility) of a person suddenly manifesting new or latent abilities or skills in cases suggesting survival.

Another (possibly deeper) set of problems concerns the way even sophisticated writers on survival (such as Stevenson and Gauld) generalize about skills. For example, Stevenson asserts, "Practice does not just make perfect; it is indispensable for the acquisition of any skill" (Stevenson, 1984, p. 160). There are at least two related problems with that claim. First, skills differ dramatically in many respects, one of which is the importance of practice in skill development. The second problem is that the *acquisition* of skills may not be the issue. All we're entitled to discuss, strictly speaking, is the *manifestation* of skills. We have no idea whether or to what extent new skills have been acquired by mediums or by subjects of reincarnation investigations. This isn't a trivial distinction, because although practice seems essential to *perfecting* a skill, it's *not* always needed to manifest skills for the first time.

And to see that, we need only to consider child prodigies and cases of savantism. In fact, musical prodigies such as Mozart, Mendelssohn, and Schubert, and mathematical prodigies such as Gauss, usually manifest exceptional skills *prior* to perfecting or developing them through practice. It's not simply that prodigious skills are rudimentary at first and then evolve with amazing rapidity. The skills of prodigies can be amazing even at the beginning. The same is true of savants. For example, one fascinating musical savant was reportedly able to read music without ever receiving instruction. She was also able to improvise in the styles of various composers at the piano the first time this feat had ever been requested. In fact, she found that she could play in different composers' styles at the same time, the right hand playing in one style and the left hand playing in the other (Viscott, 1969). Similarly, Mozart was able to write down a complex piece of music while composing another one in his head; but to my knowledge there's no evidence that he first had to practice that skill. But more important, we have no reason to think that the subjects in survival cases demonstrate levels of expertise more impressive than (say) Mendelssohn's initial displays of musicianship. Quite the contrary: the suddenly emerging skills of savants and child prodigies often far exceed anything displayed by the subjects investigated in xenoglossy cases or other cases suggesting survival. But then, how do we know to what extent certain conditions (e.g., dissociation) may unleash impressive (if not prodigious) capacities latent in many (or all) of us?

Of course, we don't need to consider prodigies and savants to appreciate this point. Ordinary folk demonstrate it all the time. Consider, for example, the skill of playing tennis. Many people are naturally athletic, even though they may not be prodigiously gifted. And to the occasional consternation of those who are more athletically challenged, natural athletes can, on their first try, play a game of tennis reasonably well—at least without looking hopelessly foolish. In fact, on their first try they might even play as well or better than others who have played for years, taken lessons, etc. But more important, the natural athlete's beginning level of tennis skill would arguably be at least as good, and probably better, than the language skills exhibited in the most compelling cases of responsive xenoglossy.

Probably, some will protest that tennis is a much simpler skill to acquire than speaking a new language. But that's doubtful. For one thing, skill difficulty is relative to a person's native capacities. And for another, there's actually an interesting parallel between conversing in a language and playing tennis. Responsive xenoglossy involves more than the ability to form sentences in a new language; it also involves understanding and responding appropriately to sentences in that language. Similarly, the skill of playing tennis goes beyond being able to get the ball over the net and inbounds. It also requires being able to return shots and placing those shots appropriately.

Behind these various considerations lurks a more sweeping problem, one that stands in the way of *ever* concluding confidently that mastering one skill is more difficult than mastering another. First of all, we have, at best, only a rudimentary understanding of what skills are. For example, we don't know whether the various things we call skills are similar enough to permit useful generalizations. In fact, we don't even know to what extent we can generalize about *individual* skills. The things we identify as specific skills (e.g., the skill of speaking a language, or composing music) typically *consist* of other skills and capacities. But those subsidiary skills, etc., may also be organized collections of other skills, etc., and at no point along the way is there some preferred set or arrangement of lower-level endowments necessary for exhibiting the more general capacity.

For example, those who can compose music have various other musical abilities that make their skill in composition possible. But compositional skill can be expressed in a great variety of ways. Many composers notate their compositions; others lack that ability. Some composers have absolute pitch, some only good relative pitch, some neither. Some composers can compose directly onto paper without the aid of a piano or some other instrument; many others can't. Some composers work well with large forms; others don't. Most composers write particularly well or idiomatically only for certain instruments, and only some composers demonstrate a keen ability to set words to music. Some composers are particularly skilled in harmony, rhythm, melody, or instrumental color, but those secondary skills take different forms and exist in different degrees and combinations with different composers. So there's no reason to assume that the skill of musical composition will allow many useful generalizations. And perhaps most important, there's no reason to think that this is a unique feature of that particular skill. It seems to be the rule rather than exception. People who possess a general skill may exhibit it in various ways and to varying degrees, depending on which subsidiary skills they possess and the manner in which they possess them. Presumably, then, there's no reason to assume that what we identify as a skill enjoys a deeper theoretical unity.

But in that case, certain familiar arguments in the survival literature seem hopelessly simplistic. For example, when Stevenson argues that skills can't be communicated or manifested without practice, he mentions riding a bicycle, dancing, and speaking a foreign language as examples. Similarly, Gauld writes,

> The ability to play bridge well is not simply a matter of learning (whether normally or by ESP) the rules (considered as a set of facts together with the precepts given in some manual). It can only be acquired by practising intelligently until things fall into place. And it is the same with learning a language. (Gauld, 1982, p. 102)

But if there are serious disanalogies between linguistic competence and these other skills, they may be deep enough to prevent us from generalizing usefully across abilities. And if we can't say how difficult or easy it is, *generally*, to learn or develop a new skill (including learning a new language), then this sort of survivalist argument is dead in its tracks.

Let's take second things first and consider some aspects of language learning. Language use, like musical composition, encompasses a variety of other capacities and manifests in quite different sorts of contexts. So it's not surprising to find persuasive reasons for thinking that we can't say, *in general*, how difficult it is to learn a new language. The degree of difficulty seems to depend on many things, including linguistic aptitude, a good "ear," the context in which the language is learned, and how different the language is from one's native tongue. I take my cue here from a recent, interesting, and sensible review of the research on second-language acquisition by Bialystok and Hakuta (Bialystok & Hakuta, 1994).

Bialystok and Hakuta observe, first of all, that new languages are learned in many different contexts, some more demanding than others, and some more conducive than others to general linguistic proficiency. For example, the wife of an American businessman in Japan might, with the help of her new Japanese neighbors, learn enough Japanese to do her shopping and banking and also to have conversations over tea. Despite her many grammatical errors, she speaks well enough to be understood. The family's children might seem to have a good working knowledge of Japanese, despite attending an American school. They can play with their Japanese neighbors, discuss comic books, order their own food in restaurants, and do these things in ways that strike their father, who has not learned the language, as very fluent. A Vietnamese carpenter's assistant in Toronto might learn English in a way suitable to his work needs. So he might learn the appropriate technical terms, and possibly even words unknown to many native speakers of English. But his command of English may be largely receptive; he may know the language well enough to understand orders and carry them out, but not well enough to assume responsibilities as a foreman. A student at Yale might earn top marks in a course in Russian, know his vocabulary and rules of grammar, but be unable to converse with or even understand a Russian exchange student he meets.

Although each of these scenarios is a legitimate and familiar example of second-language learning, the language users have acquired different skills.

> The American businessman's children learned conversational skills adapted for interaction with other children in play situations. The mother learned a mode of speech particular to the interaction of women in Japan and the kind of conversation used in shopping. The Vietnamese carpenter mostly learned receptive vocabulary specialized to the routines of his daily work. The Yale student learned a lot of grammar and vocabulary. (Bialystok & Hakuta, 1994, pp. 205–206)

Bialystok and Hakuta conclude,

> When we learn a new language, we invariably gain exposure to that lan-

guage in a more limited range of contexts than those in which we regularly use our first language...Therefore, the aspects of language proficiency that we need to master or even have the opportunity to learn depend on the particulars of these circumstances. (p. 206)

They also note that there is no clear, single, or privileged standard of linguistic proficiency. What counts as linguistic proficiency varies widely with context. And they observe that there is no single set of abilities in virtue of which people are able to learn and speak a new language. Different people draw on different aptitudes and skills, which they possess in distinctive combinations and in varying degrees.

> Learners come with an assortment of different abilities, but what is acquired during language learning, and the situations in which that knowledge is demonstrated, also vary enormous[ly]. Accordingly, proficiency, or success in learning a new language, has many facets. Language is far too complex a system to reveal itself through a single skill, a single experience, or a single test. People, too, are complex; and it is reasonable to conclude that just as an individual's makeup reflects a large number of strengths and weaknesses, so are these different attributes reflected in the multiple dimensions encompassed by language. There is no Good Language Learner, but neither is there perfect mastery of a language. Proficiency depends on use. If language is needed to navigate the streets of a new country, then social and communicative knowledge, a particular vocabulary, and some fluency are at the top of the proficiency list. If language is needed to read academic documents in a foreign language, then grammar and literacy become more important. (pp. 158–159)

In the same spirit, Bialystok and Hakuta also caution against generalizing about the difficulties of learning a new language. In most cases we can't make reliable predictions on the basis of age, personality, or aptitude. Out of "methodological necessity" (p. 206) formal studies of second-language acquisition focus on only a small range of contexts in which people learn a new language. In fact, the usual "tests of overall ability seem to correspond only to classroom success" (p. 158). But once we look beyond the "limited circumstances that provided the data for study" (p. 206), we find (as we might expect) that

> not all people learn well in all instructional (treatment) settings, and any given learning situation may be good for some people, but not for others. Putting learners who are highly successful in one context into a situation that requires a different set of skills could well reveal the limitations in that learner's achievement. (p. 207)

Nevertheless, Bialystok and Hakuta hazard a few generalizations about situations either conducive or resistant to second-language acquisition. And appropriately, they seem to recognize that these are, at best, useful *statistical* generalizations that can accommodate a variety of exceptions. They suggest (p. 213) that a second language will be most difficult to learn in those respects in which it differs significantly from the

first language. The problems are most likely to concern grammar or vocabulary, but presumably they could also concern the language's general
descriptive categories (and their embedded metaphysics). Moreover,
Bialystok and Hakuta concede that "exposure to the language and practice in its production seem to be essential to phonological mastery" (p.
210), and "there is no shortcut for learning words. They need to be
studied, memorized, encountered, and reflected upon" (p. 210).

So, how does all this help us get a handle on xenoglossy generally
and the Sharada case in particular? First of all, it seems clear that learning a second language is a significantly different process from learning a
language for the first time. It also seems clear that many sorts of people
can easily attain various kinds of minimal second-language competence,
even when the new language is grammatically and semantically novel,
but especially when the new language isn't radically different from their
own. And since formal tests of linguistic aptitude don't measure real-life
linguistic adaptability, we can't expect to be enlightened by administer-
ing such tests to subjects in xenoglossy cases (e.g., as Stevenson did in
the Jensen case, Stevenson, 1974b). Contrary to what Stevenson claims,
it seems false that the best tests measure "the ability to learn a modern
language easily" (Stevenson, 1974b, p. 50).[5] Moreover, even if there is
no shortcut for learning words, we can't specify, in general, how much
and what sort of exposure to a new language is necessary for low-level
linguistic proficiency. That seems to vary widely from person to person
and context to context. In fact, it seems reasonable to assume that, as in
many other areas of life, some people learn much more quickly than
others. Given the right combination of needs and natural aptitudes,
some people might require only a very brief exposure to elements of a
language, while others might require repeated exposure over a long period. And as cases of MPD/DID demonstrate dramatically, it may only
be under very special circumstances that we exceed our ordinary capacities or demonstrate otherwise latent natural gifts (for more on this, see
chapter 5).

But in that case, the crude linguistic competence displayed in most
cases of xenoglossy may not be all that impressive. The context of answering simple questions put to a medium (probably in a dissociated
state) seems, in many respects, far less demanding than real-life social
situations where important personal and professional relationships are
at stake and where complex issues are being discussed. Mediumistic
xenoglossy may require little more than some native (and possibly latent) linguistic aptitude, and also rudimentary knowledge (that) of vocabulary and grammar, at least some of which could be acquired
paranormally. In fact, since we're considering exotic explanations, we
can't rule out the possibility that subjects gain the needed exposure to
the new language unconsciously and psychically. And of course, if those
subjects have a knack for this sort of thing, they might be able to learn a

surprising amount with only the most meager information.

For example, in the Gretchen case (Stevenson, 1984), the subject D. J. introduced at least 237 German words before they were spoken to her, and 120 of these were uttered by "Gretchen" before any of her interlocutors addressed her in German. But according to one skeptical estimate, less than 20 percent of Gretchen's German comments (28 of them) were appropriate to the questions asked in German. Now I think we can agree with Almeder that a person who can do this in some sense knows German (Almeder, 1992, p. 30). And I agree that we need to explain "how somebody who has never been taught German can successfully understand the language enough to respond successfully to unrehearsed questions 28 times" (p. 30). But Almeder claims that this level of proficiency can't be explained, for example, "by appeal to World War II movies or casual glances at German books, because one would need to know what was being said in such movies or books" (p. 30). The problem with this claim is that some people might be able to learn a great deal from such limited material, and it's often not too difficult to discern the meaning of words or phrases in foreign movies (especially if the movies have subtitles). We can agree that the Gretchen case is intriguing and perhaps not easily dismissed. But given the complexities, discussed above, in generalizing about second-language acquisition, and considering the actual achievements of good dissociators, savants, and the more common skills of the linguistically gifted, we need to be more circumspect about this case. (This conclusion can only be reinforced by considering the astonishing, although somewhat different, linguistic skills surveyed in chapter 5.)

In the Jensen case, a Philadelphia doctor discovered that his wife T. E. was a good hypnotic subject who "could enter deep trances readily" (Stevenson, 1974b, p. 25). To explore that capacity further, he began conducting hypnotic age-regression experiments on T. E., during which she began speaking in Swedish, manifesting a personality named "Jensen." The Jensen persona spoke in a somewhat archaic language, which, together with the details provided about his life, suggested a previous existence in Sweden during the seventeenth century. But this case offered little (if any) non-linguistic evidence that Jensen corresponded to a real previous personality. Moreover, during the first five sessions, no one present spoke a Scandinavian language, and at those sessions Jensen uttered only occasional Scandinavian-sounding words or phrases. Session four was recorded, and at that session Jensen spoke two phrases that were later "identified clearly from the tape recordings" (p. 26). However, once Swedish speakers began attending the sessions, Jensen spoke a great deal of Swedish (or perhaps a mixture of Swedish and Norwegian). (Of course, this is precisely the sort of scenario that raises the specter of telepathic sitter-influence.) Jensen's pronunciation and grammar were good, but he "rarely responded in full sentences, and when he did his sentences were short" (pp. 28–29). Several Swedish speakers listened to the tapes or interviewed Jensen themselves, and they concurred that Jensen introduced words into the conversations that hadn't previously been used by the interviewers in T. E.'s presence.

T. E.'s command of Swedish (or Norwegian) seems clearly superior to D. J.'s mastery of German. But neither seems outlandish for an adult with previously untapped linguistic aptitude, who is a good dissociative subject, and who might have been exposed to elements of those languages unconsciously (and even psychically). Interestingly, Stevenson himself seems to make a crucial concession on this point. Citing a case reported by Dreifuss (Dreifuss, 1961), he says that it shows "that an ability to speak intelligibly (not merely to recite) a foreign language may remain dormant and emerge later in life" (Stevenson, 1974b, p. 53).[6] Of course, the Sharada case confronts us with a kind of linguistic fluency far beyond that demonstrated in the Jensen or Gretchen cases. But we've already noted that the linguistic competence of Sharada would have been more of a feat (a) had her language been *radically* different from that of Uttara, (b) had Uttara not already demonstrated an ability to learn new languages, and (c) had she not already learned some Bengali.

So as far as I can see, the research on second-language acquisition tends to undermine, rather than support, the survivalist position. It discredits the usual survivalist generalizations about linguistic proficiency and second-language acquisition; it reinforces the commonsense view that some people can accomplish a great deal with relatively little effort, input, or support; and it reminds us that impressive (if not prodigious) abilities may lurk under the surface, awaiting an appropriately fertile ground for expression. That's not to say that we can clearly or justifiably *reject* a survivalist interpretation of the good xenoglossy cases. But the evidence isn't nearly as persuasive as some seem to think.

A similarly cautious attitude seems appropriate to another type of case. Strictly speaking, cases in this group wouldn't qualify as examples of xenoglossy, but they raise issues analogous to those we're currently considering. The parapsychological literature contains scattered reports of children producing automatic scripts, even though they haven't yet learned the alphabet. For example, Myers mentions two cases (Myers, 1903, vol. 2, pp. 484–486). The first concerns a girl of five who wrote a few words, ostensibly in a lady's (not a child's) handwriting. But the case is poorly described, and many details cry out for further explanation and probing. Quite apart from the issues, discussed above, of latent abilities, cryptomnesia, and psychic influence from persons nearby, it's interesting that the girl had been watching her older sister produce automatic writing. So first, we need to know more about the possibly competitive relationship between the sisters. And second, we need to know whether the young sister's family life was such that she might have picked up rudiments of writing by age five, independently of formal instruction, simply through exposure to the usual activities of normally literate people. That would require only a modest degree of linguistic precocity (see chapter 5 for a detailed discussion of related issues). In the second case, a girl of four who had never been taught the alphabet or even how to hold a pencil, scribbled "your Aunt Emma," a tracing of which Richard Hodgson described as "resembling the planchette-writing of an adult rather than the first effort of a child" (p. 486). This case, too, is not thoroughly described. It may be that the child had never attended school or been taught the alphabet. But it's unlikely she had never seen a written word or observed the act of writing. And we're given no information about her visual acuity, manual dexterity, and ability to draw or copy what she had seen. So we have no idea what the child might have learned or accomplished on her own. In fact, in both cases, it would be good to know how quickly the girls exhibited linguistic mastery once formal instruction began. Moreover, Hodgson's statement in the second case is misleading. The four year old's writing, which he saw, was the last of several attempts to write the name "Emma."

Returning to cases of xenoglossy proper, I should note that in some, mediums reportedly speak languages (e.g., Hungarian, Chinese, African dialects) which are quite different from their own and to which they presumably had no normal exposure. But these cases haven't been carefully documented; and sometimes, upon closer inspection, the evidence crumbles (see West, 1948 for a good example). But quite apart from serious questions concerning the reliability of the data, in every case I'm familiar with some sitter present knew the language, and either they or someone else could have benefitted psychologically in obvious ways from receiving communications in those languages. For example, the entranced Hafsteinn Bjornsson (whom we met in chapter 2) reportedly spoke in an Eskimo language he had never learned, and which is quite different from Icelandic. But the sitter at the séance, a Danish professor, knew the language well, and the ostensible communicator was a person the professor had known when he lived in Greenland (Haraldsson & Stevenson, 1975b, p. 36). Similarly (as I noted above), in the Jensen case "Jensen spoke more and better Swedish in the presence of Swedish-speaking people and extremely little in their absence" (Stevenson, 1974b, p. 78). In these cases, then, we can't rule out the possibility of telepathic interaction between medium and sitter, and it would obviously be hasty to draw survivalist conclusions from the medium's surprising linguistic competence.

I realize that many recoil from the suggestion that telepathic sitter-influence might account for mediumistic xenoglossy. And the reasons given are usually those noted in chapter 1—in particular, (a) we have no independent evidence for such refined or powerful psychic functioning, and (b) this type of super psi is simply antecedently implausible. But in that chapter we also noted the proper replies to these objections. And perhaps most important, we observed that survivalists require the same kind and degree of psychic functioning in these cases as do non-survivalists. The only difference is that survivalists posit telepathic influence from the surviving minds of the communicator, rather than the minds of sitters. So survivalists are in a uniquely bad position to reject this type of super-psi explanation of xenoglossy.

One final matter, before moving on. Although we won't look closely and more generally at the topic of reincarnation until chapter 6, we need to consider a point about reincarnation and prodigies or savants. When I mentioned the cases of Mozart, Gauss, etc., above, I assumed that their prodigious skills required no paranormal explanation. I assumed that prodigious skills simply represent one end of a continuum of natural abilities demonstrated throughout the animal kingdom. But some suggest that reincarnation accounts nicely for the appearance of unusual or prodigious skills in children from very ordinary backgrounds. So, for example, if a child in a poor working-class family exhibits prodigious musical abilities, and if no one else in the family has ever demonstrated so much as an interest in music (much less a gift or proclivity for it), the hypothesis is that the child is a reincarnation of a deceased musician.

But this explanatory strategy has little to recommend it. First, it's not very promising. It faces the obvious problem of accounting for the *first appearance* of the prodigious abilities allegedly passed on through reincarnation. Presumably, those can't (or at least needn't) be explained in terms of reincarnation. But then subsequent occurrences of the abilities needn't be explained by appealing to reincarnation. Second, the strategy seems deeply misguided. Granted, it may be defensible to posit reincarnation if other data in the case already suggest survival (or reincarnation). But in the absence of that data, the strategy simply seems gratuitous. In fact, I suspect that advocates of reincarnation may be asking the wrong questions in these cases. Rather than trying to locate exotic hidden sources of talent, the real challenge may be to explain what dampens the average intelligent child's expressive or creative potential. This is a very big topic, and it probably deserves a treatise of its own. For now, then, let me at least stake out my own position on the matter.[7] The discussion can then be continued at some suitable later occasion.

I think we're entitled to assume that children have many natural aptitudes or potentials, most of which are never expressed or developed. And I think we may assume that these undeveloped aptitudes *would* have found suitable outlets if only they had been properly reinforced. In fact, it's a plausible general hypothesis that complex organisms are inherently creative and that unless they're constrained (or psychologically trampled), they'll tend to exhibit a variety of surprising behaviors.

Children are naturally curious and exploratory, and it seems likely that they would exhibit an assortment of unusual skills if only we responded positively, early on, to activities that delighted them. Instead, various influences suppress or redirect a child's creativity and natural predilections. Foremost among these, probably, are the fears, prejudices, and other beliefs and assumptions of caretakers, the prison-like atmosphere of schools, and the mind-numbing ordinariness and stupidity of teachers (themselves victims of the same psychic constraints they impose on others). These forces turn out children whose minds are, to a great extent, distortions and restrictions of natural potential. We seldom allow children free reign to express their native curiosity, and we seldom encourage them or reinforce their spontaneous interests. If those interests are in directions others regard as objectionable, and if they're not expressed at what others consider an appropriate time in the child's development, we'll nip them in the bud. So children quickly become truncated spirits, conforming to the limitations imposed by those around them. Consistent with this, interestingly enough, is a body of evidence showing that children's ESP scores decline as they age (and presumably learn that others consider displays of ESP to be unacceptable or impossible) (Winkelman, 1980, 1981).

Furthermore, a child's creativity and unusual skills might be elicited under stressful or otherwise repressive conditions, and those features of the child's background might come to light only after intimate and persistent questioning. The musical savant described by Viscott illustrates this nicely (Viscott, 1969). Viscott discovered how the savant's musical skills played a critical role in her overall psychology. He showed how those skills provided reassurance in the face of deep-rooted insecurities stemming from infancy and early childhood—in particular, a kind of sensory deprivation in which the sounds of her music lessons taught by her mother took the place of physical contact and recreated "a motherly presence...[that helped her deal] with feelings of loneliness and emptiness" (p. 508). But of course those insights were possible only after extensive and sensitive interviews with the savant and members of her family—precisely the kind of probing seldom (if ever) undertaken in connection with survival investigations.

6. Xenoglossy and Dissociation

In his second book on the subject (Stevenson, 1984), Stevenson discusses several potentially important, and certainly intriguing, linguistic features of xenoglossy (pp. 161ff). One feature is that when communicators respond in their native language to questions posed to them, the questions are not always in those languages. Sometimes, the language is that of the person asking the question, and in some of those cases this different language is one that the communicator was not supposed to know. For example, the trance personalities Jensen and Gretchen responded in their alleged native languages to questions posed in English. Along the same lines, some communicators speak their alleged native languages with the distinctive accent of someone whose original tongue is that of the *medium*, and occasionally they speak with the characteristically stilted or botched grammar of someone trying to master a second language.

I agree with Stevenson that these features are fascinating. But I'm not sure Stevenson has asked the right questions about them, or that he has asked enough of the important questions. Stevenson seems concerned only with making sense of these phenomena on the assumption that the communicators or trance personalities are what they purport to be. Now I agree that we can't seriously entertain the survival hypothesis unless we address that issue squarely. And that means we must consider, as sympathetically as we can, (a) what the experience of communicating might be like from the communicator's point of view, (b) to what extent there might be translation problems between different languages, and (c) what other factors might aid or hinder the process of communication. But those topics need to be discussed as part of a broader inquiry. After all, we're considering the xenoglossy cases in order to *decide* whether there's any compelling evidence of survival. Under the circumstances, then, the more fundamental question is: Do the peculiar linguistic phenomena discussed by Stevenson make more sense from the survivalist or non-survivalist point of view? And the reason that question is especially important is that those features of xenoglossy seem clearly to support a non-survivalist interpretation.

Stevenson imagines that the hypnotic subjects, T. E. and D. J., engage in what he calls "layering," a kind of subsurface interaction between those subjects and the discarnate minds or personalities of Jensen and Gretchen (respectively). He proposes (a) that interlocutors' English words evoke certain images (or other causally efficacious mental states) in the subjects' minds, and (b) that those states then trigger appropriate mental states in, and eventually verbal responses from, the communicators. Of course, it's far from clear how (a) would work, if the languages of the previous personality and the subject are different. Translations can't be automatic, and meanings aren't Platonic entities. So would we have to posit a translation "program" to make the appropriate transformations? And if so, where would it come from? In any case, if the communicators are what they purport to be, and so long as the apparently required translation process is possible (which I doubt—see, e.g., Goldberg, 1982), we must concede that something similar to what Stevenson proposes might in fact occur. So perhaps Stevenson has at least specified a process in what we could call "logical space." But we need to consider whether there's any reason to regard Stevenson's proposed process as actual, rather than merely possible. And curiously, Stevenson illustrates the process by citing research on a dissociative phenomenon—that is, a phenomenon we can naturally and fairly easily explain in terms of just one living agent. But that suggests strongly that Stevenson's proposed survivalist explanation is gratuitous.

Stevenson mentions a case of hypnotic age regression reported by Spiegel and Spiegel (Spiegel & Spiegel, 1978). The subject was a twenty-five-year-old man who learned English only after emigrating from Austria at age thirteen. When he was regressed to any age younger than thirteen, he could apparently speak no English and required the hypnotist to communicate through a German-speaking interpreter. However, the subject was still able to respond correctly to some instructions given in English, even though he had been regressed to age ten. Similarly, Orne reports that a subject

> who spoke only German at age six and who was age regressed to that time answered when asked whether he can understand English, "Nein." When this question was rephrased to him 10 times in English, he indicated each time in German that he was unable to comprehend English, explaining in childlike German such details as that his parents speak English in order that he not understand. While professing his inability to comprehend English, he continued responding appropriately in German to the hypnotist's complex English questions. (Orne, 1972, p. 427; see also Orne, 1951, pp. 219 and 222–223)

Contrary to what Stevenson seems to think, these examples pose a problem for the survivalist interpretation of xenoglossy, because they seem to show clearly that the subjects didn't actually regress to a previous stage in their mental life. Instead, their behavior seems obviously to be dissociative and to *presuppose* their knowing both German and English. In fact, the subjects' behavior seems continuous with similar behavior reported frequently throughout the history of hypnosis. Hypnotic suggestion can produce significant alterations in the experience and thought processes of good hypnotic subjects, and often those changes make it difficult for the subjects to comply with apparently simple requests (e.g., pronouncing words containing the letter "r"). Moreover, as researchers in hypnosis and dissociation are well aware, although dissociation can erect perceptual or cognitive barriers, those barriers tend to affect only some aspects or levels of a person's awareness and performance. In fact, researchers know that dissociated systems are never completely independent of one another, no matter how isolated they might appear in some contexts.

Presumably, the subjects just mentioned were doing something similar to what has been reported in cases of negative hallucination. For example, subjects in some recent studies were hypnotized *not* to see the chair in front of them, and good hypnotic subjects behaved differently from those asked merely to simulate hypnosis in the same situations.

When the hypnotized subjects were asked to walk around the room, some walked into the chair and evinced surprise that something touched them, and others avoided contact with the chair by walking or stumbling around it (Orne, 1962, p. 218). When asked to explain their surprise or curious chair-avoidance behavior, the subjects seemed genuinely puzzled and offered transparently lame excuses, frequently described as examples of "trance logic." Similar behavior has been reported in recent studies of hypnotic blindness and visual conversion disorder (a.k.a. hysterical blindness), in which subjects seem to be influenced by objects or information of which they are apparently unaware (Bryant & McConkey, 1989a, 1989b, 1989c; Oakley, 1999). These cases raise a number of interesting issues (see Orne, 1959; 1972). But for now, the crucial point about them is that they are paradigmatic examples of conflicting dissociated systems *within a single subject*. And as such, they *discourage* the sorts of survivalist explanations Stevenson offers for the analogously odd linguistic features of xenoglossy.

In fact, the examples cited by the Spiegels and Orne resemble another famous example of ostensible age regression (Orne, 1951). Orne regressed a subject to age six, and in that state the subject's handwriting changed to the immature style of a young child. Nevertheless, when the experimenter asked the subject to write the sentence "I am conducting an experiment which will assess my psychological capacities," the subject complied exactly, even correctly spelling the polysyllabic words no six-year-old would know. Again, this makes clear sense so long as we assume that the subject is not genuinely regressed, but is drawing on creative capacities perhaps manifested most easily in a hypnotic or dissociated state (see also O'Connell, Shor, & Orne, 1970).

Similar observations apply to the aforementioned peculiarities in communicators' accent and grammar. Stevenson proposes an underlying tension between two linguistic systems: the native language of the medium or subject and that of the communicator. He writes,

> A secondary personality—such as we may call Jensen, Gretchen, and Sharada—who tries to speak his native language, must nevertheless express it through the linguistic apparatus (mental, cerebral, and vocal) of the primary personality. The conflicting pulls of the two different phonemic systems give the impression of a nonnative speaker. (Stevenson, 1984, p. 164)

Now, first of all, even if we accept the reality of survival, I'm not sure why communicators "must" express their native languages through all three of the mental, cerebral, and vocal systems of the host (or why communicators would be equally dependent on each of them). And in fact, Stevenson notes (with an example from the case of Mrs. Leonard) how the tug between aspects of the host and communicator's linguistic systems seems to vary. But if communicators can be more or less free of the host's linguistic system, it's unclear why they can't sometimes be *entirely* free of it, or free enough for the tug to be negligible. In any case, let's grant tentatively that Stevenson is correct and that communicators can't liberate themselves from the mental, cerebral, and vocal systems of the host. The question still remains: are the peculiarities in communicators' accent and grammar most easily viewed as dissociative phenomena?

What Stevenson doesn't mention is the similarity between these linguistic aspects of xenoglossy cases and certain common features of MPD/DID—in particular, a phenomenon often called "co-presence" (Braude, 1995). Co-presence is a condition in which alters share executive control of the body. During periods of co-presence, those alters seem to blend or partially integrate, even if only temporarily, so that it's difficult to decide whether alters *A* and *B* are two distinct centers of consciousness or just one. And multiples themselves seem to experience co-presence as a state of variable blending. In one memorable conversation I had with a multiple whose personalities were vying for executive control of the body, she said to me, "I'm mostly Karen right now." So the tug Stevenson postulates between host and communicator linguistic systems resembles the tug and interference between personality or identity systems in MPD/DID, and the latter often exhibits the varying degrees of blending and interference noted by Stevenson in the Leonard case. As before, we can't rule out Stevenson's explanation if we're taking the survival hypothesis seriously. But also as before, the phenomena in question seem more parsimoniously explainable in terms of relatively common dissociative processes in a single subject.

To sum up, then: although Stevenson's proposed explanations may ultimately turn out to rest on an unacceptable conception of meaning and an incoherent account of translation, that remains to be demonstrated. The proposals can't simply be dismissed out of hand. But because of the many similarities between the phenomena he wants to explain and dissociative phenomena which don't even tempt us to posit the activities of an agent other than the subject, Stevenson's proposals also don't seem particularly attractive. Granted, it usually strengthens an hypothesis to have explanations at hand for the relevant phenomena, and admittedly it's useful to have an idea how a survivalist might handle the peculiar linguistic behavior Stevenson discusses. But in the absence of any other compelling reason to interpret the evidence for xenoglossy along survivalist lines, I think we must conclude that Stevenson's survivalist proposals do little to tilt the scales in that direction. On the contrary, they seem only to reinforce the plausibility of appealing to dissociation and latent creative capacities.

To pursue these issues further, let's now turn to one of the most puzzling cases in the history of parapsychology. This case will force us to take a very hard look at the mysterious and challenging topic of latent capacities.

NOTES

1. Actually, it's difficult to judge from Stevenson's and Akolkar's accounts whether Uttara's interest in F was expressed with the same intensity and insistence she displayed in her behavior toward Dr. Z. In his all too brief discussion of the possibly significant relationship between Uttara and F's father, Bhau, Akolkar suggests that there may not have been much of a difference. He notes that Uttara implored Bhau to intervene in her behalf, and one gets the impression that Uttara was fully occupied emotionally over her relationship with F and her desire to be part of his family.

2. It's unfortunate that Akolkar again omits crucial details when relating this information. Was Uttara having these episodes during her period? Might she have found passages in her reading so arousing that she experienced contractions that promoted serious bleeding? Obviously, these questions must be addressed in order to determine whether Uttara's bleeding was psychosomatic. Akolkar seems to interpret Uttara's menstrual problems generally and some of her other physical afflictions as intimations of an emerging and genuine previous personality (Sharada). He seems not to consider that Uttara's persistent physical problems might have been psychosomatic, or that as a hypnotically gifted individual she might have been expressing her emotional turmoil somatically, as multiples often do.

3. Hughes's study might be somewhat misleading in another respect as well. The multiples surveyed in her analysis seem to have exhibited the now-classic symptoms one finds in cases in North America and Western Europe. One can only wonder, then, what Hughes's results might have been had she included in her study cases of MPD from (say) Brazil, Turkey, Israel, or India, where the symptom language of multiple personality seems to assume culture-specific forms, and where the similarities between MPD and mediumship may be more striking. See, e.g., Berger, Ono, Nakajima, & Suematsu, 1994; Downs, Dahmer, & Battle, 1990; Escobar, 1995; Krippner, 1987; Sar, Yargic, & Tutkun, 1995; Sar *et al.*, 1996; Somer, 1997; Steinberg, 1990; Takahashi, 1990; Tutkun, Yargic, & Sar, 1995; Tutkun *et al.*, 1998; Varma, Bouri, & Wig, 1981; Yargic, Tutkun, & Sar, 1995.

4. It's not altogether clear whether Ducasse endorsed exactly the principle Stevenson attributes to him. Certainly he never states it explicitly. But something very much *like* that principle seems to be implied by his discussion. With this caveat in mind, I'll continue to regard the principle as Ducasse's, if only for the sake of easy reference.

5. Stevenson seems more cautious when he observes that the Modern Language Aptitude Test "predicts...which students will perform well in modern language courses" (Stevenson, 1974b, p. 51). But he incorrectly infers from this that the test predicts whether one can learn a foreign language "more or less easily" (p. 51).

6. Curiously, Stevenson doesn't cite this report in his later opus on xenoglossy (Stevenson, 1984), although it would have been relevant there as well.

7. My views here, as on many other topics, have benefitted from illuminating discussions with Jule Eisenbud.

Chapter 5

The Case of Patience Worth

1. Introduction

In the summer of 1913, a St. Louis housewife named Pearl Curran sat before a ouija board with her mother, Mrs. Pollard, and her good friend, Mrs. Emily G. Hutchings. Emily was fascinated with these explorations. At her urging, she and Pearl had experimented with the ouija board for the past year. However, Pearl was neither intrigued nor impressed. Apparently, her attitude wavered between indifference and antipathy, and nothing in the first year's messages changed her mind. The ostensible communications (purportedly from different persons) were banal and non-evidential.

But on June 22, the letters "p-a-t" were spelled several times, and then the following statement came through the board. "Oh, why let sorrow steel thy heart? Thy bosom is but its foster-mother, the world its cradle and the loving home its grave." Recognizing that this was considerably more poetic and articulate than their usual fare, the three women decided to keep a written record of the event and of any further words from the ouija board. So they designated Mrs. Pollard as note taker, and Pearl and Emily continued to operate the ouija board. On July 2, the board yielded several more messages of similar quality, and after one of the women requested the identity of the communicator, the board responded, "Should one so near be confined to a name? The sun shines alike on the briar and the rose. Do they make question of a name?"

Despite these protestations, on July 8 the board answered the request for a name. It spelled, "Many moons ago I lived. Again I come, Patience Worth my name." The women expressed wonder at this, and the board continued,

> Wait, I would speak with thee. If thou shalt live, then so shall I. I make my bread[1] at thy hearth. Good friends, let us be merrie. The time for work is past. Let the tabby drowse and blink her wisdom to the firelog.

These events launched a series of remarkable communications that lasted for nearly twenty-five years. By the time they ceased in 1937, twenty-nine volumes of recorded communications had been deposited in the Missouri Historical Society in St. Louis (for a total of 4,375 single-spaced pages of material). These included novels, short stories, plays, thousands of poems, witty epigrams and pithy aphorisms, and many clever, penetrating, and often acerbic conversations. The quality of the literature ranged from decent to spectacular, and Patience's compositions were produced with astonishing fluency. With only a handful of exceptions, Patience's literary works emerged apparently without struggle and without undergoing the overt process of correcting and refining demanded even by the most prolific and articulate authors. In fact, Patience could improvise poems, without hesitation, on any topic suggested to her and without any deterioration in the overall quality of her work. She could also interrupt writing at any time (often in mid-sentence) and continue later (sometimes much later) exactly where she had left off.

Before long it became clear that Pearl's presence, but not that of Emily Hutchings, was necessary for the Patience Worth communications (apparently, this led to some friction between the two women and the eventual cooling of their friendship). And it's because the phenomena are, in some sense, productions of Pearl Curran that this case is so important. It challenges us to determine what, exactly, Pearl's role was. And as we'll see, the two most plausible explanations leave many big questions unanswered.

For our purposes, the significance of the Patience Worth communications lies in two central facts. First, although they present the usual trappings of a survival case, the communications aren't even remotely evidential. The personality, "Patience Worth," gave a few details about her alleged earthly life, but despite attempts to track down someone matching the descriptions Patience supplied about herself, there's no evidence that the communicating personality corresponded to any real person. Second, the writings of Patience Worth are unprecedented, both in style and in literary quality. Not only are they dramatically superior to anything Pearl Curran seemed able to produce herself; they also seem to be unique in literary history.

2. Pearl Curran's Background

Pearl was born in Illinois in 1883, the only child of George and Mary Pollard. Her father had been educated at military school, but afterwards he tried unsuccessfully to make a living as an artist. Then, after a series of jobs in Texas with railroads and newspapers, he finally found steady employment with a lead company in Missouri. Mary Pollard once had some ambition to write, but she made no effort to do so after her marriage at eighteen. At that point she focused instead on her musical abilities. Pearl claimed that her mother was talented as a singer, and she also described her as "nervous, keen, ambitious" (Prince, 1927/1964, p. 11).

Pearl tells us about herself in a short autobiographical sketch, and also in answers to questions from W. F. Prince (Prince, 1927/1964). But neither she nor her interlocutor take us very deeply into her psyche. So we must read between the lines and look for inadvertently revealing comments to get a sense of Pearl as a person and to determine how she felt about her family and her life. The surface details are clear enough. Pearl never traveled beyond the Midwest until the Patience Worth communications were under way. She described herself as "impudent" and already bored with school by the age of five or six (p. 12), and by her own admission she continued to be a mediocre student. She found her teachers either dull or detestable, and it appears that her mother pushed her in directions that didn't interest her. Perhaps most tellingly, Pearl writes that during high school she "had become quite a 'show-off'. I hated it but mother desired it" (p. 13). Around that time, Pearl found the stresses in her life to be unbearable, and she writes that at age thirteen, she "broke down...of too much piano, elocution, Delsarte, school and entertainments" (p. 13) and was sent to a Catholic academy for a "rest." When she resumed her education the next year and was put back a grade, she became discouraged and simply dropped out of school. After that, Pearl lived with her parents or with other relatives in various locations in Missouri and Illinois. She earned a little money playing piano, teaching voice, and also addressing envelopes and selling music for some music publishers. And throughout this period she continued her vocal studies as well. When she was twenty-four she married John Curran, a respected land developer.

Pearl's primary interest seemed to be music. She played piano reasonably well and aspired to be a singer. But her interests in literature were minimal, and apparently she had little exposure to poetry, fiction, or general history—much less relatively arcane studies in philology. For example, Pearl thought Dickens wrote *The House of the Seven Gables* (which she said she had heard of but never read), she thought Henry VIII had been beheaded, and she didn't know who Andrew Jackson was. In response to W. F. Prince's question about her early exposure to poetry, Pearl remarked, "When Mr. Curran was engaged to me he gave me 'Thanatopsis', and it was away over my head and he laughed at me and I was ashamed" (p. 16). (This is one of the very few comments in Pearl's autobiographical statements concerning her relationship with her husband.)

Pearl also had little interest in religion or biblical literature or history. In fact, Pearl claimed that she had never even read a complete Bible chapter. Nor were her parents "of a religious turn" (p. 15). According to Pearl, if she asked her father "Is there a God?" he would answer, "My dear, I don't know" (p. 20). Moreover, Pearl claimed that she "was

raised to think spiritualist séances taboo" (p. 15). Interestingly, Pearl
had an uncle who was a spiritualist medium, and at age eighteen she
played piano for a month and a half at his Chicago church. But Pearl
remarked, "I didn't like the crowd that came, and the whole thing was
repulsive to me" (p. 21). From that time until the Patience Worth communications began, Pearl claimed to have no contacts with the world of
spiritualism.

W. F. Prince collected testimony from people who knew Pearl and
her husband well. They support Pearl's contention that she was neither
interested in nor exposed to the sort of literature that most would consider necessary for producing the Patience Worth communications (see
Prince, 1927/1964, pp. 21–30). And Prince's investigation of Pearl's
background seems to have been quite thorough. Not only did he personally solicit testimony from many who had known Pearl and her family;
he also wrote an article entitled "The Riddle of Patience Worth" in the
July 1926 issue of *Scientific American*, in which he made a direct appeal for information that might shed light on the case. Prince said later
that the object of this appeal

> was to provoke some of the half million readers scattered throughout the
> United States to write to me in some such terms as these: "You credulous
> chump, you are grossly deceived. I knew Mrs. Curran __ years ago, and
> used to see her grubbing in the reading room of __ Library, where she was
> probably reading up on history or philology." Or, "She used to write poetry,
> to my knowledge." Or, "She boarded with a professor of English literature
> who had a fad for using archaic words." Or, "She used to say, 'O that I
> could be a famous writer!'" (Prince, 1927/1964, p. 445)

Prince noted that he did receive responses from some readers, but "all
who wrote added weight to [Pearl's] own testimony" (p. 446). He continued,

> It cannot be, in a world so full of people ready to expose imposture and to
> correct mistaken claims, that everybody is under a spell as regards the case
> of Mrs. Curran, so that, there being persons who remember adverse facts,
> not one is willing to report them, even anonymously. (p. 446)

3. The History, Style, and Personality of Patience Worth

The Patience persona seemed reluctant to share details about her alleged corporeal life. In fact, Patience frequently remarked that the only
thing about her that really mattered was contained in her writings and
other utterances. On one occasion, she commented, "Behold, my wares;
herein am I." Nevertheless, Patience occasionally supplied nuggets of
information about herself, and in casual conversation she sometimes
made remarks about her life. Patience claimed that she was born in
England in the seventeenth century, lived and worked there (apparently

in Dorset) until she was an adult, and then migrated to America. Shortly after that, she was allegedly killed in some sort of battle with Indians. Prince nicely summarizes the portrait of Patience that emerges from her casual remarks. He writes,

> We get an absolutely consistent picture of an individual humble career, and a most vivid sense of a distinct personality...We see a small red-headed peasant girl, toiling at the humblest tasks, often chided by her mother and sometimes by the parish minister, a young woman of voluble and witty propensities, fond of finery and not averse to the other sex, considerably curbed in all these inclinations, because of the ideas of the day and the narrowness of the religion, but with a sense of humor which largely sustained her. She loved her mother, though she was "filled o' righteousness and emptied o' mercy"...
>
> According to her intimations she was something of a heretic, and much of her reminiscent humor is at the expense of the church and its minister.[2]
>
> "Well I remember a certain church, with its wee windows and its prim walls, with its sanctity and meekness, with its aloofness and chilling godliness. Well I remember the Sabbath and its quietude of uneasiness, wherein the creaking of the wood was an infernalism, the droning and scuffing of the menfolk's shoes and the rustle of the clothes of the dames and maids, the squeaking of the benches, and the drowsy humming of some busy bee who broke the Sabbath's law. Aye, well I remember the heat that foretold the wrath of God, making the good man [minister] sweat. Aye, and Heaven seemed far, far." (Prince, 1927/1964, pp. 34–35)

The Patience Worth communications reveal a consistent and robust personality, different in many respects from that of Pearl. In fact, from the very beginning the personality of Patience Worth emerged clearly and displayed a distinctive set of traits, opinions, and interests. Patience had a sharp tongue, quick wit, a deep love of nature, a reverence for infancy, and even at her most humorous and acerbic, an underlying moral seriousness and (as Prince put it) a "lofty spirituality." And although she demonstrated a love of both God and wisdom, Patience was highly suspicious and critical of organized religion and formal education. She was contemptuous of the various forms of academic and religious posturing, and she taught (again, as Prince puts it) that "wisdom is derived from sincere contemplation of the things which are simplest and nearest at hand" (p. 36).

But while Patience's personality remained consistent and distinctive, her style of writing varied considerably, ranging from an extremely quaint and simple language—even simpler English than in Chaucer—to one appropriate to the nineteenth century. As the examples given earlier indicate, the language of Patience's first communications wasn't particularly archaic or obscure. According to Patience, that was because she wanted to ensure that her audience understood her. Then, she said, in order to assert her individuality and distinguish her personality from that of Pearl, she adopted a strikingly antiquated linguistic style, liberally sprinkled with words of Anglo-Saxon origin (but from no locale in particular). At those times, Patience could make long speeches in words of one or two syllables (not an easy thing to do; I encourage the reader to try it). Eventually, Patience relied less frequently on her most obsolete vocabulary, apparently convinced that she had achieved her goal. The following comments from Patience explain her communication strategy and also provide a handy sample of her idiosyncratic English.

> When I first singed, I stripped the burr frae my tongue, 'nough for to sing, that I might be known in the tongue o' them that I singed unto. I taked me this and that, and created o' it a petticoat o' words—mine ain—not the tongue o' him o' this day or that. Sirrah, I had na' flesh, and made me flesh-cunnin' 'nough for to stand the blade o' inquiry. For na' man may create such an one, and he who kens it may ne'er be tricked.
> Look ye into the words o' me. Ye shall find whits o' this and that ta'en from here and there—yet foundationed upon the salt which flavors it o' my ain land. (Prince, 1927/1964, pp. 342–343)

The reliance on Anglo-Saxon root words characterized even her more up-to-date utterances, imparting to all of them an unusual, and to many a quite beautiful, rhythmic, and musical character.

The distinguished and influential literary critic William Marion Reedy made a careful study of the Patience Worth scripts, and he spent a great deal of time with Pearl at the ouija board. Like many others, he was captivated by the Patience Worth personality that emerged consistently in the poetry, fiction, and conversation transmitted through Pearl Curran. And, like others, he considered the literature to be first rate, irrespective of its origin. Indeed, to this day many still regard the Patience Worth writings as undoubtedly the finest literature and the most interesting material ever to be produced in an ostensibly mediumistic context. Fortunately, we needn't plunge into the murky waters of literary criticism. As we'll see, what matters is that Patience Worth's poems, novels, and conversations betray an intelligence and psychological style profoundly different from that of Pearl, and also abilities well beyond those Pearl seemed to possess.

Reedy was also intrigued by Patience's distinctive lexicon. He consulted an authority on the English language, who studied the case thoroughly, and who confirmed that

> the words are not of any given period, nor are they all from one early English locality. They are from almost all the counties and shires and many of them peculiar locutions to those subdivisions of England. They are always used in their exact original sense. The language, as a whole, is of such a consistency of word-texture as no mere student could use through hundreds and hundreds of thousands of words without an occasional break into the speech of today...not the most practiced writer of the speech of any special period, except one's very own period, can keep out of his writings the words in which he does his ordinary thinking. (Litvag, 1972, p. 58)

Eventually, Pearl Curran was able to abandon the ouija board and continue to transmit Patience's words through a kind of automatic speech. At first, she uttered Patience's communications letter by letter, but after a few years she saw the complete words in her mind's eye. Moreover, in many or most cases, Patience's communications were apparently accompanied by vivid inner imagery. Pearl described the process as follows. "When the poems come, there also appear before my eyes images of each successive symbol, as the words are given me. If the stars are mentioned, I see them in the sky. If heights or deeps or wide spaces are mentioned, I get positively frightening sweeps of space" (Prince, 1927/1964, p. 394).

If Pearl was in trance during the Patience Worth communications, it was very light. It would probably be more accurate to say that she experienced a state of "abstraction," as Cory put it, or perhaps distraction (Cory, 1919, p. 401; Prince, 1927/1964, p. 431). Pearl claimed that while she was spelling, she was keenly (and perhaps unusually) aware of her bodily sensations and the reactions of those around her, and she could think about such things as what she would be eating later in the day. Moreover, Pearl noted that "while I am writing there seems to be no definite place where my consciousness ceases, and that of Patience comes in" (Prince, 1927/1964, p. 398).

4. Writing Samples

The literature produced by Patience Worth received very favorable, and sometimes lavishly complimentary, reviews. But apparently because of the works' unusual origin, they were dismissed by many and eventually forgotten altogether. To help the reader appreciate the import of this case, I offer the following selections from Patience's oeuvre. They illustrate the diversity and peculiarity of her linguistic styles, and also the beauty, humor, and depth of her expression. I also take the liberty of quoting at length, because the theoretical difficulties posed here, which concern the quality of the material and the virtuosity of its production, can be savored no other way.

First, however, we should keep in mind that ouija boards have no provisions for indicating capitalization, punctuation, or parsing into lines, stanzas, and paragraphs. Therefore, all the published and unpublished versions of Patience's communications represent a joint creative venture, involving the source (whatever or whoever it was) of the words and the editor who parses and punctuates them. And because there are no strict or clear guidelines to follow in these cases, every rendering of Patience's words is inevitably tentative and presumably possible to improve. I've often felt dissatisfied with the way Patience's writings have been presented, and for that reason I reparsed and published some of her poems in a noted literary publication (Braude, 1980). So I encourage readers likewise to consider alternative parsings and punctuation. And in case words of encouragement are needed, consider the following lines from Patience. They seem to address precisely this issue.

> I am molten silver, running.
> Let man catch me within his cup.
> Let him proceed upon his labor,
> Smithing upon me.
> Let him with cunning smite my substance.
> Let him at his dream,
> Lending my stuff unto its creation.
> It shall be no less me.

From conversations:

(1) "Nay, 'tis not the put o' me, the word hereon. 'Tis the put o' me at see o' her. I put athin the see o' her, aye and 'tis the see o' ye that be afulled o' the put o' me, and yet a put thou knowest not." [In part, at least, this seems to mean that when Patience spells out words on the ouija board, it's not by controlling Pearl's hands. Rather, she communicates directly with Pearl's mind or inner vision,[3] and then Pearl spells out what she has "seen."]

(2) [Pearl commented that she deserved some credit for serving as the instrument of Patience's writing. Patience replies,] "So doth the piggie who scratcheth upon an oak deem his fleas the falling acorn's cause. The soap-kettle needeth not a shape. I cut my soap to fancy."

(3) Mrs. P.: The world is crying for proofs of immortality.
P.W.: To prove a fact, needst thou a book of words, when e'en the sparrow's chirp telleth thee more?
   A tale unfolded by the Bishops' drudge may hold the meat for thousands, while dust and web are strong on his Eminence. The road to higher plains leadeth not along the steeple.
   Drop ye a coin and expect the gods to smile? Chant ye a creed and wordy prayer, reeking with juice squeezed from thy smug fat store of self-love, expecting a favor from the God who but enjoys the show?

From *Telka*:

Chapter 4 opens:
   A-drip, and drops a-slide 'pon stone walls to pool aneath. A-chill the moon air and mist doth hang 'bout hill like white smock 'bout the shoulders of a wench. Smudge-scant upon the air, and brown fat reeking from crack o' door. A grunt, a shuffle, and door doth ope, and Telka wriggleth bare toes in pool-drip.

Chapter 5 begins:
   And hours a-drag, and drip did trickle, and maid a-rosied did baste, and sire a-drowse, 'till moon did timid seek its way through teasing cloud. Through long night hours she shuttleth 'twixt mist a-hang and clear, 'till it doth seem that sky be wove o' gold at morn.
   The morn's star hangeth 'pon a sun's beam and showeth white its light.

Soft-wrapped, the hills do lie a-cradled in a veil o' mist. The herds aroused do patter 'pon the sod like to a summer's rain, and tree tops wallow in morn's sweet breeze. But threaded smoke doth tell o' life athin the cot.

From *The Sorry Tale*:

The morn spread forth, the golden tresses of the sun, and lo, a star still rested upon a cloud bar. And Jerusalem slept. The temples stood whited, and the market's place shewed emptied. Upon the temple's pool the morn-sky shewed, and doves bathed within the waters at its edge.

Beside the market's way the camels lay, sunk upon their folded legs, and chewed, their mouths slipping o'er the straw, and tongues thrust forth to pluck up more for chewing. The hides shewed like unto a beggar's skull, hair fallen o'er sores.

The day had waked the tribes, and narrowed streets shewed bearded men, and asses, packed. The temple priests stood forth upon the stoned steps and blew upon the shell that tribesmen come. From out the pillared place the smoke of incense curled, and within the stone made echo of the chants and sandals-fall of foot.

And tribes sought out the place, and lo, like unto ants they swarmed up and o'er the steps, to sit and make wisdom of the wording of the priests.

And merchants spread forth their wares upon the temple steps that they who came from out should see. Bent and shrunk like unto the skins of ox, they sat and whined, hands spread forth o'er the wares. Filthed hands bore fruits, and faces dead looked out from swathing of cloth; and they whined, and shewed sores and twisted limbs.

Beside the pool stooped women who put therein their hands and cast drops upon withered greens. One, dark and black-locked, held between her knees a youth of young years and searched within his locks for abominations, but stopping that she eat from off a fruit that lay beside. Within the market's place the merchants brought forth cloths and hung, spread wide o'er the bins, and shewed of breads and fishes and jewels and cloths and skins. And made word unto one another of the wares.

A beggar squatted at the road's skirt plucking at his scabs, and grinned unto the passers through his whines. (Worth, 1917, p. 109)

From *Hope Trueblood*:[4]

"The man should be held up before the people. He is clothed in the garb of the hypocrite." I sucked the plum stone and wondered what a hypocrite was and if they were upon the road at night. "Sally Trueblood's brat!" I looked to the sampler and read slowly, "God is Love." And I wondered what a brat was.

Mr. Passwater seemed not to relish his port, and Miss Patricia sipped hers gingerly. I sneezed and Miss Patricia seemed not to hear me, but continued, "'Tis shameful."

I got from off the hassock and tiptoed over to the castle beneath the glass and stood wrapt. Beside it lay a book of prayer. It was thin and flat and black, and I knew it was Miss Patricia's. From this I went up to the what-all, and the lights played o'er it and I stood before it filled with wonder. Upon the third shelf was a china dog, with a babe upon its back. Oh, to touch this! I turned stealthily and looked to Miss Patricia. She did not see. I reached forth one hand and tip-toed and it was mine. I hugged it close to make sure and the what-all shook and rattled. Miss Patricia was upon her feet in an instant and pounced upon me, taking me within her grasp so suddenly that I let fall the china dog. Miss Patricia gasped:

"A thief! My dear brother William's pet! Oh, that the earth should be so sinful! Rueben Passwater, take this brat out of this house! Shut her out!"

And Miss Patricia shook me. I whimpered, and stooped to pick up the dog, tenderly, leaving my tears to fall upon it, and offered it to her hand sniffing. Miss Patricia took it and placed it upon the third shelf where it had stood and I backed away staring, my fingers within my mouth and the tears coursing down my cheeks. I knew what a thief was. Miss Patricia stared at me and looked at my feet, crying out:

"Why does your worthless mother leave you free in night's hour to visit Christian homes? Your feet are upon the ground. Where are your better shoes?"

"I haven't none, thanks. She has promised 'em at Mayin'."

This seemed to send Miss Patricia into a storm, for she rocked and shrieked and beat her bosom, crying out that the tongues of the village were lashes and that no Christian might dwell among them, stopping only to shout: "Take her away! Take her away!"

Mr. Passwater stooped slowly and took up a shoe and put it on, then the other just as slowly. He arose and buttoned his vest, sighed, went for his greatcoat and made a sign for me to follow. We went out of a narrow hallway that smelled of mutton. Mr. Passwater opened the latch and we stepped into the night. I followed him, frightened, and he did not speak. I did not seem to fear Mr. Passwater, but the dark. He seemed silent, and, as I write, I see his dark form stooped and hear him step heavily and my light footfall following, pattering. (Worth, 1918, pp. 8–10)

Poems

THE SOUNDS UNHEARD BY MAN

I have heard the moon's beams sweeping the waters,
Making a sound like threads of silver, wept upon.
I have heard the scratch of the pulsing stars,
And the purring sound of the slow moon as she rolled across the night.
I have heard the shadows slapping the waters,
And the licking sound of the wave's edge as it sinks into the sand upon the shore.

I have heard the sunlight as it pierced the gloom with a golden bar
Which whirred in a voice of myriad colors.
I have heard the sound which lay between the atoms which danced in the golden bar.
I have heard the sound of the leaves reclining upon their cushions of air,
And the swish of the willow-tassels as the wind whistled upon them,
And the sharp sound which the crawling mites proclaim upon the grasses' blades,
And the multitudes of sounds which lie at the root of things.
Oh, I have heard the song of resurrection which each seed makes as it spurts.

I have heard the sound of the night's first shadow when it intermingles
   with the day,
And the rushing sound of Morning's wings as she flies o'er the Eastern
   gateway.

All of these have I heard.
Yet man hath not an ear for them.
Behold, the miracle He hath writ within me,
Letting the chord of Imagination strum!

THE SOUNDS OF MEN

I have heard the music men make,
Which is discord proclaimed through egotry.
I have heard the churning of water by man's cunning,
And the shrieking of throttles which man addeth unto the day's symphony.
I have heard the pound of implements and the clatter of blades.
I have heard the crushing blasts of destruction.
I have heard old men laugh,
And their laughs were rusted as old vessels in which brine were kept.
I have heard women chatter like crows o'er carrion
And laugh as a magpie o'er a worm.

I have beheld all of these and heard them.
Men have ears for such.
And the mystery of man is that he should present them and cry,
"Sing! Sing, poet! Sing!"

THE NOTE OF BRASS

In that first pale hour
Still blushing from the night's embrace,
When the moon dips o'er the earth's rim
And the sun come slowly forth;
When the lark opeth its throat
And singing, climbs the still starry sky;
And the brook slips through the dew-wet field,
Whispering cool words, little calm troths;
And the reeds bend low in the marsh;
And the trees are heavy-swaying;
And the sweet scent of the damp grain floats from the valley;
At this holy instant I have oft heard
An ass bray.

THE DECEIVER

I know you, you shamster.
I saw you smirking, grinning,
Nodding through the day,
And I knew you lied.
With mincing steps you gaited before men,
Shouting of your valor.
Yet you, you idiot,

I knew you were lying.
And your hands shook
And your knees were shaking.

I know you, you shamster.
I heard you honeying your words,
Licking your lips and smacking o'er them,
Twiddling your thumbs in ecstasy
Over your latest wit.

I know you, you shamster.
You are the me the world knows.

CHILD'S PRAYER

I, Thy child forever, play
About Thy knees this close of day;
Within Thy arms I now shall creep,
And learn Thy wisdom while I sleep.
Amen.

PATIENCE WORTH

A phantom? Weel enough,
Prove thyself to me!
I say, behold, here I be,
Buskins, kirtle, cap and pettyskirts,
And much tongue!
Weel, what hast thou to prove thee?

WHO SAID THAT LOVE WAS FIRE?

Who said that love was fire?
I know that love is ash.
It is the thing which remains
When the fire is spent,
The holy essence of experience.

FATHER, IS THIS THY WILL?

Father, is this Thy will?
God, the din!
Blood, thick-crusted, still living,
I saw it fall unto the dust.
Hunger, gnawing like a wolf
Whose teeth do whet upon my vitals,
Crouching before me—
A hideous thing, whose hands show dripping,
And whose tongue doth feed upon the new-sprung streams,
Licking life from living things!

Father, is this Thy will?
Damn the discord garrulously belched forth from burning throats!
Hell is within the eyes that look across the wastes!

Hell crawls upon the earth, dragging her robe of fire,
Sprinkled of scarlet, its hem;
And the sound it makes upon its trailing way
Is like the shriek of womankind in labor!

Aphorisms

The road to higher plains leadeth not along the steeple. [This is reminiscent of the more familiar "So near to church, so far from God."]

To catch a flea needs be a dog? [This was Patience's response to the charge that because she had not been Catholic, she couldn't have written a metaphor in which the rosary was mentioned.]

No man is wearied sorer than he who is weary of himself.

Resolve is a lazy workman.

No man whose belly is soured thinketh sweet.

When a fool becomes wise he falls silent.

Jealousy is the blade that slays love.

He who lacketh the power to rage, damneth silently and rotteth his own heart.

Have faith in men but keep thine eye slitted. [Compare to "Trust, but not too much."]

Stunts of Composition

Part of the mystery of the Patience Worth case stems from the intellectual and literary merit of Patience's productions. We need to explain how outstanding literature and penetrating, scintillating conversation could emerge spontaneously in a person apparently lacking the requisite training, interest, and general background, and in the absence of prior indications of even similar creative abilities. The mystery deepens, however, when we examine the virtuosic and possibly unprecedented compositional feats Patience was able to perform on demand. These go beyond the already impressive ability to improvise poems on whatever topics her sitters proposed, and they may reveal a level or type of creativity never before recorded. They also go beyond the astonishing mnemonic ability to continue work on a novel or long poem which Patience had interrupted several days before, sometimes in mid-sentence.

Some of the challenges presented to Pearl/Patience resemble others noted in the literature on automatic writing—in particular, the simultaneous carrying out of more than one task (see Braude, 1995, and Gauld, 1992). However, it's probable that the tasks requested of Pearl/Patience demand a higher level of creativity than those traditionally performed by even the best automatists. For example, on May 6, 1920, W. F. Prince asked Patience to dictate a poem to John Curran while Pearl simultaneously wrote a letter to a friend. Before beginning,

Patience said, "I shall set a wee whit o' a singin' while she sets the ban-
nock."

The poem and letter are as follows:

WILL O' THE WISP
Oh you marshlight, flashing across the marshes, beckoning!
Is thy light that I see a beacon to tomorrow?
Give me a sign, oh you banshee! Give me a sign!
Make tomorrow's question marked against the sky
Fitfully, as thy flash, oh you marshlight flashing.
Then shall I be more accustomed to the questioning that I live.

Oh you marshlight, fitful as the hours!
If I lose you or stray, then I shall be tonight
In no worse plight than I shall be in tomorrow.
For my hope is but a shuttling fancy,
And I, following then, but learn the path unto tomorrow.

Beacon me then, make me a sign of questioning.
Blindly I follow, wishing, seeing thee shuttling,
As I, in despair, follow.
Look, I am blind, stumbling in the fog.
I am following, with persistence, a phantom.

This is no less than I do through the day's hours,
For the phantom, Hope, is but a swinging Will-o'-the-wisp
Which fades and reappears, spelling my undoing.

Dear Dotsie:
  I am writing you while I write a poem. It is a new trick. Do you like it?
See here honey, my hands are full! I don't like it, honey. It's like baking
bread and stirring soup! I am sick of the job. I wish you were here and that
we could go over this together. This is a mess of a letter, honey bug. I'm
nuts! This is some chase! Slinging slang and purring poetry! Jack is doing
his best in this Marathon. This is fine business and I'm up against it.
  "Finis" honey, and I call it going some!
                                        Pearl

On several occasions, Patience accepted the challenge of composing,
and alternating passages between, works in different styles. For example, on May 19, 1919, Patience produced a literary stew in which she
wrote about 200 words of the novel *Merry Tale*, then wrote a portion of
another story, *Samuel Wheaton*, and then began a poem which she interrupted with passages from the *Merry Tale*. And on February 18,
1926, she accepted a challenge from W. F. Prince to switch between
two literary tasks. First, Patience was to produce a dialogue, in her characteristic archaic dialect, between a lout and a wench at a fair. Then
she was to intersperse passages of the dialogue with the lines of a poem,
to be written on The Folly of Atheism. About eight seconds passed before dictation began, and it continued without interruption as quickly as
it could be written down. The two compositions were produced in the

following sequence.

Ha'e ye seen the mummers settin' up a puppet show, athin the fieldin'?
Nae.

> Who doubts his God is but a lout;
> Who piths his wisdom with egotry
> Hath lost his mark.

Aye, I see'd 'em fetchin' past, and buyed o' a ribbon and a new latchet, and
a shoon-bucklin and tasseled thongs.

> To doubt is but to cast thee as a stone
> Unto the very heart of God.

Aye, and I fetched me a whistle; and heared the doings of the village—that
Mark, the smithy, haed a new wench; And she be heft.

Aye, a wide tale. I heared it, but heeded it nae. I been feastin' 'pon the new
thong.

> Who doubts his God
> Hath but announced his own weak limitation;
> Hath tied his hand and fettered of his foot.

Weel, 'gad! Did ye see the dominie wi' his new breeks, and a sabba' shirt?
Weel, can ye heed it, and him at the fair?
A wide tale, eh?

> To doubt thy God
> Is but to stop the everlasting flow of mercy;
> To die of thirst and lose thee in the chaos of thyself.

The day before, Prince had challenged Patience with an even more
daunting task. He asked Patience to write lines beginning with each of
the letters of the alphabet, except X, in order. This, too, was produced
as quickly as it could be taken down in shorthand.

> A task is
> Before me.
> Can I, O God, perform it?
> Dole me patience
> Enough that I be sustained,
> For I am indeed in need of strength.
> Give me, O God, thy grace.
> Hear my suppliance;
> I am a beggar for a crumb;
> Justly deal in mercy;
> Keep me within the pale of judgment.
> Leave me wit, that I may perform the duty;
> Make the task perfect,
> Neither constrained nor o'er done.
> O beloved God, keep tryst with me;
> Prithee give ear unto my prayer.
> Quiet the turbulence of my heart.
> Righteously shall I endeavor,
> Steeling me against the tongue of irony,
> That I suffer not upon the judgment of this.
> Upon me distil thine aid;

Vouchsafe thy succor.
Wound not with thine indifference,
Yea, this thy servant upon the path of folly,
Zealously endeavoring that she follow a fool.

5. The Theoretical Challenge

As we reflect on the significance of this case, we should remember that
it offers no real *evidence* for the existence of a person corresponding to
the Patience Worth persona. Since the case began, investigators have
tried unsuccessfully to locate a real Patience. And today, despite the
availability of extensive computerized records and the very able and generous assistance of Donald West and Alan Gauld in the United Kingdom., the evidential value of the case remains the same. West reports "I
have found only one entry of the name Patience Worth among the many
thousands of English Parish Register records contained in the Mormon's collection available on microfiche in Cambridge" (personal communication). That individual was married to a James Symonds on September 11, 1698, at Paignton, Devon. Gauld examined the *Passenger
and Immigration Lists Index* (1982) with two supplements (1982-85 and
1986-90). But he found neither a Patience Worth nor a Patience Symonds (or, for that matter, Symons, Simmonds, Simons, Simonds, or
any other variation he could think of). I conducted a computer search at
one of the Mormon historical centers in the United States, looking both
for a Patience Symonds (and its variations) and a Patience Worth (with
variations such as Werth and Wirth). I found a record of a Patience Symonds in New England, from approximately the right period. But Symonds was her maiden name, and her parents were also New England-
ers. The name "Patience Worth" came up a number of times in my
search, from the early and mid-1700s in various parts of New England,
but again the parents were from New England as well. At any rate, it
seems that the name is common enough for it to have been subconsciously or psychically singled out by Pearl Curran.

With all this in mind, the Patience Worth case is remarkable and
important to this inquiry for several related reasons.

(1) The Patience Worth phenomena began suddenly in a thirty-one
year-old woman, and the evidence is overwhelming that Pearl's previous
behavior never suggested that she possessed the intellectual, mnemonic,
and creative powers of Patience Worth. Nor had she ever expressed an
interest in literature, the Bible, or arcane areas of linguistic and historical research. Nor had she associated with scholars or others particularly
interested in those subjects.

(2) Naturally, it takes time for the complex patterns, dispositions,
and idiosyncracies of a personality to manifest in behavior. But whereas
personalities typically *develop gradually* over extended periods of time,

the robust and talented persona of Patience Worth apparently emerged fully formed from the beginning. Patience's humor, rich imagination, characteristic wisdom, and perspectives on life were apparent from the outset, and even more important, so were her creative abilities. For example, although it's very difficult (if not impossible) for most people to compose a good, pithy aphorism, some of Patience's most memorable aphorisms were produced in the earliest sittings. Furthermore, Patience's ability to write in different literary forms and styles underwent no detectable period of development. From the start, she seemed able to write whatever she wanted, in any style she chose (and on any subject suggested), as soon as she attempted it. W. F. Prince remarked that

> only in one respect was there the appearance of *acquiring* facility and that was in the matter of spelling out the words; and if Patience Worth is what she claims to be, that was because *Mrs. Curran* had *to get used* to the process. (Prince, 1927/1964, p. 488)

(3) The Patience Worth scripts reveal an extensive knowledge of obsolete, archaic, and dialectical locutions, some probably never used in the United States. Thouless claimed that some of those words "have only been tracked down by scholars *after* they had appeared in the Patience Worth scripts" (Thouless, 1959, p. 142). But I'm not sure what his evidence is for that claim. Prince (and others) claimed only that Patience used some very rare words that display a philological expertise greatly incommensurate with Pearl's background. And Prince indicated that *he* had some difficulty tracking some of them down. Actually, that's impressive enough; Prince's command and knowledge of English (old and new) was considerable. We also know that experts in English dialects were occasionally consulted for their opinions regarding the scripts. So it seems clear that many of Patience's locutions were unfamiliar even to well-educated readers. But I can't verify that Patience used words known to *no* scholars at the time the scripts were written, and only then tracked down (which is what Thouless seems to say). Still, it's probably fair to say that Patience used words which, at best, were known only to relatively few, and that it took a fair amount of digging to confirm correspondences between Patience's dialect and what was probably spoken in the area of Dorset around the time Patience claimed to live.

Moreover, Patience's writing revealed enough historical and geographical knowledge to provide convincing background to her works. For example, it was sufficient to persuade English readers that the Victorian novel *Hope Trueblood* was written by a native and to make *The Sorry Tale* a historically credible (although not infallible) depiction of biblical times. Ordinarily, the knowledge needed to accomplish this requires years of study, and there's no reason to think that Pearl Curran ever had either the interest in or the requisite exposure to the subjects.

(4) The Patience Worth scripts illustrate special, and possibly unprecedented, creative and intellectual capacities. Pearl/Patience had the

> [a]bility to compose poetry, or long and complex narratives, with perfect
> continuity and ordered development, (a) by a stream of letters issuing with
> lightning rapidity from the lips, (b) in the presence of groups of people, (c)
> paying attention at the same time to a vivid visual accompaniment, (d)
> stopping with ease to describe the imagery, to converse on relevant or irrel-
> evant matters, or to answer the telephone or the doorbell, and to resume
> without breaking the connection, (e) and thus to compose, on one occa-
> sion, about 5,000 words, within three hours, on a difficult and dramatic
> part of the narrative, (f) laying the story aside and sometimes lending it out
> of the house, and resuming without difficulty, whether two days or two
> weeks later. All this involves phenomenal memory, phenomenal speed, and
> phenomenal complexity of mental operations. Also ability to pass at will
> from a style which is ninety per cent Anglo-Saxon...to a style as different
> and as modern as that of *Lorna Doone* or *Jane Eyre*. Also the ability to com-
> pose in the presence of an audience in almost instant response to subjects
> given her, with no declension in average quality, and also, in response to
> chance remarks to fling off aphorisms of unsurpassed quality, sounding as
> though derived from the lore of ages. And also ability to perform a variety
> of intellectual stunts impossible to at least most people, such as the inter-
> mingling of two compositions on two widely different subjects given her,
> and in widely different styles. (Prince, 1927/1964, pp. 487–488)

One feature of the case deserving special mention is Patience's ability to compose both poetry and fiction without need of revision. I don't
think there are even five instances in the entire history of the case in
which Patience demonstrated any compositional hesitancy or back-
tracked to make corrections. (The most conspicuous instance of literary
uncertainty was her apparent struggle to compose a brief and apparently
simple poem: the Child's Prayer, reproduced above.) This facility may
be most remarkable in connection with Patience's longest works, *The
Sorry Tale* and *Hope Trueblood*, novels of more than 630 and 360 pages
(respectively). One needn't be a veteran of the publishing business to
recognize how astonishing it is to produce finished works of such length
without amendment or alteration. Nevertheless, it's worth noting that
after forty years in publishing, William Targ, former editor in chief of
G.P. Putnam & Sons, remarked, "There's no such thing as a publishable
first draft."[5]

Notice, moreover, that this ability seems no less remarkable if we
suppose that most of the composition *and corrections* were made subconsciously, in a dissociated part of Pearl's mind. In that case we'd have
to suppose that Pearl possessed the ability to write and revise intricate
and lengthy works without the visual aid most authors receive from seeing their work before them. And of course Pearl would also have needed
an amazing (though perhaps not unprecedented) ability to remember
what she was doing, so that she could produce several thousand words

of finished product in a single session, and then tie together a series of such sessions into a long novel. It seems that, no matter what the underlying process might have been, Pearl/Patience's literary facility has no parallel in literary history.

6. Non-Survivalist Conjectures

So how are we to account for this complex constellation of traits and abilities? Since the Patience Worth communications offer no real evidence of survival, let's begin by considering the merits of non-survivalist explanations.

Some might think that Patience represents an improvisational ability that many people possess, but which ordinarily requires a certain amount of courage, and also the support of an accepting and nurturing environment, in order to emerge and develop. W. F. Prince considered that suggestion. He noted that many people may have largely undeveloped improvisational ability. He also granted the possibility that at one time people often extemporized verse for informal gatherings, and that because this is no longer a common activity, we're now less accustomed to exercising that skill and less comfortable attempting it. Nevertheless (he noted), it's one thing to improvise free verse, and another to do it to a degree that would attract the attention and praise of literary experts. Even if we grant that many can do the former, it's unlikely that more than a few have ever been able to do the latter. So even if Patience Worth is a creative *tour de force* of Pearl Curran, it's unlikely that Patience was produced by nothing more extraordinary than our relatively mundane and widespread improvisational capacities. And (I would add) to ad-lib poetry and compose fiction without the need of revision, and to perform the virtuosic stunts of composition Patience accomplished so frequently and so readily, is (arguably) an ability of a higher—or at least a different—order still.

Prince also considered whether Patience's literary ability was a (possibly latent) type of facility which many people might possess, but which might only be fostered or revealed in dissociative or other altered or highly unusual states. He wrote,

> I have seen hundreds of automatic, dreamed and "inspirational" compositions, and some of them seem to indicate sporadic transcendence of normal and conscious ability. But the rule is that such compositions, whether of unliterary and normally ungifted persons or literary and normally gifted ones, transcend their usual output by about the same ratio. That is, *sometimes* persons of the former class can automatically or semi-automatically do a little better than they can by conscious effort, and *sometimes* persons of the latter class can do a little better than *they* can by conscious effort. It was Coleridge, a man of manifested poetic genius, a voluminous reader and a scholar, who dreamed out "Kubla Khan." It was Stephen Crane, a man of

marked literary ability, out of whom a sheaf of poems "boiled" without effort, surpassing his average excellence. But neither these nor any other literary men of whom I have heard was able to depend upon, and to command such a method habitually, as does Mrs. Curran. (Prince, 1927/1964, p. 473)

Prince's observations are appropriate and important. But contrary to what some might think, they don't show that Patience's literary ability was something other than a latent capacity of Pearl (in particular, something that must be attributed to a discarnate being). And indeed, it would be a mistake to argue that because all previously known cases of exceptionally good automatic or inspirational writing have been relatively infrequent or sporadic, Patience's/Pearl's consistently excellent productions are *not* examples of automatic writing. After all, Pearl's compositional gift might simply have been the first and only instance of a rare talent.

Now Prince never made that error (although he came perilously close to it at times[6]). Most of the time he merely seemed uncertain how to classify the mind and capabilities of Patience Worth, and he suggested that it might be a mistake to put it into any conventional category. According to Prince, the mind presented by Patience Worth is so novel and impressive in its range and virtuosity that we have no idea what its limits (and presumably its origin) might be (see, e.g., Prince, 1927/1964, pp. 458–459).

Of course, that shouldn't deter us from healthy speculation. And one of the first issues to confront is the apparent disparity between Pearl's demonstrated abilities and those of Patience. Does that suggest that Patience's skills must be ascribed to an intelligence other than Pearl? Presumably not. I've already noted that savants exhibit striking discrepancies between skills, even within the same domain of abilities. But now we should take a closer look.

The curious limitations or boundaries of a savant's skills are of two sorts. First, savants may be profoundly dysfunctional except for their musical, artistic, mathematical, or mnemonic abilities. One well-known savant suffers from cerebral palsy, but his almost constant spasticity disappears when he plays the piano. Another savant can read or write nothing except his name and is just barely able to care for himself, but he can repair virtually any mechanical device presented to him. Others are similarly or more severely handicapped, yet they draw, paint, or sculpt works of considerable sophistication and beauty. The second limitation found in savants exists within their special areas of expertise. For example, calendar calculators tend to be accurate only within specific ranges of years, and those ranges differ from one individual to another. And although calculators might be able to perform rapid and complex operations concerning dates or remember extremely long numbers, they might be unable to do simple addition or change a dollar bill. The famous calculating twins, George and Charles, amused themselves by exchanging 20-digit prime numbers, and they could factor any number presented to them; but they could not count to 30 (Sacks, 1985). Another savant could rapidly solve complex algebraic problems in his head, but he seemed unable to comprehend even simple principles of geometry (Treffert, 1989).

Of course, Pearl had none of the deficits of a savant. In fact, she seemed not only normal but also quite intelligent. Prince commented, "her intelligence is above the average, and in ordinary conversation she shines more by virtue of that intelligence than many who have received a greater education" (Prince, 1927/1964, pp. 492–493n). But it turns out that the surprising disparity of abilities noted with savants occurs also among the exceptionally gifted. For instance, in Baumgarten's study of nine child prodigies (Baumgarten, 1930), she found that

> violinists and pianists demonstrated poor hand coordination in bending wire, drawing, and folding and cutting—though one girl violinist had a talent for drawing. Additionally, a 6-year-old boy showing difficulty in making a circle out of two or three sections or a pentagon from two sections was, at the same time, extraordinarily good at map drawing. (Morelock & Feldman, 1991, p. 353)

Moreover, various converging lines of research show that "giftedness, rather than being a generalized endowment [i.e., extending to all or most aspects of cognitive development], is *domain-specific*" (Morelock & Feldman, 1991, p. 354, italics in original). But in that case, it would be a mistake to infer that Pearl couldn't possess Patience's literary gifts simply because she failed to demonstrate talent in other areas.

This isn't the only intriguing similarity between Pearl's history and the life-profile emerging from research into exceptionally intelligent and gifted people. Morelock and Feldman note how highly gifted children "may fail to exhibit the interest and enthusiasm others expect of gifted children" (Morelock & Feldman, 1991, p. 351). That seems clearly to have been the case with Pearl. In fact, Pearl also exhibited a related characteristic of the gifted child: namely, troubles at school. As Pearl admitted, from a very early age she found school boring and her teachers uninteresting. That, too, often happens with prodigiously bright children whose education is geared toward those of only average intelligence (and whose teachers, needless to say, may likewise be distressingly ordinary and uninspiring). Perhaps Pearl's teenage breakdown reflected, among other things, the stress of trying to make herself far more ordinary and conventional than she really was. Morelock and Feldman also observe an important tension in the life of extraordinarily gifted children: between (on the one hand) developing and expressing one's gifts and (on the other) establishing peer relationships. They note that in some cases the former yields to the latter. It wouldn't be surprising if

something of the sort happened to Pearl. Perhaps the pressure to conform and Pearl's desire to be accepted outweighed the development of
her intellectual and creative gifts.

Admittedly, these speculations are highly conjectural. I offer them
merely to illustrate that Pearl's life fit certain patterns noted in the histories of the exceptionally gifted. Obviously, if more details about Pearl's
life were available, it would be easier to determine whether the similarities are only superficial.

But why did Pearl give no signs of Patience's literary and intellectual
gifts until she was an adult? According to Prince, "it is in the nature of
genius to give signs of itself, as it is in the nature of an apple tree to
bear scented blossoms" (Prince, 1927/1964, p. 499). More specifically,
he wrote that "poetical genius...begins to show signs at an early age,"
and "it is the first instinct of a poet to write" (p. 496). But Prince offered no evidence to support those assertions, and in fact the evidence
may count against them.

Still, we can understand Prince's concern. There seems to be little
doubt that "marked talent during the childhood years is fairly commonplace among [both] mathematicians...[and] musicians" (Walters &
Gardner, 1986, p. 316). And interestingly, even the exceptions to this
rule differ significantly from the Patience Worth case. For example, Jo-
seph Haydn didn't exhibit anything like the astonishing precocity of Mozart or Mendelssohn. He was never a virtuoso instrumentalist, and his
skill as a composer seems to have developed gradually and partly as the
result of much labor. But unlike Pearl Curran, Haydn demonstrated an
early affinity for his art and an "unusual musical aptitude" (Schonberg,
1970, p. 62).

The problem with Prince's assertion about poetical genius is this.
There have, of course, been many great poets. But as far as I can determine, there have been no prodigies in poetry—at least nothing on the
order of musical prodigies such as Mozart, Mendelssohn, Saint-Saëns,
or Yehudi Menuhin. Interestingly, current research suggests why this
might be the case, and it indicates how Pearl Curran's gifts might have
remained largely latent until the Patience Worth communications began. For example, there's reason to think that Pearl's literary and other
intellectual gifts were *unlikely* to emerge early. As Morelock and Feldman observe,

> Prodigious achievement can only occur within domains accessible to chil-
> dren. This means that the domains must require little prerequisite knowl-
> edge and be both meaningful and attractive to children. Equally important
> is the adaptability of the domain's media and techniques to children (e.g.,
> child-size violins are necessary for child prodigy violinists). Given these
> prerequisites, music performance and chess seem especially amenable to
> budding prodigies—as is substantiated by the fact that the largest propor-
> tion of child prodigies in recent decades emerge from these fields. Other

fields produce comparatively few prodigies." (p. 355)

So one might argue that the gifts of Patience Worth required mastery of skills and bodies of knowledge that were unlikely to be accessible or attractive to Pearl in her youth.

Moreover, it was only in adulthood that Pearl was exposed to the ouija board. So perhaps that provided a first opportunity for attaining the dissociative states necessary for producing the Patience Worth scripts, and perhaps that accounts for the emergence of the Patience Worth personality relatively late in life. We might even conjecture that if Pearl's mastery of biblical, linguistic, and historical knowledge occurred unconsciously and in part psychically, that this might not even have begun until other aspects of Pearl's life fell into place—for example, having the opportunity to manifest these sides of herself through the ouija board.

So perhaps we should view Pearl Curran as a kind of gifted underachiever, at least until Patience Worth emerged at the ouija board. Are there any other clues in the literature on the exceptionally gifted to support that view? I've already hinted at one possibility. Perhaps Pearl was an unusually intelligent child whose abilities and potential were stunted, at least temporarily, by traditional turn-of-the-century expectations regarding appropriate female behavior. For example, Pearl may have been a victim of a "general cultural undervaluing of feminine achievement" (Morelock & Feldman, 1991, p. 355) and nonsupportive childrearing patterns passed down in the family through many generations. In fact, it's plausible that many would have found Patience's feisty personality, acerbic wit, and unorthodox views on both formal education and organized religion unacceptable coming from Pearl. But since Pearl seemed merely to be a medium for those personality traits and views (however charming some may have found them), she didn't have to accept responsibility for their expression. Furthermore, mediumship was an already familiar and acceptable female role; women had been attaining some prominence as mediums since the mid-nineteenth century. So we can conjecture, reasonably, that Patience allowed Pearl to express deeply felt but unpopular opinions, and also otherwise hidden and potentially abrasive personality traits, without taking any personal risk and without having to break from her relatively safe and conventional female roles.

But even if these larger social and familial forces hadn't played a role, the home environment is still critical. Morelock and Feldman observe,

> In each of the cases of prodigiousness contained in the research literature, there was, first of all, a child of unquestionably extraordinary native ability. This child was born into a family that recognized, valued, and fostered that ability when the child's introduction to the culturally available domain re-

vealed its presence. The child was invariably exposed to the instruction of master teachers possessing superior knowledge of the domain and its history and imparting that knowledge in a way most likely to engage the interest and sustain the commitment of the child. (p. 355)

It's reasonable to think that Pearl's natural gifts would have received little if any support of this sort from her family. Mozart, Mendelssohn, and Menuhin were born into families that appreciated their gifts and also had the means and desire to nurture them. If these musical prodigies had been raised in much less supportive family environments, it's probable that their gifts would either (a) not have surfaced at all, (b) manifested in less flamboyant and impressive ways, or (c) surfaced only later, after the musicians found an environment in which their gifts could be discovered and nurtured. But Pearl was raised in conditions that one observer described as "strained..., financially speaking" (Prince, 1927/1964, p. 22). He also noted, "Her [early] surroundings were such as to be anything but 'inspiring'" (p. 23). Pearl also wrote how at one point "Father had lost everything financially and mother was ill and nervous" (p. 14). Moreover, she commented on how depressing and uninspiring her environment was. For example, she wrote, "we moved to Palmer, Mo., where my father was secretary of the Renault Lead Co. I did not like it there; I wanted to learn, to know and to see life...I wanted life and here was desolation" (p. 14).

Prince, too, commented on Pearl's environment. Although he was remarking on the absence of opportunities for acquiring Patience's distinctive vocabulary, his observations apply generally to Pearl's intellectual development. While mentioning "the extreme unlikelihood of [Pearl's] acquiring a taste and pursuing studies...under the circumstances of her life" (Prince, 1927/1964, p. 492), Prince asked,

> Where was she likely to have done so, in the common schools of Texas and on the prairies? In the school in St. Louis where she was put back for deficiency in studies, and which she left at fourteen, going to Palmer? In the mining villages of Palmer and Potosi? While in Chicago laboring as a clerk and spending her spare time in practicing music? In her intervals back from Chicago in the uninspiring little towns of Potosi, Irondale, and Bismarck...? (p. 492)

Unfortunately, Pearl revealed little about the nature and quality of her home life. So it's difficult to determine how readily her intellectual and literary gifts would have been detected and cultivated. But from the few clues Pearl and others provide regarding her upbringing, it appears that Mary Pollard might have been more concerned with imposing her own ambitions on her daughter than with discovering and nurturing Pearl's distinctive talents.

To the extent that there's a received view about Pearl Curran, it's that she was really interested in music, not literature, the Bible, history, religion, or philosophy. For example, Litvag says that Mary Pollard "passed on her love of music to her daughter" (Litvag, 1972, p. 4). But that may be a somewhat romanticized perspective on a rather different, or at least more complex, state of affairs. For one thing (and somewhat surprisingly), it's doubtful that Pearl had a love of music; and for another, it appears that Mary Pollard's influence may have taken the form of enforcement or coercion rather than inspiration.

Pearl's autobiographical sketch, as well as the questions put to her by Prince, offered many opportunities for Pearl to comment on her real interests. After all, Pearl indicated at length how *un*interested she was in the material over which Patience Worth exhibited mastery. And she remarked often on what her interests and ambitions were. For example, she mentioned that she had an "ambition to be a prima-donna and loveress" (Prince, 1927/1964, p. 14), and she also said "I never wanted to be a missionary or do good in any particular way. I wanted to go on the stage and sing" (p. 20). But not once does Pearl mention that music, rather than performing, meant anything to her.

In fact, although Pearl's own testimony contains many comments about her musical activities, not one of them refers to her love of music or evinces any real interest in or passion for the art. I'm surprised that commentators seem to have missed this feature of the testimony. Sometimes—for example, when describing her jobs or her studies, she speaks of music matter-of-factly, not as something to which she was drawn and which she deeply desired to pursue. Even more interesting, however, are comments in which Pearl speaks of music pragmatically or as a duty. For example, she wrote, "I had in my teens the desire to be successful as a singer. Mostly to lift myself out of a hopeless future—not so much for fame itself...[After she got married] Mr. Curran made me go on with my music lessons" (p. 20). Elsewhere, Pearl commented, "mother gave me music lessons because she wanted me to be attractive. I practiced an hour or two a day, which I didn't like, though I wanted to play the piano. Then mother gave me elocution lessons" (pp. 19–20).

Moreover, as the last remarks in particular suggest, Pearl's maternal influences were probably not entirely benign or selfless. I find no indications that Mary inspired Pearl musically or instilled in her any appreciation or love for the art. Instead, she seems to have pushed Pearl into music, as she pushed her into elocution and performing. Perhaps she hoped to realize her own thwarted ambitions through her daughter. As we noted earlier, Mary Pollard had some musical talent herself, and Pearl described her as "ambitious." Moreover, Pearl claimed that her mother wanted her to be a performer or "show-off," and she mentioned that she felt neglected as her mother sang and played at night.

Regrettably, W. F. Prince didn't probe these aspects of Pearl's life in the additional testimony he collected from those who had known the Pollards well. Nevertheless, one wrote that "Mrs. Pollard...was never satisfied with living in Palmer"(p. 25). Another said that Pearl's "mother was a worrier, and very nervous" (p. 25). Moreover, Pearl herself raises additional questions about her relationship with her mother and her home life generally. She wrote, "I recall some 'paddlings' by my mother over which my father would almost weep. I recall little of the home life. Mother sang or played at night and I felt 'in the way' and neglected" (p. 12).

Again, these suggestions are highly speculative. But they aren't outlandish, and they knit together comments made by Pearl and others that might otherwise remain unconnected and mysterious. Perhaps the most we can say, given what little evidence we have, is that in many respects it's credible to regard Pearl as someone whose creative genius and philosophical proclivities had few opportunities for expression early in life, but who found a means for expressing them through the ouija board. And as I noted earlier, the "cover" of mediumship enabled Pearl to avoid personal responsibility for the sharpness of tongue, the politically incorrect behavior (for a middle-class housewife), and the unorthodox views expressed by Patience.

As long as we're speculating, a series of related conjectures deserves attention.[7] These all concern the name "Patience Worth." First, the name "Patience" might symbolize Pearl's need to wait before cultivating or revealing her literary interests and abilities. It's possible (if not likely) that Pearl's real interests were not those her mother encouraged (or cajoled) her to pursue. So Pearl might have suppressed or dissociated a desire to write and simply waited patiently, yielding to her mother's wishes for her to be a musical performer, until she found the right opportunity to explore and cultivate her literary skills and allow her deeper wisdom to emerge. The pair of names, Pearl/Patience, might also be a clue to the nature of the case. It calls to mind the tendency of many MPD/DID patients to choose alliterative names for their alters.

Moreover, the surname "Worth" may be symbolic as well. Although Pearl's self-reports are neither extensive nor especially probing and revealing, she was quite clear about her desire early on to be a performer or prima donna. So despite her apparent initial lack of interest in ouija board "communications," the Patience Worth productions may have given Pearl's life a value or purpose—or worth—it had lacked in her traditional and perhaps tedious existence as a housewife. If so, this might be a non-traumatic analogue to the functional specificity of alter personalities or identities in cases of MPD/DID.

Also, when Pearl began to use the ouija board, a year before Patience Worth appeared, she may have experienced something like the "crystallizing experience," which Walters and Gardner note often precedes the emergence of an intellectual gift (Walters & Gardner, 1986). Of course, that can't be the whole story, because it doesn't address Patience's mastery of historical and linguistic material. But it does address the apparent lateness in the appearance of Pearl's presumed literary gifts. Crystallizing experiences don't always occur in childhood, and one sort of crystallizing experience is *choosing the instrument* in the domain of one's talent or potential. For example, some musicians go from one instrument to another until they find the instrument for which they have the greatest natural affinity, or with which they seem to "click." In Pearl's case we'd have to assume that her use of the ouija board was analogous to finding an appropriate instrument. And we'd also have to assume, perhaps implausibly, that the resulting crystallizing experience occurred subconsciously and remained buried for some time. The problem is that Pearl's interest in the ouija board seems to have been minimal at best during the many months of experimentation preceding Patience's first appearance. Prince claims that Pearl "kept on only to oblige her friend, and finally became so bored that...it was necessary almost to drag her to the ouija board" (Prince, 1927/1964, p. 461).

Moreover, a very important feature of the Patience Worth case seems to resist a satisfying explanation. Even if we grant that Pearl's innate and prodigious gifts remained latent until her thirties, it's still mysterious how those putative gifts could have emerged conspicuously for the first time in a mature, developed form. Perhaps Prince was right in claiming that Pearl's intelligence was so unprecedented and novel that we can't imagine its range or limitations. And perhaps it's significant that Pearl's presumed gifts would be of a kind that seldom if ever appear early in life (unlike a talent for music or chess). Nevertheless, we can't ignore the fact that even the greatest known prodigies required a gestation period in which they practiced and trained their extraordinary creative gifts. Granted, the initial emergence of their talents was remarkable, and far in advance of what most people can achieve even with years of practice. But their abilities didn't appear initially in a mature form, as did the literary and improvisational gifts of Patience Worth. For example, in the cases of Mozart and Mendelssohn, we find a clear and steady development from their early compositions to their later works.

Does it help to suppose, as Cory does (Cory, 1919), that Patience Worth existed for some time as a self-conscious alternate personality and gradually developed the cognitive powers and characteristics that emerged full-blown in 1913? Prince objected to this proposal for two reasons, the first of which is fairly easy to dismiss. He argued that

> in none of the recognized and studied cases of dissociation has a secondary personality shown power and facility amounting to genius in any field of human endeavor wherein the primary personality has not manifested talent, lavished thought and practice, or even been known to cherish ambitions. (Prince, 1927/1964, p. 452)

It may, indeed, be true that there's no precedent in the history of dissociation for the disparity between Pearl's apparent abilities and those of Patience. Nevertheless, Prince's claim isn't *obviously* true. One conspicuous problem is the vagueness of the term "genius" and the related problem of assessing the dimensions of a person's natural aptitudes. Debate over Prince's claim could easily bog down in endless disputes over the magnitude and quality of Pearl's or Patience's abilities. Of course, to challenge Prince it's not necessary to find another case as extreme as that of Patience Worth. It would be enough to show that one case or another comes at least *close* to demonstrating the requisite disparity between alter and host personality. But that strategy faces formidable obstacles. Multiple personality (or dissociative identity) systems can be very complex, and functional divisions between personalities (or identities) can change over time. For that reason and others, it becomes nearly impossible to reliably identify a *historically* primary personality (see Braude, 1995). And that, in turn, compromises efforts to compare dissociative subjects' manifested abilities with their native abilities. Fortunately, we can sidestep these thorny issues. The main and overriding problem with Prince's concern is that it may simply be irrelevant. Even if no other known instances of dissociation display features found in the Patience Worth case, we must always remain open to the possibility of novelties and exceptions to the rule.

But Prince had a stronger objection to the hypothesis that Patience was an alter personality of Pearl Curran. He wondered, reasonably, whether the personality, Patience Worth, could have existed for so long with *no* prior signs of its existence, or any other indications of Pearl being dissociative. That is, he doubted whether an alternate personality could have been practicing and developing literary skills for years, never doing anything detectable by ordinary observation, until a year after Pearl began experimenting with the ouija board. In fact, if Patience was an alter personality standing in the wings (so to speak), why wait a year before appearing? That delay might make sense if Patience was a product of latent skills. For example, one could argue that the skills could be expressed only after breaking down barriers to creativity that had taken years to erect, or as Prince colorfully put it, only in "certain periods of exaltation, when all the valves of the subconscious were, so to speak, open" (Prince, 1927/1964, p. 502n). In that case, Pearl's introduction to the ouija board might finally have afforded her that opportunity and provided the necessary crystallizing experience. But I think we can agree with Prince that if Patience had been a lingering, hidden, alternate personality of Pearl Curran, one would expect some sign of that personality's existence before 1913.

Of course, the problem here is: can we reliably determine whether there *were* any such signs? If Patience had been an alter personality, it's unclear whether anyone in Pearl's life would have known how to detect its presence, especially if Pearl's dissociative episodes weren't histrionic.

Dissociation and even MPD/DID may go unnoticed even by clinicians and spouses (Braude, 1995). Nevertheless, isn't it likely that at some time before 1913 Patience's activities (as an alter personality) would attract attention—for example, by clouding Pearl's mind to a degree that would have been apparent to people close to her, or by producing dramatic behavioral shifts? We know that dissociative systems aren't as fully independent as they sometimes appear to be (see, e.g., Hilgard, 1986; Messerschmidt, 1927-28; Eich, Macaulay, Loewenstein, & Dihle, 1997). So one would think that at some point Pearl might have appeared unusually confused or distracted. And we know that various types of odd behavior tend to be reported by those who unknowingly have a friend or spouse who had MPD/DID. They might not realize their friend or companion has dissociated personality states. But they usually find that person to be noticeably eccentric and changeable, or unusually moody.

However, that's not the picture of Pearl Curran that emerges from the testimony. Granted, one of Pearl's frequent sitters, Humanities Professor Otto Heller from Washington University, described Pearl as "capricious and of uncertain temper" and remarked on the "instability of her promises and decisions in important as well as trivial affairs." He also claimed that Pearl "was weak about the truth" (Litvag, 1972, p. 256). But as Litvag noted, that characterization of Pearl is isolated and contrasts sharply with the many other descriptions of Pearl as completely honest and forthcoming. The only other comment I have found that might bear on this issue is one made by Prince, who conceded that Pearl "is sensitive and perhaps somewhat 'high-strung'" (Prince, 1927/1964, p. 449). But there is clearly too little here to support the view that Pearl's long-standing dissociative behavior had simply gone unrecognized.

7. Latency and Creativity: The Case of Hélène Smith

Before evaluating a survivalist interpretation of the evidence, we should digress briefly to consider another unusual example of automatism. Here, too, we find a subject who exhibited a novel and quite striking degree of linguistic proficiency and creativity. But unlike the Patience Worth case, the question of survival (or of genuine mediumistic communication with another individual) simply doesn't arise. In the present instance, there's no doubt that a remarkable set of automatic productions issued from the subject's subconscious. And that can only strengthen the conviction that the Patience Worth scripts, likewise, were manifestations of Pearl Curran's latent creative talents.

The case in question is extremely complex, and fortunately it's been documented in a careful, penetrating, and detailed book by the Swiss psychologist Théodore Flournoy (Flournoy, 1900/1994). The automatist described in the book is Élise Müller (1861-1929), a woman from Geneva to whom Flournoy assigned the pseudonym Hélène Smith. Mlle. Smith's father was a Hungarian merchant with a facility for language, but apparently his daughter had no comparable proficiency or interest in foreign languages. The linguistic ability manifested during her mediumship occurred only for a relatively brief period of time.

The case divides neatly into several interesting phases, which Flournoy described and whose psychogenesis he traced in great detail. Mlle. Smith's mediumship began in the winter of 1891-92, and communications took the form of visual and auditory messages, automatic writing, and also table tipping. Her original spirit control claimed to be Victor Hugo, but after about six months he was replaced (following a struggle for supremacy) by a control calling himself Leopold. Flournoy began sitting with Mlle. Smith in the winter of 1894-95, and to his surprise the medium gave him accurate information about his family life during the period before he was born. Flournoy concluded, therefore, that Hélène's apparent psychic talents merited further scrutiny. After making friends with Leopold, he persuaded the control to reveal his real identity, which Leopold said was Guiseppe Balsamo—a.k.a. Count Cagliostro. Evidently Flournoy was the only member of Mlle. Smith's circle who didn't believe that Leopold was actually a discarnate spirit.

In Flournoy's view, the Leopold persona originated in a traumatic experience suffered during an attack by a big dog when Hélène was ten years old. The attack was interrupted when a mysterious figure, dressed in a long brown robe with flowing sleeves and a white cross on his breast, suddenly appeared and chased the dog away. The figure then disappeared before Hélène could thank him. Leopold claimed that this was his first appearance to Mlle. Smith, and on many occasions afterwards she felt that he accompanied and protected her during unpleasant or threatening situations.

Although Leopold's personality was quite different from Hélène's, Flournoy found no evidence of survival in Mlle. Smith's control persona. Indeed, he noted serious discrepancies between Leopold's behavior and knowledge and what was known about Cagliostro. It's unclear whether Hélène suffered from a dissociative disorder, much less MPD/DID, and Flournoy wisely resisted that conclusion. Nevertheless, Leopold's origin and function are strikingly similar to those in classic cases of alternate personalities, and those similarities seem to justify Flournoy's conjecture that Leopold was a kind of secondary personality or self, created through a process of autosuggestion.

Mlle. Smith's mediumship underwent a series of what Flournoy called "romances," the first of which he dubbed the "Royal Cycle." According to spirit messages, Hélène was the reincarnation of Marie Antoinette, and in trance, Hélène's behavior as Marie Antoinette was vivid and dramatically appropriate. But as with Leopold/Cagliostro, there were persuasive reasons for believing that Hélène's trance persona was constructed subconsciously by the medium. Nevertheless, Flournoy remained open to the possibility that Hélène used ESP to acquire information incorporated into her seances.

The next phase of Mlle. Smith's mediumship, called the "Hindu Cycle," began in October 1894. In this romance, Hélène assumed the role of a fifteenth-century Indian princess, Simandini, who was burned alive on her husband's funeral pyre. During her trance states, Hélène spoke and wrote a kind of ersatz Hindu language, which Flournoy described as "a mixture of improvised articulations and of veritable Sanscrit words adapted to the situation" (Flournoy, 1900/1994, p. 195). Here, too, Flournoy found good reasons for thinking that Hélène's mediumship was a subconscious production. For example, Sanskrit experts concurred that Indian women didn't speak Sanskrit at the time alleged or at any other time, and also that the language spoken in what was ostensibly Simandini's home was the quite different language, Dravidian (Flournoy, 1902; Schiller, 1902). Nevertheless, Flournoy considered the historical and linguistic knowledge displayed by Hélène in this phase of her mediumship to be a "psychological enigma." He thought it might at least partially be explained as an example of cryptomnesia, or subconscious memory of material learned at an earlier time.

For our purposes, the most interesting phase of Hélène's mediumship is the "Martian Cycle," which began in November 1894, apparently in response to an inadvertent remark by Prof. Lemaître, who had said during a séance that it would be interesting to know about activities on other planets. During this phase of her mediumship, Hélène's spirit was ostensibly transported to Mars. While there, she described the human, animal, and plant life of the planet, and she spoke and wrote fluently in a Martian language.

Because Mlle. Smith's spirit guide provided word-by-word translations of the written messages, Flournoy and colleagues were able to examine the structure of the language carefully. Like the Hindu "language" invented earlier, this, too, was more intricate and creative than a collection of senseless or random phrases. But unlike its predecessor it exhibited a very high degree of syntactic and semantic consistency. The written alphabet was novel, and the spoken sound of the language was apparently distinctive as well. However, grammatically and phonetically the language was clearly modeled on Hélène's native French. Flournoy concluded that "the Martian language is only French metamorphosed and carried to a higher diapason" (Flournoy, 1900/1994, p. 156). As an intellectual achievement, he considered it to be as "infantile and puerile" (p. 156) as other features of the Martian romance. Nevertheless, Flournoy regarded the language as an impressive feat of memory and subconscious creativity. Reflecting on the linguistic facility of Hélène's father, he wrote, "the question naturally arises whether in the Martian we are not in the presence of an awakening and momentary display of an hereditary faculty, dormant under the normal personality of Hélène" (p. 163).

The following example illustrates some of the correspondences between the Martian language and French. The Martian texts are written in bold type as phonetic French; the French translations are italicized below them; and the English translations follow.

cé êvé plêva ti di bénèz éssat riz tés midée durée cé
Je suis chagrin de te retrouver vivant sur cette laide terre; je

ténassé riz iche éspênié vétéche ié ché atèv hêné ni
voudrais sur notre Espénié voir tout ton être s'élever et

pové ten ti si éni zée métiché oné gudé ni zée darié grêvé
rester près de moi; ici les hommes sont bons et les coeurs larges.

(I am sorry to find you again living on this wretched earth; I would on our Espenié see all thy being raise itself and remain near me; here men are good and hearts large.)

Compare this to the much more rudimentary unknown language of the automatist Albert Le Baron (pseudonym), an American writer and member of a spiritualist community (James, 1896). His linguistic specimens were either written down himself or dictated into a phonograph in the presence of William James and Richard Hodgson. The language clearly lacks the consistency and coherence of Hélène's Martian, and (as James confirmed after consulting several philologists) it has no clear connection with any known language. Indeed, it's doubtful that it deserves to be considered anything but gibberish. Here's an example; Le Baron supplied the translation.

Te rumete tau. Ilee lete leele luto scele. Impe re scele lee luto. Onko keere scete tere lute. Ombo te scele te bere te kure. Sinte te lute sinte Kuru. Orumo imbo impe rute scelete. Singe, singe, singe, eru. Imba, Imba, Imba.

(Translation: The old word! I love the old word of the heavens! The love of the heavens is emperor! The love of darkness is slavery! The heavens are wise, the heavens are true, the heavens are sure. The love of the earth is past! The King now rules in the heavens!)

Flournoy expressed his doubts to Hélène about the genuineness of the Martian language and the truth of her descriptions of Martian life. As if to circumvent those criticisms, Hélène invented an ideographic Ultra-Martian language (described more fully in Flournoy, 1902). The strange hieroglyphs of this new language represented words rather than letters, but unlike some hieroglyphs they didn't resemble the objects for which they stood. Flournoy regarded this development as a somewhat childish attempt to construct a language which he would be unable to analyze. He thought it "brilliantly corroborates the idea that the whole

Martian cycle is only a product of suggestion and autosuggestion" (Flournoy, 1900/1994, p. 168). The Ultra-Martian cycle was quickly followed by a series of messages from the inhabitants of Uranus, and the Uranian language and writing differed greatly from the Ultra-Martian. But Flournoy found that the Uranian language copied the phonetic and alphabetic system of the original Martian language. In fact, he said it differed less from French than French differed from the languages of neighboring countries. Mlle. Smith also inaugurated a Lunarian phase of her mediumship, introducing several different Lunar languages about whose authenticity Schiller wryly commented, "Mr. H. G. Wells does not yet seem to have been consulted" (Schiller, 1902, p. 247).

Although the mediumship of Hélène Smith is enormously interesting as a psychological study, and also as an account of apparent psychokinesis and ESP, it differs in crucial respects from that of Pearl Curran. The first difference concerns the degree of creative spontaneity demonstrated in the two cases. As we've seen, one of the lingering challenges of the Patience Worth case is to determine when, if ever, the personality and literary skills of Patience developed. By contrast, the creation of the Martian language (and Hélène's various trance personas) underwent fairly obvious periods of subliminal incubation. In fact, whereas the presumed psychogenesis of the Patience Worth persona remains highly conjectural at best, the origins of Hélène's productions can be traced fairly easily. Moreover, the productions of Mlle. Smith lack the maturity and complexity of the Patience Worth communications. And by comparison to the language of Patience Worth, about which Schiller remarked that "we are face to face with what may fairly be called a philological miracle" (Schiller, 1928, p. 574), Hélène's linguistic productions seem clearly to be of a lower order, and perhaps (as Flournoy repeatedly observed) childish and puerile. Nevertheless, in fluency, thoroughness, and the originality of its written alphabet, Hélène's Martian language is still something of a creative *tour de force*.

Therefore, the Hélène Smith case seems to occupy a kind of middle ground between (on the one hand) humdrum varieties of subconscious inventiveness and (on the other) the talent and originality displayed in the Patience Worth case. It shows that the gap between the former and the latter is neither as great nor as unbroken as some might have thought. So perhaps my earlier speculations about latent creativity can't be dismissed as facile appeals to powers-we-know-not-what. Still, I recognize that there's always the danger, when appealing to creative capacities of a subliminal self, of "entering a land of darkness where all analogies fail us and where anything may happen" (Schiller, 1902, pp. 248–49). And I strongly endorse McDougall's admonition that "the phrase 'the subliminal self' may prove detrimental...if we do not sternly resist the tendency to use it as a mere cloak for our ignorance" (McDougall, 1906, p. 431). (And obviously, the same may be said about easy recourse to the spirit hypothesis.) But the history of psychology provides considerable empirical grounding for speculation about latent capacities. And the history of automatism in particular suggests strongly that "the advantage of relegating voluntary ends to automatic execution...[is] getting the needed thing done...with a verve and completeness which conscious effort finds it hard to rival" (Myers, 1900, p. 415). So the Hélène Smith case seems to help us focus more constructively on the *empirical* question: What are the limits of our subconscious, latent creativity? And it makes it more plausible to treat the Patience Worth case as providing a partial answer to that question.

8. Other Cases of Mediumistic Creativity

We're still not quite ready to consider survivalist interpretations of the Patience Worth case. We need first to review two other interesting cases of artistic creativity in a mediumistic context. This additional digression should help us to appreciate further the distinctive and exceptional aspects of the Patience Worth communications.

The first case is that of Rosemary Brown, a British medium who ostensibly channeled compositions from famous composers (e.g., Liszt, Chopin, Debussy, Berlioz, Schubert) (see Brown, 1971). The works are primarily for the piano, and they've been studied by a number of very prominent musicians (see, e.g., Parrott, 1978; and see Hastings, 1991 for a summary of opinions). Although musical authorities disagree over the merits of the compositions, some judge them to be similar in both style and quality to the known works of their purported authors. Moreover, as Hastings properly observes, the critical appraisals of Mrs. Brown's works have all been made by people who know the circumstances surrounding their production and who undoubtedly have biases or predispositions concerning the possibility of survival. So it's difficult to know to what extent their assessments of Mrs. Brown's production reflect those predispositions.

But I think we needn't worry much at this point about the quality of Rosemary Brown's channeled compositions. Most mediumistic communications fall short of the quality of their ostensible authors' antemortem productions, sometimes hilariously so (for a good example of the latter, see Smith, 1974). Moreover, an open-minded appraisal of mediumship demands that we consider the possibility of noise in the channel, or psychological or physical obstacles to unimpeded communication. Indeed, that's one reason why the Patience Worth case is so remarkable; it seems entirely free of the hesitancy, roughness, and variability in quality characteristic of most mediumistic productions. In any case, it's clear that Mrs. Brown's compositions are good enough for at least some musical experts to regard them as credible evidence of survival. So what we must consider is (a) whether this case differs significantly from the case of Patience Worth and (b) whether it's plausible to attribute the compositions to Mrs. Brown, never mind how good they are. That should help us determine whether the case of Rosemary Brown sheds any light on that of Patience Worth.

As far as the differences between the cases are concerned, Mrs. Brown's compositions weren't produced with the fluency of Patience's poems and novels. Nor were they produced with the fluency exhibited by many great composers. Thus, the case doesn't present what may be the most intriguing puzzle emerging from the mediumship of Pearl Curran: namely, what to make of an apparently unprecedented level of compositional facility. Moreover, although Mrs. Brown's musical education had been modest, and although she claimed she rarely attended concerts or listened to classical music on the radio, it's likely that she had a greater exposure to classical music and to the composers she channeled than Pearl did to research in history or philology, and to works of great literature. Even more important, Mrs. Brown knew how to play the piano and read music before she began channeling musical compositions. We don't detect, in her case, the (perhaps only superficial) gap between background knowledge and creative ability found in the Patience Worth case.

It may also be relevant that Mrs. Brown's first mediumistic experiences preceded her channeling of famous composers. In fact, Mrs. Brown claimed that Liszt first appeared to her when she was seven years old, telling her that when she grew up he would return and give her music. Furthermore, by that time Mrs. Brown had also been tested for her ESP abilities, which also first surfaced in childhood. So unlike Pearl Curran, whose psychic experiences apparently began with the Patience Worth communications, Mrs. Brown was already something of a psychic and mediumistic veteran.

However, the two cases may share an important common feature: the lack of any clear *verifiable* information suggesting survival. Unlike some reincarnation and mediumistic cases where subjects apparently display both knowledge-*that* and knowledge-*how*, the Rosemary Brown case offers no evidence for the personal survival of famous composers *except* the compositions themselves. Granted, the mediumistic portrayals of the composers' personalities are consistent with what we know of the composers. But those portrayals offer no revelations of information. Mrs. Brown didn't provide, in addition, obscure bits of information about the composers to which she had no normal access and which later had to be confirmed by investigators. So although nothing in the Rosemary Brown case rules out survival as an explanation, nothing strongly favors that hypothesis either. Certainly, the case isn't as strong evidentially as some of the better cases described elsewhere in this book.

In my view, the most plausible and parsimonious hypothesis is that Mrs. Brown was a naturally gifted impressionist, a musical version of those who can mimic the speech and mannerisms of famous actors and other performers. And of course, that hypothesis is not undermined by the apparent originality of some of Mrs. Brown's compositions. In fact, it's precisely what one would expect of a good impressionist. Although stage impressionists copy the verbal and behavioral style of other people, the best of the lot do this, not simply by copying their subjects' *exact* words, inflections, gestures, etc., but by producing *original* and sometimes worthwhile performances in the appropriate style.

Some might think, along with Hastings (Hastings, 1991, p. 166), that first-rate musical mimicry requires extensive musical training or experience. But as prodigies and savants demonstrate, impressive musical abilities don't have any such prerequisite (see, e.g., Hermelin, O'Connor, & Lee, 1987, Kenneson, 1998, Treffert, 1989, Viscott, 1969). Moreover, it's as implausible to claim that training or experience are necessary for musical mimicry as it is to make a similar claim about the verbal mimicry of gifted impressionists. Impressionists needn't go to impressionist school; some people simply have what it takes. Nor are musical training and experience *sufficient* for being able to play or compose in the style of various composers. Not all composers can do this, and indeed, relatively few musicians have this ability (just as relatively few speakers of English can successfully imitate major movie stars). What *is* required is a good memory and a certain kind of good "ear." Just as some people have an ear for accents and dialects, or an ability to discriminate idiosyncratic speech patterns and bodily movements, others have an antenna (so to speak) for musical styles. And that musical ability is just one of many musical abilities that not all musicians (including extremely talented musicians) enjoy. Moreover, it's one which is relatively independent of musical training.

So does the Rosemary Brown case shed any particular light on the case of Patience Worth? If Mrs. Brown's compositions are examples of refined (and presumably unconscious) musical mimicry, then the case would illustrate once again that dissociative states foster both novel and unusually high levels of creative functioning. But if that interpretation of the case is correct, then Mrs. Brown's "musical impressions" may be no more extraordinary than the performances of other gifted impressionists. And in that case, the compositions of Rosemary Brown don't help us get a handle on Patience Worth's unprecedented compositional facility.

A similar conclusion seems warranted in the case of Luiz Gasparetto, a Brazilian medium who ostensibly channels artwork from famous deceased painters, including Monet and Toulouse-Lautrec. The parallels between this case and that of Rosemary Brown are instructive. Gasparetto already had some training in art; he began automatic drawing in his teens; and although his work resembles that of various deceased artists, it's of distinctly lesser quality. As Hastings points out, Gasparetto's methods of production suggest that he paints in a dissociative or similar altered state in which he is "bypassing the ego and drawing with less habituated, more intuitive responses" (Hastings, 1991, p. 167). In fact, Gasparetto's state of mind may resemble those reportedly elicited by Vladimir Raikov, who claims to have improved subject's artistic skills hypnotically, by suggesting to them that they are famous artists (see, e.g., Raikov, 1976).

Before moving on, I should briefly mention a case that connects, at least superficially, with the others considered in this chapter. This is the Thompson-Gifford case, presented originally in a 469-page report by James Hyslop (Hyslop, 1909). The subject here was a thirty-six-year-old goldsmith, Frederic L. Thompson, who seemed to be possessed or obsessed by the recently deceased artist Robert Swain Gifford, and whose sketches and paintings corresponded closely to works by Gifford which Thompson had never seen. However, this case sheds little light on the issues we're considering at the moment. For one thing, Thompson had already demonstrated some skill at sketching before the phenomena began. So, as in the case of Rosemary Brown, Thompson's mediumistic productions don't exhibit an artistic flowering radically discontinuous with the subject's known abilities. What makes Thompson's ostensible "Gifford" paintings so interesting is their resemblance to Gifford's works, and in fact the case is quite strongly evidential, unlike the others considered in this chapter. For these reasons, we'll examine the case in detail later (chapter 6).

The case of the Portuguese poet Fernando Pessoa (1888-1935) may offer a closer parallel to that of Patience Worth than any of the other cases considered above. But Pessoa's case clearly has no direct bearing on the topic of survival. Pessoa's works were written as products of distinct literary alter egos or "heteronyms." Accordingly, his case seems more closely linked to cases of dissociative automatism, and it may reveal a nonpathological form of multiple personality.

Pessoa's early years were marked by tragedy and loss. His father died in 1893 and his younger brother died the following year. Apparently to compensate for the loss, the young Pessoa invented a pen pal, the Chevalier de Pas, with whom he maintained a correspondence. In 1896, two more significant events occurred. Pessoa's maternal grandmother was institutionalized for insanity, and Pessoa was uprooted to South Africa to join his mother's new husband, a Portuguese consul in Durban, whom she had married the year before. So Pessoa now found himself in a significantly different culture, where people spoke many unfamiliar languages, and no Portuguese. And because he was enrolled in an English school, Pessoa resolved to learn the language well. But the language he mastered was not vernacular English; it was that of literature. In a

sense, Pessoa had adopted another persona, this time a literary one. After producing a number of works in English (including sonnets written
in the style of Shakespeare), Pessoa—under one or another of his
heteronyms—began writing poems in Portuguese.

Apparently, Pessoa considered the heteronyms to be expressions of
an inherently and deeply divided self. In fact, one of the principal
themes of Pessoa's poetry is the obscure and fragmentary nature of personal identity. So, since Pessoa had three major heteronyms in addition
to his "original" self or ego state (which he called an "orthonym"), he
considered himself to be at least four poets in one, each with its own
personality, biography, philosophical perspective, and metrical style.
The initial appearance of the major heteronyms took place in a kind of
ecstatic rush of creativity in March 1914 (interestingly, about a year
after Patience Worth's appearance). Pessoa also produced works using
numerous lesser heteronyms and what he termed "semi-heteronyms"
(analogous, perhaps, to alter-fragments in cases of MPD/DID). Since
I've only seen the poems in translation from the Portuguese, I find it
hard to determine whether Pessoa's works match the brilliance, grace,
or profundity of Patience's better productions. And unlike Pearl Curran,
Pessoa displayed his literary gifts and his interest in poetry early in life.
Nevertheless, this case provides additional ammunition for those who
would explain Pearl Curran's creativity in terms of a dissociated release
of previously hidden talents. (See, e.g., Pessoa, 1998; Zenith, 1998.)

9. Survivalist Conjectures

We may now return to the case of Patience Worth. At this stage it may
be surprising—although perhaps something of a relief—to learn that the
survivalist explanation of the case can be treated fairly quickly. The advantages of a survival hypothesis are clear enough. It would explain the
sudden appearance in Pearl Curran of Patience's mature talents. We
would simply posit that the fully developed personality already existed in
a discarnate form and simply manifested through Pearl at a propitious
time. Moreover, a survivalist hypothesis could presumably explain
Pearl's anomalous knowledge of ancient and Victorian times as well as
archaic locutions. But that also seems explicable in terms of (a) Pearl's
intelligence and mnemonic abilities, (b) her perhaps only passing exposure to relevant information from books and conversations, and (c) ESP
of other pertinent facts. At any rate, I think these are the only advantages of the survival hypothesis. Too many other serious questions remain unanswered, perhaps even more than arise in connection with
non-survivalist explanations.

First of all, we can't forget that the Patience Worth case, unlike
those considered in previous chapters, is non-evidential. Despite dili-

gent research, no one has discovered a previously existing individual even roughly corresponding to the Patience persona. So the Patience Worth case is ostensibly a case of survival only in form, not in substance. Still, we might wonder how much the discovery of a real Patience Worth would bolster a survivalist interpretation of the case. And perhaps surprisingly, I suspect that it would make almost no difference. Here's why. Let's suppose that we discover the existence of someone named Patience Worth, who lived at about the right time and place. Now we know that no one, from that or any time, was ever reputed to have demonstrated the creative gifts manifested by Pearl Curran's Patience persona. So how do we explain why, if a corresponding Patience Worth actually existed, no one remarked on her improvisational prowess and no body of works survived? It seems extremely unlikely that Patience would have exhibited those abilities without someone documenting them and without Patience leaving a legacy of compositions for posterity.

So if Patience Worth existed, presumably she never demonstrated any striking literary or creative talents. And if so, that seems to leave two options. First, the real Patience might have had the abilities of the persona "Patience" but never expressed or demonstrated them to anyone. I suppose that option is a real possibility, and I suppose it's no less plausible than supposing that the abilities were latent in Pearl and simply awaited an appropriate "trigger" in order to be liberated. We'd simply need to suppose that in the case of the real Patience, no triggering event occurred. However, a second option strikes me as more plausible. We could regard the real Patience as someone without any notable literary or creative talent. And in that case—unless the correspondence to Pearl's "Patience" is merely a coincidence—she would simply be a "hook" (so to speak) on which to hang Pearl's latent abilities and deflect responsibility for behavior which would have been personally risky for Pearl to present as her own. Recall that the Patience persona gave very few confirmable details about her alleged former life. Even if all of those details were subsequently confirmed, we could easily suppose them to have been obtained by a relatively modest application of ESP. The only way the discovery of a real Patience would actually strengthen the survivalist view would be if there were additional evidence that the real Patience had creative gifts roughly comparable to those exhibited by Pearl. Otherwise, the discovery of a real Patience is, at best, neutral with respect to the two options just mentioned.

Moreover, we might wonder "why, if Patience Worth is a discarnate spirit, she did not manifest herself until two hundred and fifty years after her alleged death" (Clowe, 1949, p. 76). We might also wonder, along with Clowe, "why, among the many millions of living persons during the two hundred and fifty years after the alleged death of Patience Worth, only Mrs. C. was found as a medium of manifestation" (p. 76).

No doubt survivalists could propose various scenarios to accommodate the facts, but they'd have to be even more speculative than the proposals considered in section 6, concerning the relatively humdrum psychogenesis of the Patience persona. Furthermore, Patience's literary and mnemonic virtuosity remain a mystery on the survival hypothesis. There's no evidence that anyone—medium or otherwise—has at any other time produced works of literature with comparable rapidity and without making significant revisions. And that level of proficiency is all the more remarkable and unprecedented when we consider the consistently high quality of the work.

Granted, survivalists might suggest that intellectual abilities can continue to develop while one is discarnate and under those conditions exceed the documented abilities of any living person. But unlike the conjectures about latent creativity examined earlier, that survivalist proposal has no independent support; it seems totally ad hoc. So although admittedly we have no idea how a living person could attain Patience's high level of creative facility, the survival hypothesis has no more, and arguably it has less, success in explaining how a discarnate individual could attain such an unprecedented level of inventiveness.

In fact, if it's reasonable for a survivalist to claim that a discarnate individual can attain unrivaled levels of compositional fluency, it seems at least as reasonable to claim that a living person can do the same in dissociative or other states that unleash latent abilities or remove normal barriers to optimal functioning. In fact, the latter claim has a kind of empirical support. As I've noted already in connection with the literature on savantism, prodigies, hypnosis, and multiple personality, we find eruptions of creativity in non-survivalist contexts that at least begin to approach Patience's level of virtuosity.

Furthermore, as Schiller noted, the spirit-possession theory (as he called it) "seems too good to be true" (Schiller, 1928, p. 575).

> Never before has a "spirit" found such complete and unobstructed expression through a "medium"; never before has a "spirit" given such convincing proofs of the reality of progress in the spirit-world, as those which have turned "Patience Worth" from an illiterate servant girl of the seventeenth century into the literary character of the twentieth. If she is indeed a spirit she must be congratulated on her success in surmounting difficulties which have baffled many more pretentious communicators. (p. 575)

Of course, as we noted earlier, survivalists can't argue against the latency (in Pearl) of Patience's literary talents just because those talents are unprecedented. So presumably we can't make an analogous argument *against* the survivalist and in favor of latency—that is, on the grounds that no other case of mediumship has ever demonstrated anything like a comparable level of unimpeded communication. In both cases we must remain open to the possibility that a phenomenon is making its first appearance, even if we're inclined to assign it a very low probability. But the problem here for the survival hypothesis is that it must accept a greater number of marvels (or miracles) than the non-survivalist hypothesis. The latter posits only one: the first and only recorded case of automatism at such a high level of creativity, fluency, and initial maturity. By contrast, the survival hypothesis has to accept two marvels: (1) the first and only documented case of literary and mnemonic abilities at such a high level of creativity and fluency, and (2) the first and only recorded case of mediumistic communication with virtually no "noise in the channel" (and for nearly twenty-five years at that).

Nevertheless (and perhaps ironically), Patience's literary fluency might still count against the survivalist. If our earlier speculations (in chapter 3) about crippling complexity were on target, we'd actually *expect* psychically produced (or transmitted) material to encounter serious obstacles. Even if causal preemption isn't as frequent as I had suggested, we'd still expect intervening causal processes to disrupt "transmission" from time to time. In fact, even at its best (i.e., under conditions of optimal transfer of information), we'd expect Patience's communications to Pearl to be far more erratic or intermittent than what actually occurred. Perhaps communications would be somewhat more fluent and consistent than what Mrs. Piper or Mrs. Leonard achieved. But it seems unlikely that they would occur with the spontaneous eloquence and uniformity of Pearl's actual conversations and mediumistic writings. But that facility seems less remarkable if we attribute it to Pearl's own latent gifts.

In section 6 we considered whether Patience should be regarded as a kind of alter personality, and we noted that it's somewhat difficult to square that hypothesis with the apparent lack of evidence for previous dissociative behavior on the part of Pearl. But we should also note that Patience's personality seems more complex in depth and breadth than what one finds both in the best mediumistic communications and probably also in the most compelling reincarnation cases (including the most protracted cases, where the previous personalities have extended opportunities to express themselves fully). In its robustness and multidimensionality, Patience's personality more closely resembles those of well-developed alter identities. So to the extent that cases of MPD/DID and ostensible mediumship or reincarnation can serve as guides here, I think we must conclude that Patience Worth looks very little like other cases of apparent surviving personalities and somewhat more like cases of dissociation.

10. Concluding Remarks

The Patience Worth case seems no less mysterious today than it did initially. That's probably why commentators tend to endorse Prince's conclusion that

> *either our concept of what we call the subconscious must be radically altered,*
> *so as to include potencies of which we hitherto have had no knowledge, or*
> *else some cause operating through but not originating in the subconscious-*
> *ness of Mrs. Curran must be acknowledged.* (Prince, 1927/1964, p. 509,
> italics in original)

I, too, sympathize with Prince's assessment, although I believe we can
be somewhat less noncommittal about the interpretation and import of
the Patience Worth case.

For the reasons considered above, it seems that a survivalist interpretation of the case simply leaves too great a residue of mysteries. By contrast, we can formulate a credible, although largely unsubstantiated,
account of the psychogenesis of the Patience Worth persona, and we
can explain Pearl's creative facility and anomalous knowledge in terms
of latent capacities and (presumably psychic) processes for which we
have independent evidence. For that reason, I'm inclined to echo Schiller's comment that "it is...*safer* to credit 'Patience Worth' to the unconscious and to classify her, officially, as Mrs. Curran's 'secondary self'"
(Schiller, 1928, p. 576).

Thus, the Patience Worth case illustrates why we must take very seriously non-survivalist interpretations of more evidential cases. If Pearl
Curran could tap into the latent creative capacities needed to produce
the Patience Worth scripts, and if she could use her psychic abilities to
access obscure but relevant chunks of historical and linguistic information, then presumably similar feats can occur in cases where verified
information is provided about a previous personality. So the Patience
Worth case reminds us that we should be alert to the superficial treat-
ments of the evidence noted in earlier chapters, and also very circumspect in rejecting non-survivalist explanations of the better cases. Moreover, and perhaps most important, the case is a humbling reminder that
there's much still to learn about the human mind.

NOTES

1. "Bread" is one of the terms that Patience used to denote her writings and
other communications. For example, she frequently referred to her productions as
the "bread o' me," and her readers and hearers as people who "eat o' my loaf."
2. Criticism of the church—and in particular its skewed values, pretensions of
wisdom, and pompous solemnity—were one of Patience's recurring themes.
3. Presumably, that is why Pearl Curran was able to abandon the ouija board in
favor of speaking the letters, and finally whole words.
4. This novel is particularly interesting, in that it's clearly intended to be a Victorian novel, the style of which Patience captured quite successfully. But of course,
Patience claimed to live in the seventeenth century. Interestingly, the publisher of

this work had a sense of humor, noting on the book's dust jacket that it's "A Mid-Victorian Novel by a Pre-Victorian Writer."

5. Personal communication to his son, Russell.

6. For example, Prince seems to argue that because all other great poets exhibited some literary talent relatively early in life (a claim that may be unfounded), what Pearl exhibited was not an inherent literary gift (see, e.g., Prince, 1927/1964, pp. 496–499).

7. I thank Joyanna Silberg and Harvey Irwin for reminding me of these points and stressing their potential significance.

Chapter 6

Reincarnation and Possession

1. Introduction

In this chapter we examine another motley set of cases, which some divide into at least two distinct categories: reincarnation and possession. But as we'll see, the boundaries between these two general classes may not be very clear. Besides, for the present purpose of evaluating the merits of the survival and super-psi hypotheses, the issues they raise are largely the same, and we can afford to treat them together.

The classic instances of apparent reincarnation rest on fairly distinct types of evidence (Gauld, 1982, p. 164). One general category consists of statements made by psychics, during psychic readings, about their clients' previous incarnations. For example, Edgar Cayce was famous for making past-life claims of that sort. But these cases are evidentially much weaker than those falling into the second broad category, which consists of subjects' apparent *recollections* of past lives. Cases in this second category may be subdivided into three groups: (a) evidence from hypnotized subjects "regressed" to a past life, (b) cases in which unhypnotized adults seem to recollect previous lives, and (c) evidence of children apparently recalling earlier lives. In this chapter we'll examine all three types of ostensible memory. We'll also look at cases usually classed as instances of possession, which nevertheless resemble the reincarnation cases in many respects, including evidential strength.

Although spontaneous (i.e., nonhypnotic) displays of apparent reincarnation aren't common anywhere, they seem to occur most often in parts of the world where belief in the phenomenon is widespread—notably, in south and southeast Asia, western Asia, west Africa, Brazil, and Alaska. And although the cases differ somewhat from one culture to the next, certain features recur with great regularity.

Typically, the subject in a reincarnation case is a child, and the phenomena begin between the ages of 2 and 4. During that time, the child either begins speaking about a previous life or else behaves in unusual ways later found to correspond to that life. These behaviors then diminish or disappear a few years later, usually between the ages of 5 and 7.

In the majority of cases, investigators identify a person who (almost always) died before the child's birth and the details of whose history corresponds to the child's statements. Moreover, in most cases children report that they died a violent death in their previous life, and they tend to offer details, later verified, about the mode of death. In many cases, the families of the subject and the previous personality live in widely separated communities (geographically, socially, and sometimes temporally), so that it's reasonable to conclude that the families had no contact before the child's unusual behavior began.

And that behavior isn't limited merely to reports about a former life. Subjects also exhibit traits, beliefs, and behaviors similar to those of the previous personality, many of them unusual for that family or community, or for the child's age. For example, subjects often exhibit phobias appropriate to the previous personality's mode of death. So if the previous personality died from a snakebite, drowning, or gunshot, the child might seem unusually afraid of snakes, water, or guns (respectively). And in some of those cases, the children's phobias manifested even before they began speaking of a previous life. Along the same lines, some children display interests or cravings inappropriate for them but characteristic of the previous personality (e.g., sex, intoxicants, or certain foods). Some have tried or pretended to smoke cigarettes.[1] Others, apparently remembering the lives of heavy drinkers, have either requested or surreptitiously imbibed alcohol. In a sizeable portion of cases, children seem to remember lives of people of the opposite sex, and they behave accordingly (e.g., by cross-dressing or showing an interest in play characteristic of the opposite sex). In fact, Stevenson writes, "the subjects who have shown behavior appropriate for the sex of a previous life have nearly all remembered lives that ended during the usual years of greatest sexual activity" (Stevenson, 1997a, p. 1911).

More generally still, there's a substantial and growing body of evidence that child subjects engage in various forms of unusual play. This play often corresponds to features in the life and death of the previous personality (usually, the previous personality's profession or vocation), and in the most impressive cases the play "seems to have no contemporary model in the child's life or other normal explanation" (Stevenson, 2000b, p. 559). Similarly, some children display a surprisingly mature degree of piety or religiosity, or (in cases where they apparently remember lives of criminals) an interest in violence or stealing. Moreover, when children claim to remember being murdered in a previous life, they often exhibit great hostility toward the alleged murderer, in some instances reaching for a weapon when they see that person.

As that last comment indicates, subjects also suggest reincarnation through the act of recognition. Usually, this occurs when subjects are introduced to family, friends, or acquaintances of the previous personality, or when they visit the previous personality's village or home, or when someone shows them photographs pertaining to the previous personality's life. At those times, subjects identify people, places, or objects they've never seen before, and often they exhibit the sorts of emotions we might expect of a previous personality. For example, subjects reportedly weep bitterly or display great joy at being reunited with loved ones, or they might exhibit antipathy toward the previous personality's enemies, or they might display reticence about discussing matters that the previous personality would have considered sensitive. Moreover, when they encounter the previous personality's friends, relatives, or spouse for the first time, subjects often use locutions (e.g., nicknames) which had special or intimate significance to the previous personality and the other person, but which (presumably) they hadn't learned normally.

In about one-third of reincarnation cases, the children have physical features (e.g., birthmarks or deformities) corresponding to birth defects, wounds, or other notable physical features of the previous personality. Stevenson notes, further, that

> in 18 cases in which the death in the previous life was caused by a gunshot wound, the subject had two birthmarks corresponding to bullet wounds of entry and exit. In 14 of these, one birthmark was appreciably larger than the other; this accords with the almost invariable fact that gunshot wounds of entry are small and round, those of exit larger and irregular in shape. (Stevenson, 2000a, p. 656)

A common belief about reincarnation cases is that subjects usually display *abilities* characteristic of the previous personality. Nevertheless, and despite the interest Stevenson and others have shown in ostensible xenoglossy, that belief seems to be false. Indeed, Stevenson observes,

> untaught skills have rarely occurred among the children we have studied. They often show...precocious interests and sometimes unusual aptitudes, but not fully formed skills, such as geniuses like Mozart and Gauss manifested in childhood. (Stevenson, 2000a, p. 658)

Of course, we've already considered examples of anomalous skills suggestive of (but not strongly supporting) survival—for example, Rosemary Brown's or Gasparetto's skills (see chapter 5). But those look like cases of possession rather than reincarnation. The difference between reincarnation and possession is not entirely clear, and in some cases they may be observationally indistinguishable. Nevertheless, there's a distinctive profile for at least a large set of possession cases, enough so that mental health professionals and anthropologists recognize and study discrete possession syndromes or ritualistic patterns of behavior.

However, many of those behaviors fall outside the scope of this inquiry. The full range of possession cases includes many examples of apparent spirit or demonic possession, and those cases seem clearly to be examples of dissociative phenomena (see, e.g., Braude, 1995; Crabtree, 1985; Crapanzano & Garrison, 1977; Lewis-Fernández, 1994; Suryani

& Jensen, 1993; and the entire issue of *Dissociation*, vol. 4, no. 4, 1993). But our concern here is with possession cases suggesting the persistence of *personal* consciousness following bodily death. Of course, examples of demonic or spirit possession aren't irrelevant to this inquiry. They remind us that dissociation can unleash a variety of astounding behaviors, some apparently having a psychic component. And that reminds us, once again, to be alert for similar processes in cases suggesting postmortem survival. However, by now that's a familiar refrain, and we needn't dwell on it again.

So, restricting our attention only to possession cases suggesting personal survival, we see some, but not many, respects in which they differ from typical reincarnation cases. For example, subjects in possession cases are usually older than in reincarnation cases (often teens or adults), and the previous personality tends to be someone who died after the subject's birth. Moreover, although displacement of the host personality is usually temporary in both possession and reincarnation cases, in possession cases it's frequently sporadic, as if the possessing personality periodically retreats or loses control of the body. Also, personality displacement in possession cases may be *voluntary*. That's why mediumship (and shamanism) can be classified as types of possession.

But perhaps the main difference between reincarnation and possession cases is that the "main personality in reincarnation cases generally has a strong sense of identification, present whenever he thinks about it, with the past personality; whereas in possession cases the main or host personality has no sense of identification with the parasitic personality" (Alan Gauld, personal communication, October 21, 2000). So in reincarnation, there seems to be a blending of the host and previous personality, which we do not see (at least to the same degree) in possession cases. However, that difference may be no more theoretically or ontologically significant than it is in cases of MPD/DID, which also exhibit varying degrees of personality or identity blending. We'll revisit this topic in the next chapter.

Another difference between reincarnation and possession cases concerns their susceptibility to motivated super-psi interpretations. Subjects in typical reincarnation cases are children. So at the age when they start speaking about a former life, it's unlikely that they're strongly motivated to simulate the behavior of a previous personality. Therefore, super-psi explanations of those cases will usually have to posit relevant motives in people other than the subject—probably, one or the other set of parents or members of the immediate families. But because subjects in possession cases are older, they're undoubtedly grappling with psychological baggage, internal conflicts, etc., appropriate to their age and more robust than we'd find in young children. So it's fairly easy to imagine why they might be motivated to simulate the appearance of survival, even unconsciously.

That's not to say that possession cases can't be impressive, and as we'll see, some of them are. But it does suggest that the best survival evidence from this general class may come from reincarnation cases and also the small number of possession cases whose subjects are young children. These pose a clear problem for the super-psi hypothesis. As I noted, if we can't plausibly attribute relevant unconscious motives for simulating survival to the child subject, then the next most likely culprits will be members of either the subject's or the previous personality's family. But it's not easy to defend treating these family members as psychic agents, even if we find plausible motives for them. For one thing, their presumed motives may not mesh neatly with other observed facts (e.g., see the comments in section 7 on Griffin's argument). And for another, we may have to posit even more hopelessly convoluted and complex causal chains than we'd need if we treated the subject as the psychic agent.

Consider what these explanations might look like. For reincarnation cases we can imagine two principal versions, one for the subject's family, and the other for the previous personality's family. And to make the explanatory challenge as clear as possible, let's consider cases in which the subject has birthmarks corresponding to prominent features of the previous personality. In broad outline, super-psi explanations might look something like this.

For the subject's family: The subject (*S*) is born with one or more birthmarks. Then a member of *S*'s family, for whom a reincarnation in that family serves a deep need or interest, psychically finds an individual whose features or mode of death provides correspondences to the birthmarks. Through ESP, the family member also learns about the previous personality's history, and then through telepathic influence manages to shape *S*'s behavior accordingly.

For the previous personality's (*PP*) family: Some member of *PP*'s family is vitally interested in having *PP* reincarnated (e.g., to identify *PP*'s killer, or to relieve the grief over *PP*'s death). That person psychically finds an infant born with appropriate birthmarks. The child's subsequent behavior would then be explained by means of telepathic influence from someone who already knew the *PP* well.

I think we're entitled to be suspicious of the complexity of these scenarios (especially, perhaps, the first one), even if we take seriously magic wand types of super-psi hypotheses. Still, we should remember that the psychic snooping or telepathic influence required here may be no more extreme than the psychic achievements *survivalists* often require of discarnate personalities. So, as we've noted before, survivalists are in a uniquely bad position to protest about the complexity, scope, or refinement of the psi posited in the above scenarios.

However, for reasons similar to those presented in chapter 3, there may be other grounds for preferring survivalist to super-psi explana-

tions, at least when we need to explain a long string of verified statements or behaviors suggesting survival. Under those circumstances, we
might be justified in applying the *Argument from Crippling Complexity*
to the reincarnation scenarios mentioned above. In fact, we might be
entitled to apply that argument even when the behaviors suggesting survival occur only sporadically. For reasons that will emerge as we examine individual cases, super-psi explanations posit a great range and number of successful psychic efforts, arguably far greater than what survivalists require. And that seems only to increase the mystery of the best
cases. It makes it harder to see why the phenomena occurred with any
regularity at all.

Despite their intriguing regularities, reincarnation and possession
cases vary considerably in their details and also in their empirical cre-
dentials. And not surprisingly, different cases exhibit different sets of
strengths and weaknesses. Some are impressive even though investigators collected the evidence under less-than-ideal conditions, and we'll
review some examples below. But consider first what would be optimal
conditions for gathering evidence in these cases. Ideally, we want what I
like to call *early-bird* cases. In these, investigators record subjects' statements *before* anyone attempts to find a corresponding previous personality, or at least before the case is "solved." That helps counter predictable worries, even in the best cases, about distortions and evidence-contamination. When investigators interview subjects only after the apparent previous personality has been identified, we can always wonder
about the extent to which they've tailored their testimony (possibly inno-
cently) to fit the information already gathered. Fortunately, a number of
early-bird cases exist (see, e.g., Haraldsson, 1991, 2000b; Haraldsson &
Samararatne, 1999; Mills, Haraldsson, & Keil, 1994; Stevenson, 1974a,
pp. 67–91, 274–320). In fact, thirty-three of them are on file in the
large database at the University of Virginia's Division of Personality
Studies. That might seem like a large number, but according to a recent
estimate it's only 1.5 percent of the total number of recorded cases
(Haraldsson, 2000b, p. 82). Nevertheless, there doesn't seem to be a
suspicious or notable excess of correct statements in cases investigated
only after they were solved (Schouten & Stevenson, 1998). So even
though early-bird cases remain preferable, there's no conspicuous sign
of evidence-contamination in the remaining cases.

In most good reincarnation and possession cases, subjects provide an
impressive number of detailed and subsequently verified statements
about the life and location of the previous personality. However, many
of those statements are elicited from the subjects through direct questions—for example, of the form "Do you know who this is?" or "What
was the name of [the previous personality's] uncle?" We have good reason to be impressed when subjects successfully answer many of these
questions. Nevertheless, there's a problem assessing the information

provided under direct questioning.

Once we grant the possibility of telepathy, and also the relevance of motivations for specific outcomes, these scenarios present a clear context for telepathic success, even if they provide no guarantee. Presumably, the survivalist's case would be strengthened if subjects *spontaneously* provided verifiable information prior to any such requests or other stage setting. Of course, explicit requests for information aren't the only contexts pregnant with hope or expectation for verifiable statements. For example, suppose subjects visit the previous personality's house or village and spontaneously identify faces in the crowd (or mention obscure details about the location). If witnesses verify these statements on the spot, then someone present knew the information already and quite possibly hoped that the subject would volunteer that sort of—and perhaps even that specific—information. A subject's achievement under these conditions would be no more remarkable, and no more indicative of survival, than those instances in which Mrs. Piper or Mrs. Leonard provided recent information about their sitters, and to which deceased communicators would have no privileged access (chapter 3).

In fact, mediumistic "hits" about the living may be especially impressive as psychic achievements, because often there's no reason to suppose that sitters were looking for recent personal information. Presumably, mediums use their ESP to either dig into a sitter's subconscious or else simply to bypass the sitter's immediate or overt concerns. Therefore, since it's clearly gratuitous to interpret such mediumistic hits along survivalist lines, we should be open to similar non-survivalist interpretations of subjects' hits in reincarnation or possession cases. That's a major reason why the most strongly evidential statements in these latter cases are those volunteered in early-bird investigations, before the previous personality has been identified.

With these considerations in mind, let's now look at specific cases.

2. The Case of Bishen Chand

And let's begin with a classic reincarnation case, exemplifying much of what makes the best cases so intriguing. Many of the subject's statements were written down before they were verified; the subject's behavior was often inappropriate to his age and socioeconomic setting; and the subject reportedly displayed abilities which he had not been taught but which were characteristic of the previous personality. Like many of the better cases, this one comes from India (Sahay, 1927; Stevenson, 1972; 1975).

Bishen Chand was born in Bareilly in 1921. He was the youngest of three children (another sibling died in early childhood), and his father earned a very modest living as a railway clerk. His parents reported that

when Bishen Chand was ten months old and barely able to speak, he
would utter something sounding like "Pilvit" or "Pilivit." It turns out
that a large town, Pilibhit, was located about fifty kilometers northeast
of Bareilly, and as Bishen Chand's command of the language increased,
he began speaking of a previous life in Pilibhit. Among many other
things, he said that his name had been Laxmi Narain, that his uncle was
named Har Narain, and that his father had been a wealthy landowner.

At about the age of four, Bishen Chand's father took him and his
brother to a wedding party in a town beyond Pilibhit. As they were returning by train to Bareilly and stopping at Pilibhit, Bishen Chand
heard the announcement of the station's name. He demanded to leave
the train, claiming that this was where he used to live. His father refused, and the boy cried.

About eighteen months later, word of Bishen Chand's behavior
reached a lawyer from Bareilly, K. K. N. Sahay, who was already in the
process of investigating a reincarnation case involving his son. Sahay
then visited the child and wrote down some of his comments about a
former life. Afterwards, he persuaded Bishen Chand's father to visit
Pilibhit to verify those claims, and on August 1, 1926, the two men took
the boy and his brother, Bipan Chand, to Pilibhit. Once there, Bishen
Chand correctly identified various places and people, and he made
other statements about his former life in Pilibhit. Those statements corresponded nicely with the life of Laxmi Narain who died in 1918, more
than two years before Bishen Chand was born.

Sahay's original report of the case was published in 1927. From 1964
to 1971, Ian Stevenson conducted several additional interviews with
Bishen Chand and surviving members of the two families (including
Bipan Chand). Also in 1964, Stevenson's associate, Professor P. Pal,
interviewed Bishen Chand's father, who was eighty-two at the time and
who died two years later. These interviews confirmed and supplemented
the information initially reported by Sahay.

It turned out that Laxmi Narain's maternal uncle, B. Upendra
Narain, lived in Bareilly, about two kilometers from Bishen Chand's
home, and this uncle's sister (Laxmi Narain's mother) would visit there
occasionally. But for reasons mentioned by Stevenson, it seems unlikely
that the two families had any contact or that information about Laxmi
Narain somehow reached Bishen Chand's family from that source. For
one thing, if Bishen Chand's family or Sahay had known that the previous personality's uncle lived in Bareilly, they could easily have verified
the child's statements by consulting him, rather than by traveling fifty
kilometers to Pilibhit. So the fact that they first went to Pilibhit to
check out the story suggests that they were unaware of the uncle's presence nearby. Moreover, Bishen Chand never conclusively identified
Laxmi Narain's family as "his" former family until that first visit to Pilibhit, where (among other things) he identified Laxmi Narain and his fa-

ther in a photograph, as well as Laxmi Narain's former home and the home of his former neighbor. And it was during that visit that the party learned that Har Narain was Laxmi Narain's father, not his uncle.

Laxmi Narain's life had been brief, but colorful. His father, Har Narain, was indeed a wealthy landowner, and probably because Laxmi Narain was his only son, he spoiled the boy and helped him develop "a taste for luxury and extravagance" (Stevenson, 1975, p. 180). Laxmi Narain dropped out of school after his father died and "freely indulged his fondness for good food, fine clothes, beautiful women, and alcohol" (Stevenson, 1975, p. 180). Despite a short stint working at the railway service, he never found (and quite possibly never sought) a career other than hedonism. Between his personal indulgences and his generous contributions to charities and needy individuals, he quickly exhausted his inheritance, so that when he died at the age of 32, his mother had almost no resources to sustain her. Accordingly, she moved in with her brother in Bareilly, abandoning the family house, which then deteriorated rapidly and was partly in ruins by 1926.

Laxmi Narain was particularly fond of a prostitute named Padma, whom he apparently regarded as his property. Because of that possessiveness, and probably also because of his quick temper, he once shot and killed a man he saw emerging from Padma's apartment. Laxmi Narain then went into hiding for a while and apparently bribed his way out of difficulty.

Judging by Sahay's report, Bishen Chand was impressively accurate in his initial (early-bird) statements as well as those made on his August 1 visit to Pilibhit. The boy noted that he (i.e., Laxmi Narain) was of the Kayasth caste, that he lived in Pilibhit, that his father was a wealthy landowner, that he had studied up to the sixth class in the Government School, that he knew Urdu, Hindi, and English, that his house had two stories and also separate apartments for men and women, that he used to listen to and watch nautch (dancing) girls, that he drank wine and liked rohu fish, and that he had a neighbor, Sunder Lal, whose house had a green gate. These claims were all true of Laxmi Narain. And on the visit to Pilibhit, Bishen Chand correctly identified Sunder Lal's home, the courtyard where nautch parties had been held, and also Har Narain's now abandoned house. When he saw the decrepit condition of Laxmi Narain's former home, Bishen Chand reportedly wept bitterly and lamented that no one had maintained the place after his death (an odd complaint, since Laxmi Narain had squandered most of his fortune). And although the house was at the time mostly a pile of bricks and mud, the boy also correctly identified where the house's staircase had been. He also recognized his old school and one of his former classmates (who was in the crowd), and he stated correctly where class VI was held in his time. Furthermore, people in the crowd asked him to name the prostitute with whom he associated in his previous life, and although he gave Padma's name, he reportedly did so reluctantly.

Later, Laxmi Narain's mother interviewed Bishen Chand, and the boy provided additional details that convinced her that he was indeed the reincarnation of her son. For example, Bishen Chand claimed that he had thrown away some pickles his mother wanted him to eat, even though they had become rotten and worm infested. The mother confirmed this. She admitted throwing away the worms but then keeping the pickles in a jar, and she said she was annoyed when Laxmi Narain threw the pickles away.

Also, when he was given a pair of tablas (drums) to play, Bishen Chand reportedly played them "with ease" (Stevenson, 1975, p. 184, 199), even though tablas are difficult to play well and although Bishen Chand allegedly had never seen tablas before. But this feature of the case should be treated with caution. For one thing, it's hard to know how accurate the reports are. We don't know whether the observers could reliably distinguish decent or passable tabla playing from impressive (or even ordinary) childish twiddling, especially when performed in a context in which observers have high expectations for behavior indicating a former life. Also, I don't believe we know how unprecedented it would have been, under ordinary conditions, for Bishen Chand to have demonstrated some modest musical or rhythmic ability. Sometimes individuals manifest those abilities spontaneously, even though their families have never previously displayed any such proclivities. Moreover, Stevenson notes that there's no clear evidence that Laxmi Narain ever played the tablas, much less that he played them with any skill.[2] All we know is that he had a fondness for singing or dancing (Stevenson, 1975, p. 199). So even if Laxmi Narain puttered away at the tablas during moments of lubricated enthusiasm, we must be cautious about inferring that he actually knew how to play the tablas. In the West it's all too common for patrons of bars or lounges to try, usually incompetently, to play the house piano or sit in or sing along with the band. We don't know whether Laxmi Narain did anything more notable.

More impressive, perhaps, are reports of unusual linguistic competence, corresponding to Laxmi Narain's competence in Urdu. Bipan Chand reported that his brother, as a child, had been able to read Urdu (written in Arabic script) before receiving instruction in the language. Bishen Chand's father claimed, more modestly, that his young son surprised them by using two Urdu words which he presumably had not been taught. He referred to the ladies' quarters in the house in Pilibhit with the word "masurate" instead of the Hindi word "zenana." Then, pointing to a door on that house he said, "There was a kofal [lock] on this." Stevenson reports that the Urdu word "kofal" is used by upperclass people in Pilibhit. But Bishen Chand's family used only the Hindi word for "lock," "tala."

Occasionally, Bishen Chand's behavior was surprisingly adult and apparently similar to that of Laxmi Narain. For example, although the boy's parents didn't drink, they kept brandy in the house for medicinal purposes. And apparently the family discovered that the brandy supply was diminishing even during periods of good health. Then at one point, Bishen Chand's sister caught her brother drinking the brandy. At the time he was probably between the ages of four and six, and when asked about this behavior, he reportedly replied "I am used to drinking."

Furthermore, Bishen Chand's father claimed that when his son was less than five and a half, he said to him, "Papa, why don't you keep a mistress? You will have great pleasure from her." Apparently, the father managed to contain his surprise and asked his son quietly, "What pleasure, my boy?" Bishen Chand answered, "You will enjoy the fragrance of her hair and feel much joy from her company." Later, on their first visit to Pilibhit, the police superintendent asked Bishen Chand about his wife and children. The boy replied, "I had none. I was steeped in wine and women and never thought of marrying." Also during this period, Bishen Chand would proudly relate the story of how Laxmi Narain murdered the man coming from Padma's apartment, and he boasted that his family's influence allowed him to escape prosecution.

Assuming the accuracy of the reports, this case poses a substantial challenge to anti-survivalists. Bishen Chand evidently produced a long string of verified statements (many of them early-bird statements), along with various behaviors appropriate to the previous personality but unusual (if not unprecedented) for a young child. Moreover, if the reports can be trusted and observers weren't simply projecting their hopes or expectations onto the boy's behavior, Bishen Chand's emotions on certain occasions seem difficult to square with the super-psi hypothesis. For example, if he really wept *bitterly* upon seeing Laxmi Narain's decrepit former home, that reaction is very interesting. Weeping bitterly is probably difficult to describe precisely, but it's clearly distinguishable from childlike crying. The two types of crying have a different feel and presentation, and only one of them seems appropriate to an adult.

3. A Recent Early-Bird Case

Sri Lanka has been the source of a number of interesting recent cases, featuring not only early-bird testimony, but also phobias appropriate to the previous personality's mode of death and (in a few cases) birthmark correspondences (Haraldsson, 2000a; 2000b; Stevenson, 1977). They demonstrate nicely what makes many reincarnation cases simultaneously intriguing and frustrating.

For example, in evaluating 33 early-bird statements in the case of Chatura Karunaratne (Haraldsson, 2000b), 15 were false. Of these, 5 (possibly 6) were attempts to provide personal names. But the subject,

Chatura, was never correct in giving personal names. From one point of view, that clearly reinforces skepticism about the case's paranormality or its value as evidence for survival. However, Haraldsson says this "is almost the rule in Sri Lankan cases" (Haraldsson, 2000b, p. 88). Stevenson agrees, noting that Sri Lankan subjects "appear to be blocked mainly with regard to the remembrance of proper names, especially personal ones" (Stevenson, 1977, p. 8). He notes that this is probably not connected to the Buddhist disinterest in personal identity, because if that were the underlying cause, we'd expect to see a similar regularity in cases from countries likewise dominated by Theravada Buddhism, such as Burma and Thailand. So Stevenson traces this peculiar deficiency to a more overt regularity among the Sinhalese. Unlike the Burmese, who use personal names very freely, Stevenson says the Sinhalese "seem almost to have a national phobia about calling anyone by his given name" (Stevenson, 1977, p. 9). Apparently, this holds even between spouses.

Consider now the following case, also from Sri Lanka. Like some other cases it's strong (but not overwhelming) in several respects. First, the subject had a relatively high proportion of verified early-bird statements (higher than Chatura), and many of them were unusual, quite specific, and corresponded clearly to the life of the previous personality. Second, the subject exhibited a phobia appropriate to the previous personality's mode of death. And third, at least one member of the subject's family apparently didn't welcome her past-life revelations, and the family seemed to make only one, evidently cursory, effort to solve the case. That helps undercut skeptical appeals to the Usual Suspects and at least one type of motivated super-psi explanation (Mills *et al.*, 1994).

Thusita Silva (pseudonym) was born in 1982 in the small town of Elpitiya in southwestern Sri Lanka. Six years later (apparently after the death of Thusita's father), the family moved to Panadura, located 18 miles south of Colombo. In June 1990, Tissa Jayawardane (T. J.), interviewed Thusita and her mother, and then the following November Haraldsson (E. H.) independently interviewed Thusita and her family. According to Thusita's mother and grandmother, Thusita was two and half years old when she began speaking about a former life in Akuressa, located 30 miles from Elpitiya and 78 miles from Panadura. The story she told them, and then repeated later to the investigators (before they identified the previous personality), is the following. She and her husband were walking on a narrow suspension footbridge near their home in Akuressa. But the bridge broke down and Thusita fell into the river and drowned. Thusita also claimed that she was pregnant at the time. Moreover, she said her husband nearly drowned as well, after throwing himself into the river in order to save her. All these claims turned out to be true of a woman named Chandra Nanayakkara (born Abeygunasekara) from the village of Akuressa (population 20,000).

Thusita's family claimed they had no connection with Akuressa, and apparently they hadn't even visited there until well after Thusita began talking about a former life. Eventually Thusita's brother traveled to Akuressa to look for confirmation of Thusita's statements, but he found nothing. Evidently angered by this, he scolded Thusita for lying, and he beat her for talking to T. J.

It was T. J. who learned the identity of a person corresponding to Thusita's story. He visited Akuressa in the summer of 1990, but he was unable to meet any of Chandra's family members. The following November E. H. visited Akuressa after interviewing Thusita, and he interviewed Chandra's husband, her brother, two of her sisters-in-law, and a close family friend. They confirmed that Chandra drowned in 1973 at the age of 27, after falling from the suspension bridge she and her husband were crossing. Chandra, who at the time was seven months' pregnant, stepped on a plank that gave way, and she fell into the river. Her husband then jumped into the swollen river to rescue her, but he failed and almost drowned in the process. Chandra's body was found down river three days later. The coroner's office confirmed that Chandra died in December 1973 "by choking after swallowing water when the deceased fell into the River Nilwala from the suspension bridge." That bridge is the only suspension bridge in the area.

Thusita made other claims as well, generally less interesting and less distinctive than those already mentioned, not all of which were true. For example, she said her father's name was Jeedin Nanayakkara. This probably counts as a partial hit because (a) her father-in-law's name was Edwin (not Jeedin) Nanayakkara, and (b) it's customary for a married woman in Sri Lanka to refer to her father-in-law as father. Thusita also stated that her family owned a car, which was true of her in-laws and which is uncommon in Sri Lanka. She also claimed correctly that the family owned a bicycle, that their house was larger than Thusita's home, and that it had a big front gate. By contrast, she claimed falsely that her bicycle was yellow (it was black), that she had worked in a hospital (a cousin and close friend had been nurses), that her husband was a postman (he was a bus driver, but his elder brother was a postman), and that her sister had a daughter (perhaps a partial hit: her sister-in-law had a daughter).

According to Thusita's mother, her daughter had a phobia of bridges and water. She also claimed that Thusita had at one time remembered more names than she mentioned to the investigators. But by the time T. J. and E. H. interviewed Thusita, neither she nor her mother could remember them. At that time Thusita was eight years old, an age at which most reincarnation subjects have lost many of their apparent past-life memories.

It's curious that Thusita's brother failed to discover the previous personality during his visit to Akuressa. Haraldsson's team apparently managed it without too much difficulty. Granted, Haraldsson and his associates are veteran investigators, and Haraldsson modestly wrote me that luck always plays a role in these inquiries (personal communication, September 27, 2000). Nevertheless, Akuressa is a town of only 20,000, and I'd think that if Thusita's brother and family had been genuinely interested in discovering a previous personality corresponding to Thusita's statements, they would have tried harder, made more than one trip to Akuressa if necessary, and asked the sorts of questions that led Haraldsson and his team to Chandra's family. After all, the number of relevant people to interrogate or appropriate offices at which to inquire was presumably quite small. And there was only one suspension bridge in the area. So their efforts don't strike me as those of a family anxious to confirm their daughter's ostensible past-life memories.

If we're wondering whose motivated super psi might have simulated evidence of Chandra's survival, we should probably focus on Chandra's family, not Thusita's. But that strategy would be more promising if Thusita had been born closer to the time of Chandra's death. Instead, Thusita was born nine years afterwards, and reportedly she began speaking of a former life more than two years after that. But by that time, presumably, Chandra's family was no longer grieving intensely, if at all.

Moreover, the hostility and violence of Thusita's brother may also be revealing. If (as it seems) he was angry because he thought Thusita was lying and had sent him on a wild goose chase, then it seems clear that he had failed to discover a previous personality. And in that case, his behavior helps secure early-bird status for Thusita's statements to T. J. and E. H.

4. The Antonia Case

This case is difficult to classify. Probably, we should view it as an instance of apparent reincarnation, with the phenomena emerging through hypnotic past-life regression rather than spontaneous behavior in a child subject. Of course, regression cases are problematic. Some therapists think that if they trace present behavioral problems to a past life, and especially if they then manage to rid their patients of their problems, then this demonstrates the truth of their patients' stories. Unfortunately, many laypersons fail to see that this is simply a non sequitur, and they don't realize that hypnosis provides no guaranteed or reliable access to the truth.

In fact, as a large body of research has documented in detail, it's clear that hypnosis often liberates a person's latent creativity and imagination (see, e.g., O'Connell, Shor, & Orne, 1970; Orne, 1951, 1972; Spiegel & Spiegel, 1978; and the discussion of regression in chapter 4). Moreover, that creativity may embellish material which the subject has forgotten and which hypnosis helps recover, and it may take considerable research to demonstrate that nothing paranormal was going on (see Venn, 1986, for a good example). Nevertheless, we shouldn't be blindly skeptical about hypnotic regressions. As the present case illustrates, hypnosis may lead to behavior that apparently can't be explained away in terms of latent capacities and for which some sort of psi hypothesis seems mandatory.

This case is also difficult to summarize briefly, because it's exceptionally rich in intriguing detail, and because it can't be assessed without considering those details carefully. The subject's name is Laurel Dilmen, and her reported former life was investigated by psychotherapist Linda Tarazi (Tarazi, 1990). Laurel was born and raised in the Chicago area during the Depression, and she lived in that general vicinity all her life. After attending public schools, she graduated from Northwestern University with a degree in education. Her ancestry is German and her religious background is Lutheran, although at the age of twenty she became a Methodist. Laurel embarked on her teaching career after a few years in show business, and at the time of Tarazi's report she was married with two children.

In the mid-1970s Laurel investigated hypnosis for controlling weight and headaches. She joined some amateur hypnosis groups, which Tarazi also had joined, and eventually they and some other members began exploring past-life regressions. During Laurel's first round of hypnotic sessions, she related former lives from a variety of historical periods and geographic locations. But the one that interested her the most, and the one to which she kept returning, was that of a sixteenth-century Spanish woman named Antonia. During eight sessions conducted between June 1977 and January 1978, Laurel gave a great deal of information about Antonia's life. Three years later, between June 1981 and March 1983, Tarazi conducted thirty-six more sessions, which she tape-recorded and transcribed.

Because Antonia's story was an erotically charged romantic adventure, Tarazi initially believed that Laurel's regression was a fantasy, rooted in cryptomnesia and the demand characteristics of the hypnotic experiment. And indeed, Tarazi at first found most of the facts Laurel provided by consulting history books and encyclopedias, "albeit with difficulty" (Tarazi, 1990, p. 311). But Laurel also mentioned names and events that Tarazi was unable to trace at the time, and as her investigation progressed, she discovered that Laurel was providing an astonishing amount of detailed and exceptionally obscure information about the appropriate period and locale of Antonia's alleged life. Occasionally, that information even conflicted with authoritative sources, but Tarazi later confirmed Antonia's claims by diligently tracking down even more obscure and reliable sources. Interestingly, she was never able to find evidence of a person matching Antonia's description and alleged history. However, if Antonia's story is true, that fact wouldn't be especially remarkable.

And that story certainly seems like the stuff of a romance novel. In fact, in 1997 Tarazi published Antonio's story as a 650-page first-person narrative (Tarazi, 1997). According to Antonia, her full name was Antonia Michaela Maria Ruiz de Prado, and she was born November 15, 1555, on the island of Hispaniola to a Spanish office and his German wife. After her mother's death in 1569, Antonia was raised in Germany by her uncle Karl, a former priest who had left the clergy to marry. By the time Antonia arrived he was a university professor and widower, and he successfully imparted to his niece his love of learning and his independence of thought. In 1580 Karl and Antonia moved to Oxford, and although Karl had by then abandoned Catholicism, he never imposed his views on Antonia, who remained a devout Catholic.

After Karl's death, Antonia went to Spain to join her father (Antonio) at the inn he now owned and managed in Cuenca. But when she arrived there in May 1584, she learned that her father had died ten days earlier and that the inn was seriously in debt. Despite her grief, Antonia worked hard to integrate herself into the community and make the inn a success.

Antonia was unaware that the Inquisition had been observing her carefully during this period. In fact, because her father had been a close friend of Inquisitor Arganda, the Inquisition knew a great deal about Antonia from the moment she arrived in Spain. The dying Antonio had feared that his daughter would not fare well on her own, and Arganda promised to care for her as if she was his own daughter, at least so long as it didn't conflict with his duties as Inquisitor. As a final (but perhaps unwise) gesture of trust, Antonio handed over his daughter's letters to Arganda. These detailed uncle Karl's heresies and the tradition of free-thinking to which Antonia had been exposed. But Antonio also knew that the letters documented his daughter's loyal Catholicism. He hoped that Arganda would be impressed by this and realize that although Antonia had been exposed to unacceptable ideas, she remained steadfast in her devotion to the Church and to Spain.

Arganda and his fellow Inquisitor were, indeed, impressed by Antonia's piety and loyalty to Spain. They were also impressed by her sensuous beauty. But they remained suspicious of her background, her failure to confess voluntarily to the Inquisition (Antonia hadn't realized that was the law), and her associations with suspect individuals. So they summoned Antonia three times for typically intense questioning, and once they arrested her. After several months in prison and a full confession, Antonia paid a heavy fine, performed other penances, and eventually returned to her business. Normally, an arrest by the Inquisition would have disgraced Antonia and all her descendants. But because of her special relationship with one of the Inquisitors (more on this later) and an important personal favor she performed for the other, a spilled bottle of ink "accidentally" obliterated her folio. As a result, the Inquisition records, otherwise scrupulously detailed, contain no mention of Antonia.

Antonia lost her virginity around the age of twenty-nine, when a man took her by force in the torture chamber. The eroticism of this assault aroused all her passions and revealed her masochistic tendencies. She had secretly adored this man before, and now she fell madly in love with him and eventually bore him a son. Their relationship evolved from lustful self-indulgence to a deep and all-consuming physical and spiritual union. (This romantic and erotic aspect of Antonia's life was unlike anything reported during Laurel's other past-life regressions.) Together, they traveled widely and enjoyed many adventures, including encounters with Satanists and pirates, and culminating in a visit to Peru, where Antonia met her previously unknown uncle, Inquisitor Juan Ruiz de Prado. On their return voyage, Antonia drowned near a small Caribbean island. Her lover tried desperately to save her, nearly drowning in the process.

Of course, Tarazi wondered whether Antonia's story was true. She claimed that Antonia's narrative is correct for several hundred historical facts mentioned over the forty-four hypnotic sessions. Many of the facts and historical figures are likely to be known by any well-read person—for example, the existence of a Spanish Inquisition and Spanish Armada, and the monarchs Queen Elizabeth and Mary Queen of Scots. Moreover, Tarazi estimated that fifty or sixty details of Spanish, English, or Dutch history were relatively easy to find in books and encyclopedias—for example, concerning Don Bernadino de Mendoza (Spanish ambassador to England) or the Duke of Parma. However, it's difficult to see how someone could spontaneously relate these facts, or provide them in answer to direct questions, without a substantial education in sixteenth-century European history and a very good memory. Furthermore,

> Another 25 to 30 highly specialized facts were located with much greater difficulty. Even though these are published in English, it was necessary to check the Chicago Public Library, Newberry Library, and several university libraries (Northwestern, Northeastern, Loyola, DePaul, University of Illinois, and University of Chicago) to verify them all. Examples include: Date of the first publication of the Edict of Faith on the Island of Hispaniola; Spanish laws governing shipping to the Indies; types of ships used in the Mediterranean and the Atlantic, and details about them; dates and contents of the Spanish indexes of prohibited books and how they differed from the Roman Index; names of priests executed in England in 1581 and 1582, and the method of execution; and information about a college in Cuenca. Over a dozen facts did not seem to be published in English at all but only in Spanish. A few could only be found in the Municipal and others in the Diocesan Archives in Cuenca, Spain. (Tarazi, 1990, pp. 316–317)

Concerned that the apparent obscurity of these facts merely reflected

her lack of expertise in history, Tarazi sent a questionnaire to nine professors at the six largest universities in the Chicago area. For each of
sixty alleged facts, it asked them to rank the likelihood of a nonhistorian
being able to find the information revealed by Antonia. Seven of the
nine professors replied, and the responses confirmed Tarazi's suspicion
that Antonia was indeed supplying extremely recondite information.

Some of the material concerning Cuenca is especially interesting. On
two of the questionnaire items Laurel contradicted Spanish authorities,
and in both cases research showed that she was correct. Antonia's description of the building housing the Inquisition didn't match the one
supplied by the Government Tourist Office in Cuenca. But Tarazi found
an obscure Spanish book on Cuenca, which mentioned that in December 1583 the Tribunal moved from the address given by the Tourist Office to an old castle overlooking the town. That event was five months
before Antonia claimed to arrive in Cuenca (in May 1584), and the castle fit Antonia's description very closely. Moreover, in a follow-up visit
to Spain in 1989, Tarazi found additional information in the Episcopal
Archives that also corresponded to Antonia's account.

Antonia's reference to a college in Cuenca was also controversial.
Both Tarazi and the history professors thought this matter would be
easy to check. But it wasn't. Tarazi found no college in Cuenca, nor any
reference to one in encyclopedias, history, or travel books. Not even the
archivist at the Municipal Archives in Cuenca claimed to have heard of
a college there. But Antonia insisted that students and faculty from the
college met regularly at her inn. Then at the suggestion of a consultant
at Northwestern University, Tarazi called Loyola University and was
told that if there was a college in Cuenca, it might be mentioned in an
old seven-volume work in Spanish (Astrain, 1912-1925). In Volume 2
(pp. 131, 595) of that work Tarazi found references to the founding of a
college in Cuenca in the mid-sixteenth century. She states, plausibly,
that "Even a person who reads Spanish is not likely to wade through this
tome unless involved in historical research" (Tarazi, 1990, p. 321).

A similar disagreement concerned Antonia's claim that Cuenca had
only two Inquisitors. This conflicted with the opinion of Tarazi's experts
that there should have been three Inquisitors and that the Inquisition
always used three. Once again, Antonia was right. During the period
Antonia claimed to live in Cuenca, from 1584 to 1588, there were only
the two Inquisitors she mentioned (Ximines de Reynoso and de Arganda). Before that there were the customary three.

Perhaps the most interesting part of Antonia's story concerns her
claim that, for a time, she became the mistress of one of the Inquisitors.
Initially, Antonia resisted and tried appealing to the Inquisitor's sense of
honor as a conscientious agent of the Church. As she tells it,

> "Can you honestly believe that such a willful and deliberate sin will not
> alter your decisions as Inquisitor?" I asked cooly. He sighed: "I suppose in a

way it already has. In reviewing my cases recently, I noticed that they indicate a far more lenient view of fornication since I decided to indulge myself. To me the liberality was so striking that I feared it might arouse suspicion in the Suprema. I suppose I shall have to revert to my sterner judgments." (Tarazi, 1990, p. 339)

The Inquisition records for Cuenca seem to bear this out. During the
period when Antonia claimed to be the Inquisitor's object of desire,
there was a sharp decline in the percentage of people penanced for fornication. Presumably, those arrested for fornication were instead re-
leased for insufficient evidence or granted a suspended sentence. The
figures are interesting. In 1582, 73% of those arrested for fornication
were penanced. In 1583 it was 75%. In 1584 (but before Antonia's arrival): 60%; for the next five months: 10%; for the end of the year (when
she was under suspicion): 100%. Then in 1585, when Antonia worked
for the Inquisitors and had her affair with one of them, the figure is
11%. In 1586 it was 35%, and in 1587 it was 50%.

Although Tarazi found no evidence that Antonia ever existed, I
should note that she didn't even look for certain records. Tarazi argued
that if Antonia's story is true, it's highly unlikely that crucial records
were ever made, or that they survived. Antonia claimed to be born on an
isolated plantation on Hispaniola and baptized at a small local church
whose name she couldn't recall. It's also unlikely that there would be
records of her marriage by an unofficial priest at her husband's home,
or of her death by drowning off an unnamed Caribbean island.

Tarazi was appropriately cautious about there being no mention of
Antonia in the otherwise meticulous and accurate Inquisition records.
She noted that Antonia's explanation for this, while plausible, seems
suspiciously convenient. She wrote,

> When I checked the Inquisition records, I found no missing number where
> her folio should have fit, and asked her about this. She said that the Inquis-
> itors had probably foreseen the desirability of eliminating her file and prob-
> ably gave it a number identical to another but with an "A" after it so that
> there would be no gap in the record. A check showed that this practice was
> indeed sometimes followed, although probably not usually for this reason.
> (Tarazi, 1990, p. 323)

Alan Gauld remains justifiably suspicious about the evidential value
of this case. One concern is the possibility that Laurel once read (and
then later forgot) an obscure historical novel rich in accurate details of
the period. Certainly, there's a precedent for that concern; there's at
least a small body of evidence for this sort of cryptomnesia—for example, the "Blanche Poynings" case (Dickinson, 1911; see also Kampman,
1976; Kampman & Hirvenoja, 1976). However, Gauld's search for such
a novel has so far been unsuccessful. Tarazi, likewise, found no book
with the relevant information. For reasons of space, I can't review all
the considerations leading Tarazi to rule out the Usual (and Unusual)

Suspects as explanations for this case. Commendably, she seems sensitive to relevant psychological subtleties, and she appears to have investigated Laurel's background carefully to determine the likelihood of either fraud or cryptomnesia. To see why she rules out those options, I urge readers to look closely at Tarazi's report and examine her detailed summary of Laurel's history.

Once again, our concern has to be with the viability of a motivated super-psi explanation, assuming the Usual and Unusual Suspects have been eliminated. And in that connection, what matters particularly is the lack of evidence, not only for the existence of Antonia, but also for her uncle Karl. I'm greatly indebted to Gauld on this matter. With his customary tenacity and resourcefulness, he's embarked on a careful search for traces of Antonia and Karl in England. He assumes, reasonably, that such traces would exist given Karl's academic affiliations and Antonia's alleged political activism. But that search, too, has turned up nothing.[3] Perhaps in light of the Patience Worth case, we should be especially wary of treating the Antonia case as evidence of survival. Both Pearl and Laurel exhibited surprising amounts of recondite background knowledge—in Pearl's case, of biblical history.

Now it's not difficult to imagine why Laurel (or virtually anyone) might have been motivated to be obsessed with a highly romantic, adventurous, and erotic life history. But as Tarazi recognized, psychodynamics won't account for the factual material in the story. Considering the accuracy, abundance, and obscurity of details, and their disparate and varied sources, I think it's fair to say that positing super psi for this case raises the problem of crippling complexity in an especially acute form.

A few more details are worth mentioning. To emphasize the difficulty of learning the relevant information by normal means, Tarazi writes,

> Even some material from American libraries would have been difficult for her to obtain. Not only were the books old, rare, highly specialized, and in a language which L.D. did not read, but they contained many quotes from 16th-century Spanish that present a problem to the average native Spanish speaker and even for the Spanish teachers whom I contacted. Nor were there only a few such books; rather, about 30 each contribute new facts. (p. 329)

Moreover, Tarazi noted that this case was impressive right from the start, both in its specificity of information and in the way it was revealed. Whereas Laurel's other regressions had a nebulous quality, "Antonia came through as a proud, independent woman who knew exactly who, what, and where she was" (Tarazi, 1990, p. 320). Laurel's hypnotist for the first set of sessions was a person born, raised, and educated in Holland, with a good command of Dutch history. His pointed questioning of Antonia led to some interesting revelations early on. Tarazi writes,

Most persons who know the Dutch history of the period would have said, as many history books do, that the governor at the time was the Duke of Parma. Asked about this, Antonia said that he was the son of Margaret of Parma, but not the Duke. She was correct for that date. Alexander Farnese did not succeed to that title until 1586. (p. 320)

That was in Laurel's first session. Also in that session she displayed

some knowledge of a few battles in which her father had reportedly partici- pated in 1567-1569, under Don Fernando de Toledo who, she claimed, was then the Spanish Governor. The hypnotist told her she was wrong: the Duke of Alva was governor then. She replied: "Of course. That is his title. I gave his name." The title is much more well known. Even some history books neglect to give his name. It was the extreme accuracy of the numer- ous details that affected Antonia's "life" together with relative ignorance of contemporary events unrelated to it that presented such an intriguing con- trast from the very first session. (p. 320)

The foregoing exchange is interesting for another reason. It illus- trates why Tarazi ruled out explanations in terms of familiar hypnotic compliance and demand characteristics of the regression. Laurel clearly resisted overt pressure from her interlocutors, on this and on other oc- casions, to give the responses they encouraged or believed to be correct. In fact, Tarazi agreed to accept Laurel as a client because she wanted to help her break free of her preoccupation with Antonia, which had led her to neglect other people and activities in her present life. Tarazi hoped to convince Laurel that this past life was pure fantasy and that the love reportedly experienced by Antonia was merely the stuff of fic- tion and dreams. Her plan, at least initially, was to confront Laurel with errors in her depiction of the facts.

Some of Laurel's (or Antonia's) emotions during her regressions are noteworthy as well. They tend to strengthen the conviction that her re- sponses weren't artifacts of suggestion and hypnotic compliance. For example, when she saw the building identified incorrectly by Spanish authorities as the one housing the Inquisition tribunal,

she was stunned. All present observed her dramatic change in mood from eager anticipation to a deep depression. It never occurred to her to ques- tion the authorities. In quiet resignation she said her whole story must have been imagination. (p. 329)

Later, Tarazi found the obscure Spanish book, containing the correct information, in the Newberry Library. Laurel claimed never to have vis- ited Newberry, and besides, the library there doesn't circulate books, and it keeps a record of all visitors.

Eventually, Tarazi used hypnosis to help her client let go of Antonia's story. She asked Laurel, under hypnosis, to live out the unfinished part of Antonia's life, telling her that Antonia's son had not died and that Antonia had been rescued from her near drowning. Tarazi suggested,

further, that Antonia and her lover returned to Spain and lived out a
healthy life there. Laurel complied with the suggestions, and Tarazi's
therapeutic strategy seems to have worked. Laurel finally lost her desire
to have further regressions, and she took a renewed interest in her own
life. But what's noteworthy is that her newly

> fantasized story was of an entirely different quality than the original one.
> No new facts could be produced. No more adventures occurred....Most
> descriptions were far less vivid and lacked the emotion of the original nar-
> ration. (p. 328)

Curiously, perhaps, there's little evidence of xenoglossy in this case.
Tarazi said Antonia spoke no Spanish spontaneously, and only a little
Spanish and Latin responsively. Regrettably, Tarazi didn't provide details of the few apparent instances of responsive xenoglossy. But she
noted that Spanish-speaking persons at the sessions claimed that Antonia pronounced Spanish words and names very well. Moreover, Antonia
"recited the prayers required by the Inquisition in Latin, referred to special methods of making the sign of the cross, the *signo* and *santiguado*,
unknown to most Spanish-speaking priests today, and composed words
and music to a song in Latin" (p. 323). At the very least, that's not what
one would expect of a person of German ancestry and a Lutheran or
Methodist religious background.

5. The Sumitra/Shiva Case

Let's now examine a specimen of ostensible possession (described in
Stevenson, Pasricha, & McLean-Rice, 1989, and also Pasricha, 1990a,
pp. 256–268). I select this case for several reasons. First, it's recent; unlike many other intriguing cases it hasn't been scrutinized *ad nauseam* in
the literature. Second, it's good, illustrating clearly why survivalist explanations of possession cases are seriously tempting. And third, it also
illustrates why super-psi counter-explanations must also be taken seriously, and not simply as mere theoretical possibilities. In particular, this
case raises, perhaps more clearly than most, the sorts of concerns about
motivations that may well extend to other, more superficially straightforward, cases.

In this case, the subject, the previous personality, and their respective families lived in an area about five hundred kilometers southeast of
Delhi, most less than one hundred kilometers from one another, and
within fairly easy access by railroad. The subject was a seventeen-year-
old married woman named Sumitra Singh. When the case developed,
she resided in the village of Sharifpura with her husband and one child
in her husband's family home. As Stevenson and colleagues report,
"Sumitra's early life was unusual in the degree to which she lived separated from one or both of her parents" (Stevenson *et al.*, 1989, p. 87).

In fact, Sumitra's experience of loss or separation occurred not simply with respect to her parents. She was separated from her father for long periods, because he found steady employment in a distant city, and Sumitra was eleven years old when her mother died. Only two years later, at age thirteen, Sumitra married, but since her husband (like her father) worked in another city (Delhi), she was once again separated from a major figure in her life.

Sumitra had also been separated from both her parents for long periods, apparently as her father sought work in neighboring villages. During these intervals, Sumitra lived with an older cousin who taught her the elements of reading and writing. But that seems to have been the extent of Sumitra's education; she never attended school. And since Sumitra's cousin had attended primary school only for a year or two, Sumitra's mastery of the written language was rudimentary. Nevertheless, she was able to read, and she could compose a simple letter.

Sumitra gave birth to her son at age sixteen, and a month or two later she began to experience periods of unconsciousness accompanied by eye rolling and clenching of her teeth. She claimed on some of those occasions that she had been possessed by a Hindu goddess, and twice she acted as if she was possessed by more mundane discarnate personalities. A visit by a local healer seemed to calm Sumitra, but it didn't halt the periods of trance. During one of those trances, in July 1985, Sumitra predicted that she would die three days later. When that day came (on July 19), Sumitra did in fact seem to die. Eyewitnesses reported that her respiration and pulse stopped, and her face drained of blood. Because there was no doctor in the vicinity, we have only reports of friends and family that Sumitra was in this state for at least five minutes (some said it was much longer). It was certainly long enough to convince many that Sumitra had died, and some began to cry and discuss arranging the appropriate Hindu ritual.

When Sumitra revived, she was apparently unable to recognize her family and surroundings, and she spoke very little for the next day or so. But then she began to say that her name was Shiva and that she had lived with her husband and two children in the village of Dibiyapur, about one hundred kilometers southeast of Sharifpura. She also claimed that she had been murdered by her in-laws, and she mentioned many details that were subsequently found to correspond to the life of a young married woman named Shiva Diwedi, who had died violently two months before Sumitra's apparent death and revival. The evidence of Shiva's death leaves it open whether she died from murder or suicide. Shiva's father, Ram Siya Tripathi, believed it was the former. He filed a complaint, charging that Shiva's in-laws had murdered his daughter and then placed her body on nearby railway tracks in order to simulate suicide. Apparently, this case received very little press coverage, although newspaper reports appeared in the town of Etawah, where Shiva's father lived. That district town lies about fifty kilometers west of Dibiyapur and sixty-five kilometers south of Sharifpura.

Sumitra's in-laws claimed to know nothing about Shiva, and they thought at first that Sumitra had gone mad. Before long, they thought she might have become possessed by a vagrant and hopefully transient discarnate personality, like those who had apparently possessed Sumitra before. But except for a few hours in the autumn of 1986 when the Sumitra personality resumed control, the Shiva persona remained dominant. It was still dominant when the investigators conducted their last interviews in October 1987.

Initially, Sumitra's in-laws made no effort to verify her statements about Shiva. And when Shiva's father learned about Sumitra's statements—a month after Sumitra's apparent death—it was apparently coincidental. During a visit to Dibiyapur, Ram Siya Tripathi heard a rumor that his deceased daughter had taken possession of a girl in another village. Two months later, he had this information verified, when someone from a village near Sharifpura visited Sumitra and her family. Because the information gathered from Sumitra corresponded to facts in Shiva's life, Ram Siya personally visited Sharifpura in October 1985. During that visit, Sumitra recognized Ram Siya and claimed to be his daughter. And in the days that followed, she also recognized at least thirteen members of Shiva's family and circle of friends. These identifications were made both in Sharifpura and in Etawah (where she had gone to visit Ram Siya).

Sumitra's behavior also underwent a dramatic change during this period. Her family belonged to the Thakur caste and were mostly uneducated villagers. But Shiva's family were Brahmins and middle-class urbanites. In fact, Shiva's father was a college lecturer, and Shiva had earned a B.A. degree. After reviving, "Sumitra's behavior changed from that of a simple village girl to that of a moderately well-educated woman of higher caste and more urban manners, who could now read and write Hindi fluently" (Stevenson *et al.*, 1989, p. 84).

Stevenson and his colleagues learned about the case in October 1985, after a report was published in the *Indian Express*, and shortly after Sumitra's and Shiva's families first exchanged visits. About three weeks later, they began interviewing those who had witnessed Sumitra's apparent death and subsequent behavioral changes, as well as the members of Shiva's family. Their interviews continued, off and on, for the next two years.

The members of Sumitra's and Shiva's families denied any previous knowledge of each other. This is credible, considering how the families were separated by differences in caste, education, and economic position, as well as geography. Additional support comes from "the slow and roundabout manner in which Shiva's family learned about the personality change in Sumitra" (Stevenson *et al.*, 1989, p. 86). The investigators suggest, plausibly, that if the families had been previously acquainted or had acquaintances in common, they would have exchanged information relatively soon after Sumitra's revival, and it would not have taken Ram Siya three months before his initial meeting with Sumitra.

Investigators learned that some information about Shiva's death had made its way to Sharifpura, although Sumitra's relatives claimed to have heard nothing about that incident. Nevertheless, it's wise to assume that Sumitra's family might have learned of Shiva's death and the surrounding allegations, even if they had since forgotten the matter. The important question is whether Sumitra/Shiva demonstrated knowledge about Shiva's life and behavior that went beyond the published accounts of Shiva's death and the subsequent judicial proceedings.

With that constraint in mind, we should be wary of Sumitra's ability to identify persons, places, or events reported in the newspaper. Moreover, although a good deal of circumstantial evidence points to the murder of Shiva by her in-laws, some of Sumitra's statements about Shiva's life and death were never verified. These include (a) an account of Shiva's final quarrel with her in-laws, (b) Shiva's sister-in-law then hitting her on the head with a brick, and (c) the family then depositing her body on tracks at the railway station to simulate suicide. However, a third group of statements has more evidential value. These concern nicknames and private matters never mentioned in published accounts, and of which Sumitra probably had no normal knowledge. Sumitra/Shiva noted, among other things, "a particular yellow sari that Shiva had owned, a watch that had belonged to Shiva and the box [in Ram Siya's home]...in which it was kept, the respective order of birth of Shiva's maternal uncles (although one who was younger actually looked older than one of the older uncles), one of Shiva's nicknames familiarly used in the home..., the names of two educational institutions where Shiva had studied..., the pet names of Shiva's two children..., the names of two friends of Shiva who happened to have the same name, and the names of Shiva's two brothers, two of her sisters, two of her maternal uncles, a maternal aunt (by marriage), and a nephew" (Stevenson *et al.*, 1989, p. 91).

Obviously, it's important to consider whether Sumitra might have made these identifications with the aid of subtle and unconscious cues provided by her interlocutors. And ideally, Sumitra's identifications should be made spontaneously, without prompting by such statements as "Do you know who this person is?" or "Tell me who I am." Stevenson and colleagues cite what they regard as the most compelling of Sumitra's identifications, and then they consider various explanations competing with the possession hypothesis. Regrettably, however, they don't consider psi among the living, which in this case may be more than a mere theoretical possibility. Of course, as in every case, if the subject's statements can be verified by normal means, then the relevant information was also accessible to ESP. That's why super-psi explanations seem always to be options in logical space. And perhaps that's why Stevenson and colleagues didn't bother to discuss super-psi alternatives. However, although Sumitra made some correct early-bird statements about Shiva, it may be significant that most of Sumitra's true statements were known to be true to someone at the scene. As good mediumistic cases suggest, that context may be more conducive than most to successful ESP. Furthermore, although I agree that fraud is highly unlikely, the investigators' discussion of possible secondary gain is quite superficial. But as we've seen (e.g., in the Sharada case), the possible role of secondary gain is crucial in framing plausible motivated super-psi hypotheses.

Let's consider how these matters influence our evaluation of the evidence. And let's begin with the recognitions that Stevenson and colleagues regard as most strongly supporting the possession hypothesis.

(1) When Sumitra was first introduced to Ram Siya (whom she had been told was "her"—that is, Shiva's father), she called him "Papa," which Shiva had also done, and she wept. And after he asked her, Sumitra gave two pet names by which Shiva was known in her family. One of these, Shiv Shanker, had not been published in the newspaper report of Shiva's death.

(2) Sumitra recognized Shiva's maternal uncle by marriage when he accompanied Ram Siya to Sharifpura. Sumitra was asked to identify him, and at first she got it wrong, claiming he was the father of one of Shiva's maternal uncles. Asked again, she correctly identified him.

(3) Sumitra recognized Ram Rani, Shiva's mother, when she paid her first visit to Etawah. Ram Siya tried to mislead Sumitra. Ram Rani was inside the house, and Ram Siya told Sumitra that she was in a group of women standing near the house. But Sumitra insisted that "her" mother was not in that group, and when she went inside the house and found Ram Rani, she embraced her tearfully.

(4) Sumitra recognized another of Shiva's maternal uncles, even though he had grown a beard after Shiva's death. Sumitra recognized him as Shiva's mother's brother, but could not give his name. Then he finally spoke, and Sumitra, apparently recognizing his voice, correctly identified the uncle by name.

Sumitra also recognized fifteen members of Shiva's families in photographs shown to her by Ram Siya, including one of his wife and children taken eighteen years earlier. Sumitra recognized the picture of the young Shiva, saying "This is me." She also recognized a picture of Shiva's sister-in-law, identifying her as the person who had hit "her" with a brick.

So long as we consider these recognitions individually, they pose no problem even for a very conservative version of a super-psi hypothesis. The interlocutor (or someone else at the scene) knew the correct answers; so telepathy among the living is a live option. But if we consider

Sumitra's correct identifications collectively, that option loses some of its force. The consistency of Sumitra's correct identifications becomes an issue, and crippling complexity casts a shadow over our deliberations.

Several of Sumitra's responses are more difficult to evaluate than those mentioned above, and they are probably less impressive. But overall, Sumitra seems to have done rather well in identifying people in Shiva's life, either in person or from photographs. However (as we've noted), accuracy is only one part of the story; motivation is another. Super-psi explanations shouldn't be taken seriously unless they explain credibly why someone might be motivated to simulate survival with their psychic abilities. Similarly, survivalist explanations need to provide good reasons for thinking that no such motivations existed. That's especially important in cases like that of Sumitra/Shiva, containing clues as to what those motivations might be. And in that respect, Stevenson and colleagues seem not to have met their explanatory challenge.

For example, they considered whether Sumitra or her family had anything substantial to gain from the apparent possession by Shiva. Naturally, they considered whether the increased status of having a Brahmin in the family might have mattered. And I think we can agree that there's no evidence supporting the hypothesis of fraud. But that still leaves open the possibility that increased status might have meant a great deal to Sumitra, and that the Shiva persona was constructed unconsciously (rather than fraudulently) to satisfy that need or desire. The investigators dismiss this possibility as "minuscule" (p. 98), although they offer no supporting argument for that judgment.

More seriously, they dismiss as minuscule—again, without supporting argument—the interesting fact that Sumitra's husband, "who had been away a lot prior to the change, was staying at home more than he had before and presumably giving her more attention" (p. 98). Of course, in light of Sumitra's history of abandonment and isolation (which the investigators acknowledge was unusual), it's unacceptable simply to assume that this was a relatively unimportant state of affairs. Clearly, something sensitive and penetrating needs to be said about Sumitra's feelings of separation, not simply from her primary caretakers, but from the major male figures in her life. That would be especially important for the period during and after her son's birth, when her husband's presence might have been especially welcome. So in the absence of persuasive reasons for discounting these matters as deeply urgent, a motivated super-psi hypothesis remains a viable option.

Another aspect of Sumitra/Shiva's psychology seems particularly troubling for the survivalist. It's intriguing that Sumitra/Shiva apparently didn't want to return to Shiva's family (including her children), preferring instead to remain with Sumitra's less affluent and cultivated circle.[4] Of course, we can easily imagine why a surviving Shiva would rather not return to the family that (she believed) murdered her. But even though married women in India more commonly live with their in-laws than with their own family, presumably the real Shiva could still have retreated to her father's home. And in fact, it's not unprecedented in possession cases for the subjects to move in with the possessor's family—for example, in the famous case of Lurancy Vennum (Hodgson, 1901; Myers, 1903, vol. 1, pp. 360–368; Stevens, 1887).

But quite apart from that issue, it's striking that Sumitra/Shiva apparently felt a greater duty to Sumitra's children than to Shiva's. After her revival, Sumitra initially showed no interest in her husband and child. In fact, she refused to acknowledge her child as her own and asked about Shiva's children instead. Then, during the following weeks, she gradually accepted Sumitra's husband and child as her own, even though she continued to insist that she was Shiva. According to Stevenson and colleagues, Sumitra worried that God would punish her if she failed to care for Sumitra's child (Stevenson *et al.*, 1989, p. 95). Now is this concern, or shift in allegiances, more appropriate to Sumitra or to Shiva?

Survivalists have at least one answer. They could argue that the surviving Shiva recognized that she "inhabited" Sumitra's body, and that this fact alone created a *prima facie* duty to Sumitra's family rather than Shiva's. And they might argue that Sumitra/Shiva gradually came to recognize and accept this obligation. But that response isn't entirely convincing. Since the Shiva personality remained dominant, we could just as easily expect Sumitra/Shiva to have preferred maintaining a relationship with Shiva's children. In fact, we might have expected that even from the survivalist's perspective. As I noted, a survivalist would presumably have to say that Sumitra/Shiva recognized a duty to Sumitra's husband and child, simply in virtue of the bodily criterion of controlling Sumitra's body. But psychologically Sumitra/Shiva appeared to be Shiva rather than Sumitra, and we can only wonder why—if a surviving Shiva was possessing Sumitra—that fact didn't create a competing and equally compelling *prima facie* duty to Shiva's husband or children. From the survivalist's point of view, we might reasonably have expected Sumitra/Shiva to be torn between two competing *prima facie* duties, one based on a bodily criterion, and the other based on a psychological criterion. Now granted, at one point Sumitra/Shiva cried when shown a photograph of Shiva's children. But there seems to be a striking discontinuity between that outburst and Sumitra/Shiva's relative lack of interest in (or indifference to) pursuing a relationship with the children. That seems most strongly to favor a non-survivalist explanation.

Moreover, we have the mystery of Sumitra/Shiva's enhanced literacy. On the surface, that seems to favor a survivalist explanation, because it was a competence that Shiva possessed. But Sumitra exhibited only one enhanced ability after her transformation, and we have to wonder why that is and why Sumitra didn't manifest other new abilities that were characteristic of Shiva. It seems unlikely that the appropriateness of Sumitra's new skill is merely a coincidence, and survivalists can accommodate it neatly as part of the postmortem Sumitra persona. However, Stevenson and colleagues note that this change "was not in [Sumitra's] basic ability to read and write but in her fluency in these activities and in her interest in writing" (Stevenson *et al.*, 1989, p. 97). Presumably, then, this change is of the same sort observed, to a much higher degree, in the case of Patience Worth (chapter 5). It's similar also, in both degree and kind, to the enhanced fluency of linguistic and artistic skills observed in many cases of MPD/DID (where survivalist explanations are usually—and transparently—superfluous).

So we need to be cautious in our interpretation of Sumitra's new literacy. As we noted in chapter 5 (and to some extent in chapter 4), we shouldn't underestimate our latent knowledge, creativity, and resourcefulness. And here, once again, we must be alert for three things: first, the possibility that skills can ferment under the psychological surface; second, that they can then find expression in dissociative or other unusual states that bypass ordinary resistances or barriers to optimal performance; and third, that (as with MPD/DID patients) given the right motivation we can selectively tap into exactly the skills we need, drawn presumably from a much larger reservoir of latent faculties.

Clearly, then, this case falls short of ideal in a number of respects. But despite its shortcomings, a survivalist interpretation is at least tantalizing, and it may well be our best choice. Altogether, "Sumitra recognized 23 members of Shiva's family and acquaintances either in person or in photographs, some of them in both ways" (Stevenson *et al.*, 1989, p. 95). And of seventeen persons identified in photographs, Sumitra identified twelve of them without hesitation, another three with some hesitation, and she failed to recognize two persons. Moreover, Sumitra often made these identifications with accompanying expressions of emotion more appropriate to a surviving Shiva than to Sumitra. Of course, if we assume that Sumitra closely identified with a kind of alter ego constructed from psychically derived information, those emotions might be explained away fairly easily. But the information she provided may be more refractory. It's questionable whether Sumitra could have made so many correct identifications, and *so many without hesitation*, if she were relying solely on telepathy from the living, aided occasionally by superior mnemonic abilities (e.g., when she had previously identified people in photographs). As we saw in chapter 3, even if ESP is (in principle) unlimited in range and refinement, there are reasons for expecting it to be less consistent than this.

In fact, quite apart from the considerations advanced in chapter 3, we might find Sumitra's identification scorecard better than expected even for a great virtuoso. For one thing, psychic capacities seem clearly to be situation-sensitive, even under the most favorable conditions. And for another, great virtuosi in other domains suffer similar or greater lapses of reliability. As is often the case, the clearest examples come from music and sports. Consider, for instance, great basketball players whose ability to score (or even make foul shots) probably doesn't achieve a comparable degree of consistency, or great tennis players who frequently miss shots, or great musicians who have memory lapses or miss notes.

Moreover, as with good drop-in cases like that of Runki (chapter 2), psychodynamic considerations point most clearly to a survivalist interpretation. Granted, the super-psi hypothesis can be applied to the case, at least in principle. Anti-survivalists can claim that Sumitra suffered from a kind of attachment disorder. They could argue that her experience of abandonment impelled her to locate psychically and then personate a suitable deceased subject. They could then argue that Sumitra (a) learned psychically what she needed to know about Shiva, and (b) drew upon a previously untapped linguistic fluency to make the Shiva persona more convincing. By contrast, survivalists have a much simpler story to tell, even if we don't know quite what to make of it. They need only claim that Shiva somehow survived bodily death, and "indignant at having been added to the flourishing Indian bride-murder statistics, was not prepared to go quietly" (Mary Rose Barrington, personal communication, September 16, 2000).

Finally, we should note some intriguing similarities between the case of Sumitra and that of Jasbir (Stevenson, 1974a). In both cases, the subjects seemed to die. Then, after reviving and passing through a period of not speaking (or being unable to speak), they exhibited profound behavioral changes corresponding to a subsequently identified previous personality. Furthermore, in both cases the emerging personality appeared only gradually to accept that it "occupied" an unfamiliar body, eventually settling down (more or less grudgingly) with the new family. Perhaps the most important difference between the cases is the age of the subject. Sumitra was in her teens, but Jasbir was three and a half years old. So it might be more of a stretch to explain the Jasbir case in terms of the *subject's* motivated psi. The same problem arises in the less well-documented case of Sudhakar Misra (Pasricha, 1990a, pp. 104–109). In this case the subject was not even a year old when the previous personality died, and here too the apparent possession began around the time of the subject's illness.

In fact, it's intriguing that subjects in reincarnation and possession cases often begin speaking about a previous life after suffering a fever, serious illness, or apparent death. And it's unclear whether this makes more sense in terms of survival or in terms of super psi. The survivalist can always say that the illness, etc., weakens the subject's personality structure and provides an "opening," either for a possessing entity to take control or for the emergence of a previous personality's latent characteristics. But partisans of super psi might see the illness, etc., as belonging to the class of unusual or altered states that are both psi-conducive and favorable to the emergence of latent knowledge or abilities. If the survivalist has the advantage here, it will be in cases, like those of Jasbir and Sudhakar Misra, where the subject seems too young to have the motivations needed for a plausible super-psi explanation.

6. The Thompson-Gifford Case

Let's pass finally to a case that's somewhat difficult to classify. Although we could reasonably catalog it as an example of possession, we might also regard it as an instance of what many call *obsession* (the Antonia case might also fall into this category). Gauld distinguishes the two sorts of phenomena as follows.

> In cases of possession the supposed intruding entity displaces or partly displaces the victim from his body, and obtains direct control of it—the same sort of control, presumably, as the victim himself had....In cases of obsession, the victim remains in immediate control of his body, but the supposed intruding entity influences his mind. It establishes a sort of parasitic relationship with his mind, whereby it can to an extent see what he sees, feel what he feels, enjoy what he enjoys, etc., and can also change the course of his thoughts and actions to conform with its own desires. (Gauld, 1982, pp. 147–148)

But how significant is this difference? Interestingly, it resembles the different degrees and types of trance found in mediumship (chapter 3). In both cases, the variability concerns the extent to which, and the manner in which, the intruding entity displaces the host personality. In fact, these differences also parallel some of the varying relationships between ego or personality states in cases of MPD/DID. So I question whether we need to regard obsession as anything other than a type of possession. We don't need to make comparable taxonomic divisions in cases of mediumship or MPD/DID. Just as mediumship and MPD/DID fall along continua of trance-depth and personality-displacement, the same seems to be true in cases of possession.

But this is a side issue. What matters here is the extent to which good obsession cases challenge the super-psi hypothesis, and the case described in this section is about as good as they get. But because many others have discussed it, sometimes at great length, we'll review it fairly quickly (see, e.g., Gauld, 1982; Rogo, 1987; Roy, 1996). The principal investigator was James Hyslop, whom we first encountered in chapter 2, and whose meticulous and painstaking account of the case consumed 469 pages in the 1909 *Proceedings of the ASPR* (Hyslop, 1909).

The subject of this case was a thirty-six-year-old goldsmith from New York City, Frederic L. Thompson. During an earlier apprenticeship as an engraver, he had exhibited some talent for sketching. But apart from a few art lessons during his school years, he had no formal training in art. However, throughout the summer and autumn of 1905 he often found himself seized by powerful impulses to sketch and paint in oils. These impulses began to dominate Thompson's life, and (as his wife confirmed) during these periods he often felt that he was the artist Robert Swain Gifford. Thompson had met Gifford before, but only very casually. For example, they spoke briefly during an encounter in the marshes of New Bedford, where Thompson was hunting and Gifford was sketching. And once Thompson visited Gifford in New York to show him some jewelry. But their acquaintance seems to have gone no deeper than this, and apparently Thompson knew almost nothing about Gifford's work.

When Thompson attended an exhibition of Gifford's work in January 1906, he learned that Gifford had died a year earlier, approximately six months before Thompson's apparent obsession began. Moreover, as he looked at one of Gifford's paintings, he had an apparent auditory hallucination. A voice said to him, "You see what I have done. Can you not take up and finish my work?" This experience seemed only to strengthen Thompson's urge to paint, and he began having frequent auditory and visual hallucinations. Most of the visions were of landscapes with wind-blown trees, and one of these haunted him repeatedly. It was a view of gnarled oaks on a promontory by raging seas, and Thompson made several sketches of it as well as a painting called "The Battle of the Elements." In fact, Thompson painted several of his visions, and although opinions divided over the skill demonstrated in the paintings, he sold a few of them on their merits. Moreover, some noted a similarity between these paintings and Gifford's work.

Thompson had always been somewhat dreamy or distracted, but his current situation was more extreme. He painted in mental states ranging from slight dissociation to nearly complete automatism, and as these episodes became more common, he began neglecting his work. Before long, his financial situation deteriorated badly, and both Thompson and his wife Carrie feared that he was becoming insane. So on January 16, 1907, Thompson sought advice from Hyslop, whom an acquaintance had recommended and who at first also suspected that Thompson might be insane.

Nevertheless, Hyslop was intrigued by Thompson's obsession with Gifford. Recognizing that Thompson's experiences resembled others in which psi apparently play a role, he decided to pursue the matter by taking Thompson to a medium. Thompson claimed to be skeptical about mediumship and spiritualism, but he was desperate enough to go along with Hyslop's suggestion. So on January 18 they visited the medium Mrs. "Rathbun," to whom Thompson was introduced anonymously. Without prompting, Mrs. Rathbun mentioned a man behind Thompson who was fond of painting, and her descriptions of this man resembled Gifford in several intriguing respects. Thompson remarked that he was trying to find a certain scene of oak trees near the ocean, which Mrs. Rathbun then seemed to describe, noting that it needed to be reached by boat.

Both Thompson and Hyslop were encouraged by this sitting. Thompson, now feeling that he wasn't insane, continued to sketch and paint his visions. And Hyslop continued to arrange anonymous sittings for Thompson with other mediums. The most significant of these sittings, on March 16, 1907, was with Mrs. Chenoweth, whom we also encountered in chapter 2. Thompson entered the séance room only after Mrs. Chenoweth's trance had begun, and the session was preserved in full stenographic records. The medium's control mentioned numerous specific items that seemed clearly to apply to Gifford, many of them subsequently confirmed by Mrs. Gifford. These included Gifford's distinctive clothing and mannerisms (Hyslop, 1909, pp. 117, 121–122), the oil skins he wore when boating and painting (p. 126), his fondness for rugs (pp. 118, 127), his color preferences (pp. 119, 126–127), his love of misty scenes (p. 126), his two homes (p. 130), and his unfinished canvases (p. 124).

Mrs. Chenoweth's control also claimed to relay the following statement from Gifford: "I will help you, because I want someone who can catch the inspiration of these things as I did, to carry on my work" (p. 125). That statement certainly fits Thompson's obsession, and assuming that we're dealing here with a case of possession, it's the sort of statement we'd expect Gifford to convey to Thompson. But it may instead have a more mundane origin. Earlier in the sitting, Thompson had already provided Mrs. Chenoweth with enough information to concoct the statement on her own, consciously or unconsciously. When she invited Thompson to pose a question to the communicator, Thompson said, "Well, I just wanted to know if I should go on with these feelings that come to me and carry out the work as I feel he would like to have me" (p. 122).

A few months after this sitting, Thompson set out to locate and paint the actual scenes that had appeared before his mind, and he kept a daily diary of his efforts. But on July 2, 1907, before departing, he deposited a collection of his "Gifford" sketches with Hyslop. He had drawn these in the summer and autumn of 1905, and Hyslop locked the pictures away for safekeeping, along with notations indicating how and when he received them. Thompson's first stop was Nonquitt, Massachusetts, the location of Gifford's summer home. Because it was inaccessible except by boat, Thompson hoped to find there some of the scenes from his visions. And in fact, he located and photographed several apparently familiar scenes. Thompson also called on Mrs. Gifford, who allowed him to inspect her late husband's studio. That studio had been disturbed very little in the two-and-a-half years since Gifford's death, and Thompson discovered several works that seemed to be of scenes he had sketched or envisioned previously. According to Hyslop, a few of these were identical with some of Thompson's earlier sketches.

But that alleged identity is difficult to evaluate. Not all of Thompson's earlier sketches had been deposited with Hyslop, and Hyslop's published photographs of Gifford pictures are sometimes small and unclear. Moreover, even when Gifford's pictures are reproduced more adequately, it's sometimes questionable whether they correspond closely to Thompson's sketches (see Hyslop, 1909, pp. 385–386). But we should also remember, as Gauld observes, that the black-and-white reproductions in Hyslop's report may be a bit misleading. They may not do justice to similarities that would be more impressive in color.

But quite apart from these more questionable correspondences, one piece of evidence is exceptional. Thompson found on an easel a painting that matched, both closely and unmistakably, one of the sketches he had left behind with Hyslop. Because Thompson's impulse to paint this scene first arose six months after Gifford's death, the obvious question was whether he could have seen Gifford's painting before producing his own sketch. To address that issue, Hyslop printed a letter from Mrs. Gifford, who noted that the picture was placed on her husband's easel only after his death. Before that it had been rolled up and put away. Hyslop also confirmed that Gifford's painting had never been exhibited or offered for sale (Hyslop, 1909, pp. 65ff). So Thompson had no opportunity to see the painting before this visit to Gifford's studio.

Mrs. Gifford told Thompson that he might find even more of his visualized scenes on the Elizabeth Islands, off Buzzard's Bay, and especially on Naushon Island (where Gifford had been born). Thompson headed for those locations shortly thereafter, and he claimed to find several landscapes that matched his visions. In fact, he felt that something was directing him to the scenes. On one occasion, while sketching a group of trees on Naushon Island, he heard a voice telling him to look on the far side of the trees. There he found Gifford's initials carved into a tree, along with the year 1902.

Also on that island Thompson located and painted the group of trees he had depicted earlier in "The Battle of the Elements." Thompson had already deposited one of his initial sketches of this scene with Hyslop, and that sketch of Thompson's vision closely matched his new painting of the scene. Of course, that proved nothing. Hyslop needed to ascertain whether the scene really existed. So he accompanied Thompson back to the island, and eventually they located and photographed the spot (for the grubby details of the difficulties they encountered, see Hyslop, 1909, pp. 64–85). However, the photographs could only be taken from angles different from that represented in Thompson's sketches and painting. And two of the most strikingly curved oak limbs had been broken off and were lying on the ground (Hyslop photographed these for his report). Nevertheless, it takes little effort to see that the scene corresponds quite closely to the sketch left with Hyslop. In fact, Hyslop noted that this early sketch is a more realistic depiction of the scene than the later painting, which is more idealized. Moreover, it's worth noting that in a sitting with one of Hyslop's psychics prior to discovering the real scene, the medium predicted that one limb of the trees in question would be missing.

Thompson claimed that he had never visited these islands before his visions began. However, he had lived near the islands in his childhood. So although Thompson's veracity generally seemed beyond reproach, Hyslop also obtained statements from Thompson's mother, sister, and wife, confirming that Thompson hadn't visited the islands.

Hyslop was encouraged by these developments to arrange more sessions with his team of mediums. The new round of sittings began in April 1908, and Hyslop continued to introduce Thompson anonymously. Regrettably, nothing much of interest "came through" until May 1908, by which point the press had gotten wind of this case. Although the newspaper stories were rather cursory, their appearance raises the possibility that the mediums knew enough about the case to dig up additional information on their own. I'm aware of no reasons to doubt the integrity of Hyslop's mediums. Nevertheless, because Thompson's obsession had begun to receive public attention, we need to consider whether furtive information gathering could explain correct details revealed in the sittings. If so, that detracts somewhat from their impact.

For example, Mrs. Chenoweth's controls mentioned Gifford's practice of holding something "like a little cigarette" (p. 245) in his mouth while painting. Although Gifford didn't smoke, he did hold a stick in his mouth, and he rolled it around and chewed on it as some people do with cigarettes or cigars. Now even if that habit of Gifford's was not well-known, probably many people besides Mrs. Gifford had seen Gifford paint. So many people would have been in a position to observe Gifford with the stick in his mouth, some of whom might have spoken to one of the mediums. Similar concerns apply to other details mentioned in the sittings. For example, Mrs. Chenoweth also mentioned Gifford's two studios, one in town and one in the country (p. 267), and she provided some correct details about the latter. She also correctly described, among other things, some of Gifford's old-fashioned furniture (pp. 287–288), his habit of keeping a pile of old brushes to paint "rocks and things that were rough" (pp. 289–290) and (somewhat more obliquely) the fact that Gifford had lost a child whose face he tried to incorporate into his pictures (p. 309). That last item seems less likely than the others to have been known beyond Gifford's most intimate acquaintances. But it was probably no secret, and probably many people knew that Gifford had lost two sons.

Of course, the strength of this case doesn't rest on the later sittings. So even if we can explain some of the material from those sittings by appealing to one or more of the Usual Suspects, that strategy won't work for the earlier sittings, and it certainly won't help us account for the similarities between Thompson's sketches and Gifford's paintings.

Another intriguing incident comes from a sitting with Mrs. "Smead" (also a trance medium) on December 9, 1908. Gifford purported to control the medium, drawing what looked like a cross on top of a pile of rocks, and then writing that his name was on the cross. Interestingly, Thompson had encountered such a cross near the sea, one month before this sitting. The cross was part of a wrecked ship, and although Thompson thought he saw Gifford's initials R. S. G. on the cross, they disappeared as he approached. However, the scene impressed him so much that he painted it. He also described the incident in a letter to his wife, which Hyslop obtained prior to the December 9 sitting.

Overall, this case is undoubtedly impressive, and it poses a clear challenge to the super-psi hypothesis. Nevertheless, partisans of super psi can raise legitimate concerns. First, there are the usual worries about the subject's ESP. Could Thompson have exercised refined clairvoyance to "view" Gifford's original works, and could he then have painted his resulting visions? Moreover, although some of Thompson's sketches are strikingly close to Gifford's pictures, others are less so. In fact, some seem to represent fairly generic New England landscapes. So it's unclear how much psychic functioning Thompson's sketches and paintings represent, and perhaps this case doesn't challenge us—as the best mediumistic cases do—to explain highly prolific and consistent psychic functioning.

Similarly, we can question the amount and quality of psi demonstrated by Hyslop's mediums. Although several mediums provided nuggets of correct and occasionally obscure information about Gifford, these didn't occur with the impressive regularity found in the very best mediumistic cases. It's also curious that none of Hyslop's mediums managed to come up with Gifford's name, although Mrs. Smead came up with the initials R. S. G. (after first producing them as R. G. S.). That seems puzzling on both the survivalist and super-psi hypotheses. If the mediums could get other fine details, either from the deceased Gifford, Mrs. Gifford, Thompson, or Hyslop, why not Gifford's name?

Moreover, we need to look closely at the relationship between Hyslop and his mediums. Consider, first, Mrs. Chenoweth. Although we're probably entitled to regard her as being a good psychic, this case and the Cagliostro case (and perhaps others) suggest that she may have been more thoroughly "tuned" to the living than to the dead. In particular, Mrs. Chenoweth may have been unusually sensitive to Hyslop's unspoken needs and interests. Therefore, since experimenter (or sitter) influence can't be ruled out, we need to consider the possibility that Hyslop's knowledge of Gifford contributed to the verifiable portions of the mediumistic communications. And of course, other parts, beyond Hyslop's knowledge, could be attributed to the medium's ranging ESP of other sources, such as Mrs. Gifford and (especially in the later sittings) Thompson.

Furthermore, the relationship between Hyslop and Mrs. Smead only fuels this sort of concern. Before Hyslop's involvement with this medium, none of her mediumistic productions were remotely evidential. Once again, Hyslop seems to have been a catalyst for apparently evidential communications. All this suggests either outright experimenter psi, or some other sort of medium-experimenter psychic interaction. Moreover (as I already noted), we can't rule out psychic interaction between the medium and Mrs. Gifford or Thompson. For example, the incident mentioned above, about the hallucination of Gifford's initials on a cross, could be explained in terms of telepathy between Mrs. Smead and either Thompson or Hyslop. And of course, since Mrs. Gifford confirmed the various details about her husband's habits, clothing, favorite locations for painting, etc., she might have been a prime target for psychic snooping.

Another troubling feature of the Smead sittings is that Hyslop helped this medium by allowing her to handle Gifford's brushes. Now there's plenty of anecdotal evidence, and some experimental evidence, that *psychometry* is possible. That is, we have good reason to believe that handling a person's objects helps some psychics home in on relevant facts about those objects or about the person's life (see, e.g., Besterman, 1933; Dingwall, 1924; Osty, 1923; Pagenstecher, 1922; Pollack, 1964; Prince, 1921). For the moment, it doesn't matter how we explain that phenomenon. And for reasons I mention briefly in the next chapter (in connection with transplant cases), we can probably rule out one leading theory: namely, that information is impressed or encoded into the psychometric object. What matters here is that however psychometry works, survivalist conjectures are gratuitous or irrelevant. Whatever the mechanism for psychometry may be (if there is one—see Braude, 1997), it seems clear enough that the psychometric object plays a crucial role. Somehow, it enables the psychic to focus or pick out verifiable bits of information. So when psychometry is practiced successfully on objects belonging to the *living*, presumably our explanations won't require appealing to postmortem entities. But then we don't need to do so when the objects in question are those of dead people. So why suppose that Mrs. Smead's verifiable remarks when handling Gifford's brushes indicate Gifford's survival?

Of course (as we've seen), super-psi explanations must do more than indicate *how* psi among the living might create the appearance of postmortem survival. They must also indicate *why*. They must posit a plausible underlying *motivation* for simulating survival. In correspondence with D. Scott Rogo over an early draft of Rogo's book *The Infinite Boundary*, Eisenbud attempted such an explanation (Rogo, 1987, pp. 272–274). Eisenbud's conjecture is based in part on his interpretation of Thompson's interactions with Gifford. Thompson himself admitted that after meeting Gifford in New Bedford he made a "few attempts at art work" (Hyslop, 1909, p. 30). But, he writes, "beyond the copying of prints my efforts were so crude and laborious I soon gave it up" (p. 30). Thompson also claimed that Gifford didn't encourage painting as a profession, but that he did take an interest in his metalwork and spoke of its artistic possibilities. Later, when he called on Gifford in New York, Thompson says Gifford didn't recognize him at first, and (apparently mistaking Thompson for an artist) he spoke of how difficult it was for an artist to succeed in New York. He then encouraged Thompson to pursue his activities in glass and metalwork (p. 31).

Now it's unclear whether Thompson idolized or even respected Gifford as a painter before his obsession began. According to Thompson, he'd seen only one of Gifford's paintings before his fateful visit to the gallery (one year after Gifford's death), and he claims that he didn't particularly like that painting. We can't know whether this disavowal is sincere or self-aware, but if we consider that it isn't, then Gifford's later remarks to Thompson might have been taken as a kind of slap in the face. They might have struck Thompson as a refusal to encourage him as a painter, capped by a dismissive suggestion to stick to his metalwork. If this interpretation of events is plausible, then Eisenbud's proposal needs to be taken seriously. He wrote,

> These slights may appear to be meager enough data upon which to base a serious supposition concerning the underlying dynamics of the Thompson-Gifford case. However, psychiatrists regularly see the far-reaching and sometimes quite astonishing effects of what might superficially seem to be slight enough rejections. If in fact Gifford had become a kind of admired ideal image for the youthful Thompson, a target for unconscious identification—and we are certainly not postulating in this anything at all uncommon between a young man aspiring to a vocation and an older one with considerable gifts along the lines aspired to—such treatment could be crushing. On one hand it might well have resulted in what might superficially appear to have been a complete withdrawal of interest on Thompson's part in Gifford's subsequent life and work. (There is some ambiguity on this point, but there were several years during which Thompson is alleged neither to have sought nor to have had any further contact with Gifford, not even learning of his death until almost two years [sic] after it had occurred.) But it could at the same time have resulted in a compensatory strengthening of the unconscious bonds of identification with Gifford. This would have amounted to an unconscious attempt to capture and hold the rejecting ideal figure through a kind of psychic incorporation, which psychiatrists commonly see in similar situations. And this could well have led ultimately to a delusion on Thompson's part that Gifford's spirit had actually invaded and informed his own by way of singling him out to be the

vehicle for continuing his work.

This type of feeling-idea is consistent with a wide range of phenomena commonly seen when people feel rejected or abandoned by someone whose love and appreciation they desire. It is perhaps most often—in fact classically—seen in the subtle kinds of identifications which develop during and after mourning for a love object lost through death or other type of desertion. (Rogo, 1987, p. 273)

Apparently, then, both the survival and super-psi hypotheses can account for the motivations behind Thompson's obsession and paintings. Survivalists would appeal to Gifford's intense desire to complete the work he left unfinished. And they could claim that Gifford selected Thompson as his medium because of Thompson's native artistic abilities and perhaps also (as Rogo suggests, partly in the spirit of Eisenbud) because Thompson "was both psychically and psychologically bonded" to Gifford (Rogo, 1987, p. 275). Anti-survivalists could claim that Thompson's paintings resulted from (in Eisenbud's words) "a natural, if psi-mediated, projection of Thompson's unconscious fantasy...[rather] than...a kind of emanation from someone who in life found Thompson uninteresting both as a person and as an aspiring painter" (Rogo, 1987, p. 274).

But even if we go along with Eisenbud, partisans of super psi must still explain the clear correspondence between some of Thompson's sketches and Gifford's works. In fact, that may be the most intransigent feature of the case, from any point of view. We can probably sidestep the issue of the apparently anomalous skill demonstrated by Thompson. Although Thompson wasn't a trained artist, he was clearly an artistic person, and he had previously demonstrated skill in sketching. But (leaving aside the clearly untenable hypotheses of fraud or coincidence) how should we explain the best of the correspondences?[5]

A multiple-process super-psi explanation would probably posit something along the following lines. Thompson might have (a) acquainted himself clairvoyantly with Gifford's works and sketched directly from those clairvoyant impressions, or (b) "learned clairvoyantly (perhaps from Mrs. Gifford) of Gifford's favourite hunting grounds, clairvoyantly investigated them, and selected from them, as the themes of recurrent visions, the sorts of spots which might appeal to a painter" (Gauld, 1982, p. 154). And I suppose a magic-wand explanation would claim simply that Thompson worked directly from corresponding or appropriate mental images, but it wouldn't posit any feedback-producing underlying process. From this point of view, Thompson needn't undergo any search at all, either for Gifford's works, Mrs. Gifford's mental clues, or Gifford-friendly scenes along the coast. The required images would simply be there in his mind, given (a) the appropriate needs and desires, and (b) a confluence of psi-conducive background conditions. And then, to explain Thompson's other psychic experiences (e.g., during island

expeditions to locate scenes from his visions), the magic-wand explanation would posit additional spurts of ESP.

Undoubtedly, some will dismiss both types of super-psi explanation
as wildly incredible. But (as we've noted before) survivalists may not be
able to take that position. They too must posit a rather amazing psychic
achievement to explain the correspondences, and arguably it's no less
super and no less incredible than whatever the super-psi hypothesis requires. Let's grant (as I believe we should) that Thompson had no normal knowledge of the Gifford works he replicated. In that case, survivalists must suppose either (a) that the surviving Gifford telepathically supplied Thompson with detailed information about those works, and that
this allowed Thompson to construct sufficiently detailed visions from
which to sketch and paint, or (b) that Gifford controlled Thompson's
body and mind to produce the needed visions and to guide his hand in
the production of the sketches and paintings.

So as far as the correspondences are concerned, I see no clear reason
to prefer either the survivalist or super-psi explanation. Neither seems
conspicuously simpler or antecedently less incredible than the other.
Nevertheless, for reasons similar to those discussed in chapter 3, we
might give the survival hypothesis a slight edge here, especially if we
decide that Thompson's paintings correspond *consistently* to those of
Gifford. In that case, the consistency of Thompson's mediumistic
achievement is another crucial datum in need of explanation, and it's
precisely on that point that super-psi explanations may falter.

At any rate, when we look at the case as a whole and recognize that
Thompson's achievements have to be explained *along with* the material
gleaned from several mediums, crippling complexity clearly becomes an
issue once again. Gauld expressed a similar point when he wrote that
the super-psi hypothesis, "applied to this case...is *messy* in a way not to
be equated with mere complexity. If the survivalist theory were tenable
it would immensely simplify things" (Gauld, 1982, p. 155). On the
super-psi hypothesis, the evidence needs to be explained in terms of
the psychic successes of, and interactions between, many different individuals. And it must also posit multiple sources of information, both
items in the world and different people's beliefs and memories. But on
the survival hypothesis, we seem to require fewer causal links and one
individual—a surviving Gifford—from whom all information flows.

7. Concluding Remarks

Taken individually, the most impressive reincarnation and possession
cases seem at least to tilt the scales toward the survivalist, even if we
can't demonstrate conclusively that the super-psi hypothesis is false.
Moreover, when we look at the totality of those cases and feel the cu-

mulative force of the best of them taken together, the survivalist position seems stronger still. Now, partisans of super psi might still be correct on some critical issues. Psi might be sneaky and naughty, and perhaps it often is. And perhaps psi can also be more refined and far-ranging than critics usually allow. Nevertheless, the best reincarnation and possession cases raise a major problem for the super-psi hypothesis, the same problem we discussed in connection with mediumship. I've argued that completing a psi-task requires avoiding an underlying and unimaginably complex nexus of potential obstacles. Some of the obstacles may be preexisting, and the rest may emerge spontaneously from others' ongoing psychic activity. So psychic success would be analogous to walking carefully through a minefield while also managing not to be caught in the crossfire of continuing hostilities. And this would be true even if psi works like a magic wand; we must still avoid various intentional or inadvertent obstacles to success. But if that's right, then the processes posited by the survivalist seem less vulnerable to interference or preemption than those required for super-psi explanations. So even if psi works like a magic wand, partisans of super psi apparently have more trouble than survivalists explaining the abundance and consistency of verified information revealed in the strongest cases.

Moreover, crippling complexity may favor the survivalist in another way. In reincarnation and possession cases (and in mediumship as well), manifestations of the previous personality (or possessing or communicating entity) are often sporadic or diluted by intermittent or simultaneous behaviors more appropriate to the host. In these cases, it seems as if the previous personality is interrupted by intrusive thoughts or memories characteristic of the subject, or displaced by the full-blown reappearance of (or repossession by) the subject. In fact, as in many cases of MPD/DID, subjects sometimes seem to exhibit a kind of copresence of the previous and host personalities. These various occurrences suggest something like competition for expression, or at the very least something like partial or inadequate filtering. Now if these really are cases of survival, and therefore if they illustrate difficulties facing an unimpeded demonstration of reincarnation or possession, the causal picture seems relatively straightforward. For one thing, if barriers are preventing full or continual manifestation of the previous personality, those barriers seem largely *internal* to the subject. Presumably, they result from the subject's own preexisting dispositions or ongoing thoughts, which may be difficult to displace (at least for extended periods). And for another, whether the obstacles are internal or external, only one causal connection seems to be disrupted: namely, the link between the subject and the previous personality. By contrast, to explain the best cases in terms of super psi, we may need to posit either implausibly successful ESP links between the subject and multiple sources, or even more incredible psi on the part of the parents, involving both information gathering and telepathic influence over the subject. The causal lines here seem to be far more complex and vulnerable to interference than in cases where most of the action takes place entirely or mostly within the subject.

As far as I can see, appealing to crippling complexity is by far the most forceful line of reasoning in favor of survival. But for the sake of completeness, we should also examine a position advanced by David Ray Griffin. Griffin is one of the few who appreciates the force and subtlety of super-psi alternatives to survival. Nevertheless, he believes certain considerations decisively rule out motivated super-psi explanations of reincarnation.

In considering the possibility of motivated super psi by members of the subject's or previous personality's family, Griffin writes,

> Such explanations seem to entail that multiple reincarnations of the same personality should be common and, in fact, that reincarnations of individuals while they are still in the prime of life should be common. Neither of these expectations is supported by the evidence. I take the nonfulfillment of these two predictions to be the most decisive disconfirmation of [a super-psi interpretation]. (Griffin, 1997, p. 265)

However, I find this puzzling, especially if we regard psychic functioning as deeply need-driven. In fact, it seems psychologically counterproductive for psi to work as Griffin suggests. If parents selected *living* persons as previous personalities, then presumably we'd conclude that the case only *seemed* to be one of reincarnation when in fact it was something else—most likely, a kind of possession or telepathic influence. Of course, beliefs about reincarnation vary. For instance, they vary with respect to whether there's an interval between bodily death and reincarnation, or how long that interval can be, or whether one can exist somehow between incarnations. But believers in reincarnation converge on one important point: namely, that reincarnation can only take place *at or before* the new body's birth or conception. Presumably, that's why many people attach great cosmic or karmic significance to reincarnation, but not to possession. So if parents psychically but mistakenly selected a living (and even more so, a *healthy*) person as previous personality, the case would lose its primary source of meaning to them. Moreover, if the parents investigated the case, they would risk uncovering their mistake and depriving the case of its deepest value.

Griffin suggests that these pseudo reincarnations might be explained in terms of the *intensity* of the previous personality's life (Griffin, 1997, pp. 204-205). However, the second prediction also appears to rest on the following tacit assumption, which I'll call the *Whoops!* assumption.

> (Whoops!) If all apparent evidence of reincarnation results from psi among the living, we'd expect occasional psychic errors, some of which involve picking out living persons by mistake.

Now that assumption is interesting and not obviously outlandish. But I'm not sure it's ultimately defensible. Even if we grant that psychic errors are possible (or even likely), it's far from clear what forms those errors should take. We have little choice but to reason by analogy here, and on some plausible analogies, the type of pseudo reincarnation Griffin mentions seems highly unlikely.

To see why, suppose I asked someone to do any of the following:

(a) distinguish corpses from the living in a wartime hospital,
(b) from a huge stack of medical files pick out only the records of those listed as deceased,
(c) distinguish headstones in a cemetery from the people moving about in the cemetery,
(d) distinguish pictures or video clips of people from real people,

and perhaps most relevantly,

(e) distinguish clothing currently being worn from clothing still on hangers or on display.

Now according to at least the multiple-process super-psi hypothesis, parents in reincarnation cases locate and choose a deceased individual, rather than a living person, to serve as previous personality. So they face a selection process that roughly parallels the five projects listed above. Of course, in those five projects it's hard to imagine how people could make mistakes, much less frequently. Their required choices are between objects of clearly distinct categories. But to make the error mentioned by Griffin, parents would need to confuse individuals differing even more dramatically than those in the analogies. In fact, if the Whoops! assumption is correct, parents would be confusing members of radically distinct ontological types. Somehow, they would mistake an embodied soul for a disembodied soul. So if the Whoops! assumption is tenable, we should be able to find alternative analogies, at least as strong as those above, for the errors leading to the pseudo reincarnations posited by Griffin. But I'm not sure what those would be. They would have to be selection tasks at least as clear-cut as (but preferably, even more obvious than) those above, but with a greater potential for error. And in the unlikely event that we wound up with competing and equally compelling analogies for the parents' selection process, we probably know too little about the operations of psi to have a clear and justifiable preference for one set rather than the other.

Of course, *mediums* occasionally seem to err along the lines predicted by Griffin, apparently producing trance communications from the living as if those individuals were dead. But the evidence for this isn't particularly strong or abundant. In fact, the best of these cases, that of Gordon Davis (Soal, 1925), is suspect for several reasons (see Gauld, 1982, pp. 137–138; Harris, 1986; and West, 2000). Nevertheless, assuming it's reliable, the case is instructive, because its psychology differs significantly from that of reincarnation cases. The sitter (Soal) apparently believed that his friend Gordon Davis had been killed in World War I, and that is how the medium presented Davis's ostensibly postmortem communication. Now from the perspective of the super-psi hypothesis, the false beliefs of sitters (and even their proxies) might telepathically influence the medium, either by conveying those beliefs to her directly or by "pointing" her psychic antennae (so to speak) toward a living person. So we could easily appeal to telepathy among the living to explain how the medium picked out Gordon Davis and portrayed him as if dead. But there's no clear parallel to this dynamic in reincarnation cases. If it counts as a psychic error on the part of the medium, it differs considerably from the error posited by Griffin.

At any rate, although I can't find reincarnation or possession cases where the "previous" personality was in the prime of life, we've noted cases in which the subject's birth preceded the death of the previous personality (section 5). And there are even more cases where the previous personality died after the subject's conception. Now perhaps we should interpret these as psychic errors committed by the living, and arguably they make better candidates for psychic errors than picking out someone in the prime of life. After all, if parents are psychically on the lookout for promising subjects for simulating reincarnation, it's possible that they might occasionally err *slightly* and select someone who died a bit too late. In fact, if the parents' unconscious desire to simulate reincarnation began or peaked only after the child's birth (a plausible scenario), then this sort of mistake is even credible. Indeed, from the parents' point of view, it wouldn't clearly be a mistake. By the time of the child's birth, the previous personality would already be dead. So from the parents' perspective, they would accurately have selected a deceased person. But I don't see why we should expect the gross error of mistaking an intense ongoing life for an intense previous life.

Granted, it's tempting to assume, along with Griffin, that certain kinds of evidence for reincarnation (or for survival generally) are more plausible than others. No enquiry into survival can be free of presuppositions, some of which concern our explanatory standards and our gut instincts about which theories make sense and tie things together in a credibly systematic way. All these come into play as we weigh rival hypotheses in terms of empirical adequacy, explanatory simplicity, and conceptual cost. But we should remember that we're largely clueless about the range, reliability, or accuracy of psi in daily life, and likewise we can only speculate about the nature of an afterlife and how it might influence the evidence for survival. The situation here is the same as in the case of physical mediumship, where some argue, unjustifiably, that the data *should* have taken some form other than what we actually find (Braude, 1997).

Besides (as we've noted), if the "previous" personality dies after the subject is born (or conceived), then presumably we'd interpret the case as an instance of possession rather than reincarnation. So for all we know, some of the possession cases described in the literature might be attempted reincarnation-simulations gone awry, but in a way that still has psychological utility for the relevant families. And I doubt that Griffin could defend the claim that there should be more of these cases than we've discovered. From the perspective of a super (but fallible)-psi hypothesis, the number of ostensible possession cases seems about right, or at least reasonable.

But should we, on the super-psi hypothesis, expect multiple reincarnations of the same personality? Although Griffin suggests that this would be another likely type of psychic error, once again his predicted scenario seems psychologically far-fetched and counterproductive. When evaluating (or formulating) motivated super-psi explanations, we always need to ask: Whose interests would be served by the appearance of evidence of survival? And since most subjects are too young to be burdened by the right kinds of motivations, the most plausible conjecture is that the psychic agent is a parent (probably the previous personality's parent). But from that parent's perspective, presumably the whole point of having the previous personality manifest in a new body is to take care of some unfinished business, either of the previous personality or of the family. For example, the parent might need to identify the previous personality's killer, say a proper good-bye, tie up financial loose ends, or demonstrate that karmic processes were well under way. If the psychic agent is the *subject's* parent, the relevant unfinished business would probably assume other forms. For example, it might concern social or financial status (e.g., caste membership), or (if the subject has deformities or prominent birthmarks) it might relieve the parent from responsibility and guilt over having a child with those features or handicaps. In any case, if the previously unfinished business was taken care of the first time and the parent or family experienced emotional "closure," then it's not clear whose interests would be served by *another* ostensible appearance of the previous personality. And it's even less clear why we should *predict* multiple reincarnations of the previous personality. Given how little we know, not only about psi, but also about the inner lives of the people involved in reincarnation and possession cases generally, Griffin is in no position to insist that we should expect more return appearances of the same person.

Granted, in the context of formal lab experiments, psychic functioning seems neither dazzlingly accurate, refined, nor consistent. But we haven't a clue what to expect of psychic efforts in uncontrolled, natural settings, with genuinely and deeply motivating real-world interests. Perhaps Griffin is right that we might reasonably expect at least *some* psychic errors of this kind. And in fact, there are cases of mediumship and spirit possession where the same individual ostensibly takes over a series of people. But as far as I can tell, these don't occur in cultures with a strong belief in reincarnation, where they could be interpreted as attempted reincarnation-simulations gone awry. Once again, I suspect that we know too little about both psi and the relevant family dynamics in reincarnation cases to have clear or defensible ideas of what to expect. So at the very least, the failure (as far as we can tell) of Griffin's prediction can hardly be decisive for the survivalist.

It seems, then, that the issue of crippling complexity is what makes the reincarnation and possession evidence most compelling. And as we've seen, that might be enough to tilt the scales toward the survivalist.[6] So let's turn, now, to another class of cases, and see whether they shift the balance one way or the other.

NOTES

1. Compare this to the medium Hafsteinn Bjornsson going through the motions of using snuff, mentioned in chapter 2.

2. Almeder reports this inaccurately, and he's apparently too generous in his description of Bishen Chand's tabla-playing ability. He claims that both Bishen Chand and Laxmi Narain played the tablas "skillfully" (Almeder, 1992, p. 7). But I find no comparable claims in the source material.

3. I can only gape in admiration at Gauld's industry and command of the relevant material. He filed two reports with me on the matter. Although they overlap somewhat, both deserve to be quoted at length. In his first report, Gauld writes,

> There are no hints of [Antonia or Karl] either in Conyers Read's *Mr. Secretary Walsingham* (3 Vols., Oxford UP, 1925) - Walsingham was Elizabeth's spy-master, and Read treats the plots in detail. I searched the *Calendar of State Papers (Domestic), 1581-90,* which lists quite a lot of Catholics who were arrested for suspect activities, but no-one around Jan. 1854 seemed to be a possible Antonia-candidate. Likewise with the corresponding *Cal. S.P. (Foreign)*...There is quite a lot of Mendoza's correspondence in Vol 86 of *Colección de documentos inéditos para la historia de España* (112 vols), but it is mostly with Philip II and a bit above the routine work of spies....
>
> I also looked at Anthony à Wood's *Fasti Oxonienses* 3rd edn (enlarged), London F.C. and J. Rivington, etc., etc., 1815. Had Uncle Karl been an accredited scholar visiting Oxford, he would have been admitted to the University under one heading or another. The only remotely possible German candidate I could discover over the relevant period (indeed there were only two Germans altogether) was one Hieronimus Schlick, Count of Passan or Passaun and Lord in Weiskerchen (Weiskirchen, Weisskirchen), neither of which places I have been able to locate with certainty, who was admitted to the degree of B.D. on 4th May 1579—no College listed and one doesn't know how long he stayed in Oxford. The *Alumni Oxonienses* adds a bit more—he had studied (divinity) for two years in the University of Prague and five in Lips, and had been Rector of the University of Marpurg. Heironimus translates as Jerome so he is not a Karl; I can't identify Passaun (Passau?) Or Weiskirchen, though standard German biographical works mention various distinguished Schlicks who were counts of those regions; however, Lips (Liptzi, Lipsi) is Leipzig, so he scores two out of three universities, which is curious. No date of death is given, which I think there would have been had he died in Oxford or even England—a death date around 1584 would have set one thinking (maybe he appears in the burial registers of some Oxford church). Had he changed from Catholicism to (say) Lutheranism it would

have been between Prague and Leipzig (Leipzig and Marburg were both in Lutheran territory), not between Heidelberg (Catholic) and Oxford. He wrote a Latin pamphlet in 1578 which, from its title, appears to be a justification of his resigning from the Rectorship of Marburg, but I haven't looked for the original yet. (personal communication, October 21, 2000)

In his second report, Gauld summarizes his results as follows.

Firstly Antonia: Had Antonia been detained (and then escaped!) around the time of the Throckmorton plot as a suspect Catholic agent, I should think there would have been a fair chance that she would have been mentioned in the standard records, especially if she had been disguised as a man [These were claims made by Antonia—SB]. Walsingham's network was pervasive and he was particularly keen on tracking down anyone who might have had dealings with Mary Queen of Scots. The *Calendar of State Papers (Domestic), 1581-90* mentions many suspects who had been arrested or were under observation, especially around the times of the various plots, but there is no hint of Antonia. Nor is there any in Conyers Read's three volumes on Walsingham, or in Alan Haynes's *Invisible Power: The Elizabethan Secret Services 1570-1603* (1992). Walsingham's published diaries end in April 1583. The *Calendar of State Papers, Spanish, Elizabeth* has got quite a lot of Mendoza's correspondence with Philip II, which is mostly above the level of common agents, though one letter (26th Nov 1583) refers to a list of sympathizers who have been apprehended sent by Mendoza in his previous letter (Nov. 18th). But this letter isn't there (along with lots of other Mendoza letters)....

As for Uncle Karl: Had Uncle Karl been a distinguished scholar, attending lectures etc. at Oxford he would have had to have been incorporated into the University (i.e., accepted into Oxford University in whatever rank or status he had achieved in his own University). This was done either by direct incorporation (mostly for very distinguished persons) or by the award of an appropriate degree. Persons thus incorporated are listed, with a few details about them, in Anthony à Wood's *Fasti Oxonienses* (3rd edn. enlarged 1815). For the relevant period (widely interpreted) I can only find two candidates, that is to say persons from German-speaking lands. They also appear in the *Alumni Oxonienses* (standard Oxford biographical dictionary up to 1886). They are Johann Barnardus, a Moravian of University College (B.D. 1583, aged 28), who is said to have afterwards gone into Scotland to study at Universities there, and Heironymus Schlick, Count of Passan or Passaun (which, it appears from other sources, may be Bassano in N. Italy), Lord in Weiskerchen (Weisskirchen, etc.) who received his B.D. in 1579 but does not seem to have been attached to a college.

Only the latter appears to be even a remotely possible candidate for Uncle Karl. From the above-mentioned works one gathers that he studied for two years at the University of Prague (Catholic), five at Leipzig (Protestant), and at least one at Marburg (Protestant), where he became rector (he published a religious pamphlet in 1578). There is a little bit more about him in A. Clark (ed.) *Register of the University of Oxford, Vol. II, 1571-1622, Part I* (Oxford Historical Society, 1887), p. 377. His family had suffered a lot in the wars of the Schmalkaldic League, he came to the University recommended by great princes, and he studies at Oxford for several months in theology, "audiendo legendo disputando et concionando [speaking before audiences]."

There is a lot about the Schlick (or Schlik) family, which seems to have been rather distinguished, in *Biographische Lexicon der Kaiserthums Oesterreich* (Vienna), vol. 30, 1875. There are no Karls, but our Heironymus appears briefly on p. 111. No birth or death dates are given for him, but it is apparent that, as a zealous Protestant convert and proselytiser he was a bit of a black sheep in his Catholic family. He married Anna Salomao, Grafin v. Oettingen but had no progeny.

This Heironymus has some curious points of similarity with Uncle Karl. He had been to three of Uncle Karl's four universities, he travelled a lot, he was a convert from Catholicism to Protestantism, and he was married but left no progeny. None the less I think there are nearly decisive objections. He does not seem to have stayed long at Oxford. He has the wrong Christian name. And since his father only married in 1547 he could have been at most only a few years older than Antonia. Even worse, he could not have had a sister, at any rate a legitimate one, who could have had a child old enough to be Antonia (unfortunately the extensive genealogical trees in the article leave out the females of the line).

I did enquire about Oxford burial registers which might have shown Heirony-mus's death had that been in Jan 1584 and in Oxford. Unfortunately there are about thirty Parish Churches whose records would require searching, and in addition the various Colleges kept their own! I haven't got that much time, and I rather think that if he had died in Oxford so soon after coming there, that fact would have found its way into the printed records. (personal communication, December 5, 2000)

4. I'm grateful to Mary Rose Barrington for reminding me of this.

5. I encourage readers to examine Hyslop's report (or the possibly more accessible reproductions in Gauld, 1982, and Rogo, 1987), to appreciate how close those correspondences are.

6. Tucker (Tucker, 2000) applied a reasonable strength-of-case scale to 799 ostensible reincarnation cases. Although it doesn't clearly help us choose between survivalist and super-psi explanations of the data, it offers further evidence that strongest cases require some sort of paranormal explanation. For example, Tucker found intriguing correlations between strong cases and various factors (e.g., distance in kilometers between child subject and the previous personality, degree of association between the subject's and previous personality's families before the case developed, and unusual skills or aptitudes related to a previous life). Some of these correlations are at least consistent with a paranormal (or more specifically, a reincarnation) explanation, and some run counter to what non-paranormal explanations would predict.

Chapter 7
Lingering Spirits

1. Introduction

By now we've considered a fairly wide variety of cases, exhibiting distinctive strengths and weaknesses. But despite their differences, they share an important common feature: an apparent postmortem agent trying to identify itself and communicate actively through gifted (or perhaps afflicted) individuals. Now we examine cases of a different sort, in which surviving personalities seem to manifest only (or primarily) *dispositionally*. Here we don't find, at least to the degree we did in other cases, indications of entities actively attempting to make themselves known, discuss their histories, or express their needs and interests. Rather, we see apparent postmortem entities or remnants of personality merely *attached* to things, without attempted self-identification and without the conversational and behavioral self-expression displayed in most cases of mediumship, reincarnation, and possession.

It's not surprising to find such cases. In some ways they seem to be stripped-down variants of the case-types considered earlier. After all, in mediumship, reincarnation, and possession, postmortem entities seem to do two things. First, they apparently attach to or "hover" around people. And second, they apparently try to identify themselves and communicate. But why should the second of these always happen? If survival is a fact, it seems reasonable to think that postmortem individuals might do no more than hover or linger. And in that case, we might expect to find traces or remnants of their activity. Like more ordinary loiterers and hangers-on who simply won't go away or who have trouble letting go, they might make their "presence" felt without actively trying to communicate. And if postmortem individuals can attach to (or hover around) people, then presumably they can attach to other things as well.

We'll now look at two classes of evidence suggesting this sort of persistence. First, we'll consider cases of apparent haunting, in which postmortem agency seems to attach to a location (rather than a person). And then we'll examine transplant cases, in which agency or remnants of personality seem linked to bodily organs.

2. Haunting: Preliminaries

Haunting phenomena resist neat classification. In one direction they shade off by degrees into *poltergeist phenomena*, and in another direction they morph gradually into cases of *haunting ghosts* or *recurrent localized apparitions*. One crude way to distinguish hauntings from poltergeist cases is that most of the former are place-centered, whereas most of the latter are person-centered. That is, we can usually trace poltergeist phenomena to the (presumably unconscious) psychic activity of a poltergeist-*agent*. In fact, the phenomena sometimes follow the presumed agent from one place to another. But generally speaking, no living agent seems causally linked to haunting phenomena. Instead, those phenomena apparently attach to a location, never mind who happens to be there.[1]

Gauld offers a useful profile of haunting phenomena.

> The leading characteristic of hauntings are these: the phenomena centre round a place, usually a house, rather than round a person, and often continue off and on for several years (which is not generally so with poltergeists). The phenomena take place mainly at night, and prominent amongst them are what may be called imitative noises—sounds resembling those which normally accompany people treading on the floorboards or opening doors or breaking crockery or dropping heavy weights or banging walls, but to which no observable breakages, displacements, marks, etc., correspond; or sounds like human whispers, groans, distant conversations or articulate phrases. Other phenomena not infrequently reported in such cases include the appearance of luminosities and balls of light; disturbance of and tugging at bedclothes; and the actual opening of room and wardrobe doors with visible turning of handles or lifting of latches. (Gauld & Cornell, 1979, p. 178)

Gauld recognizes that these cases make a smooth transition into haunting ghost cases, where subjects repeatedly see apparitional *figures*, sometimes nondescript, sometimes distinctive and apparently resembling previously living persons. And those cases may also include some of the haunting phenomena noted above.

Haunting ghosts may also be classified as a subset of *apparitions of the dead*, and not all of these are recurrent. Like apparitions of the living, they may be unique episodes in the life of the percipient. Moreover, these apparitions often seem *purposive*, even if they don't attempt to identify themselves. For example, percipients frequently identify apparitional figures as relatives, and sometimes the apparitions apparently manage (or at least try) to deliver crucial information to the percipient, such as the existence of a hidden will or a piece of timely advice. (See the examples noted in Gauld, 1982, pp. 233–235. See also MacKenzie, 1982; Myers, 1889, 1903; Podmore, 1890, 1910/1975; Sidgwick, 1885; Tyrrell, 1942/1961.)

But unlike the best cases of mediumship, recurrent haunting apparitions don't provide a regular (much less long-term) stream of *verified* material. So the problem of crippling complexity doesn't seem to arise, at least in an acute form. Nevertheless, the best of these cases (both recurrent and unique) pose a clear problem for the super-psi hypothesis, even if they don't strain it to the breaking point. When apparitions (like drop-in communicators) provide obscure information and manifest a clear agenda, I agree with Gauld that it seems

> obviously simpler to suppose that...there was at work some further agency, to be identified with a still surviving portion of a formerly incarnate human being, which somehow shaped the experience of the percipient or percipients in accordance with its own persisting knowledge and purposes. (Gauld, 1982, p. 235)

In fact, insofar as apparitions exhibit purpose and supply information unknown at the time to the percipients, they present many of the challenges we've considered already in connection with mediumship. And although the best veridical cases are quite impressive, space limitations prevent me from covering what is by now familiar ground. We need to focus here on what makes haunting cases *distinctively* puzzling: namely, the status of the apparitional phenomena themselves. These may be visual, auditory, olfactory, or tactile, and in some instances at least, they seem best explained as genuinely external, intersubjectively perceptible physical objects (however peculiar their causal histories might be). But we need to consider why that conclusion sometimes seems so promising and how it affects our assessment of the survival evidence.

In order to appreciate the theoretical challenge posed by these cases, let's look briefly at examples of the phenomena in question.

Case 1 (Myers, 1889, pp. 25–29; Myers, 1903, vol. 2, pp. 326–329):

In this case the apparition is purposive and collectively perceived. The percipients were Mr. and Mrs. P., the latter of whom, once before and in answer to a prayer, had experienced a non-veridical apparition of her father.

The time was approximately 9:30, and Mr. and Mrs. P. had retired early that night, about 30 minutes before. Mrs. P. was resting in a near-sitting position on top of her bed waiting to feed her baby, who usually awoke around that time. Mr. P. was asleep under the covers, and because Mrs. P. anticipated arising soon to feed the baby, a lamp had been left burning in the room. Mrs. P. writes that she was

> thinking of nothing but the arrangements for the following day, when to my great astonishment I saw a gentleman standing at the foot of the bed, dressed as a naval officer, and with a cap on his head having a projecting peak. [Because of the position of the lamp]...the face was in shadow *to me*, and the more so that the visitor was leaning upon his arms which rested on the foot-rail of the bedstead. I was too astonished to be afraid, but simply wondered who it could be; and, instantly touching my husband's shoulder

(whose face was turned from me), I said, "Willie, who is this?" My husband turned, and for a second or two lay looking in intense astonishment at the intruder; then lifting himself a little, he shouted "What on earth are you doing here, sir?" Meanwhile the form, slowly drawing himself into an up-right position, now said in a commanding, yet reproachful voice, "Willie! Willie!"

I looked at my husband and saw that his face was white and agitated. As I turned towards him he sprang out of bed as though to attack the man, but stood by the bedside as if afraid, or in great perplexity, while the figure calmly and slowly moved *towards the wall* at right angles with the lamp...As it passed the lamp, a deep shadow fell upon the room as of a material per-son shutting out the light from us by his intervening body, and he disap-peared, as it were, into the wall.

Mr. P. said he would look throughout the house for the figure. But Mrs. P. recalled that the bedroom door was locked, and she reminded her husband that the figure hadn't exited through the doorway. Never-theless, Mr. P. unlocked the door and searched unsuccessfully through the house. During his absence, Mrs. P. speculated to herself that the apparition might have been her brother Arthur, who was in the navy at the time and en route to India. She suggested this to Mr. P. after he returned from his unsuccessful search, still "looking very white and mis-erable." But Mr. P. declared that the figure was his father, who had been dead for fourteen years, and who had also been in the navy.

Mr. P.'s health declined in the following weeks, and he eventually disclosed to his wife that the apparition discouraged him from taking what would have turned out to be disastrous financial advice. Mr. and Mrs. P. agreed that the apparition was a "direct warning to my husband in the voice and appearance of the one that he had most reverenced in all his life, and was the most likely to obey." Mr. P. confirmed the de-tails recorded by his wife.

Case 2 (MacKenzie, 1982, pp. 196–200; Zorab & MacKenzie, 1980):

This is a modern case of recurrent apparitions. The home, occupied by Mrs. Graham (pseudonym) and her family during the period in ques-tion, was built in 1871 and is located in a prosperous London suburb. Mrs. Graham wrote her account of the haunting while still in residence, adding notes as additional phenomena occurred. Mr. Graham and two of their three daughters later signed the account (the third daughter was away at the time), as did Mrs. Turner (pseudonym), their housekeeper. Evidently, the two eldest daughters experienced few or no phenomena. But Mr. and Mrs. Graham, their youngest daughter Thelma, and Mrs. Turner experienced quite a few. At least one visitor to the home also experienced an apparition. Both Zorab and MacKenzie conducted follow-up interviews with Mrs. Turner and the family members.

The Graham's home was formed from what were originally two cot-tages. Zorab and MacKenzie describe the house as "a substantial detached building, standing on high ground facing a park, and the exterior does not contain any cracks such as would occur had the house been affected by subsidence or 'settling' of the foundations." The Grahams moved into the house in 1946 and remained there until 1977.

According to Mrs. Graham, she and her husband often sat in the downstairs lounge, and "countless times" they heard the sound of footsteps going upstairs, followed by noises in the five upstairs bedrooms as if someone was walking around. Invariably, Mr. Graham investigated, checking every room for signs of a burglar. But he never found traces of an intruder, and the doors to the house would also be locked.

In December 1973, the eldest daughter Helen and her husband George Wells (pseudonym) moved into the house temporarily, as their own house underwent alterations. One morning around 3 or 4 a.m., while Helen slept, Mr. Wells awoke

> to see the seemingly solid figure of a young woman reaching upwards toward the wardrobe as though she were dusting. She was wearing a long, faded, washed-out-looking rust-coloured dress and a long white apron. Her sleeves were rolled up and her hair was dressed in an upswept fashion. The dress suggested that of a domestic of the last century.

Mr. Wells didn't wake his wife. He simply watched the apparition from a sideways view for several minutes, after which it faded away. This was Mr. Wells's first apparitional experience, and he claimed that until this time he had always been very skeptical. The next morning he told Mrs. Graham what had happened, and Mrs. Graham then realized that the footsteps she and her husband had been hearing might have been those of a ghost.

In the meantime, however, Mrs. Turner had been experiencing various odd phenomena around the house, but she hadn't mentioned that to her employers. She came to the home two or three mornings each week, beginning in 1965, and from the start she felt that there was some sort of presence in the house. In fact, she often felt that someone wanted to pass her on the stairs. But Mrs. Turner never mentioned those experiences to Mrs. Graham, until by chance they both heard a noise and Mrs. Graham joked "Perhaps it's our ghost." Mrs. Turner then said, "Oh, so you do know." In 1975 Mrs. Turner apparently had her closest encounter with the ghost. As she walked along the upstairs landing she experienced what she described as a "physical push" and "quite a nasty experience." When Mrs. Graham returned home she found Mrs. Turner in "an extremely shocked state."

Thelma Graham had numerous apparitional encounters, the majority of which seem to have been exclusively auditory. She heard footsteps on many occasions. And in 1972, as she lay in bed one evening when she was alone in the house, she heard noises, apparently from the kitchen below her room. It sounded as if at least three people were talking, and their conversation was accompanied by bangs and crashes resembling the sound of saucepans being placed on metal shelves. Then she heard heavy footsteps coming up the creaking stairs and stopping outside her door. Thelma was "absolutely petrified," convinced that burglars were in the house. She hid under the blankets, and eventually she fell asleep. The next morning, she went downstairs expecting to find "total destruction," "but everything was absolutely normal. Nothing had been moved. I could not believe it."

Another type of phenomenon concerned the opening and closing of doors. Sometimes, either Mr. or Mrs. Graham simply heard the sound of a door banging shut, even though they ascertained that the windows were closed and nobody else was in the house. On one occasion Mr. Graham was standing on the landing at the top of the stairs. He was alone in the house, and the street doors and all the windows were closed. Nevertheless, he saw the five open bedroom doors bang shut one after the other. And in 1976, while Mrs. Graham spoke to a friend on the telephone upstairs, she observed the bedroom door open about a foot, close again, and then open again. After this repeated several more times, Mrs. Graham stopped her conversation and checked the windows, which were firmly closed. Mr. Graham was downstairs at the time, and when Mrs. Graham went to tell him what had happened, she found him watching the television and their two cats were curled up peacefully in the hall. No one else had been upstairs.

Case 3 (Podmore, 1890 pp. 255–270; Gauld & Cornell, 1979, pp. 186–195):

This older case from Brighton was examined carefully by two of the SPR's original leading researchers, Edmund Gurney and Frank Podmore. The phenomena consisted mostly of imitative noises, but they were reported by four groups of witnesses, the second of which for a long time knew nothing of the first group's experiences. Moreover, two diary records of the phenomena exist, one of them very detailed.

The first two residents of the house, Miss Morris and Mrs. Gilby, had been told that a woman had hanged herself in the upstairs back bedroom, and they both tended to believe that this was connected to the phenomena they and their families experienced. But although the story of the suicide was later confirmed, this case can't be considered veridical. In fact, even though the two women reported seeing a female phantasm, the experiences were too indistinct to establish a clear connection between the apparitions and the person who committed suicide.

Miss Morris was the first to provide testimony in the case (the previous tenant told her that nothing abnormal had occurred in the house). She rented the house from October 1882 to December 1886, and her written statement is dated June 1888. Miss Morris shared the house with her aunt and a maidservant, and two of Miss Morris's sisters visited occasionally. Podmore interviewed Miss Morris and one of the sisters in July 1888. Gauld and Cornell describe Miss Morris as "a fairly strong-minded person, who did not hesitate to search the house, poker in hand, to discover the source of persistent heavy footsteps and banging" (Gauld & Cornell, 1979, p. 190).

Those noises began the first evening Miss Morris spent in the house. Both she and her sister Charlotte experienced them, and so Miss Morris took up her poker and explored the house to make sure that no one else was there. That night, the "ceaseless and unwearying footsteps" (Podmore, 1890, p. 256) kept Miss Morris awake. Three weeks later,

> it was about five o'clock one afternoon in November, and so light that I had no need of the gas to enable me to read clearly some music I was practicing, and which engrossed my whole attention and thought. Having forgotten some new waltzes I had lain on the music shelf in the back drawing-room, I left the piano, and went dancing gaily along, singing a song as I went, when suddenly there stood before me, preventing me getting the music, the figure of a woman, heavily robed in deepest black from the head to her feet; her face was intensely sad and deadly pale. There she stood, gazing fixedly at me. (Podmore, 1890, p. 257)

Soon afterwards, the figure vanished. Miss Morris rushed upstairs looking for her aunt and found her alone in her room. Her sisters and the servant were out at the time. Miss Morris's aunt told her that she had been in her room the entire time and hadn't entered the drawing-room.

Miss Morris also records that in June 1884

> our hall-door bell began to ring incessantly and violently. We had frequently heard at intervals a ring, and discovered no one was at the door, but this especially annoyed us, and puzzled everyone inside and outside the house by the noise repeatedly made. We had always put it down to a "runaway ring" [i.e., a prankster] and took no notice, but for three weeks, at intervals of a quarter of an hour or half an hour, it rang unceasingly, and such peals, it electrified us. We put ourselves on guard and carefully watched, believing it a trick. We had everyone up from the basement, out of connection with the wire, in the front drawing-room, and placed the hall door and our doors wide open; it was the same result: loud and piercing peals from the bell, which, at last, after three weeks, we had taken off, when we saw the wire in connection with it vibrated as if the bell was attached to it.

After Miss Morris moved away, in December 1886, the house remained vacant until November 1887, when it was rented by Mrs. Gilby, a widow with two girls (ages 9 and 10) and one maidservant. She had moved to Brighton only six months earlier and apparently knew nothing about the phenomena reported by Miss Morris. During her tenancy, the phenomena were so extreme and incessant that they drove her from the house in May 1888. The following month, at Gurney's request, Mrs. Gilby provided a detailed account of the family's experiences, which included many reported sightings of apparitional figures. That account was compiled with the help of a diary in which Mrs. Gilby had recorded the unusual phenomena. The maid also provided an account. Gurney spoke at length with Mrs. Gilby and wrote,

> She struck me as an excellent witness. I have never received an account in which the words and manner of telling were less suggestive of exaggeration or superstition. There is no doubt that she was simply turned out of a house which otherwise exactly suited her, at very serious expense and inconvenience. (Podmore, 1890, p. 264)

Mrs. Gilby's account contains many interesting (and spine-chilling) passages. A few extracts will have to suffice.

> We had not been more than a fortnight in our new home...when I was aroused by a deep sob and moan. "Oh," I thought, "what has happened to the children?" I rushed in, their room being at the back of mine; found them sleeping soundly. So back to bed I went, when again another sob, and such a thump of somebody or something very heavy....I sat up in bed, looked all round the room, then to my horror a voice (and a very sweet one) said, "Oh, do forgive me!" three times. I could stand it no more; I always kept the gas burning, turned it up, and went to the maid's room. She was fast asleep, so I shook her well, and asked her to come into my room. Then in five minutes the sobs and moans recommenced, and the heavy tramping of feet, and such thumps, like heavy boxes of plate being thrown about. She suggested I should ring the big bell I always keep in my room, but I did not like to alarm the neighborhood....I told her to go to bed, and hearing nothing for half-an-hour, I got into mine, nearly frozen with cold and fright. But no sooner had I got warm than the sobs, moans, and noises commenced again....Three times I called Anne in, and then in the morning it all died away in a low moan. (Podmore, 1890, pp. 259–260)

Like her predecessor, Mrs. Gilby experienced problems with the door bell. Her diary for March 3 reads, "Heard the bell ring about 11. No one at the door." In her subsequently written account, she elaborated,

> March 3rd I was writing in the drawing-room, when the front door bell rang violently. I asked who it was; "No one ma'am." I thought I would stand by the window, and presently it rang again; down the servant came, no one there, and after the third time I told her not to go to the door unless she heard a knock as well. I knew no one had pulled the bell, as I was standing by the window. (Podmore, 1890, p. 263)

Also in June 1888, Anne, the servant, provided her own, much more economical, account of the phenomena. Here are some extracts,

> We used to hear noises in the roof of a night as if someone was up there throwing something about; then it would seem to give a great jump down, and run up and downstairs, and they tried the handle of the children's door; we heard something move across the room and back again....Then we heard that screaming again; we heard it in the children's room this time; it was most dreadful. Then we heard some door shook as if to shake it down;

then it kept banging all night long....Then we used to hear a great crash every night about 10 o'clock; it was downstairs in the kitchen....Then the same night as mistress went to London I heard that screaming again as if they was knocking someone about dreadfully. There was such a row. Father was in the house; he did not hear anything; then he felt something breathing on his face; got a light and looked about, but he could not see anything. (Podmore, 1890, p. 266)

The house was not rented again until August 1888. But shortly after Mrs. Gilby's departure, four men interested in psychic matters obtained access to the house on May 23 and 28. They also reported some unusual experiences, but they "were clearly such dedicated believers in the supernatural that their evidence is of very little value" (Gauld & Cornell, 1979, p. 191). The next residents were Mr. G. A. Smith, an associate member of the SPR, his wife, and a maidservant. Smith left the house in September 1889, and during those thirteen months 137 guests slept in the house. He also kept a diary of occurrences, extracts from which can be found in Gauld & Cornell, 1979, pp. 192–195. The reported phenomena are similar to those noted by Miss Morris and Mrs. Gilby, including ringing of the door bell while no one was at the door.

3. Haunting: Comments

Looking generally at the class of ostensible hauntings, anti-survivalists have several explanatory options. If they shun any kind of paranormal explanation, they must claim either that the apparitions are mistakenly identified normal physical objects or (possibly shared) hallucinations. And in fact, some cases seem amenable to this approach. For example, recent studies plausibly trace some non-veridical haunting experiences to the effects of infrasound standing waves at the relevant locations (Tandy & Lawrence, 1998; Tandy, 2000). Others have suggested—with varying degrees of plausibility—that the culprits might be movements of the earth, magnetic fields, or sudden changes in the magnitudes of such fields (see, e.g., Persinger, 1985; Persinger & Cameron, 1986; Persinger, Tiller, & Koren, 2000). Not surprisingly, however, good cases allow us to rule out geophysical causes, malobservation, and other Usual Suspects.

Of course, even if every haunting apparition was mediated by localized geophysical processes, those processes alone wouldn't explain why some cases are veridical. And it's dubious that geophysical explanations would work for phenomena that seem to be products of design or human intelligence—for example, the neat or artistic arrangement of moved or overturned objects, or the utterance of distinct sentences or phrases (especially those heard by more than one witness). Geophysical explanations may also have difficulty explaining the variety of haunting phenomena at a given location. In case (2), for example, these include the sighting of apparitional figures, crashing and banging sounds similar to those produced by kitchen implements, physical pushes, sounds as of footsteps, and the opening and closing of doors. In case (3) the phenomena include sounds of thumps, banging doors, sobs, moans, screams, identifiable English phrases, and also the tactile experience of breathing on one's face. (For recent cases boasting a wide variety of phenomena at a given location, see Maher, 2000; Maher & Hansen, 1995).

In the most refractory haunting cases, the *content* of the hallucinations seems to be shared, either between several individuals at the same time, or between independent observers at different times. Moreover, sometimes pets and other animals seem to be aware of something happening at the locations where people experience haunting phenomena. So apparently, psi-unsympathetic accounts of hauntings won't get us very far; an appeal to telepathy, at least, seems unavoidable.

But even the appeal to telepathy has limited utility. In an earlier book (Braude, 1997, chapter 4), I looked closely at the puzzles presented by collective apparitions, and I explained in detail why telepathic theories are unsatisfactory. I'll also discuss the matter again, briefly, in the next chapter. But for now, we'll have to settle for more cursory remarks still. The problem, in a nutshell, is that telepathic explanations have trouble accounting for the similarity and simultaneity of the different percipients' experiences. That's why I proposed interpreting collective apparitions as products of PK, at least when survivalist explanations seem unwarranted. We could view those apparitions as being analogous to the materialized figures reported throughout the history of mediumship.

Apparently, then, a viable anti-survivalist account of hauntings must appeal to super (or just dandy?) psi. It will need to interpret at least some apparitional figures either as telepathic constructs or as products of PK. Of course, we've noted that apparitions may also be veridical. Sometimes apparitional figures reportedly resemble people who previously occupied (or were connected with) the place where they appear, and sometimes those figures provide information unknown to the percipients. So in those instances, super-psi explanations also require an appeal to percipient ESP.

But for now, we can ignore the issues posed by the veridical nature of haunting cases. We've already discussed their counterparts in connection with mediumship. Besides, the vast majority of haunting cases provide no verifiable evidence of survival, and most veridical cases are not much better. However, that still leaves us with the following problem, unique to cases of haunting. As I noted above, the fact that some apparitions are perceived collectively counts against telepathic explanations and in favor of interpreting them as paranormally produced *physical* objects. Moreover, some other haunting phenomena (e.g., object

movements) seem undoubtedly to be physical, irrespective of the number of observers. So, assuming that some psi hypothesis is called for in
these cases, several related questions arise: First, do we have any reasons, apart from these haunting cases, for thinking that enduring physical objects can be paranormally produced? And second, is it more plausible to trace these putatively physical objects and phenomena to living
or to deceased agents?

I think the first of these questions has a fairly easy answer, although
few are likely to find it satisfying. In my view, we have ample evidence
that people can paranormally influence events at a distance. Although
some disagree (inscrutably, in my view), let's suppose for the sake of
argument that we're maximally sympathetic to the evidence for PK and
that we accept not only the laboratory evidence (see, e.g., Radin, 1997),
but also evidence for the large-scale phenomena surveyed in Braude,
1997. What we then need to consider is: How long can those effects
linger, and how autonomous can they be? For example, would we be
entitled to conclude that PK can produce localized *processes* that attach
to a location and which may be activated by various nearby events (e.g.,
the presence or movements of living persons)?

As far as I can tell, there is no evidence, outside of the haunting
cases themselves, for such processes. Granted, there's an interesting
body of data on materialization phenomena. But those phenomena seem
invariably to be short-term. Typical reports describe objects materializ-
ing gradually (or appearing suddenly) and then dematerializing (or dis-
appearing suddenly). There are also many accounts of so-called *apports*,
where objects seem suddenly to move from one location to another, and
those objects don't subsequently disappear or dematerialize. But haunting cases seem to suggest something quite different from "standard"
materializations or apports. Of course, survivalists would say they suggest the continuing presence at a location of a discarnate intelligence.
But if we reject that, we'd presumably have to interpret recurrent haunting phenomena as being produced by something like a tape loop or remotely activated playback device.

So how serious a problem is this for advocates of super psi? It seems
undeniable that some haunting phenomena are physical and
intersubjectively perceivable. It also seems clear that some must be considered paranormal. But once we've made that concession, it may be irrelevant (even if it's unfortunate) that no other body of evidence in
parapsychology—that is, apart from apparition cases—provides evidence
for similarly long-term phenomena. We can't reject evidence for a phenomenon *P* just because *P* is unprecedented, and there's nothing inherently peculiar or suspicious about a phenomenon that occurs only in a
restricted range of situations. Presumably, then, we can't reject a super-
psi interpretation of recurrent localized haunting phenomena just because we'd have to interpret them as forms of PK unique to haunting

cases. And remember, they'd be unique only with respect to their duration or persistence, not to their magnitude.

Still, some may feel that survivalists can tilt the interpretive scales in
their direction, because they have systematicity on their side. That is,
recurrent haunting phenomena seem to connect nicely with other bodies of survival evidence suggesting the influence of postmortem intelligence or agency on the physical world. In fact, recurrent haunting phenomena seem continuous with mediumistic phenomena suggesting the
direct influence of surviving agency on a person. The principal difference between haunting and mediumistic cases is that in the former, the
direct influence in question would be on a location rather than a person. Living persons (i.e., those who observe the phenomena) would be
influenced only indirectly.

However, advocates of super psi can also appeal to a kind of systematicity. Apart from the persistence of observable effects, haunting phenomena connect to the extensive body of evidence for large-scale PK.
Of course, most of that evidence is from cases of ostensible physical
mediumship, but in many of those cases the effects have no distinctive
association to a deceased person. In fact, as cases of apparent postmortem survival most of them aren't remotely evidential. So there's no reason on the face of it to treat them as survival cases, and it's perfectly
legitimate for anti-survivalists to see them as supporting their position.
(There are, however, good reasons for thinking that spiritistic beliefs are
unusually conducive to the production of large-scale PK. See Braude,
1997, chapter 2.)

4. Transplant Cases

These cases are valuable for several reasons. First, they constitute a significant body of *new* evidence. Although reincarnation and possession
cases continue to appear, cases of mediumship declined sharply in the
last half of the twentieth century along with interest in Spiritualism.
Second, transplant cases reinforce the impression, easily gained from
cases of mediumship, reincarnation, and possession, that the *form* of
survival evidence is influenced by surrounding cultural and social
forces. Mediumship is tied to spiritistic beliefs of some sort, and reincarnation and possession cases occur primarily in communities whose
belief systems accommodate the phenomena. That doesn't show that
the phenomena are nothing but social constructs. But it suggests that
survival evidence varies in its *symptom language*, like the varying and
culturally specific forms of dissociative disorders. Not surprisingly, the
evidence from transplant cases seems distinctively restricted to more
technologically developed and affluent parts of the world, where transplant operations are accessible and affordable. And with the decline of

mediumship, they might even act as a continuing counterweight to the large and growing body of reincarnation and possession cases, which cluster in less-industrialized societies.

Third, transplant cases introduce evidence of a new *type*. They expand the empirical horizon in our search for evidence of survival, and they present us with a distinctive network of needs and interests to which we can apply both the super-psi and survival hypotheses. When we think along survivalist lines, it's easy to imagine why, after their tragic and premature deaths, organ donors might cling to their earthly connections. Of course, advocates of super psi would emphasize a different set of causally relevant motives. Donors would not be the only individuals with apparently burning needs. Organ recipients and the families of both donor and recipient will also have deep concerns, and they must be addressed as well. For example, we need to consider not simply how much the recipient and recipient's family knew about the donor, but how much they *wanted* to know. Similarly, we need to consider whether members of the donor's family urgently seek evidence of the donor's survival. And of course, organ recipients tend to feel a deep bond with their donor, and that bond may be expressed in a variety of ways, both flagrant and subtle.

Some try explaining transplant cases in terms of cellular memory (e.g., Pearsall, Schwartz, & Russek, 1999). I suspect that approach is deeply flawed (in fact, incoherent), but space prohibits a critical discussion of the problems with the hypothesis of cellular memory. For now, it's enough to note that it seems to face the same fatal difficulties confronting all trace theories of memory (Bursen, 1978; Heil, 1978; Malcolm, 1977; Braude, 2002). But more important, if cellular memory were to account for the transplant cases, then those cases wouldn't be evidence of the type of survival concerning us in this book. The appeal to cellular memory is actually an attempt to *explain away* the evidence for postmortem survival by (a) recasting it in what its proponents believe are scientifically credible terms, and (b) linking personality (or at least a limited set of dispositions) to still-functioning body parts. So of course, that strategy won't apply to types of survival evidence in which relatively robust personality, active agency, and clear postmortem agendas seem to persist even after all parts of the body cease functioning or decompose. Thus, explanations in terms of cellular memory treat transplant cases as *limiting cases* (given today's technology) of *antemortem* survival. So long as (at least certain?) organs continue to function, bodily death hasn't occurred, although of course bodily integrity has been seriously compromised.

So I propose that we try evaluating transplant cases as another potential source of evidence for noncorporeal survival. As I noted earlier, we can construe both transplant and haunting cases as indicating that surviving personalities *hover* around objects (bodily organs and locations, respectively). And as we'll see, some transplant cases support that interpretation more clearly than others.

Public awareness of transplant evidence probably began with the publication of *A Change of Heart* in 1997 (Sylvia, 1997). In this book, Claire Sylvia described the personality shifts she experienced after her heart and lung transplant in 1988. She noted these changes before meeting her donor's family and learning about his character. For example, she found herself craving food she had previously disliked, but which her donor, Tim, had enjoyed. Among these were beer (which Claire felt like drinking shortly after her surgery), green peppers, and Kentucky Fried Chicken nuggets. The last of these seemed particularly odd, considering that Claire was a dancer and choreographer who had always been very careful about her diet. Moreover, KFC nuggets were found in Tim's jacket when he was killed. Claire's color preferences and level of aggressiveness also changed in ways that seemed more Tim-like.

Claire's changes were accompanied by some interesting dreams during the first few months after her surgery. In one dream, she met a man named Tim L, who (it turned out) resembled her donor, and at the end of the dream she kissed and inhaled Tim into her. In another dream she changed from a woman to a man, and then back to a woman.

But Claire's experiences aren't unique, and other cases seem even more remarkable. Consider the following case summaries, taken from a review of ten similar cases involving heart or heart-lung recipients (Pearsall *et al.*, 1999).

Case 1

The donor was a 17-year-old black male student victim of a drive-by shooting. The recipient was a 47-year-old white male foundry worker diagnosed with aortic stenosis.

The donor's mother reported:

"Our son was walking to violin class when he was hit. Nobody knows where the bullet came from, but it just hit him and he fell. He died right there on the street hugging his violin case. He loved music and his teachers said he had a real thing for it. He would listen to music and play along with it. I think he would have been at Carnegie Hall someday, but the other kids always made fun of the music he liked."

The recipient reported:

"I'm real sad and all for the guy who died and gave me his heart, but I really have trouble with the fact that he was black. I'm not a racist, mind you, not at all. Most of my friends at the plant are black guys. But the idea that there is a black heart in a white body seems really...well, I don't know. I told my wife I thought my penis might grow to a black man's size. They say black men have larger penises, but I don't know for sure. After we have sex, I sometimes feel guilty because a black man made love to my wife, but I don't really think that seriously. I can tell you one thing, though: I used to hate classical music, but now I love it. So I know it's not my new heart, because a black guy from the hood wouldn't be into that. Now it calms my heart. I play it all the time. I more than like it. I play it all the time. I didn't tell any of the guys on the line that I have a black heart, but I think about it a lot."

The recipient's wife reports:

"He was more than concerned about the idea when he heard it was a black man's heart. He actually asked me if he could ask the doctor for a white heart when one came up. He's no Archie Bunker, but he's close to it. And he would kill me if he knew I told you this, but for the first time, he's invited his black friends over from work. It's like he doesn't see their color anymore even though he still talks about it sometimes. He seems more comfortable and at ease with these black guys, but he's not aware of it. And one more thing I should say: he's driving me nuts with the classical music. He doesn't know the name of one song and never, never listened to it before. Now, he sits for hours and listens to it. He even whistles classical music songs that he could never know. How does he know them? You'd think he'd like rap music or something because of his black heart." (Pearsall *et al.*, 1999, p. 68)

Case 2

The donor was a 24-year-old female automobile accident victim. The recipient was a 25-year-old male graduate student suffering from cystic fibrosis who received a heart-lung transplant.

The donor's sister reported:

"My sister was a very sensual person. Her one love was painting. She was on her way to her first solo showing at a tiny art shop when a drunk plowed into her. It's a lesbian art store that supports gay artists. My sister was not really very 'out' about it, but she was gay. She said her landscape paintings were really representations of the mother or woman figure. She would look at a naked woman model and paint a landscape from that! Can you imagine? She was gifted."

The recipient reported:

"I never told anyone at first, but I thought having a woman's heart would make me gay. Since my surgery, I've been hornier than ever and women just seem to look even more erotic and sensual, so I thought I might have gotten internal transsexual surgery. My doctor told me it was just my new energy and lease on life that made me feel that way, but I'm different. I know I'm different. I make love like I know exactly how the woman's body feels and responds—almost as if it is my body. I have the same body, but I still think I've got a woman's way of thinking about sex now."

The recipient's girlfriend:

"He's a much better lover now. Of course, he was weaker before, but it's not that. He's like, I mean he just knows my body as well as I do. He wants to cuddle, hold, and take a lot of time. Before he was a good lover, but not like this. It's just different. He wants to hug all the time and go shopping. My God, he never wanted to shop. And you know what, he carries a purse now. His purse! He slings it over his shoulder and calls it his bag, but it's a purse. He hates it when I say that, but going to the mall with him is like going with one of the girls. And one more thing, he loves to go to museums. He would never, absolutely never do that. Now he would go every week. Sometimes he stands for minutes and looks at a painting without talking. He loves landscapes and just stares. Sometimes I just leave him there and come back later." (Pearsall *et al.*, 1999, pp. 67–68)

Case 3

The donor was a 16-month-old boy who drowned in a bathtub. The recipient was a 7-month-old boy diagnosed with Tetalogy of Fallot (a hole in the ventricular septum with displacement of the aorta, pulmonary stenosis, and thickening of the right ventricle).

The donor's mother is a physician:

"When Carter [recipient] first saw me, he ran to me and pushed his nose against me and rubbed it. It was just exactly what we did with Jerry [donor]."

"I'm a doctor. I'm trained to be a keen observer and have always been a natural born skeptic. But this was real. I know people will say I need to believe my son's spirit is alive, and perhaps I do. But I felt it. My husband and my father felt it. And I swear to you, and you can ask my mother, Carter said the same baby-talk words that Jerry said. Carter is [now] six, but he was talking Jerry's baby talk and playing with my nose just like Jerry did."

"We stayed with the [recipient family] that night. In the middle of the night, Carter came in and asked to sleep with my husband and me. He cuddled up between us exactly like Jerry did, and we began to cry. Carter told us not to cry because Jerry said everything was okay. My husband, I, our parents, and those who really knew Jerry have no doubt. Our son's heart contains much of our son and beats in Carter's chest. On some level, our son is still alive."

The recipient's mother reported:

"I saw Carter go to her [the donor's mother]. He never does that. He is very, very shy, but he went to her just like he used to run to me when he was a baby. When he whispered 'It's okay mama', I broke down. He called her mother, or maybe it was Jerry's heart talking. And one more thing that got to us: we found out talking to Jerry's mom that Jerry had mild cerebral palsy mostly on his left side. Carter has stiffness and some shaking on that same side. He never did as a baby and it only showed up after the transplant. The doctors say it's probably something to do with his medical condition, but I really think there's more to it."

"One more thing I'd like to know about. When we went to church together, Carter had never met Jerry's father. We came late and Jerry's dad was sitting with a group of people in the middle of the congregation. Carter let go of my hand and ran right to that man. He climbed on his lap, hugged him and said 'Daddy'. We were flabbergasted. How could he have known him? Why did he call him Dad? He never did things like that. He would never let go of my hand in church and never run to a stranger. When I asked him why he did it, he said he didn't. He said Jerry did and he went with him." (Pearsall et al., 1999, p. 67)

Case 4

The donor was a 34-year-old police officer shot attempting to arrest a drug dealer. The recipient was a 56-year-old college professor diagnosed with atherosclerosis and ischemic heart disease.

The donor's wife reported:

"When I met Ben [the recipient] and Casey, I almost collapsed. First, it was a remarkable feeling seeing the man with my husband's heart in his chest. I think I could almost see Carl [the donor] in Ben's eyes. When I asked how Ben felt, I think I was really trying to ask Carl how he was. I wouldn't say that to them, but I wish I could have touched Ben's chest and talked to my husband's heart."

"What really bothers me, though, is when Casey said offhandedly that the only real side effect of Ben's surgery was flashes of light in his face. That's exactly how Carl died. The bastard shot him right in the face. The last thing he must have seen is a terrible flash. They never caught the guy, but they think they know who it is. I've seen the drawing of his face. The guy has long hair, deep eyes, a beard, and this real calm look. He looks sort of like some of the pictures of Jesus."

The recipient reported:

"If you promise you won't tell anyone my name, I'll tell you what I've not told any of my doctors. Only my wife [Casey] knows. I only knew that my donor was a 34-year-old very healthy guy. A few weeks after I got my heart, I began to have dreams. I would see a flash of light right in my face and my face gets real, real hot. It actually burns. Just before that time, I would get a glimpse of Jesus. I've had these dreams and now daydreams ever since: Jesus and then a flash. That's the only thing I can say is something different, other than feeling really good for the first time in my life."

The recipient's wife reported:

"I'm very, very glad you asked him about his transplant. He is more bothered than he'll tell you about these flashes. He says he sees Jesus and then a blinding flash. He told the doctors about the flashes but not Jesus. They said it's probably a side effect of the medications, but God we wish they would stop." (Pearsall *et al.*, 1999, pp. 70–71)

5. Transplant Cases: Comments

Of course, the testimony in these cases is fascinating, and it should be clear that we can't discount it simply by appealing to the Usual Suspects. Granted, the recipient in case 2 knew that his donor was female. So we might credibly interpret the recipient's use of a purse and his new interest in shopping as a kind of role-playing due to suggestion. We could claim that knowledge of his donor's gender unleashed his feminine side, which until that time had been largely latent. But other features of the recipient's behavior seem not simply less generically feminine, but rather specific to the donor—for example, his newfound interest in museums and landscapes. Similarly, it's unclear why knowledge of his donor's gender would lead to the more specific and intimate knowledge about female anatomy demonstrated during lovemaking, much less the knowledge-*how* demonstrated at those times but never before. Case 1 offers even more striking examples of donor-specific behavior, because the recipient's new interests ran counter to his expectations and racial stereotypes.

Appeals to psi among the living also have limited utility, although they seem to take us somewhat further. For example, recipient-ESP or donor-family telepathic influence might help explain the donor-specific

behavior exhibited in case 1, young Carter's Jerry-like behavior in case
3, and even the experiences in case 4 of the blinding light and image of
Jesus. And in all the cases it's easy to imagine why the donor's family
and the recipient might deeply wish for indications of the donor's postmortem persistence.

But perhaps the principal issue before us is: How well do transplant
cases support what we could call the *hover hypothesis*: that the donor's
surviving personality (or a fragment thereof) remains close (in a sense
needing to be explained) to the organ recipient (or to the transplanted
organs)? Some cases suggest this fairly clearly and even look a bit like
possession cases. In fact, apparent possession might be a relatively clear
exemplar of the sort of hovering at issue. If so, transplant cases would
be a subset of possession cases: namely, those possession cases in which
transplanted organs provide a clear motivating link between possessor
and victim. And if that's the case, then the transplant cases may not be
nearly as unprecedented as they seem at first. They would still be cases
of a new type, but that type would not differ radically from other forms
of possession.

The cases most strongly favoring the hover hypothesis are those
where the organ recipients are children. Survivalists could argue that
children will be particularly open to postmortem influence, presumably
because they haven't had their receptivity "educated" out of them. Of
course, advocates of super psi could make an analogous claim: that children are particularly receptive to ESP. And in fact (as I noted in chapter
4), there is some evidence that children score more poorly on ESP tests
as they age, pass through the educational system, and presumably learn
that others consider displays of psi to be unacceptable or impossible
(Winkelman, 1980, 1981).

Of the cases presented above, number 3 most clearly suggests hovering or possession. Young Carter attributed his behavior in church to the
donor, Jerry. He said it was not he (i.e., Carter) who ran to Jerry's father
(whom he had not met), hugged him, and called him "Daddy." Carter
said Jerry did this and *went with him*. And Carter told Jerry's parents not
to cry because Jerry said it was OK. On the surface, at least, this suggests an interaction between two distinct minds or individuals, Carter
and Jerry. In fact, it resembles a form of mediumship in which the communicator interacts with and sometimes controls the body of the medium.

Another case from Pearsall, Schwartz, and Russek's modest collection suggests a similar type of communication between organ recipient
and the surviving personality of the donor. The donor was a 3-year-old
girl who drowned in the pool at her mother's boyfriend's house. The
mother and boyfriend had left the girl in the care of a teenage babysit-
ter. Apparently, the girl's parents had been through an ugly divorce, and
thereafter the father never saw his daughter. Jimmy, the recipient, was a

9-year-old boy who claimed not to know who the donor was. He reported,

> I talk to her sometimes. I can feel her in there. She seems very sad. She is
> very afraid. I tell her it is okay, but she is very afraid. She says she wishes
> that parents wouldn't throw away their children. I don't know why she
> would say that. (Pearsall *et al.*, 1999, p. 69)

Jimmy's mother added that since the operation, her son was "deathly
afraid of the water," although he had loved it before.

Although the hover hypothesis seems to handle transplant cases fairly smoothly, one striking feature of the cases may be problematic: namely, the apparently lasting personality alterations in the organ recipient.
For example, in case 1 the recipient acquired what seems to be a new
and abiding interest in classical music, and in case 2 the recipient began to manifest a new and apparently permanent interest in art and attitude toward sex. If these cases really form a subset of possession cases,
then presumably we'd have to regard the possession as permanent, or
nearly so. Now I see no problem with that. It's a problem only if we suppose, apparently without justification, that possession (assuming it occurs) can only be temporary or sporadic. Of course, here, as elsewhere,
the evidence is ambiguous. But it's also a fertile source of clues for theory construction. So, once we decide to entertain the possibility of possession, we must try to let the data guide us, and we must try also not to
be constrained by whatever biases we had at the start. Cases of ostensible possession cover a wide range, including traditional cases of
mediumship, spirit possession in shamanic contexts, cases closely resembling reincarnation cases, and the transplant cases now under consideration. And to me at least, the totality of data suggest that possession—whatever it is—can occur in varying forms, varying degrees of
completeness, and for varying periods of time.

We might want to modify this stance later, after hammering out a
detailed and empirically adequate theory of postmortem existence. We
might then decide to taxonomize possession cases so as to draw a sharp
line between transient or temporary possession (as in mediumship or
shamanic ritualistic possession) and its apparently more permanent
forms. But for now at least, it seems that these cases all share a common crucial feature. The ostensible manifestation of another, postmortem, individual occurs well after the subject's birth, typically following
some sort of ritual, or induction, or other event (such as an organ transplant) that provides an occasion or motive for apparent possession. That
may be enough to distinguish these cases from cases of ostensible reincarnation.

We noted in the last chapter that subjects in reincarnation cases
tend to identify thoroughly with the past personality, whereas in most
possession cases the previous personality seems more parasitic and ap-

parently *displaces* the normal personality. And that distinction may, indeed, be one fair, if rough, way to distinguish most reincarnation from possession cases. But transplant cases don't fit neatly in either category. In some of those cases, the original personality of the recipient isn't displaced; instead, it's *modified* in ways characteristic of the donor. And in others (sometimes in the same cases), the recipient does identify strongly with the donor, and we see the kind of personality blending characteristic of reincarnation cases. Yet in others (and again, sometimes in the same cases), the recipient (a child in these instances), apparently interacts, seemingly mediumistically, with the donor.

So we might well find it necessary or appropriate to develop a finer-grained taxonomy, of survival cases generally and possession cases in particular. But for now at least, my recommendation is that we interpret transplant cases as supplementing the evidence for possession. Moreover, as we noted earlier in this chapter and in chapter 6, it's not unprecedented for survival evidence to take culturally specific forms. Similarly, the evidence for MPD/DID seems to vary (as a symptom language or idiom of distress) from culture to culture and from epoch to epoch.[2] Analogously, it seems plausible to interpret the transplant cases as a culturally specific manifestation of possession, appropriate to societies that are technologically advanced and in which more classic manifestations of possession are not accepted as a matter of course. Moreover, children would tend to be relatively unbiased (or polluted) by a prevailing worldview in which spirit possession plays little or no role. So if transplant cases are really disguised possession cases, we would expect young organ recipients to express their conceptual innocence by providing more conventional signs of possession. And that, in fact, is what we find. As this body of evidence grows, it will be interesting to see whether the trend continues.

NOTES

1. For a discussion of the subtleties and difficulties with the haunting/poltergeist distinction, see Gauld & Cornell, 1979, and Maher, 2000.

2. See Braude, 1995. Also Berger, Ono, Nakajima, & Suematsu, 1994; Gangdev & Matjane, 1996; Krippner, 1987; Martínez-Taboas, 1995; Middleton & Butler, 1998; Osborne, 2001; Sar, Yargic, & Tutkun, 1995; 1996; Takahashi, 1990; Tutkun, Yargic, & Sar, 1995; Varma, Bouri, & Wig, 1981.

Chapter 8

Out-of-Body Experiences

1. Introduction

People having out-of-body experiences (OBEs) feel as if they travel to, and (in most cases) observe the world from, locations outside the physical body. OBEs occur under a great variety of conditions, including ordinary waking states, times of relaxation, periods of crisis, physical trauma, and life-threatening events. Many of the latter cases are so-called near-death experiences (NDEs), but not every NDE is an OBE. Most OBEs are involuntary, although apparently some people can induce them at will. During the experience (which can last from seconds to more than an hour), subjects seem to have unusually clear but otherwise normal sense perceptions of their environment and physical body.[1] In many cases, they experience themselves as having a kind of secondary body (often called a *subtle, astral,* or *parasomatic* body). Some say this secondary body resembles the physical body, and some believe it to be infused throughout or located within the physical body. Moreover, OBErs often feel that their main consciousness is somehow centered within the secondary body, in roughly the same way as it seems to be located within the physical body during ordinary waking states. Therefore, when OBErs experience their secondary body as traveling, sometimes considerable distances, from their physical body, they experience their main consciousness as going along with it. In *veridical* OBEs, subjects acquire information about remote locations which they couldn't have gained through normal sense perception. And in *reciprocal* cases, people report seeing the OBEr at the site that person is ostensibly visiting.

Not surprisingly, some believe that all OBEs are illusory. In their view, OBEs may be unusually vivid and personally compelling, but they reveal nothing more than our sometimes formidable psychological creativity. Others regard OBEs, especially veridical and reciprocal cases, as providing evidence, not of our imaginative capacities, but of psychic functioning. They claim that OBEs demonstrate the mind's ability to influence and gather information about distant events. Still others be-

245

lieve that OBEs support the survival hypothesis, at least indirectly. From their perspective, OBEs show that the self, personality, or mind can operate apart from the body, which in turn shows that a human being isn't merely a physical system. And in that case (so the argument goes), we have a good, if not coercive, reason to believe in survival of bodily death.

This last, survivalist, line of reasoning may be traced back to the early days of the SPR.[2] But it still has adherents, and all along philosophers have taken the view quite seriously (see, e.g., Broad, 1958/1976; 1962; Ducasse, 1961; Harrison, 1976; Huby, 1976; and, arguably, Geach, 1969). In fact, in recent years philosophers have been unusually attentive to the topic of OBEs and survival, most notably Almeder, 1992; Griffin, 1997; Paterson, 1995; and Woodhouse, 1994b. However, these latest participants in the debate disagree (perhaps even more than their predecessors) on the import of the evidence. Almeder regards OBEs as providing strong support for the survival hypothesis, whereas Woodhouse argues that it provides none. Griffin and (to a lesser extent) Paterson contend that the survival hypothesis is at least more probable in light of the evidence. Despite these differences, all four philosophers concur on (or at least raise) other important points that warrant our attention.

The following passages express aspects of the position I want to examine.

> During an OBE one *seems* to be feeling, perceiving, thinking, deciding, and acting while being apart from one's body, including one's brain. This experience gives strong *prima facie* support to the idea that, when the body dies, this core of the person will continue to experience. (Griffin, 1997, p. 230)

> If out-of-the-body experiences ever give those who have them knowledge of the events they seem to witness from places in space outside their bodies, this weakens the claim that we are so tied to our bodies that our veridical perception is impossible without a suitable modification to our sense organs. It also strengthens the claim that such people were, in some sense or other, situated in a place outside their bodies, for this is the place from which they perceive. (Harrison, 1976, p. 112)

> Obviously, if people can literally leave their bodies, then human personality is something distinct from the body itself. The person who leaves her or his body and then returns to it must be something more than just the very complex organism whose properties are revealed by physical science. Such a person would need to be some sort of nonphysical being that lives *in* the body. (Almeder, 1992, p. 163)

It's clear, then, that thoughtful people have found it worthwhile to explore the possible connection between OBEs and survival, and so I propose that we take a close look at the issues. More specifically, I suggest that we examine systematically the survivalist position sketched above. Even when we consider the argument for that view in what I believe is its most careful and plausible form, the connection between OBEs and survival turns out to be more tenuous than many have supposed. In fact, as in many philosophical journeys, what we find at the end of the road may be less momentous than what we discover en route.

Ordinarily, this would be an appropriate place to offer a more detailed description of the OBE. But at best, that would needlessly duplicate what others have done quite superbly, and in any case I imagine that most readers already have a general idea what OBEs are. Furthermore, I'll discuss and illustrate crucial features of OBEs as the chapter progresses. Nevertheless, I encourage those who wish to brush up on the evidence to consult the excellent discussions in Almeder, 1992, Griffin, 1997, and (for the older cases) Broad, 1962. I also strongly recommend Gauld's brief but astute treatment of the evidence (Gauld, 1982), Irwin's careful and scholarly treatise (Irwin, 1985), and Alvarado's up-to-date survey of the research literature (Alvarado, 2000).

Explanations of OBEs tend to divide into two broad classes. According to the first, consciousness is somehow physically separable from the body; the OBEr's mind or mental states are literally *at* the sites from which the OBEr seems to perceive. According to the second, nothing of the sort happens; the experience of being outside the body is always illusory. Griffin, after more caveats than we can afford to survey, labels these options the *extrasomatic* and *intrasomatic* hypotheses. Woodhouse calls them the *externalist* and *internalist* hypotheses. Because I find the latter terms somewhat more convenient, I'll follow Woodhouse in this matter.

Many, but not all, externalists adopt a view for which Broad imported the term "animism" (Broad, 1962). Behind this view is an intuition many feel is too obvious to mention, and which most philosophers and scientists have held since antiquity. The intuition is that an individual's thoughts, feelings, and dispositional capacities can exist only so long as they are *grounded in* or *supported by* a kind of underlying substrate. Whatever that substrate turns out to be, it must (at the very least) enable our mental capacities and psychological characteristics to persist over time. For example, we assume that people have psychological attributes and traits even when those characteristics are not being expressed—for example, during periods of sleep or unconsciousness. And most believe this is possible only because these capacities and traits are somehow rooted in the body. (Of course, philosophers differ greatly over what that rooting relation amounts to.) Some might think that this substrate has another essential feature as well: namely, that it allows us to express our mental states and capacities in something like the way the physical body does. But presumably that would be denied by (among others) those who accept reincarnation. They would say that although our capacities and memories persist in a substrate between incarnations, we need a physical body in order to express them. At any rate, it's a widespread (and generally unquestioned and unchallenged) intuition that mental states must be grounded in some kind of substrate if they are to exist and persist at all. So, if our mental capacities and traits can operate apart from the body and persist even after bodily death and dissolution, it would appear that some substrate besides the normal physical body makes that possible.

The way animists handle this is as follows. According to the animist, each human mind, both before and after bodily death, "is essentially and inseparably bound up with some kind of extended *quasi*-physical vehicle, which is not normally perceptible to the senses of human beings in their present life" (Broad, 1962, p. 339). It's this vehicle that some identify as the secondary or astral body they experience during OBEs, and which observers at remote locations apparently perceive in reciprocal cases. Following Broad's terminology, we could say that a human mind "informs" its secondary body, thereby constituting the unit we could call the human "soul." So before death, a human being would be composed of two intimately but only temporarily connected things: a soul and a *physical* body. And we can denote their relationship by saying that the soul "animates" the physical body. Therefore (as Gauld recognized), the animist regards death as a kind of OBE in which one's soul never returns to animate the physical body (Gauld, 1982, p. 221). Philosophically, this view has an ancient and distinguished lineage, with roots traceable back at least as far as Plato's *Phaedo*.

We're now in a position to consider carefully what we may call the *OBE Argument* for survival. Because the difficulties of this argument emerge most clearly only from a step-by-step examination, I want to consider it in the following formulation, which I believe presents its crucial elements and does as much justice to the position as is possible. This idealized version of the *OBE Argument* is a compendium of claims taken from the philosophers mentioned above, although (as I've indicated) some of those philosophers dispute parts of the argument.

(1) Some accounts of OBEs are authentic (i.e., the experiences happened largely as reported).

(2) Some of the OBEs reported in those accounts are veridical (i.e., the subjects accurately describe objects or events that they were not physically in a position to observe normally).

(3) The veridicality of at least some of those OBEs is not fortuitous (i.e., there seems to be a kind of causal connection between certain states of affairs and the subject describing those states of affairs correctly).

(4) The nonfortuitous veridicality of OBEs can't be explained in conventional physiological terms (e.g., as a relatively infrequent neurological phenomenon) or conventional psychological terms (e.g., as a dissociative hallucination).

(5) The nonfortuitous veridicality of OBEs also can't be explained in terms of "ordinary" ESP.

(6) *Therefore*, the most plausible remaining explanation is *externalism*, the hypothesis that one's mental activity can literally *be* at locations different from that occupied by one's body.

(7) *Therefore*, at least some mental states (those at locations remote from the body) are distinct from bodily states.

(8) According to the survival hypothesis, one's characteristic mental activity can continue in the absence of corresponding bodily activity, even after bodily death.

(9) *Therefore*, externalism is at least compatible with the survival hypothesis, even if it doesn't entail it.

(10) *Therefore*, to some extent, the evidence for OBEs also supports the survival hypothesis.

This argument strikes me as deeply problematic, both empirically and philosophically. Although I would argue that steps (1) and (2) are uncontroversial, I invite more skeptical readers (or those simply unfamiliar with the evidence) to accept them provisionally. That will allow us to focus on the more interesting issues raised by the argument. Besides, if (1) and (2) are false, then the OBE Argument is dead in its tracks and there's no point in pursuing it further. Let's also grant steps (3) and (4), at least for the sake of argument. As we'll see, this in no way lets the proponents of the OBE Argument off the hook. On the contrary, the most interesting problems with the argument remain.

Before proceeding, however, I should mention that Griffin's case for the relevance of OBEs is more complex than the argument presented above (Griffin, 1997). Although Griffin realizes that the most important fact (in this context) about OBEs is that some of them are veridical, he argues—as does Broad (1962)—that it's the *totality* of features common to OBEs that externalism handles more easily than rival explanations. Griffin also argues that, although the OBE evidence by itself lends some support to the survival hypothesis, when that evidence is combined with the evidence from mediumship and reincarnation, the case for survival strengthens considerably. I'll address the first of Griffin's points, about the totality of features of OBEs, later in this chapter. For now, I prefer to focus on the apparently crucial role played by veridical OBEs. The second of Griffin's points, about the weight of various types of parapsychological data taken together, is (of course) one main focus of this book, and I'll address it in chapter 9.

2. Why Externalism?

The first question to consider, then, is: Why should we accept step (5) in the *OBE Argument*? Why is it unsatisfactory to explain veridical OBEs by appealing to ESP, rather than some sort of traveling consciousness? Almeder and Woodhouse answer this question, in part at least, by appealing to an interesting and ingenious experiment reported in 1980 by Osis and McCormick (Osis & McCormick, 1980). The subject for the experiment was psychic Alex Tanous, who induced OBEs during which he identified remote targets (optical images) that could be viewed normally only from a very specific location in front of a viewing window. In addition, a strain-gauge at that location detected perturbations when Tanous (ostensibly out of his body) was trying to identify the target. In other words, the strain-gauge was registering mechanical effects at the spot where Tanous's perceptual perspective seemed to be. Furthermore, there was significantly more activation of the strain-gauge on trials when Tanous correctly identified the targets than on trials when he did not. According to both Almeder and Woodhouse, these results support the externalist claim that Tanous's mental activity was literally *at* the location of the strain-gauge.[3]

But clearly, there's no compelling reason to accept that conclusion unless we can rule out explanations in terms of both clairvoyance and PK. Osis and McCormick reject one version of this hypothesis: a suggestion by Rhine that PK effects would occur at the surface of ESP stimuli (Osis & McCormick, 1980, p. 327). Although their results suggest that Rhine's conjecture is false, other hypotheses remain live options. Clairvoyance would explain Tanous's ability to identify the targets, and PK (from either subject or experimenters) would account for the strain-gauge readings. Although Woodhouse has little to say on the matter (apart from a few remarks in Woodhouse, 1994a), Almeder rejects this explanatory strategy, and he claims that its principal flaw is the appeal to PK. That's not because Almeder denies the existence of PK. The problem, he argues, is with the assumption that Tanous's PK would be *unintentional*. Almeder writes, "People do not produce effects consistent with action at a distance (or general PK) unless they have a deliberate intention to do so" (Almeder, 1992, p.186). And he asks rhetorically, "what evidence do we have—either in the lab or outside—that this unintentional PK works *in a regular way* consistent with the data in the Osis-McCormick experiment?" (p. 186, emphasis in original).

Unfortunately, Almeder overlooks several bodies of relevant evidence, from both inside and outside the lab. Helmut Schmidt's PK tests provide several examples of unintentional PK in laboratory experiments (see the survey of his work in Braude, 2002). For instance, in one series of experiments, significant PK effects were obtained with target systems of whose existence the subjects were unaware (at least normally) and which neither subjects nor experimenters knew were serving as targets. Some of Osty's experiments with the physical medium Rudi Schneider might be even more relevant (Braude, 2002; Gregory, 1985). The most impressive result obtained with Rudi was discovered only after introducing a kind of electronic device not originally considered appropriate for the experiment, and which was so state-of-the-art that it was unknown even to most physicists at the time. But most important, the discovered effect—the regular correlation of Rudi's breathing with the absorption of an infrared beam—was one no one had anticipated. Granted, Schneider knew he was expected to produce PK effects and where those effects were supposed to occur. But there's no reason to think that anyone was looking for the absorption of infrared beams. Additional regular, and presumably unintentional, effects have been reported in poltergeist cases (see Gauld & Cornell, 1979).

I see no compelling reason, then, for regarding the strain-gauge readings in the Osis-McCormick experiments as anything other than examples of PK, which—like the many other well-documented PK effects they resemble—neither suggest nor require the externalization or independence of mental activity from bodily states. But in that case, we must ask again: Why reject ESP explanations of veridical OBEs and appeal instead to externalism? Let's assume, as I think we must, that we have ample independent evidence for the existence of ESP. What would it take, then, to show that OBEs are an altogether different sort of phenomenon? The answer, presumably—and certainly the one usually given—is that the evidence for OBEs is radically discontinuous with the evidence for other apparent forms of ESP.

Of course, OBEs and ESP experiences might be distinct even if they are qualitatively very similar, or even if there is no systematic qualitative difference between them. As Woodhouse correctly observes, the two phenomena might simply be different ways of acquiring information about remote events (Woodhouse, 1994a, p. 32). Still, if people don't leave their bodies during ESP but do leave them during OBEs, it's reasonable to think that this difference would be apparent somehow at the level of experience. It's at this point that survivalists sometimes argue for the distinctiveness of OBEs as compared to ESP. But for that strategy to work, it's not enough merely to point out that OBEs and ESP experiences differ phenomenologically. After all, the other apparent forms of ESP also differ from each other phenomenologically. The evidence for ESP is drawn from a vast empirical menu encompassing apparitions, dreams, slightly altered states (as in ganzfeld experiments), card-guessing tests, and mundane and apparently unremarkable hunches or urges. But (we're told), OBEs differ from ESP experiences in more dramatic and thoroughgoing ways.

What impresses defenders of the *OBE Argument* is not simply *that* OBEs differ subjectively from other types of apparent ESP. What matters is the *way* they differ. OBErs have extremely vivid and distinctive types of bodily sensations. They feel intensely and clearly that they travel away from their physical bodies. And those experiences seem at least as clear as many ordinary perceptions. Still, that's no reason for concluding that the sensations are veridical and that the person is genuinely located apart from the body. In fact, that would be as unwarranted as drawing the analogous inference from lifelike drug- or hypnotically induced hallucinations. Many recreational users of mescaline or LSD experience the walls breathing, and that experience may be consistent across different sensory modalities (sight, touch, hearing). But neither the vividness nor the pervasiveness of the experience justifies concluding that the walls actually breathe.

As far as OBEs are concerned, the most we're entitled to say is that the evidence is *compatible* with externalism. But because the OBE evidence is also compatible with explanations in terms of ESP, and because we have independent evidence for phenomenologically diverse and robust forms of ESP, it would be premature (at least) to say that the OBE evidence *supports* externalism. A more cautious and parsimonious view would be that veridical OBEs are simply a particularly vivid (or imagery-rich) subset of ESP experiences. In fact, in light of the totality of evidence for ESP, we should probably *expect* some ESP experiences to take the form of OBEs.

To see why, let's review some relevant theoretical and empirical matters about ESP. First, whatever one might think about the quality of the evidence, ESP would have to be at least a two-stage process. The first stage would be a stimulus (or interaction) stage during which (to put it loosely) the subject receives some information from a remote state of affairs. In the case of telepathy, this causal interaction is with another individual's mental state; in the case of clairvoyance it would be a physical state (e.g., a house on fire). The second stage of ESP would be a response (or manifestation) stage during which the subject expresses or experiences the results of the first stage. Since the early days of the SPR, parapsychologists have recognized that subjects have an opportunity during this second stage to profoundly shape the nature of their ESP experiences. The underlying process would parallel a familiar feature of ordinary perception. We know that different people can have quite different experiences of the same event, depending on their own cognitive idiosyncracies, prevailing moods, needs, concerns, etc. Presumably, something similar would be inevitable in the second stage of ESP. At that point, subjects could impose their idiosyncratic predispositions and personality characteristics (or psychological "signatures") on the evidence. Subjects' responses to a psychic stimulus would pass through a kind of psychological filtering system, consisting of their general conceptual framework, assumptions, and state of mind at the time. This plausible conjecture also explains why subjects in free-response

ESP experiments seem to filter, distort, or symbolically transform target images according to their own distinctive predispositions, biases, needs, and histories.

The parapsychological literature contains many examples of this process. In one well-known dream-telepathy experiment, a target picture of an old rabbi was apparently altered by a Protestant subject into Christian and secular imagery (Braude, 2002, p. 138; Ullman, Krippner, & Vaughan, 1989). Subjects might also modify visual perspective or change only selected elements of a target scene. Or, subjects might fixate on minor elements of a scene that they find especially interesting or meaningful. For example, if the target is a picture of a man in front of a fence, the subject might have an image of a man behind the fence (or behind bars). Or, if a small detail of the target picture is coiled rope, images of rope might figure prominently (rather than peripherally) in the subject's experiences (see Ullman *et al.*, 1989 for examples of these and related types of apparent psychic distortions; and see Sinclair, 1930/1962 and Warcollier, 1938/1975 for earlier examples of idiosyncratic distortions). Admittedly, it's often difficult to distinguish partial hits from misses in free-response ESP tests. But this much seems clear: ESP experiences are likely to be a cognitive cocktail of accurate information and confounding material generated by the subject. And most important, the subject may contribute to this mixture by altering *or supplying* the visual perspective from which the information is presented.

In fact, we can't hope to evaluate the significance of OBE imagery until we get clear on the role of imagery in ESP generally. Defenders of the *OBE Argument* may simply have skipped this important step. Parapsychologists have known for many years that some ESP subjects experience more vivid imagery than others. They have also known that ESP may occur without *any* accompanying imagery. In many reported cases of telepathy and clairvoyance, subjects seem to experience nothing more than inexplicable and incongruous desires to act (e.g., "I should phone so-and-so"). And of course, in classic card-guessing ESP tests, subjects typically experience nothing at all that is subjectively noteworthy. So it appears that occurrences of ESP are as varied and idiosyncratic as other kinds of mental states, and that (as in the case of memory) some people's psychic experiences are regularly—and perhaps unusually—detailed, vivid, and rich in imagery.

But in that case, it's reasonable to interpret OBEs as imagery-rich manifestations of ESP, and it's reasonable to conclude that for some the information gathered is accurate and perspectival, just as it may be for ESP *not* accompanied by an OBE. But then there's no need, and certainly no compelling reason, for saying that subjects actually leave their bodies in veridical ESP *or* OBE experiences.

Now let's approach the matter from another angle. Consider, first, the ESP dramatically demonstrated by star subject Pat Price in the remote viewing experiments at SRI (Targ & Puthoff, 1977; Targ, Puthoff, & May, 1979). Price often gave accurate and detailed descriptions of the locations visited by an outbound experimenter. But he tended to describe those sites from perspectives quite different from those of the outbound experimenter. Often, he described locations as if he first looked at them from high in the air and then zoomed down toward the target. Now granted, if a person were to have a normal visual perception of the target location from that perspective, the person would initially have to be located far above it. So at first glance, this might seem to help the case for externalism. After all, externalists could argue that *both* perspectival ESP and veridical OBEs require subjects to be located somehow at the appropriate point in space. That is, they could claim that normal and paranormal forms of information acquisition have similar structures, so that clairvoyant awareness requires being located in space in roughly the same way that visual or auditory perception requires a spatial location. Therefore, externalists could argue that Price, like an OBEr, was somehow at the altitude from which he viewed the target. Unfortunately for the externalist, the parapsychological data suggest that this strategy is simply untenable.

To see why, compare ESP of card faces in a sealed deck to visual perception of those cards. Visual perception of, say, the tenth card down is physically impossible so long as the deck is sealed. When the deck is sealed, there simply is no location from which a person can view *any* card in the deck. But apparently that hasn't prevented subjects from correctly identifying cards in ESP tests. Moreover, if ESP of the card depended on some sort of emanation from the card (as visual perception requires the reflection of light rays from the object perceived), it seems impossible to explain the *selectivity* of ESP—for example, the ability to identify specific cards in the deck. As C. D. Broad recognized, the clairvoyant emanations from the face of the card would be part of a much larger package of emanations. In visual perception we perceive only the *facing* surface of an object. And because not every object is transparent to light rays, visual perception can be blocked by intervening objects. But in clairvoyance we needn't physically face the object in question, and apparently every object is transparent to clairvoyance. So if clairvoyance (like sight and hearing) is mediated by some kind of emanation, those emanations would be arriving from the identifying front of the card, but also from the back of the card, from all the other cards in the deck, from every object in the room, and (presumably) from everything in the universe. Similar problems arise in the case of subjects who can correctly identify target pictures in sealed envelopes (see Broad, 1953).

So, assuming the integrity of at least the better evidence for ESP, ESP and accurate visual perception seem to differ in at least one critical respect. The evidence for clairvoyance shows that a person needn't be

suitably situated in the vicinity of an object to have clairvoyant awareness of it, even when ordinary visual perception of that object requires
occupying a specific location in space. In fact, it shows that clairvoyant
awareness of an object or event X can occur even when there's *no* position in space from which a person could normally be aware of X. So
there's no reason to think that Pat Price needed somehow to be positioned far above the objects he described, or (more generally) that clairvoyant awareness *ever* requires being located in space in the way required for normal perspectival perception. But then we also have no
reason to suppose that veridical OBEs require subjects to be located
somehow in the vicinity of the objects apparently perceived. Therefore,
in the Osis-McCormick experiments, there's no reason to insist that "in
the case of Tanous' alleged ventures...a correct call depended on being
exactly in the right place for the optical illusion to take shape" (Woodhouse, 1994b, p. 9).

Language can be seductively misleading, and it wouldn't be surprising if a subtle misuse of language makes the *OBE Argument* more appealing initially than it deserves to be. The problem here, if there is one,
concerns the possibly improper use of perception terms. Admittedly, it's
tempting to say that the OBEr *sees* certain objects during an OBE, or
(using scare quotes to indicate that we don't really know what we're saying) that the person "sees" those objects. But strictly speaking, "perceive," "feel," "hear," "see," and "smell" are words whose customary
meaning derives from the way our sensory organs interact with physical
objects. So it's unclear whether these terms should *ever* have been used
in connection with OBEs, no matter how perspectival OBE imagery
may be. At the very least, the familiar uses of perception terms in this
context may be needlessly problematic (for similar reservations about
the use of perception terms, see Penelhum, 1970).

The following analogy illustrates why. If I hallucinate a hippo in the
corner, it would be false to say I *see* or *perceive* a hippo. Perhaps it's a
bit less misleading to say I see or perceive a non-existent hippo. But the
correct and circumspect thing to say is—not that I see or "see" a hippo
(of any kind)—but simply that I *seem* to see or perceive a hippo. Moreover, my hippo hallucination (like my dream images) will be perspectival
even though I don't stand in any corresponding spatial relation to a hippo. In fact, the objects in our hallucinations and dreams will appear *as if*
they are viewed from a point in space *whether or not* there is a location
from which the perspective is derived. That's why I can dream vividly
that I'm standing on the edge of a cliff even when I'm lying in bed. Presumably, then, we should describe the dream case as we did the hippo
case. We should say that I *seem* to be looking over the edge of a cliff,
not that I am looking (or "looking") over the edge of a cliff. So perhaps
similar caution is appropriate even in the case of veridical OBEs. Perhaps we should say that the OBEr seems to perceive or observe the ob-

jects or events described correctly. Or perhaps we could use the relatively neutral term "aware" and say that in veridical OBEs subjects are aware of remote states of affairs. That may help counter the temptation to regard "aware" as shorthand for a disjunction of ordinary perception terms, such as "perceive," "see," and "hear." After all, one of the big questions about ESP is whether or how it differs from ordinary forms of perception.[4] So, since ESP of sealed objects suggests strongly that ESP differs profoundly from ordinary visual perception, it would seem question begging to assume, from the start, that subjective states of OBE subjects are straightforwardly describable with ordinary perception terms.[5]

3. Distinctness and Independence

So far, we've been questioning step (5) in the *OBE Argument*: the claim that we can't satisfactorily explain veridical OBEs in terms of ESP. And we've considered reasons for regarding that claim as unconvincing and probably false. Let's now examine subsequent steps in the argument, to see what additional problems remain.

Assuming that the first five steps in the *OBE Argument* are satisfactory, then step (6) would perhaps be a reasonable inference. That is, if we can't explain OBEs in terms of normal or unusual bodily processes *or* in terms of ESP, then some sort of externalist hypothesis is a genuinely live option. But it's still not clear sailing for the *OBE Argument*. The next serious problem with that argument concerns the move from (7) to (9), where there may be some important (and contentious) missing steps.

Remember, first of all, the central philosophical intuition behind the *OBE Argument*. The intuition is that OBEs demonstrate a profound distinction between mind and body, and thus they show that human beings aren't simply physical systems. And that conclusion in turn suggests that our characteristic mental activity can continue after bodily death. It's this underlying intuition that steps (7)–(9) try to capture. Notice, however, that I stated the conclusion in step (9) very conservatively, so that all externalists would be likely to endorse it.

(9) *Therefore*, externalism is at least compatible with the survival hypothesis, even if it does not entail it.

This statement is modest because it avoids making the strong claim that externalism entails personal survival, or even the weaker claim that the truth of externalism lends a high degree of probability to the survival hypothesis. Step (9) is true if externalism is merely *compatible* with the survival hypothesis. But if the *most* that can be said for externalism is that it's compatible with survival, then that result is clearly underwhelming. Externalism might be compatible with survival even if there are good reasons for concluding that the survival hypothesis is *false*. For example, Woodhouse (who argues for externalism) comments,

> Externalism does not entail anything about survival of bodily death, except that it does not rule it out. It is a tremendous conceptual jump from, say, a 30-minute OBE to immortality. (Woodhouse, 1994b, p. 14)

Irwin concurs. He writes,

> Even if OBE research should support the existence of a nonphysical element of being, it might not bear directly upon the issue of whether this element is immortal. (Irwin, 1985, p. 25)

Echoing Ducasse (Ducasse, 1961, p. 164), he continues,

> it should not be assumed that during life the nonphysical element animates the body. In fact the reverse may be the case, so that destruction of the body occasions the death of the nonphysical element. (pp. 25–26)

Therefore, to show that externalism actually *supports* (or entails) the survival hypothesis, more needs to be said. That's why some proponents of the *OBE Argument*, such as Almeder, do try to say more. So we must ask: Why *exactly* would the distinctness of mind from body lead us to *accept* the survival hypothesis? As Woodhouse, Irwin, and others have noted, it's not enough simply to claim that mind and body are distinct. What matters is the way they differ.

At this point it might be instructive to recall the passage from Almeder, quoted earlier.

> Obviously, if people can literally leave their bodies, then human personality is something distinct from the body itself. The person who leaves her or his body and then returns to it must be something more than just the very complex organism whose properties are revealed by physical science. Such a person would need to be some sort of nonphysical being that lives *in* the body. (Almeder, 1992, p. 163)

Then, in the concluding section of his chapter on OBEs, Almeder writes,

> the evidence [for veridical OBEs] strongly warrants our endorsing some form of mind-body dualism that eschews a pure reduction of human personality to bodily existence as we know it... [W]e have in these best cases enough in the way of "proof" to justify a rational belief in some form of postmortem personal survival. (Almeder, 1992, p. 194)

Let's assume, for the moment, that we understand what it means to say that a person "leaves" the body. Even if we then concede that the individual leaving the body is something more than the organism described by physical science, that won't give Almeder what he needs. In particular, and contrary to what Almeder claims, it doesn't warrant the conclusion that a person can exist independently of the body.

Ducasse saw this clearly. He noted that animists consider the physical body to be causally dependent on the thing that leaves the body.
They would say that under normal circumstances, the secondary (or
astral) body animates the physical body by being infused throughout the
physical body (or co-located with it). And during OBEs the secondary
body animates the physical body in a different way, either through its
connection with a "silver cord" (according to some accounts), or by
means of an invisible and currently unidentified connection. But,
Ducasse noted, it

> could equally be that the animation is in the converse direction, i.e., that
> death of the body entails death of the conscious "double" whether the lat-
> ter be at the time dislocated from or collocated with the former. (Ducasse,
> 1961, p. 164)

Now, Almeder doesn't subscribe to the existence of astral bodies; so
he doesn't endorse a classically animist position. But Ducasse's underlying point is that mind may be causally dependent on body even if mind
and body are distinct. And that point weighs equally against Almeder's
version of externalism. Part of the problem is that there are as many
forms of dualism as there are flavors of ice cream. And many philosophers take mind and body to be different while at the same time holding
that mind can't exist without the body. In fact, some of those deny
psychophysical reductionism while remaining staunch physicalists.
They subscribe to a kind of substance-monism according to which the
world is comprised fundamentally of physical stuff, even though our
descriptions of mental events can't be translated without residue into
physical terms. But then it's clear that one can take mind and body to
be distinct while rejecting the survival hypothesis.

Fortunately, we can illustrate the problem without surveying (either
comprehensively or cursorily) the full spectrum of possible—or even
widely held—positions in this complex arena. One example will suffice.
Epiphenomenalists argue that mental events are merely by-products of
physical events. Although they differ from physical events, mental
events are entirely causally dependent on underlying physical processes,
and in fact mental events have no causal powers of their own. For example, although it seems as if our volitions cause our actions, the apparent efficacy of our volitions is misleading. Both our actions and our
volitions are caused by physical events. Volitions, according to this view,
are merely symptoms of that underlying causal network and (as it were)
signals of the physical events that follow. So in some respects, for the
epiphenomenalist the relation of body to mind is analogous to that between a thing and its shadow. The object and its shadow are distinct,
but once the object ceases to exist, so does the shadow.

It doesn't matter for present purposes whether epiphenomenalism is
a viable philosophical position, and in fact there are good reasons for

thinking it isn't (see, e.g., Braude, 1979; Goldberg, 1977; Kim, 1993). What matters is the ease with which we can drive a logical wedge between mind-body distinctness and mind-body independence. And that's not all we can learn by considering the relationship of an object to its shadow. That relationship differs in crucial respects from the body-mind relationship asserted by epiphenomenalists. In fact, the object-shadow relationship is strikingly similar to the alleged relationship between body and mind in OBEs. But ironically, those similarities work against the *OBE Argument* for survival.

Notice, first, that the object and its shadow occupy different locations in space, just as the mind and physical body purportedly occupy different locations during OBEs. Moreover, shadows are causally efficacious; they can have effects on the world around them. For example, shadows will lower the ambient temperature and affect light meter readings at their locations. Similarly, externalists claim that, in reciprocal OBEs and in the Osis-McCormick experiment, the traveling mind affects the world at remote locations. In reciprocal cases observers at the remote locations report seeing the OBEr, and in the Osis-McCormick experiment Tanous apparently activated the strain-gauge. But then, even if externalists are correct that during OBEs the mind exists apart from the physical body and can affect the world at that place, that won't advance the case for survival. After all, since the shadow will cease to exist when the object casting the shadow ceases to exist, for all we know the mind may be similarly dependent on the body. The question for the externalist at this point must therefore be: Is there any reason for thinking that the mind is more independent of the body than the body's shadow?

Before considering predictable externalist responses to that question, we should observe an important point about the connection between externalism and mind-body dualism. It's tempting to suppose that externalism presupposes a strong *substance* dualism, according to which mind and body are radically different kinds of *entities*. Almeder seems to take this view. As we've seen, he contends that the "person who leaves her or his body and then returns to it...would need to be some sort of nonphysical being that lives *in* the body." Now historically, at least, substance dualists have maintained that one crucial difference between mind-stuff and body-stuff is that the latter is extended in space whereas the former is non-extended. Thereafter, opinions diverge. For example, Descartes claimed (notoriously) that, despite this difference, mind and body interact causally. However, his follower, Malebranche, endorsed the parallelist view that mind-body interaction was merely apparent causality, with true causal connections being traceable only to God.

But these differences needn't concern us here. What matters is that, contrary to what some think, externalism presupposes neither classic Cartesian dualism nor any of its successors. Even if we grant that dur-

ing veridical OBEs the mind, or some aspect of oneself (or one's consciousness), severs its normal connection with the body, nothing follows
about what sort of stuff this might be (see also Woodhouse, 1994b, p.
11). Actually, for reasons I explain below, it may follow that whatever
leaves the body is not an unextended Cartesian mind. But apart from
that, externalism doesn't commit one to any particular view as to what
kind of substance the mind (or the relevant aspect of consciousness) is.
Externalists need only claim that this thing has certain functional properties—for example, the ability to mediate the OBEr's apparent perceptions of remote locations. It can remain an open question whether this
thing is nonphysical or possibly a kind of material stuff not currently
identified by science. That simply acknowledges a reasonable point
widely accepted within the philosophy of mind: namely, that even if
minds and bodies are not radically different types of *hardware*, they may
still differ functionally. But if this is correct and externalism doesn't
have to posit a mind-stuff that differs radically from body-stuff, then the
inference from externalism to survival (made by Almeder and others) is
weakened considerably.

Moreover, externalism seems *incompatible* with any dualism (such as
Descartes's) according to which mind is nonspatial. For the Cartesian
dualist, mind may be associated somehow with a body, and even interact causally with a body. However, mind is not contained *in* the body,
because that requires having a location in space. According to the Cartesian dualist, the mind is nowhere in particular, or nowhere at all. Perhaps if Descartes had been familiar with the trendy terms of current
physics, he would have said that mind is nonlocal. At any rate, the problem is this. Externalism holds that during OBEs a person's mental activity detaches from the body and travels somehow to a location different
from that of the body. But since only something in space can be *at* a
location, this thing can't be what many substance dualists say the mind
is: an unextended nonphysical thing.

Of course, animists avoid this last problem by positing secondary or
subtle bodies that have some spatial properties. It's curious, then, that
Almeder shows so little interest in this theoretical option. It might help
flesh out his claim (pun intended) that minds (or perhaps *persons*) are
both nonphysical and localizable. But in the absence of any such hints,
the reader is left wondering what, exactly, Almeder's view is.

4. Apparitions and Reciprocal OBEs

Fortunately, we needn't agonize now over that issue. As I've indicated
many times already in this book, in this inquiry it seems prudent to remain as metaphysically noncommittal as possible and let the data propel
us in whatever direction seems appropriate. So, let's return to the ques-

tion: Is there a reason for thinking that the mind is more independent of the body than the body's shadow? At this point in the discussion, defenders of the *OBE Argument* might appeal to the evidence from reciprocal cases. Reciprocal cases constitute a subset of veridical OBEs, in which (a) people report seeing the OBEr at the site that person is ostensibly visiting, and (b) the apparition accurately represents the condition or the surroundings of the OBEr at that time. Some reciprocal cases concern *crisis* apparitions, in which the OBEr is apparently observed at approximately the same time as the OBEr's death or other emergency. But many reciprocal cases involve *experimental* apparitions in which OBErs try consciously to project themselves to remote locations, for the purpose of being detected at those sites.

Consider the following examples.

Case 1

Early on the morning of January 27, 1957, "Martha Johnson" (a pseudonym) from Plains, Illinois, had a dream in which she traveled to her mother's home, 926 miles away in northern Minnesota. In a statement sent to the ASPR the following May, she wrote,

> After a little while I seemed to be alone going through a great blackness. Then all at once way down below me, as though I were at a great height, I could see a small bright oasis of light in the vast sea of darkness. I started on an incline towards it as I knew it was the teacherage (a small house by the school) where my mother lives.... After I entered, I leaned up against the dish cupboard with folded arms, a pose I often assume. I looked at Mother who was bending over something white and doing something with her hands. She did not appear to see me at first, but she finally looked up. I had a sort of pleased feeling and then after standing a second more, I turned and walked about four steps. (Dale, White, & Murphy, 1962, p. 29)

Martha woke from her dream at 2:10 a.m. (1:10 a.m. in Minnesota). The dream "nagged" her mind for several days, at which point she received a letter from her mother, who wrote that she had seen Martha. Martha then replied, describing her experience and asking her mother to identify what she had been wearing. A second letter from Mrs. Johnson answered that question and provided further details about her experience.

In the first of her two letters, dated January 29, Martha's mother wrote,

> Did you know you were here for a few seconds? I believe it was Saturday night, 1:10, January 26th, or maybe the 27th. It would have been 10 after two your time.... I looked up and there you were by the cupboard just standing smiling at me. I started to speak and you were gone. I forgot for a minute where I was. I think the dogs saw you too. They got so excited and wanted out—just like they thought you were by the door—sniffed and were so tickled. (Dale *et al.*, 1962, p. 30)

Mrs. Johnson's second letter was written on February 7, 1957. She wrote,

> I *was* bending over the ironing board trying to press out a seam.... You were standing with your back to the cupboard (the front of it) between the table and the shelf, you know, just sort of sitting on the edge of the lower part of the cupboard.... I looked at the dogs and they were just looking at you. I'm sure they saw you longer than I did.... I turned to go in the bedroom and you must have started to go out the door then. That's when the dogs went wild.
>
> Your hair was combed nice—just back in a pony tail with the pretty roll in front. Your blouse was neat and light—seemed almost white.... You were very solid—JUST like in life. Didn't see you from the lower bust down—that I can remember, anyway. (Dale *et al.*, 1962, p. 30)

Martha confirmed in correspondence that during her "visit" she had indeed experienced her hairstyle and clothing as her mother described.

Case 2

In October 1863, Mr. S. R. Wilmot and his friend Mr. W. J. Tait shared a cabin on the steamship *City of Limerick* heading toward the United States. Mr. Wilmot occupied the lower of two berths. Due to the sloping of the ship's stern, Mr. Tait's upper berth was not exactly above that of Mr. Wilmot. Accordingly, the lower berth was somewhat visible from above.

After more than a week of bad weather, Mr. Wilmot was finally enjoying a decent night's sleep. In his account, he wrote,

> Towards morning I dreamed I saw my wife, whom I had left in the United States, come to the door of my state-room, clad in her night-dress. At the door she seemed to discover that I was not the only occupant of the room, hesitated a little, then advanced to my side, stooped down and kissed me, and after gently caressing me for a few moments, quietly withdrew.
>
> Upon waking I was surprised to see my fellow passenger...leaning on his elbow, and looking fixedly at me. "You're a pretty fellow," said he at length, "to have a lady come and visit you in this way." I pressed him for an explanation [and he] related what he had seen while wide awake, lying in his berth. It exactly corresponded with my dream. (Sidgwick, 1891, p. 42)

Mr. Wilmot returned home to Connecticut the day after landing in New York. When he was reunited with his wife, "Almost her first question, when we were alone together, was 'Did you receive a visit from me a week ago Tuesday?'" Mr. Wilmot noted that this was physically impossible, but his wife replied that she felt that she had, indeed, made such a visit. Mr. Wilmot reported his wife's explanation as follows.

> On account of the severity of the weather and the reported loss of the *Africa* [another ship that sailed from Liverpool at about the same time as the *City of Limerick*]...she had been extremely anxious about me. On the night

previous, the same night when...the storm had just begun to abate, she had lain awake for a long time thinking of me, and about four o-clock in the morning it seemed to her that she went out to seek me. Crossing the wide and stormy sea, she came at length to a low, black steamship, whose side she went up, and then descending into the cabin, passed through it to the stern until she came to my state-room. "Tell me," said she, "do they ever have state-rooms like the one I saw, where the upper berth extends further back than the under one? A man was in the upper berth, looking right at me, and for a moment I was afraid to go in, but soon I went up to the side of your berth, bent down and kissed you, and embraced you, and then went away." (Sidgwick, 1891, pp. 42–43)

Mrs. Wilmot confirmed this story, as did her sister, Miss E. E. Wilmot, who also had been a passenger on the *City of Limerick*. Miss Wilmot wrote that, because of the stormy weather, Mr. Wilmot had been seasick for several days and unable to leave his cabin. Apparently, the weather had also been hard on Miss Wilmot, but with Mr. Tait's help, she had been able to make it to the breakfast table the morning after the incident. During breakfast, Mr. Tait asked if she had been in the stateroom the night before to see her brother. Astonished, Miss Wilmot said *"No, why?"* and Mr. Tait explained that "he saw *some* woman, in white, who went up to my brother" in his berth (Sidgwick, 1891, p. 44). (See also the brief discussion in Broad, 1962, pp. 175–178.)

Case 3

The swami Dadaji practiced OBEs as an integral part of the guru-devotee relationship. Early in 1970, he was touring in Allahabad, approximately 400 miles northwest of Calcutta. While his devotees were singing religious songs in one room of a house, Dadaji was alone in the prayer room. After emerging from the prayer room, Dadaji asked one of the ladies present to contact her sister-in-law in Calcutta to see if he had been seen at a certain address there. The Mukherjee family lived at that address, and the sister-in-law learned that they had, indeed, seen Dadaji's apparition. Osis and Haraldsson interviewed Dadaji's hosts in Allahabad, the sister-in-law in Calcutta, and also the Mukherjee family.

The Mukherjees reported that their daughter Roma had been lying on her bed studying for an English examination when she heard a noise. She looked up and through an open door saw Dadaji in the study. Initially, he seemed semitransparent, but eventually the figure became opaque. Roma then screamed, which alerted her brother (a physician) and mother. Instead of speaking, the apparition used sign language to tell Roma to be silent and to bring him a cup of tea. Roma then went to the kitchen and left the door to the study ajar. When she returned to the study with the tea, her brother and mother followed. Reaching through the partially open door, Roma handed the figure the tea and a biscuit. Roma's mother was able to see the apparition through the crack in the door, but the brother's vantage point wasn't as good. He saw only

Roma's hand reach in through the opening and come back without the tea. But there was no place for Roma to set the cup without entering the room.

At that point, Roma's father (a bank director) returned home from shopping. He was incredulous when his family told him about the apparition. But when he peeked through the opening in the door, he saw a man's figure sitting on a chair. The Mukherjees remained in the living room, within full view of the study door, until they heard a noise. They then entered the study and found that the apparition was gone, as was half of the tea and part of the biscuit. A cigarette was still burning on the table, and it was Dadaji's favorite brand. All four Mukherjees observed that the other study door was locked from the inside, by an iron bar across it and also by a bolt from above. (Osis & Haraldsson, 1976)

These cases are certainly intriguing, and at first glance it might seem as if a version of externalism makes sense of them. In fact, some form of animism would seem to be especially promising. After all, it appears as if the OBEr's secondary or subtle body—and vehicle for the person's consciousness—really traveled to another place, so that appropriately positioned observers could see it.

However, matters aren't so simple. The appeal to apparitions doesn't really help the *OBE Argument*, and it may even undermine it. Most of those who have thought carefully about apparitions explain veridical cases in terms of telepathy,[6] and for good reason. First, it makes reciprocal OBEs continuous with a massive body of similar data for ESP generally, including the many crisis and experimental cases in which there are no apparitions. Therefore, a telepathic explanation helps systematize a large and motley assortment of psychic phenomena, and there's no need to make additional externalist assumptions—much less the animistic postulate of a secondary or subtle body. And second, telepathy seems to account nicely for features of apparitions that are troublesome for externalist theories. For example, in many potentially collective cases, only some of those in a position to observe the apparition actually experience it. Accordingly, some argue that the apparition was probably not located in space and that (as one would expect) telepathic influence had succeeded with certain observers rather than others. Even more important is the familiar phenomenon of *time displacement* (what some call "telepathic deferment"). In many crisis and experimental cases, percipients experience the apparitional figure *after* the crisis or attempted projection. In fact, the experience can be delayed as much as several hours or days, and usually it occurs when the percipient is in a relaxed or apparently more receptive state of mind. This clearly suggests that percipients internally construct (i.e., hallucinate) the apparition in response to an earlier psychic stimulus.

Can externalists account for these two features of apparitions in terms of physically detachable aspects of consciousness or in terms of secondary bodies? The first feature, at any rate, might be manageable. Some physical objects, such as gases, electromagnetic fields, and rainbows, are present in or spread out in a region of space. They are also localized more intensely in certain locations than in others, and (most important) they are often *perceivable* only from certain locations. They illustrate that not all physical objects occupy space in the way a *solid body* does. Obviously, then, one could argue that apparitions might also fall into this class (see Braude, 1997, and Broad, 1962). This point has considerable merit, but it favors a PK interpretation of apparitions as much as an externalist interpretation. Nevertheless, externalist theories *can* account for failures to observe an apparition.

The phenomenon of time displacement, however, is more refractory. I suppose externalists could explain time displacement as a delayed recognition of a spatially located aspect of consciousness or secondary body. That is, they could claim that observers were at first only subliminally or subconsciously aware of the apparition, and that the experience "registered" or emerged into consciousness at a time of relatively low cognitive interference or "noise." But this strategy doesn't seem very promising. In particular, it's unclear why a delayed recognition of a formerly observed apparition would occur as if it were a *present* perception. Delayed recognitions of earlier perceptions are fairly common, but most are *retrospective*. We recognize in those cases that we *had* observed something. However, in reciprocal cases observers experience apparitions as *present* events. Even worse, externalists would presumably have to say that the apparition, a detachable aspect of the OBEr, exists in a remote region of space approximately *at the time* of the crisis or experiment, when the percipient is aware of it only subconsciously. Then later, the percipient experiences the apparition as existing at that location. But in that case, one would expect more reports of time-displaced apparitions *at multiple times*: namely, the time when they really exist in space and then later when observers have a delayed recognition of the apparitions' former presence. But as far as I know, there are no reports, from cases of apparent telepathic deferment, of apparitions having been spotted also at their presumed times of generation.

So far, then, externalism doesn't seem to be a very promising approach to explaining apparitions. But we should also note that it's not entirely clear sailing for telepathic theories either. One problem is that they seem unable to account for the percipients' perspectives in reciprocal cases. For example, Mrs. Wilmot felt she was actually in her husband's cabin, viewing its interior from an appropriate point of view, and also looking at her husband. She didn't have the experience of viewing herself looking at her husband. So, if Mr. Wilmot was simply responding telepathically to his wife, why didn't he have the experience of seeing the cabin and himself from *her* point of view?[7]

However, the greatest problems for telepathic theories are posed by collective apparitions, for two main reasons. First, given the possibility of telepathic deferment, subjects needn't experience apparitions at any particular time, much less the time of the presumed telepathic stimulus. Second, subjects may respond idiosyncratically to telepathic stimuli; their responses may betray distinctive psychological "signatures." As a result, telepathic theories have trouble explaining the similarity and simultaneity of different observers' experiences. For example, they have difficulty explaining why Mr. Wilmot and Mr. Tait saw a similar apparition at about the same time. Furthermore, the case of Dadaji is particularly difficult for the telepathic theories, because of the physical traces reportedly left behind by the apparition. For these reasons and others, I argued (in Braude, 1997) for a PK explanation of collective apparitions, according to which the apparitional figure is similar to the materializations produced by physical mediums.[8]

Of course, in the majority of these cases externalists might propose a different explanatory strategy—in fact, the same animist strategy already considered in connection with a single remote observer. If collective apparitions require positing an observable entity at the location where the apparition seems to be, that entity might be the OBEr's subtle body rather than a materialized figure. So once again, PK and externalist theories seem to be on equal footing. Ignoring for the moment their other respective advantages and drawbacks, they seem equally able to explain both collective apparitions and also the failure to observe apparitions in potentially collective cases.

So perhaps no single approach to apparitions can handle smoothly all the apparitional phenomena needing to be explained. And perhaps in that case we should regard externalism as a viable option (if not the preferred hypothesis), at least some of the time. However, there remains a nagging problem for the externalist, one that afflicts every case for which externalism seems plausible. To see why, we need to consider a modified version of the old question: Why do ghosts wear clothes? The externalist strategy we're considering is to claim that the OBEr projects something, some kind of localizable and detachable aspect of consciousness or subtle body, to a remote location where it can then be observed. And we've seen that this externalist strategy has at least *prima facie* explanatory utility when applied to reciprocal cases. But even if we grant, for the sake of argument, that each person might have a normal physical body as well as a detachable extension or astral body, it seems far less compelling to suppose that our clothes (or accoutrements) have doubles or subtle extensions as well.

For example, suppose that, while decked out in my new Armani suit, I try to project myself in an OBE to a friend, who then has an apparition of me in my sartorial splendor. If we explain my friend's ability to describe me accurately by positing a traveling secondary body, how do we explain my friend's experience of my new suit? Does my Armani suit also have a double? It seems absurd to think so. But if we can—and indeed, *should*—explain the apparition of my Armani suit without appealing to a secondary or astral suit (e.g., if we explain the apparition of my suit in terms of "ordinary," non-traveling ESP), it seems far less compelling to explain the apparition of *me* in terms of a detachable part of consciousness or secondary body.

The case of Miss Johnson, above, seems to reinforce this point. In that case, the clothing and hairstyle of the apparitional figure were not those of the sleeping Miss Johnson. They corresponded, instead, to the way Miss Johnson experienced herself during her OBE. So assuming that telepathic explanations are at least sometimes appropriate, one such explanation comes immediately to mind. Presumably, Miss Johnson's hairstyle and clothing during her OBE are mental constructs, just as they would be if her experience were merely a dream. But then it certainly looks as if Miss Johnson telepathically communicated those features of the OBE to her mother, as well as influencing Mrs. Johnson to experience her with arms folded, near the cupboard, etc.

I realize this explanation might strike some as positing an unprecedented and implausibly high level of telepathic influence. However, for reasons I discussed in earlier chapters, that position is untenable, especially for a survivalist (see also Braude, 1997, especially chapters 4 and 7). For one thing, at our current (and considerable) level of ignorance, we're in no position, theoretically or empirically, to set any limits to the range and refinement of psychic functioning. And for another, the degree of telepathic influence posited here is *not* unprecedented. It seems that way only by imposing the wrong standard: namely, the evidence gathered from laboratory experiments. Clearly, it's risky (if not futile) to extrapolate from experimentally elicited behavior to real-life behavior. In most cases that's analogous to inferring the full range of athletic abilities from the performances of people in straitjackets. But quite apart from general concerns about the scope and refinement of psychic functioning, rejecting telepathic explanations is not an option for most of those sympathetic to the survival hypothesis. As we've observed several times already in this book, survivalists must posit equally (if not more) refined telepathic influence to explain mediumistic communications. The survivalist and more conventional telepathic explanations differ mainly over the ontological status of the communicator. In the explanation sketched above, the presumed agent (Miss Johnson) is a living person, whereas survivalists contend that the telepathic agents in mediumistic settings are postmortem surviving personalities.

Of course, an apparitional experience could be a mixture of genuine perception (of an apparitional figure) with a telepathically induced quasi-perception (of the figure's attire, etc.), just as genuine and quasi-perceptions combine when I hallucinate a hippo in the real corner of the room. But if we must appeal to ESP (or PK) to explain parts of the apparitional experience, then it may simply be gratuitous to suppose that a detachable part of consciousness or astral body was actually present at the remote location.

I should add that in some reciprocal cases, it's the *percipient*, rather than the OBEr, who seems to supply the apparitional clothing, etc. In one such case (summarized in Myers, 1903, vol. 1, pp. 688–690), the Rev. Clarence Godfrey tried to appear to a friend at the foot of her bed. He made the mental effort in the late evening after retiring to bed, and he fell asleep after about eight minutes. He then dreamed that he met his friend the next morning, and she confirmed that he had appeared to her. This dream woke him, and he noticed that his clock showed 3:40 a.m. When his friend actually confirmed the experiment's success the following day, she noted that it occurred at about the time the servant put out all the lamps, which usually took place around 3:45. In her written account, she says that Godfrey "was dressed in his usual style." Podmore recognized the significance of this. He wrote that the apparition's dress

> was that ordinarily worn in the day-time by Mr. Godfrey, and that in which the percipient would be accustomed to see him, *not* the dress which he was actually wearing at the time. If the apparition is in truth nothing more than an expression of the percipient's thoughts, this is what we should expect to find, and as a matter of fact in the majority of well-evidenced narratives of telepathic hallucination this is what we actually do find. The dress and surroundings of the phantasm represent, not the dress and surroundings of the agent at the moment, but those with which the person is familiar. (Quoted in Myers, 1903, vol. 1, pp. 689–690)

In a similar case, Mr. G. Sinclair tried mentally to "visit" his ailing wife, whom he had left back at home while he was traveling (see Myers, 1903, vol. 1, pp. 697–698). At the time of Mr. Sinclair's attempt, he was undressed and sitting on the edge of his bed. Mrs. Sinclair later wrote, "I saw him as plain as if he had been there in person. I did not see him in his night clothes, but in a suit that hung in the closet at home." Because the apparitional clothing in these cases seems to be supplied by the percipient's mind, the cases clearly support the view that the apparition itself is likewise (as Podmore puts it) "an expression of the percipient's thoughts" and not an ordinarily perceived astral body.

Before leaving this topic, we should consider another issue regarding apparitional clothing, etc. If an apparition's clothing is constructed subjectively in response to telepathic influence, then what (according to externalists) would observers perceive if the telepathy were unsuccessful or deferred to a later time? If externalists want to say that only the secondary body is genuinely perceived, are we to suppose that this body is unclad and that the clothing is supplied telepathically? What would happen, from that point of view, if the telepathy were unsuccessful?

Would there be, in those cases, perceptions of naked secondary bodies? In fact, if externalists contend that our secondary bodies go forth into the world unclad, one would expect at least some reports of naked apparitions. Given the vagaries of successful ESP and PK, one would expect the genuine perception of naked secondary bodies to occur more reliably than the associated quasi-perceptions of their clothing, etc. But as far as I know, the extensive literature on apparitions contains almost no reports of naked human figures. According to Irwin, "in Crookall's extensive case collection only four such cases occur and in some of these the astral body quickly became clothed (Crookall, 1966, p. 1)" (Irwin, 1985, p. 229).

At this point, externalists might argue that one's secondary body has a certain degree of malleability, so that it can alter its age, size, and other features (e.g., whether or not it has a beard, or long hair). So perhaps this malleability can also extend to the simulation of clothing, etc. However, certain cases make this externalist strategy seem particularly incredible. Consider the following example, cited in Gauld, 1982. The two persons in this case had agreed to experiment with producing OBE apparitions.

> JAKOB: The day after our decision I drove my daughter to her job, the time was 6 P.M. I was suddenly reminded of this agreement with Eva. Then I transported myself astrally to her home and found her sitting on the sofa, reading something. I made her notice my presence by calling her name and showing her that I was driving my car. She looked up and saw me. After that I left her and was back in the car which I had been driving all the while without any special awareness of the driving.

> EVA: I was sitting alone in the room in an easy chair.... Suddenly I saw Jakob sitting in front of me in the car, saw about half the car as if I were in it with him. He sat at the wheel: I only saw the upper part of his body. I also saw the clock in the car, I think it was a couple of minutes before six. The car was not headed towards our house but in another direction. (Gauld, 1982, p. 228)

Presumably, positing the existence of a duplicate car is even less plausible than positing the existence of duplicate clothes. And as Gauld notes, even if the externalist manages to explain how a secondary body might transform its outer parts into semblances of clothing, etc., it seems excessive to suppose that our subtle bodies might also shape-shift into a half car with a clock showing the correct time. A telepathic explanation is obviously most compelling in this case, and that greatly weakens the externalist recourse to secondary bodies in other reciprocal cases.

5. Near-Death Experiences

It's here that defenders of the *OBE Argument* might appeal to the relevance of near-death out-of-body experiences. As with conventional OBEs, the most compelling examples of these experiences are veridical. Persons experiencing near-death OBEs frequently describe activities, people, objects, or locations which they were in no position or condition to observe, and which they might never have seen before. For example, they might report correctly that certain individuals were located in another part of the hospital (when there was no reason for predicting that those persons would be together in the hospital), and they might report accurately what those people were saying, wearing, or doing. Many near-death OBErs also describe various features of their immediate environment which they likewise were unable to view normally. For example, they might describe the pattern of tiles on the floor, or the color of a nurse's shoelaces. And sometimes they express surprise over the amount of dirt on the tops of lights in their operating room.

Consider the following report. The subject apparently watched his own open-heart surgery.

> I was up at the ceiling, looking down at [Dr. Traynor] and the rest of them.... There were two other doctors, a nurse assistant, I guess, and an anesthesiologist. I had the whole view, and I could look through those that I didn't choose to see what they were doing.... I saw them, but I could look through them. My vision was able to penetrate the two doctors and the table so I could look down at Doctor Traynor's boots. They looked longer than others, but I guess that's because he has such short little legs. He was standing on a pad for static electricity. He told me later that that's what it was for. And I told him that he was wearing glasses. I had never seen him with glasses before, but he said that during the operation he sometimes wears special glasses. (Lawrence, 1993, p. 125)

Apart from the reported transparency of those in the operating room, this account is quite typical. And I suggest we keep that reported transparency in mind as we evaluate the status of NDEs.

One interesting feature of near-death OBEs is that those experiences seem to differ considerably from dream states. In particular, subjects comment that their mental processes are surprisingly lucid and their sensory experiences are quite vivid—sometimes more so than during normal waking states. Cook, *et al.*, explain why this matters.

> Persisting or enhanced mentation at a time when one would expect it to be diminishing, or entirely absent, because of diminishing physiological functioning at least suggests that consciousness might not be so dependent on physiological processes as most scientists now assume. (Cook, Greyson, & Stevenson, 1998, p. 379)

But why should cognitive functioning diminish under physically traumatic conditions? Some commentators on NDEs have argued that during oxygen deprivation and certain other physiologically stressful states, one might actually expect subjective experiences to take on a kind of hallucinatory clarity and brilliance (see, e.g., Saavedra-Aguilar & Gomez-Jeria, 1989; Siegel, 1980; 1981). Granted, many of these attempted physiological or chemical explanations are clearly inadequate (see the discussions in Almeder, 1992, Grosso, 1981, and Paterson, 1995). Nevertheless, as Cook, *et al.*, concede, "we do not even know what physiological conditions are minimally required for organized, vivid cognition" (Cook *et al.*, 1998, p. 404). But that's a very important admission of ignorance. If we don't know what the physical or physiological correlates are to ordinary (much less optimal) cognitive functioning, we should be wary of taking our expectations in these cases too seriously. We simply don't know what to expect in the case of NDEs, any more than we know what to expect of savants, who display enhanced cognitive functioning despite their physiological impairments.

Paterson argues that NDEs differ systematically from illusory experiences induced by drugs, stress, or trauma (Paterson, 1995, pp. 143–145). But contrary to what Paterson seems to think, even if there are such systematic differences, they wouldn't show that NDEs are non-illusory. We can grant that experiences of type E_1 differ systematically from hallucinatory or illusory experiences E_2. Nevertheless E_1 experiences might also be hallucinatory or illusory. In fact, it's precisely because of systematic subjective differences that recreational or experimental drug users prefer certain mind-altering substances to others (e.g., peyote over LSD, or marijuana over hashish or cocaine). So one should probably expect there to be differences between NDEs and other altered states, even if NDEs are always illusory.

Paterson also argues that unlike NDEs "the structure and contents of drug-induced hallucinations are indefinitely variable and idiosyncratic" (Paterson, 1995, p. 144). However, there are several problems with that claim. First, drug-induced hallucinations aren't as relentlessly idiosyncratic as Paterson suggests. Presumably, that's one reason certain mushrooms play a prominent role in the rituals of some cultures; users know generally what sorts of effects to expect. And in our culture, too, certain specific drug-induced hallucinations can be fairly predictable—for example, the breathing walls and animated plants frequently reported by users of LSD or mescaline. Second, even if the content of drug-induced hallucinations varies more than the content of NDEs, NDEs are linked together physiologically and psychodynamically in a way drug experiences are not. NDEs all occur under at least apparently life-threatening conditions, whereas drug experiences occur under an enormous variety of social and emotional conditions. It's probably significant that OBEs, which are more variable in their structure and content, occur under a greater variety of conditions than NDEs (see section 6).

Moreover, we shouldn't overestimate the degree of similarity among NDEs generally and near-death OBEs in particular. And when we consider some of those variations, the externalist approach to NDEs loses much of its plausibility. One important difference concerns the conditions under which the experience occurs. Many reported NDEs happen when subjects are neither seriously ill nor in any life-threatening situation, and often those experiences differ little from those that take place under genuinely life-threatening conditions. In these cases, experiencers were not really about to die; they simply *thought* they were. The reason this is important is that an externalist account of the cases seems extravagant compared to the internalist alternative. The externalist would have to say that the mere fear of death causes the detachment of something from the body. Now, we can agree with Griffin that a life-threatening event "might frighten one out of one's skin" (Griffin, 1997, p. 240). And perhaps fear alone, in the absence of any real danger, can do the same thing. But the internalist proposes simply that the fear of death produces an unusual psychological state that helps reduce the fear. To me at least, that seems clearly to be the more parsimonious option. Moreover, it has systematicity on its side. It makes NDEs continuous with many other altered states (e.g., trauma-induced dissociation) that have the function of alleviating pain or fear.

Furthermore, many features of NDEs are culturally specific, and they likewise tend to undermine externalist explanations of the phenomena. The most striking differences tend to emerge from the oldest cases, where we find (among many other things) graphic accounts of Hell (Kellehear, 1995; Zaleski, 1988). But contemporary NDEs from our own culture seem no less culture-bound. For example, some subjects report encounters with the grim reaper (Lawrence, 1993). A particularly interesting case was reported recently in the magazine of the Society for Psychical Research (*The Paranormal Review*, no. 5, February 1998, p. 13). The subject is a woman, S. J., whom Alan Gauld has known for many years and whom he considers to be very reliable. Her NDE occurred following childbirth, but (as in many other cases) she was in no danger of dying. She writes,

> I remember...feeling as if I were completely weightless, and floating in space. I was surrounded by brilliant, pulsating light, the whole of space was coloured azure fading away to paler and paler shades of blue, and wonderful music was playing. I was being asked questions by someone I couldn't see. The questions were of life-and-death importance, and I knew that whether I lived or died depended on what answers I gave, even though I cannot now remember what the questions were. When I answered correctly my body would soar even higher, but if I got a question wrong my body fell down and down through space. I answered more and more questions, and suddenly I felt I had infinite knowledge and could answer all those questions about where we came from and why we are here. I knew all the secrets of the universe. I soared higher and higher in space, and the

music became triumphant because I had unlocked the secret of everlasting life!

So far, this experience enjoys a kind of generic similarity to many other mystical or transcendental NDEs. However, another feature of the case is more unusual. When the face behind the disembodied voice was revealed to S. J., it turned out to be Bamber Gascoigne, the still-living host of a popular TV quiz program, "University Challenge." S. J.'s NDE had transformed Gascoigne into a kind of "celestial quiz-master."[9] Now S. J. regarded her experience as a dream rather than an NDE, because she recognized that she wasn't near death. But as I mentioned, many NDEs occur in non-life-threatening situations. S. J.'s experience reveals clearly how the subject (and the subject's culture) can influence the content of an NDE, and it helps make a literal (externalist) interpretation of NDEs seem excessive. It can only strengthen the suspicion that all NDEs are fundamentally dreamlike, even if they are more vivid than most dreams. After all, the dreams of most people are not all equally distinct and vivid, and we might reasonably expect some dreams under unusual circumstances to be more remarkable than most. Moreover, NDEs might still genuinely reflect certain states of the experiencer, just as dream content often represents the dreamer's physical state.

But at this stage in the argument, these issues may be relatively peripheral. We're focusing on OBEs, and what matters most, right now, is that some of them seem to occur *after* the experiencers meet familiar criteria for physical death—for example, the absence of a heartbeat or breathing for a considerable period of time, and even after the diagnosis of brain death. So in these cases at least, it appears that mental activity can occur both independently of, and in another location from, bodily activity.

But once again matters aren't so simple. First, as Moody observes, in clinical emergencies physicians generally have no time to prepare anyone for an EEG; usually their concern is to resuscitate their patients (Moody, 1976, pp. 102–103). So even if a flat EEGs is obtained with a near-death OBE patient, that evidence would still be difficult to interpret. Moody writes,

> Resuscitation attempts are always emergencies, which last at the very most for thirty minutes or so. Setting up an EEG machine is a very complicated and technical task, and it is fairly common for even an experienced technician to have to work with it for some time to get correct readings, even under optimum conditions. In an emergency, with its accompanying confusion, there would probably be an increased likelihood of mistakes. So, even if one could present a flat EEG tracing for a person who told of a near-death experience, it would still be possible for a critic to say—with justice—that the tracing might not be accurate. (Moody, 1976, p. 102)

Besides, as Moody also notes, even when the equipment has been set up properly, flat EEGs have been obtained, in non-near-death OBE cases, for persons who were subsequently resuscitated (e.g., in cases of drug overdoses and hypothermia). So it's doubtful in any case that a flat EEG reliably indicates physical death. And as if that weren't enough, Moody recognizes that NDEs are, *at best*, only *roughly* contemporaneous with the cessation of vital signs. But then we can't be certain that those experiences occurred *after* the vital signs disappeared. Our ability to date the time of mental activity in NDEs depends entirely on the subject's retrospective testimony, and that measure is simply too crude for us to know when, exactly, the near-death OBE occurred.

But what if the experiencer accurately reports events that occurred, say, more than fifteen minutes after the cessation of vital signs? Forgetting (at least for now) the possibility of reasonable guesses or precognitive ESP, that would seem to indicate that the near-death OBE occurred some time after the onset of clinical death. I'm aware of only one near-death OBE case in which perhaps the most sensitive measure of clinical death, a flat EEG, was detected for any significant time. Sabom reports the case of a woman who, for about an hour, had all the blood drained from her head and her body temperature lowered to 60 degrees. During that time her heartbeat and breathing stopped, and she had both a flat EEG and an absence of auditory evoked potentials from her brainstem (Sabom, 1998, chapter 3). Apparently during this period she had a detailed veridical near-death OBE. But even in this case it would be hasty to conclude that the woman had died, or that mental activity clearly persisted independently of bodily activity. There are several reasons why we must be cautious here.

First, as Moody notes, our criteria for determining clinical death are also crude, and there may be no justification for declaring a person dead at all if the person subsequently can be resuscitated. Perhaps death can only be an *irreversible* loss of vital functions. Cook, *et al.*, agree.

> Out-of-body experiencers, including near-death experiencers, are in fact still alive at the time of their experience and have not existed independently of their bodies. Even those persons who may have been pronounced dead by medical personnel were physically intact enough to have been revivable. Consciousness may therefore *seem* to be detached from the physical body, but it may still remain dependent on it for its continued existence. (Cook *et al.*, 1998, p. 380)

Sabom concurs as well, arguing that "loss of biologic life, including death of the brain, is a process and does not occur at a single, definite moment" (Sabom, 1998, p. 50). He then cites several recent studies indicating the persistence of brain or related organic activity up to a week following the careful diagnosis of brain death, and he concludes,

> These findings indicate that even when a person is deemed "brain dead" by strict clinical criteria—that is, showing no spontaneous movements or res-

piration; no response to painful or auditory stimulation; and no brain stem, cough, gag, or respiratory reflexes—brain activity can often still be demonstrated days later, raising the question of *when*, if at all, death had actually occurred. (Sabom, 1998, p. 51)

Fortunately, we needn't debate now the complex topic of what counts as physical death. We need only concede the following, reasonable, point made by Moody.

In order for resuscitation to have occurred, some degree of residual biological activity must have been going on in the cells of the body, even though the overt signs of these processes were not clinically detectable by the methods employed. (Moody, 1976, p. 103)

But of course one can then argue, plausibly, that the near-death OBE couldn't have occurred in the absence of that residual biological activity. And in that case NDEs wouldn't show that the mind is less dependent on a body than the body's shadow.

But let's suppose, for the moment, that we had convincing evidence that mental activity in near-death OBEs occurred in the absence of *any* residual bodily activity. Not even that would lend much support, if any, to the case for survival. The issue here connects with the observation quoted earlier from Woodhouse: "It is a tremendous conceptual jump from, say, a 30-minute OBE to immortality" (Woodhouse, 1994b, p. 14).

The survival hypothesis doesn't posit that one's characteristic mental activity continues for only a few seconds or minutes after bodily death. The evidence allegedly explained by the survival hypothesis—most of it from ostensible mediumship, reincarnation, and hauntings—suggests personal survival over many years, if not eternally. Moreover, the reason many regard postmortem survival as a source of hope and solace is that they regard it as a form of prolonged noncorporeal existence. People hope that when they die they might reunite with friends and family members who had long since "passed over."

But of course, if OBEs provide evidence for any kind of survival of bodily death—which, as we've seen, is far from obvious—strictly speaking, it would be evidence only of short-term survival. OBEs provide no justification for assuming that mental activity could persist independently of the body for periods significantly longer than an OBE. Analogies are easy to come by. For example, a person's last breath may linger briefly after bodily death. But it will dissipate quickly, and certainly it won't persist indefinitely. Similarly, my farts can leave my body; they are distinct from my body; and they can affect the world outside my body. But they are also entirely causally dependent for their existence on my body. Now of course, farts can (regrettably) linger for a while after coming into existence—probably considerably longer than even the most noxious final breath. But despite an enormous database of human farts, we have no reason to anticipate the production of a fart everlasting, even if that remains an empirical possibility. So it seems that even under the most charitable of readings, the evidence from OBEs shows too little. It gives us no reason to believe that the mind is more substantial, resilient, and self-sustaining than a fart.

6. An Appeal to Systematicity

Our discussion thus far has focused on veridical OBEs, the apparitions in reciprocal cases, and NDEs. Although these are undoubtedly the most impressive features and types of OBEs, we've seen that they lend little (if any) support to externalism, much less to the survival hypothesis. But perhaps a stronger case can be made by considering how well externalism accommodates a broad range of features of OBEs. Perhaps it has greater overall explanatory power than rival hypotheses. This is an approach considered by Griffin (Griffin, 1997), and it deserves our attention. Griffin lists 13 features of OBEs most of which seem *prima facie* to be (and some of which, he says, genuinely are) problematical for internalism, but which externalism handles neatly.

However, a reasonable internalism may also have sufficient explanatory power. In view of the preceding discussion, we could expect an enlightened internalist to appeal, not simply to the creative powers of the mind and to the impressive variety of altered states, but also to the operation of psychic functioning (to explain veridicality). Presumably, then, internalists could plausibly subscribe to a kind of *altered state + psi* hypothesis. They would explain the veridicality of OBEs in terms of ESP operating from within the subject's body or embodied mind. And they could then allow the remaining, purely subjective, features of OBEs to assume any of the myriad forms noted in research into exceptional and profoundly meaningful experiences, especially those produced in traumatic, dissociative, or other altered states. As we go through Griffin's list of features, I think we'll see that an altered state + psi hypothesis handles the data at least as well as an externalist hypothesis. (For ease of exposition, I'll conflate some of Griffin's categories and reduce his list from 13 to 9.)

(1) *OBErs feel as if they leave the body, and most have a strong conviction that the experience is real.* Externalists can explain this simply by saying that subjects really were out of their bodies. But internalists likewise have no trouble here. As we noted earlier when discussing hallucinations, the vividness of an experience is no mark of veridicality. In fact, the conviction of reality in OBEs needn't be regarded as more reliable than in the case of (say) convincing illusions produced by hallucinogenic drugs, or produced for naive members of a magician's audience. I'm not totally convinced that OBEs are illusory. But it would be a mis-

take to concede the externalist's point too quickly, and in fact, an enlightened internalist does have something to say in response.

What the internalist needs to explain is why, if the experience of being out of the body is always illusory, more people seem to be fooled by OBEs than by drugs or magicians. And the answer, presumably, is that OBE illusions rest on a higher level (or more abstract form) of conceptual naivete. That is, unless OBErs consider some of the complex issues addressed in this chapter as well as some general topics in the philosophy of mind, they might not realize that the idea of literally being outside one's body is conceptually problematic. By contrast, no such theoretical preparation is required to learn why drug experiences and magicians' tricks are illusory. Moreover, the conviction of reality might also be a by-product of the OBEr's use of ESP in veridical cases. Subjects might recognize (at least subconsciously) that some details of the experience were accurate, and then they might mistakenly infer that the experience *as a whole* is veridical.

It might be helpful here to compare descriptions of OBEs to the reported body perceptions of those suffering from MPD/DID. Different alter personalities often have very clear and distinct, but illusory, experiences of their bodies. That's why they object strenuously that they are the wrong size, sex, or age to wear another alter's clothes. And in some cases, people with DID experience their alters at distinct locations in their immediate environment—for example, seated in separate chairs at therapy sessions (Braude, 1995).

(2) *Most OBErs experience a greatly altered emotional state—usually, an overwhelming sense of tranquility or joy. And most report a complete absence of pain.* But this clearly poses no problem for the altered state + psi hypothesis. And in view of the long and often extraordinary history of major surgery and other procedures performed under hypnotic anesthesia, it's clear that we don't need to posit actual separation from the body to account for the painless OBEs of accident victims and hospital patients. (For a quick history of hypnotic anesthesia and other related dissociative states, see Braude, 1995. For a more comprehensive account, see Crabtree, 1993, and Gauld, 1992.)

(3) *Most OBErs report normally or unusually clear visual experiences and also normal hearing.* Again, there is nothing here that hasn't also been reported in connection with dissociative or drug-induced states. In fact, if OBEs are continuous with the dissociative experiences reported throughout the history of hypnosis, this perceptual clarity is precisely what one would expect (Gauld, 1992).

(4) *Some OBEs are veridical.* We've covered this issue at length, and for the reasons already noted, the veridicality of OBEs doesn't require an externalist explanation. Indeed, it appears that we can account for the data at least as well in terms of ESP. But veridicality *per se* may not be what matters. As I noted earlier, some argue for externalism by ap-

pealing to an alleged qualitative difference between veridical OBEs and non-traveling ESP. They claim that "the clarity and the accuracy of the extrasensory perceptions that are reported in OBEs greatly exceed anything ever verified in intrasomatic clairvoyance (or remote viewing), whether in experimental or spontaneous cases" (Griffin, 1997, p. 253).

But there are two reasons why that claim offers no support for externalism. First, it's irrelevant whether the clarity of OBEs exceeds that of other types of ESP. As we've observed, experiential clarity is no sign of veridicality, and many drug-induced hallucinations are also routinely clearer than most ESP experiences. Second, it's highly questionable whether veridical OBEs are notably more accurate than other types of ESP, especially when we consider spontaneous cases, where the information reported is often extremely detailed (see, e.g., Sidgwick, 1922). In fact, I see no justification for claiming that the ESP from OBEs is clearly superior to the spectacularly accurate remote viewing recently declassified by the U.S. government (see, e.g., May, 1995; May, 1996; Puthoff, 1996; Targ, 1996). Furthermore, if the better mediumistic evidence can count as evidence of ESP (telepathy or clairvoyance), then the alleged superiority of the ESP from OBEs seems more dubious still.

(5) *OBErs usually report that they think clearly during OBEs, and many of those who have had near-death OBEs claim that their thought processes were clearer during the experience than during their normal waking states.* Griffin says this "would follow from the fact that the mind is free from any confusing, disorienting feelings and information from the brain" (Griffin, 1997, p. 259). That's an interesting conjecture, but our enlightened internalist can also account for the clarity of thought during OBEs. Again, the literature on hypnosis, dissociation, and altered states documents many instances in which people perform at a cognitively or creatively higher level than during normal waking states. We've already considered two very dramatic examples of that phenomenon, in the cases of Patience Worth and Hélène Smith. Although we don't know how, exactly, it works, I think it's fair to say that dissociation and some other altered states help us bypass or neutralize various psychological (and possibly physical) barriers to optimal functioning. At the very least it's clear that we needn't appeal to externalist conjectures to explain unusually high levels of creative or cognitive functioning.

Moreover, perhaps we should be wary when subjects retrospectively report their cognitive clarity during OBEs. Even if those claims are true, we must remember that drug users, dreamers, and hypnotic subjects offer similar—and presumably equally reliable—testimony regarding their earlier altered states. So once again, unusual clarity of thought seems easily compatible with internalism. We might wonder, though, how trustworthy *any* of these retrospective reports are. How do we determine whether the subjects were really thinking more clearly or whether they simply thought that they were? It would be naive or arrogant to think we know how to answer that question. Besides, I suspect that many would challenge dreamers' claims to have been unusually clear or creative in their dreams, or drug users' claims to have been unusually lucid while high. Presumably, then, to accept uncritically or without additional support the similar claims of OBErs would be to apply an indefensible double standard.

(6) *OBErs frequently report that their experiences transformed them, profoundly altering their beliefs, values, and mood. Moreover, OBErs usually report a significantly altered sense of time.* But that hardly distinguishes OBEs from many drug-induced and other experiences (e.g., see Grinspoon & Bakalar, 1979; Tart, 1983). Besides, it's important to remember that the significance of an experience is a function, not simply of the kind of experience it is, but who the subject is and the conditions under which the experience occurs. Under the right circumstances (say, an openness to change), an ordinarily minor life episode can be life changing. Similarly, a dramatic and potentially profound experience may be insignificant if the person isn't ready for it.[10]

(7) *There is "a remarkable sameness to reports of OBEs from various people from different times and places, regardless of sex, age, religion, culture, occupation, the circumstances under which the OBE occurred, or any other variable"* (Griffin, 1997, p. 237). Moreover, the belief that people can literally leave and have experiences outside their bodies is virtually universal. Again, externalists would explain this simply by noting that the OBE is what it seems to be. However, the overall similarity of OBEs strikes me as fairly unremarkable. So I'm not sure to what extent there is a datum here to be explained.

We've already considered some of the ways near-death OBEs are culturally influenced. But OBEs generally differ with regard to many apparently crucial features. OBErs disagree, for example, whether or not a cord connects the traveling self to the physical body; whether or not there *is* a perceived traveling body, or a perceptual-like awareness of the remote location; whether or not the second body is felt to be the locus of consciousness, or whether it resembles the physical body; whether or not one travels to another realm (e.g., Hélène Smith's travels to Mars) or to heavenly paradise; and whether OBE experiences seem to be at one or multiple locations (see Alvarado, 1997). If similarities remain, they can presumably be explained in any or some combination of familiar ways—for example, universality of needs and physiology, cross-cultural similarity of symbols, and perhaps even Jungian archetypes.

(8) *Despite their (allegedly) widespread similarities, OBEs have been produced under many different sorts of conditions.* Griffin argues that it's difficult for the internalist to explain how so many distinct sorts of causal chains could result in such similar experiences. Of course, external-

ists again have an apparently easy way of explaining that underlying
phenomenological unity. They would say that OBEs simply are what
they appear to be. However, the problem with this position is similar to
that raised in connection with point (7). If (contrary to what Griffin
claims) OBEs are not a nearly universal set of phenomenologically similar experiences, there may be no impressive datum demanding an explanation.

Furthermore, the conditions that produce OBEs, whether spontaneous or experimental, sleeping or waking, do *not* always result in the experience of leaving one's body. For example, crisis or experimental cases
may instead result in more traditional (or at least less dramatic) forms
of ESP. This raises again the issue discussed in section 2, where we
considered the range and variety of imagery in ESP experiences. We
noted there that ESP occurs in many different forms, some more rich in
imagery than others. And one would expect a certain subset of ESP experiences to take the form of OBEs, even if the experience of leaving
the body is totally illusory.

But perhaps most important, it's unclear why it should be difficult,
in principle, to explain how many different causal chains can result in
phenomenologically similar experiences. In fact, it's the received wisdom in various branches of psychotherapy (not to mention common
sense) that fears, phobias, obsessions, and many other types of mental
states can have diverse causal histories. Moreover, as headaches and
stomachaches illustrate, it's actually quite common for similar experiences to have a variety of causes.

(9) *We find a relatively high incidence of OBEs in the general population, especially among those in near-death situations.* But I fail to see a
problem here, except (as Griffin notes) for those internalists who offhandedly dismiss the widespread and (allegedly very) similar accounts
as "fabrications or aberrations of deranged brains" (Griffin, 1997, p.
238). As we've seen, noncrisis OBEs can be regarded as a subset of an
even more widespread set of ESP experiences. Some near-death OBEs
would also fall into that category, as a subset of crisis ESP experiences.
And quite apart from the physiological similarities among responses to
traumatic and life-threatening situations, it's reasonable to think that
near-death OBErs also have very similar needs—perhaps most notably,
a need to make an intolerable situation tolerable. So, just as many people deal with trauma dissociatively by inducing amnesia or anesthesia,
others might experience OBEs instead. In fact, it might be plausible to
interpret OBEs as forms of dissociation in which visual imagery typically plays a vital role (as it does, say, in the case of negative hallucinations—see Braude, 1995). From this internalist point of view,
OBEs aren't deranged or aberrant responses to a situation. Instead, having an OBE would be a handy adaptational strategy, and it would connect coherently with a substantial body of research into hypnosis and

dissociation generally, and traumatic stress in particular.[11]

So it's doubtful that externalists have an overall explanatory edge in accounting for the various features of OBEs. Moreover, externalists can only *conjecture* that genuinely leaving one's body would result in ostensibly clear thinking, transforming effects, and an altered sense of time. By contrast, we *know* that dissociation and drugs can produce these effects.

7. Concluding Remarks

I think we must conclude that the case for survival receives very little *independent* support from OBEs, NDEs, and apparitions. Indeed, considered apart from other types of evidence suggesting survival, there seems little reason to appeal to externalism to account for the data. We can do at least as well by appealing to phenomena—including ESP—whose existence and features have already been established. So even if survivalists can account for most of the phenomena (with the possible and nagging exception of apparitional clothing, accoutrements, and material surroundings), other explanatory strategies seem more compelling. Of course, we might find an externalist view of OBEs and apparitions more attractive in light of the evidence from mediumship and reincarnation. And we might decide that OBEs and apparitions strengthen the case for survival made by the better evidence. Whether a super-psi interpretation of all the data reigns supreme in the end is a matter we'll consider shortly.

NOTES

1. Although in the great majority of OBEs subjects apparently perceive the world from positions outside their bodies, some OBEs seem devoid of all perceptual content (see Irwin, 1985). But these rare cases needn't concern us here.

2. In the late nineteenth and early twentieth centuries, the phenomena in question weren't called out-of-body experiences. Rather, they were discussed under the headings of *veridical phantasms*, or *traveling clairvoyance*. See, e.g., Myers, 1903, who, incidentally, was already describing some cases as "reciprocal."

3. For criticisms of attempted explanations along more or less conventional internalist lines, see Almeder (Almeder, 1992), Grim (Grim, 1994), and Woodhouse (Woodhouse, 1994a; 1994b).

4. In this respect, of course, the term "ESP" (for extrasensory *perception*) is misleading. What many wonder about ESP is precisely whether it is a form of awareness that is either non-perceptual, or at least radically different from the perceptual modalities already identified.

5. Hart (Hart, 1956) offered an interesting variant of the OBE argument. Like other proponents of that argument, he claimed that OBEs (especially reciprocal cases) demonstrate that the projected figure or phantasm should be understood as a vehicle for (or center of) the consciousness of the projector. From that, he reasoned that the many common characteristics of apparitions of the dead and the living

show that they belong to the same class of objects. So, he inferred, it's reasonable to hold that apparitions of the dead are likewise vehicles for the consciousness of the deceased person. This argument may well have more problems than its initial premise. But for our purposes, we need only to note that it gets off to a very shaky start. The considerations in this section seem clearly to undermine (or at least cast serious doubt on) Hart's initial claim that projected figures in reciprocal cases seem clearly to be locations of, or vehicles for, the consciousness of the projector.

6. These telepathic theories come in several varieties, but the differences between them don't matter for present purposes (see Braude, 1997 for a survey and discussion; also Broad, 1962).

7. I thank Alan Gauld for reminding me of this (personal communication, Nov. 28, 1998).

8. Some might prefer to interpret the Dadaji case as an instance of bilocation, but the concept of bilocation needs to be made clear before that option becomes tempting. And I suspect it would be unduly optimistic to think that the analysis would go smoothly. In fact, it's not even clear that the hypothesis of bilocation adds anything new to the discussion. If bilocation is only a doubling of the body, it's unclear how this explanation would differ from that of PK (or materialization). Otherwise, bilocation seems to require a doubling of body and also a doubling or bifurcation of consciousness. And in that case, it's difficult to see how the explanation would differ from the externalist account proposed by animists.

9. Gauld, personal communication, November 28, 1998.

10. I'm grateful to Charles Tart for reminding me of this.

11. For a thoughtful and more detailed presentation of this position, as well as a recent study providing empirical support for it, see Irwin, 2000.

Chapter 9

Conclusion

1. Introduction

It's time now to take stock and also address a few remaining concerns. I've noted from the beginning that our inquiry into survival must respect the data and not be prejudiced either by philosophical fashion or by pre-theoretical biases. Even if that seems reasonable enough and in need of no more elaboration, we still need to consider the point from a few novel angles. So I want to examine, first, the significance of so-called "ideal" cases, and second, physiological data that many find incompatible with a belief in survival. Then we need to look briefly at some other fairly traditional skeptical concerns, including familiar metaphysical worries about what kind of *stuff* might survive. After that, we can return briefly to the topic of crippling complexity, and also consider to what extent the totality and variety of survival cases have a kind of cumulative force, despite their departures from a theoretical ideal.

2. Ideal Cases

We've examined an array of interesting cases, some stronger than others, but all illustrating ways in which the evidence can be both impressive and frustratingly inconclusive. Even the best cases have their shortcomings. Good mediumistic communications get diluted by twaddle or outright "misses," or by "hits" that suggest psychic interaction with the living, or by trance impersonations that too dimly resemble the individuals they purport to be. Reincarnation cases all too often suffer from a paucity of early-bird testimony, or from a shortage of idiosyncratically specific "hits" or demonstrated skills uniquely linked to the previous personality. In fact, it seems clear that no actual survival case is as coercive as the ideal cases we can imagine.

Nevertheless, it's important to remember that we *can* imagine cases so impressive that we'd have to regard them as indicating survival, even if we have no idea how to integrate that revelation into a coherent worldview. Sometimes, writers begin their survey of survival evidence by describing ideal cases, to serve as a standard against which to measure the cases they discuss next. But I prefer the perspective we gain by considering ideal cases at the end of our inquiry, after the continued frustration of examining lesser, but real, cases. Of course, this procedure still allows us to throw both the strengths and the shortcomings of actual cases into sharp relief. But we've been considering how difficult it is to weigh the survival and super-psi hypotheses against each other, and we've seen repeatedly how even the best actual cases disappoint, or at least leave many important questions unanswered. So this seems like a particularly good time to consider apparently ideal cases. It reminds us that it's not an idle enterprise to examine less-than-ideal cases, even if the exercise is consistently frustrating. The quest isn't futile; the evidence *can* point compellingly to survival, at least in principle.

Obviously, by "ideal" here we mean something like "really, really, good." No survival case can be ideal in the sense in which a triangle (say) can be ideal. Presumably, an ideal survival case would be one for which appeals to the Usual and Unusual Suspects are clearly out of the question. It would also be one for which appeals to super psi seem considerably less plausible than the survivalist alternative. I doubt whether we could compile an exhaustive list of essential features for such a case. But we can at least note some obvious candidates. Some of these apply more clearly to reincarnation and possession cases than to instances of mediumship.

(1) Our case would not have the etiological features found in cases of MPD/DID or other psychological disorders. For example, the phenomena ideally should not begin after the subject experiences a traumatic childhood incident. (2) The manifestations of a previous personality should not serve any discernable psychological need of the living. (3) Those manifestations should make sense in terms of agendas or interests credibly (if not coercively) attributable to the previous personality. (4) The manifestations should begin, and should be documented, before the subject (or anyone in the subject's circle of acquaintances) has identified and researched the life of a corresponding previous personality. (5) The subject should supply verifiable, intimate facts about the previous personality's life. (6) The history and behavior of the previous personality should be recognizable, in intimate detail, to several individuals. (7) The subject should also be able to display some of the previous personality's skills or traits—the more idiosyncratic the better. (8) In order for investigators to verify information communicated about the previous personality's life, it should be necessary to access multiple, culturally and geographically remote, and obscure sources. (9) Anomalous skills or traits manifested by the subject should be as foreign to the subject as possible—for example, from a significantly different culture to

which the subject has had no exposure. (10) Skills associated with the previous personality should be of a kind or of a degree that generally require practice, and which are seldom (if ever) found in prodigies or savants. (11) The manifestations of the previous personality should continue to provide verifiable information and credible behavioral simulations for an extended period of time, adding to the crippling complexity of super-psi explanations.

To see how an apparently ideal case might develop, let's consider two hypothetical scenarios. The first (a reincarnation or possession case) is from a former student, Amy Lynn Payne, who sketched its features in response to an exam question. Her answer was so articulate and penetrating that I borrow liberally and gratefully from her own words.

Suppose someone discovered a society of native Amazonians who had previously eluded all contact with other peoples. And suppose that the discoverer was someone who himself had little knowledge of other cultures, and certainly no knowledge of U.S. culture. Suppose, next, that one of the Amazonians went into trance and started speaking in a language the explorer didn't know. So the explorer records the utterances, has them translated, finds that they're in English, and discovers that the Amazonian was claiming to be Knute Rockne, the famous football coach of Notre Dame. (And of course, let's assume that we can rule out fraud and the other Usual Suspects.) At this point, English-speaking investigators interrogate the Amazonian, who answers them in English and responds in ways others recognize as idiosyncratically Rockne-esque.

Based on these later interviews as well as the original recordings, we discover that the Amazonian displays a level of football knowledge comparable to that of Knute Rockne, and also a set of extensive apparent memories that Knute Rockne would be expected to have. We also find that the Amazonian displays Rockne's distinctive mannerisms of speech, his customary posture, gait, gestures, facial expressions, and other physical characteristics, his apparently inspirational persona, and his peculiar attitudes on and emotions about various subjects. The Amazonian's statements will thereby demonstrate a great deal of knowledge which neither he nor the investigators possessed beforehand—not just knowledge about Rockne himself, but also about his time and culture. For example, suppose that Knute Rockne had been a devout Democrat (I actually have no idea about this) and that the Amazonian appropriately expresses dismay at a Republican in the White House. And suppose the Amazonian displays a great and seasoned coach's grasp of the subtleties of college football, not simply outside the scope of those investigating the case, but also beyond that of even ardent fans of the game. Moreover, suppose the Amazonian seems to know matters which only Rockne should have known, or which only he and close associates might have known (and which certainly no investigator of the case knew prior to lengthy follow-up investigation). For example, Knute Rockne would have known about scandals on his team that were concealed from the press. He would have had memories of games that he coached and specific memories of his players and their histories and skills. He would have had a vast reservoir of stories about specific plays in specific games, as well as stories about specific players. These would not simply be stories that could be substantiated; the Amazonian would offer an impressive quantity of stories, both substantiated and unsubstantiated. For example, Rockne was reportedly the only person who knew what "The Gipper" said upon his deathbed. Rockne told his team that the Gipper's last words were "Win one for the Gipper." But some think Rockne concocted the story to motivate his team after the Gipper's death. If the Amazonian native was really a medium for (or reincarnation of) Knute Rockne, then ideally he'd be able to resolve the debate over this incident.

Clearly, this case presents a number of features we'd look for in an ideal case. Many of them result from the geographic and cultural distance between the subject and the previous personality, something that distinguishes this case from the vast majority of survival cases. Here we find responsive xenoglossy in a language quite different from that of the previous personality. We also find extensive and refined knowledge-that appropriate to the previous personality but far outside the scope of the Amazonian's culture. Similarly, the case concerns a skill (coaching college football) that is culturally specific to the U.S.A. and which seems to require an extensive period of practice to be expressed at the advanced level of proficiency manifested by the Amazonian. The native also displays an extensive array of behavioral and physical traits of the previous personality, as well as various motives, interests, and other attitudes idiosyncratically appropriate to that individual, but irrelevant to and far outside the culture of the Amazonian. And many of these features of the case were exhibited *before* the appearance of investigators who spoke English and who knew something about the previous personality's culture and history. So at least obvious forms of sitter-telepathy seem ruled out.

Our next case illustrates a kind of mediumistic ideal. Mrs. B is a gifted medium. Her formal education did not extend beyond primary school, and her exposure to the world has been confined exclusively to her immediate small-town environment in the American Midwest. She never traveled beyond her hometown or expressed any interest in books, magazines, or TV shows about other locales. Similarly, she's had no exposure to the world of ideas, to literature (even in cinematic form), or to the arts. In fact, when she's not channeling communications or caring for her home and family, she devotes her time to prayer and developing her psychic sensitivity.

One day Mrs. B gives a proxy sitting for Mr. X, who lives in Helsinki.

Using a pseudonym, Mr. X had sent a watch, once owned by a dear friend, to the Parapsychology Foundation in New York, requesting that someone there present it to Mrs. B on his behalf. So no one at the Parapsychology Foundation knew (at least by normal means) the identity either of Mr. X or the original owner of the watch.

When Mrs. B handled the watch, she went into trance and, speaking English as if it weren't her native tongue and with a clear Scandinavian accent, purported to be the surviving personality of the Finnish composer Joonas Kokkonen.[1] She then provided detailed information, on this and subsequent sittings, about Kokkonen's life and his music, in the process demonstrating an intimate acquaintance with Finnish culture and a professional command of music generally (and a knowledge of Kokkonen's music in particular). For example, she wrote out the final bars to an uncompleted piano quintet and requested that they be given to Kokkonen's former colleague, Aulis Sallinen, who she claimed correctly had possession of the original score, so that the quintet could be assembled into a performing edition.

These sittings caused a minor sensation in Finland and elsewhere, and before long many of Kokkonen's friends traveled to have anonymous sittings with Mrs. B. Because Kokkonen was a major international musical figure and had friends and colleagues throughout the world, many of those friends were not Scandinavian. So at least those sitters provided no immediate linguistic clue as to whom they wished to contact. But in every case, Mrs. B's Kokkonen-persona recognized the sitter and demonstrated an intimate knowledge of details specific to Kokkonen's friendship with the sitter. When speaking to Kokkonen's musican friends, the Kokkonen-persona discussed particular compositions, performances, or matters of professional musical gossip. For example, with one sitter, the Kokkonen-persona discussed the relative merits of the Finlandia and BIS recordings of his cello concerto (neither of which the sitter had heard), and then complained about the recording quality of the old Fuga recording of his third string quartet. With another sitter, the Kokkonen-persona gossiped enthusiastically and knowledgeably about a famous conductor's body odor. When speaking to nonmusician friends, the trance-persona spoke in similar detail about matters of personal interest to the sitter. Some of these later sittings were themselves proxy sittings. For example, the composer Pehr Nordgren arranged, anonymously, to be represented by a Midwestern wheat farmer. Mrs. B went into trance immediately, mentioned a term of endearment by which Kokkonen used to address Nordgren, and began relating a discussion the two composers once had about Nordgren's violin concerto. Communications of this quality continued, consistently, for more than a year.

As I noted in chapter 1, if we actually encountered cases of this quality, we'd have to agree with Almeder that it would be irrational (in some sense) not to regard them as compelling evidence of survival, even if we didn't know how to make sense of them theoretically, and (in the most extreme scenario) even if our underlying metaphysics was clearly uncongenial to the idea of postmortem existence. These cases obviously comprise precisely the kind of evidence that could force us to revise, abandon, or at least seriously reconsider a conventionally materialist worldview. Philosophical intransigence in the face of such cases would not demonstrate admirable tough-mindedness. Instead, it would betray indefensible intellectual rigidity.

3. The Significance of Physiological Data

Survivalists argue that we, or something essential to who we are (our mind or soul), can persist even when our bodies die. And many believe this puts survivalists in an awkward position empirically. We noted earlier that the study of survival must respect the data, whatever they might be, and at the time, that observation was intended to caution us against our *anti*-survivalist biases. But in fact the observation is double-edged; it can work against survivalist biases as well. And on the face of it, some evidence seems to cut against the survival hypothesis.

It doesn't matter whether survivalists' underlying metaphysics are staunchly idealistic, dualistic, or nonmaterialist in some other way. Eventually, they must contend with the huge body of data pointing to the apparently intimate connection between brain states and mental states. Therefore, survivalists must say something about how mental states or characteristic chunks of personal psychology might persist in the absence of brain activity. More specifically, they must explain why, if mental states can occur independently of bodily states, they *seem* to be bodily dependent. Typically, survivalists do this by arguing that the brain is merely one kind of physical *instrument* for expressing mental activity.

Not surprisingly, most anti-survivalists find this hard to swallow (e.g., Edwards, 1996), and Richet offered an analogy to explain why (Richet, 1924). In doing so, he anticipated the sort of position many neuropsychologists (among others) would probably now express somewhat differently, but no more cogently. Richet observed how certain changes to the brain affect (and sometimes seem to obliterate) memory. He noted that survivalists hold that the brain "is only an instrument, which is unable to respond unless it is intact" (Richet, 1924, p. 109). Although Richet didn't object to that claim, he found it incredible to assert further, as survivalists do, that this instrument is not necessary for memory and other cognitive functions. He wrote,

> It is as if I were to say that in an electric lamp the passage of the current and the integrity of the mechanism of the lamp are not necessary for the

production of its light. (Richet, 1924, p. 109)

This analogy, and others like it, are initially seductive. But they might be the wrong analogies. Survivalists contend that mental states are *manifested*, but not produced (or at least not uniquely produced), through the brain and nervous system. Electric light, they could object, is simply a different sort of phenomenon. And interestingly, the survivalist position can be bolstered by different analogies and by some good, old-fashioned, but commendably cautious, metaphysics. We need only look to McTaggart to see how the argument could go.

First, survivalists obviously would reject both physicalistic reductionism and epiphenomenalism. They want to say that the self (whatever, exactly, it is) is not something identical with one's physical body or a part of the body (e.g., the brain). Nor is it merely an activity of the body, or something totally causally dependent (or supervening) on (part of) one's physical body. Presumably, survivalists would say that the self (whatever, exactly, it is), as we know it introspectively and through our earthly commerce with others, is something that *has* a body.

Of course, that way of speaking may strike some as intolerably quaint. In fact, anti-survivalists might object that it's question begging, because it presupposes precisely what's at issue: namely, that the self might not be embodied. But I think we need to grant survivalists the use of the locution that the self has a body. *Pre-theoretically*, it's no less legitimate than the competing, and equally theory-laden, terminology of physicalists (i.e., that the self is, or supervenes on, a body). Granted, physiological evidence seems to cast doubt on the survivalist position. It's precisely what draws many people to some form of the identity theory or epiphenomenalism. But according to McTaggart, survivalists can concede that physiological discoveries pose at least an initial challenge to their position. That's why Richet's analogy seems compelling. But as we've seen throughout this book, the survival evidence has a theoretical pull in the opposite direction and poses an apparently comparable *prima facie* challenge to the anti-survivalist. Moreover, McTaggart believed that survivalists could appeal to analogies of their own, and he believed that they were at least as weighty as analogies apparently favoring the physicalist.

So McTaggart granted that the physiological evidence is challenging and that our sensations and mental life *seem* invariably linked to bodily changes of some kind. Nevertheless, he argued, physicalists make various unwarranted inferential leaps when they interpret the evidence. No matter how intimate the mind-body connection seems to be, the data would show, at most, "that *some* body was necessary to my self, and not that its present body was necessary" (McTaggart, 1930/1997, p. 104). But even that may be going too far; strictly speaking, the data show us only what *is* the case, not what *must be* the case. Putting aside (as we must in this arena) our physicalistic or reductionistic biases, the data

don't establish limits on the *possible* manifestations of selfhood. Specifically, nothing in the data compels us to conclude that a self must be
linked to a physical body. So on a more circumspect or conservative appraisal of the data, we might conclude simply that *"while a self has a
body*, that body is essentially connected with the self's mental life" (p.
105). McTaggart argued,

> it does not follow, because a self which has a body cannot get its data except
> in connexion with that body, that it would be impossible for a self without a
> body to get data in some other way. It may be just the existence of the body
> which makes these other ways impossible at present. If a man is shut up in a
> house, the transparency of the windows is an essential condition of his see-
> ing the sky. But it would not be prudent to infer that, if he walked out of the
> house, he could not see the sky because there was no longer any glass
> through which he might see it. (McTaggart, 1930/1997, p.105)

McTaggart makes a similar point with regard to the more specific,
and apparently intimate, relation between brain states and mental
states.

> Even if the brain is essential to thought while we have bodies, it would not
> follow that when we ceased to have brains we could not think without
> them...It might be that the present inability of the self to think except in
> connexion with the body was a limitation which was imposed by the pres-
> ence of the body, and which vanished with it. (McTaggart, 1930/1997, p.
> 106)

I think we can supplement McTaggart's point with a contemporary
analogy, although I don't want to make too much of its physicalistic and
mechanistic features. Consider the case of portable electronic devices
that can operate either on battery power or through a connection to AC
lines, docking stations, or some other component to which they can be
joined and through which they can draw power. Typically, the latter
connections allow a portable device to perform functions it might not be
able to perform on its own, or to perform functions better than it can
perform on its own. For example, docking stations enhance the func-
tionality of laptop computers, and AC connections often permit them to
display brighter screen images. Moreover (and perhaps more important), the connections bypassing the unit's battery power also impose
constraints on the portable device's function, constraints which it lacked
as a stand-alone device. Of course, they make the device less portable.
But they also render the portable device vulnerable to processes (e.g.,
power surges or fluctuations) which can alter or impair its performance
and even disable it. For example, some audio equipment sounds better
on its battery power than when connected to AC lines.

Now I don't think it's plausible or helpful to push the analogy between electronic devices and minds (or personalities). But if we ignore
that for the moment, the connection between the portable device and

an AC source seems to mirror the familiar dependence of thought processes on brain functioning, and the analogy captures an important feature of McTaggart's survivalist position. Like connection to a wall outlet or docking station (which can both expand and constrain the device's functions), physical embodiment would simply be one possible medium for cognitive expression. And like running on battery power, disembodied existence or possession of an astral body might be others.

McTaggart's view is important and insightful. Strictly speaking, the physiological evidence doesn't show that selfhood or consciousness is *exclusively* linked to bodily processes, much less the processes of any particular physical body. Probably, physicalistic interpretations of the data seem initially compelling because physicalistic presuppositions are widespread and deeply rooted. And if so, it may be a useful intellectual exercise to try to divest ourselves of those presuppositions and then take a fresh look at the data. We might find, then, that McTaggart's (or the survivalist's) interpretation seems more immediately appealing.

Moreover, it's not clear to what extent physicalists can cite neurophysiological data in support of their position, especially when physicalism itself is in question. More specifically, they can't simply assume that the received physicalistic interpretation of that data is correct. After all, if we seriously entertain the survival hypothesis in light of the evidence initially in its favor, that would force us to consider alternative interpretations of some neurophysiological data. Besides, data don't come preinterpreted. They must always be evaluated in the light of a background theory, and our choice of background theory is always up for grabs, no matter how well entrenched it may be at the time. Often enough, apparently obvious interpretations of the data reveal more about our unexamined theoretical presuppositions (or lack of imagination) than they do about the phenomena in question. An interesting episode from the history of psychology illustrates that point nicely.

In the 1920s, Karl Lashley thought he could determine where, in a rat's brain, the rat's memories were located. He trained rats to run a maze, and then he excised the portion of the brain where he believed their acquired memory to be. To his surprise, the rats continued to run the maze. So Lashley cut out even more of the brain, but the rats still managed to navigate the maze (though with a bit less panache). Lashley continued excising portions of the rats' brains until there was only a small fraction of the brain left, and only then were the rats unable to run the maze. Unfortunately, at that point in their surgical marathon they also could do little else (Lashley, 1929; 1950; Beach, Hebb, Morgan, & Nissen, 1960). Later, others looked at these results and concluded that the rats' memories must have been diffusely localized in the brain, much in the way information is diffusely distributed in a hologram. For that hasty inference and his resulting holographic theory of memory traces, Karl Pribram has been heralded as a pundit (Pribram,

1971, 1977; Pribram, Nuwer, & Baron, 1974). But I'd suggest that Pribram's apparently easy recourse to a holographic model was merely a sign of theoretical myopia and an uncritical acceptance of physicalistic and mechanistic dogma. To those not antecedently committed to mechanistic analyses of the mental, Lashley's data take on a different kind of significance. They also support the view—held in some quarters—that the *container metaphor* (i.e., that mental states are *in* the brain) was wrong from the start and that memories are not localized *anywhere* or *in any form* in the brain. Moreover, that antimechanistic position can be supplemented by deep and apparently fatal objections to trace theories of memory generally (e.g., Bursen, 1978; Heil, 1978; Malcolm, 1977; Braude, 2002).

A similar lack of metaphysical sophistication or awareness all too frequently affects the interpretation of evidence cited in connection with survival. And in fact, that was recently demonstrated in an interesting article on reincarnation (Bishai, 2000). Bishai addressed the familiar anti-survivalist argument that "reincarnation appears to be refuted by population statistics" (Edwards, 1996, p.227). He sketched a simple "circular migration model" that does, in fact, account for the data from a reincarnationist perspective, and he showed how various assumptions about the "dwell time" between incarnations yield different predictions about the peak of human population growth. But more important, he showed that metaphysical assumptions are unavoidable no matter where one stands on the issue of reincarnation and population growth. Specifically, he showed that the alleged incompatibility between the reincarnation hypothesis and the facts of population growth rest on a very controversial assumption: namely, that "the mean duration of stay in the afterlife has been constant throughout human history" (Bishai, 2000, p. 419). Presumably, Edwards was unaware that his own position rested on that assumption. But even if he had realized what his presuppositions were, it's highly unlikely that he could have successfully defended this one against the assumptions required by various reincarnationist positions. In this context at least, he can't justifiably flaunt his empiricist pretensions and profess more respect for the evidence than those he criticizes. Ironically, Edwards's allegedly hard-nosed and condescending attack on reincarnationists is as deeply (and inevitably) metaphysical and debatable as the view he opposes.

4. The "Stuff" That Survives

So let's agree with McTaggart (at least tentatively) that the physiological evidence doesn't rule out survival. That still leaves a major puzzle: What is it, exactly, that might survive bodily death and decomposition? Can we be content to say simply that it's our mind or soul? Don't we need to say something more? As I noted in the last chapter, we tend to suppose (reasonably) that our mental states must be grounded in *some* kind of substrate. That's one reason why many find it hard to grasp the concept of *literally bodiless* survival. Another is that it's hard to understand how postmortem awareness of the physical world could be *perspectival* in the absence of a physically located body from which the perspective could be derived (see, e.g., Penelhum, 1970).

Of course, in chapter 1 I cautioned against relying too heavily on our ability (or inability) to conceive of survival or certain of its alleged features. Our imaginative capacities are notoriously unreliable, and they may well be inadequate to the task at hand. Nevertheless, many survivalists naturally want to say something specific about the sort of thing that survives. That's why some posit astral or secondary bodies, which at the very least supply the substrate for postmortem mental activity. They might also help explain how perspectival postmortem perception could occur. However, it's questionable whether astral matter would "absorb and react to ordinary electromagnetic radiation of the sort that enables embodied persons to see objects" (Alan Gauld, personal communication, November 28, 1998). So it might still be a challenge for advocates of astral bodies to explain perspectival postmortem perception without appealing to ESP—in fact, ESP of exactly the magnitude that survivalists consider implausible in the context of super-psi explanations.

Curiously, some think not only that survival and physicalism are compatible, but that we can explain survival without positing exotic types of matter like astral bodies. As a result, resurrectionist theories are staging something of a comeback at the hands of philosophically sophisticated physicalists (see, e.g., Corcoran, 2001a; Merricks, 2001). But as far as I can tell, these proposals can't accommodate the type of survival suggested by much of the evidence, which at best seems only *temporarily mediated* by a physical body. For example, the evidence from haunting suggests only

> absolutely minimal embodiment, as when a recurrent and localized voice of a recognizable tone is heard to make publicly audible remarks. The voice might give evidence of qualitative and positional continuity sufficient to treat it as an identifiable body, even if of an excessively diaphanous kind. (Quinton, 1975, p. 71)

But more seriously, both haunting and mediumship suggest that postmortem individuals continue to exist—presumably in a disembodied state—during periods of mediumistic or haunting inactivity (e.g., when the séance is over).

Of course, many view the survival evidence as providing *prima facie* evidence for a form of substance-dualism—specifically, the Platonic-Cartesian view that a person is an intimate compound of a bodily component with a mental component. But that's precisely what seems to introduce the hard-to-grasp concept of literally disembodied survival—that is, survival with *no* kind of body, not even a secondary body. Moreover, the problem seems especially acute when we consider that the survival evidence suggests not simply the existence of *occurrent* mental states belonging to a deceased individual, but also the persistence of *dispositional* states (memories, traits, attitudes, abilities, etc.).

More specifically, the problem is this. When we attribute a disposition to a thing, we commit ourselves to various *conditional* or hypothetical claims about it, stating (roughly) what *would* be the case about the thing under certain circumstances. Now perhaps we can claim intelligibly that specific, occurrent mental states can persist free-floating (as it were), detached from their owners or authors (though I doubt it). But dispositional states and their associated tendencies more clearly require a persisting, underlying something-or-other. And whatever that thing is, presumably it's something that contains (or carries or holds) the disposition and which can eventually express the disposition in occurrent states. But if it's not a physical body or a secondary body, what is it?

Many would say that Cartesian dualists have no viable response to that question. In fact, their appeal to an immaterial soul may conflict with at least one way of understanding the assumption that mental capacities require an underlying substrate. Consider C. D. Broad's version of that assumption.

> Every conditional fact about a thing must be grounded on a categorical fact about its persistent minute structure or recurrent internal processes. (Broad, 1962, p. 415; see also p. 414)

It's easy enough to grasp how we can explain the properties of both inert and animated physical things in terms of their persistent minute structures. In fact, we appeal routinely to such underlying structures to explain many sorts of dispositions, from the solubility of salt to the ability to digest food. But Broad has trouble attaching sense to the notion of a purely mental or nonphysical *structure*. Of course, he's not alone in this, and it's fairly clear why that is. It's hard to see what would count as a suitable grounding microstructure unless the substrate had something like familiar physical properties. So it's not surprising that when Broad searches for analogies to explain how our mental states might persist following bodily death, he writes,

> Nowadays we have plenty of experience concerning physical existents which are extended and in a sense localized, which have persistent structure and are the seat of rhythmic modulations, which are not in any sense ordinary bodies, but which are closely associated with a body of a certain kind in a certain state. One example would be the electromagnetic field associated with a conductor carrying an electric current. Or consider, as another example, the sense in which a performance of an orchestral piece, which has been broadcast from a wireless station, exists in the form of modulations in the transmitting beam, in places where and at times when there is no suit-

ably tuned receiver to pick it up and transform it into a pattern of sounds. (Broad, 1962, p. 416)

Along the same lines, he suggests that if something survives death, it might be like

a persistent vortex in the ether, carrying modulations imposed on it by experiences had by the person with whose physical body it was formerly associated as a kind of "field." (Broad, 1962, p. 430; cf. p. 419)

Nevertheless, despite the appeal of Broad's widely shared physicalistic intuitions, there are clear philosophical precedents for positing literally immaterial structures (in fact, it's surprising that Broad failed to acknowledge them). Leibnizian idealism is one approach, and so is a Whiteheadean process philosophy constructing physical reality out of fundamental occasions of experience (see Griffin, 1997, for an attempt to accommodate survival along these lines). I don't find either of those approaches especially appealing (and I have particular difficulty understanding the latter), but both seem to be genuine options in logical space. Another approach would be to argue for the possibility of temporally "gappy" existence, hoping thereby to avoid positing an underlying stuff to "hold" the temporally separate parts together. Merricks has offered a view of this sort, and he combines it with a defense of the view that there are no criteria of identity over time (e.g., Merricks, 1998, 2001). In fact, Merricks is willing to accept that "there is *no possible explanation* of how personal identity could hold across a temporal gap" (2001, p. 196).

I sympathize with some of Merricks's intuitions, although I would approach the issues from a different angle, one suggesting another reason why Broad's concern might be misplaced. Even if we agree that there must be some substrate or other for our mental capacities and dispositions, we needn't make the further mechanistic and reductionistic assumption that the capacities or dispositions are always analyzable in terms of the substrate's microstructure. Indeed, there are good reasons for thinking that this further assumption is false and that at least some of our mental states should be regarded as primitive and unanalyzable (I've argued this myself in Braude, 2002, 1997). I must refer the reader to those sources for a more detailed presentation of that position. But in a nutshell, the issues are as follows.

Broad seems to be making an assumption that is widely and uncritically accepted in most areas of science, and which I have dubbed the *Small-is-Beautiful Assumption*. Most scientists would agree that explaining natural phenomena in terms of lower-level processes is something that can't continue indefinitely. In other words, they assume that eventually we must reach a kind of explanatory ground level, a level where we take phenomena to be primitive. And to say that those phenomena are primitive means that no lower-level processes explain *how* they oc-

cur. These ultimate facts may be framework principles (such as conser-
vation laws in physics) or other sorts of lawlike regularities (e.g., radio-
active decay). But whatever the phenomena are taken to be, scientists
agree that the universe simply works in those ways, and no constitutive
processes explain why. (Of course, we may incorrectly take some phenomena or regularities to be primitive, and then later discover that they
can be analyzed in terms of a microstructure. But scientists nevertheless
agree that some phenomena must be genuinely primitive, and with luck
and diligence we'll figure out what they are.)

Now, it's perfectly reasonable to assume that vertical explanation (in
terms of lower-level processes) must stop somewhere. But most scientists assume, further, that when vertical explanation stops and where we
find primitive natural phenomena, it's always at the level of the very
small—for example, the atomic, subatomic, neurological, or biochemi-
cal level, but not at the observable level (say, the level of behavior). But
that assumption, the small-is-beautiful assumption, is not an empirically
established principle. It's an article of faith, and there are compelling
reasons for taking it to be false. In fact, there are good reasons for
thinking it fails consistently and dramatically in the case of psychological explanation, and accordingly, that mental states and dispositions are
not (at least in general) the sorts of things analyzable in terms of lower-
level processes.[2]

In that respect, the dispositional nature of mental states would differ
from that of (say) the solubility of salt. But if the mental states of *living*
persons have no analysis in terms of lower-level processes, presumably
mental states would continue to be unanalyzable even if they persisted
after bodily death and dissolution. And in that case, we're presented
with some intriguing explanatory options. In the case of living persons,
we can still ground the conditional nature of mental capacities in categorical facts about an underlying substrate. We would simply regard the
substrate as only *mediating* the conditional facts, rather than having a
structure that explains, or permits an analysis of, the conditional facts.
The conceptual move here parallels—at least in certain respects—what
many say (plausibly) about meaning and communication. Linguistic
communication must be mediated by one or more familiar physical
processes—for example, those involved in writing or speaking. But it
doesn't follow that the meaning of our words or sentences can be analyzed in terms of those mediating processes—much less in terms of allegedly more fundamental underlying categorical facts (e.g., atoms of
meaning or minimal meaning-bearing units; see, e.g., Goldberg, 1982).

So let's suppose (if only for argument's sake) that we require only
that there be some *mediating substrate* for the expression of dispositions
and other conditional facts about a person's mental life. That may open
the way for a kind of Platonic-Cartesian explanation of survival in terms
of an immaterial soul. The substrate in this case would simply be imma-

terial, and we needn't appeal to any underlying structure of souls to explain how the dispositions, etc., persist and get expressed. But how plausible is this? After all, in the case of unanalyzable features of communication we can pick out clear mediating processes—for example, those involved in the production and transmission of sounds and images. And in the case of living persons' mental states we can pick out living organisms the integrity of whose processes seems necessary for mediating those mental states. But it's unclear whether Cartesian dualists can make analogous claims. It's unclear whether they can specify *any nonphysical processes* that mediate the survival of dispositions.

However, it's also unclear that Cartesian dualists *need* to say more at that point. Our tendency to look for underlying explanations of phenomena is very strong, and it persists even in areas of science (such as physics) where we find a broad consensus about the phenomena taken as primitive. Even there, it's hard to shake the suspicion that something more can be said, something about how underlying processes allow the universe to exhibit just those features we consider fundamental. Perhaps we need to remind ourselves that it needn't be a failure of understanding to bring vertical explanation to a halt—that is, to claim that a phenomenon has no explanation in terms of subsidiary processes or mechanisms. In fact, it would seem to be a *victory* of understanding to realize that vertical explanation is no longer appropriate and that other forms of explanation may be more useful (e.g., covering-law explanation, or explanation by analogy).

There's no doubt that accepting some survival evidence as legitimate and compelling increases the temptation to posit the existence of immaterial souls. And in the last chapter we examined some ways in which that philosophical intuition has been defended. But there's also no doubt that many strongly resist that conceptual move, more or less for the reasons expressed by Broad. I'm certainly not lobbying here for a form of Platonic-Cartesian dualism. Nevertheless, I suggest we remember that when physicists posit the existence of an undetected particle with unusual properties, or a type of undetected matter (dark matter), few bat an eye. Clearly, then, positing novel and even radically different stuff has a legitimate scientific pedigree. We might simply have to be equally generous or open-minded about positing souls, even if we're not sure, initially, how to flesh out the hypothesis (pun intended). If the best survival data, and the totality of good evidence, can't be handled satisfactorily along non-survivalist lines, we may have no choice but to entertain a variety of metaphysical theses we would previously have dismissed out of hand (probably with a disdainful flourish).

It might be tempting to follow Quinton's lead and take the soul to be "a series of mental states connected by continuity of character and memory" (Quinton, 1975, p. 65). As we saw in chapter 1, that provides a pragmatically viable basis for making both antemortem and postmortem identity judgments. And it's at least agnostic with respect to the question: What (if anything) undergirds these continuities? But as modest as that approach may be, it may still rule out reincarnation as a coherent interpretation of the sorts of cases examined in chapter 6.

From Quinton's neo-Lockean point of view, a soul is identified by means of psychological continuities. But theories of reincarnation take the soul to be the thing or stuff that *has* or *supports* idiosyncratic psychological continuities. In fact, on standard interpretations of reincarnation cases, souls are things that, as they persist through successive incarnations, take on and lose distinctive psychological regularities. Ostensibly, that explains why a child subject's past-life memories typically disappear before the age of ten. But on a view like Quinton's we might have to say (implausibly, it seems) that a formerly living person survived for a time and then gradually became someone else.

Of course, if we're sympathetic to Quinton's approach but don't like the idea of souls morphing into new souls, we might be content to reject all reincarnationist theories. That still leaves the option of treating all ostensible reincarnation cases as evidence of possession. Possession (including mediumship) *is* compatible with Quinton's view. And perhaps some would find it more palatable to believe that souls simply change bodies. (We should also remember, as we noted in chapter 6, that the differences between reincarnation and possession cases may be no more than superficial. They might be analogous to similar surface variations in types of MPD/DID. So we're not compelled to interpret the cases differently.)

5. The Almeder/Hales Debate

A recent exchange between Robert Almeder and Steven Hales raises a slightly different set of concerns about the evidence suggesting postmortem survival (Almeder, 1996b, 2001; Hales, 2001a, 2001b). Hales disputes Almeder's defense of the reincarnation hypothesis. He argues first "that a necessary condition for justifiably accepting the hypothesis of reincarnation is a theory that embeds the cases" (2001b, p. 361). That is, "we are epistemically justified in accepting the reincarnation hypothesis only if someone shows us exactly how reincarnation works" (p. 361). Almeder replies that we may know that a fact is true without being able to explain it, and Hales concedes that *if* the reincarnation hypothesis were the only available hypothesis, we'd have to give it serious consideration. But (he claims) we can't "blindly venerate data over theory" (2001a, p. 339), and in fact reincarnation is inconsistent with our best physical theories of the mental. So,

> if there is some other hypothesis that explains the cases ostensibly suggestive of reincarnation as well as the reincarnation hypothesis, and if this

other hypothesis is consistent with materialism about the mind, and other well-established theories, then we should prefer it. (2001a, p. 342)

One such hypothesis, according to Hales, is this:

> that there are intelligent, technologically advanced extra-terrestrials who regard humans with great amusement, and secretly monitor and occasionally interfere with our lives. One thing they enjoy is performing super-advanced psychosurgery on select humans that provides these humans with quasi-memories of having lived past lives, verifiably true beliefs about where ancient bracelets are hidden, and previously non-existent linguistic or musical talents. Unlike a Cartesian evil genius, the ET hypothesis is perfectly testable by empirical means—if the aliens were to land and reveal themselves and their techniques, this would serve to confirm the hypothesis. If we were to completely survey the universe and find no such aliens, this would falsify it. Moreover, the ET hypothesis is entirely consistent with materialism about the mind, and explains the cases as well as the reincarnation hypothesis. Even better, the probability of there being some sort of extra-terrestrial life is quite high. (2001a, p. 342)

I agree with Hales that Almeder's response to this challenge is unconvincing, although it's better than Hales allows. However, since space prohibits further discussion of their exchange, I'll simply mention my own additional reservations about Hales's view. First, I believe there's little reason to share Hales's optimism or confidence in materialist theories of the mental, which he claims are "well-developed, systematic, and highly justified" (2001b, p. 359). For reasons I and many others have discussed—and which have nothing to do with the survival debate—those theories seem to be little more than bad philosophy usually dressed up in obscurantist technical terms. And they're certainly not well developed; in fact, I'd argue that they remain little more than promissory notes and account for almost nothing of interest about the mental. At any rate, I and many others would argue that there's no antecedent credibility in Hales's conjecture that aliens could analyze and surgically implant complex memories and (perhaps especially) skills (particularly of the sort typically requiring practice). But this is not the place to argue those big issues.

For present purposes, a different feature of the Hales/Almeder debate is more interesting. Almeder argues for reincarnation and for the Platonic-Cartesian view of the soul most people associate with it. In fact, reincarnation is at least a crude *theory* of survival, positing the existence of soul-stuff which can successively take on and lose different distinctive psychologies. By contrast, it's considerably less committal metaphysically to say merely that there's evidence—not for reincarnation—but for postmortem personal survival. It's noncommittal with respect to *how* survival occurs, whether it be through the mediation of immaterial souls, monadic rearrangements, occasions of experience, astral bodies, ET interventions, or something else. In fact, it's apparently compatible with a view that takes survival or identity to be unanalyzable.

Moreover, Hales's ET hypothesis, like many thought experiments, is woefully underdescribed. We don't know to what extent the aliens' psychosurgery simulates the deceased persons' psychology—for example, how it compares to good cases of mediumship and reincarnation. But if aliens could do what Hales suggests, and if their resulting simulations were convincing in minute detail, we might want to say that people *survive* when the aliens mischievously implant their memories and skills into unwitting victims. Hales's ET hypothesis would simply be an unorthodox (nondualistic, nonspiritistic) proposal about the processes underlying postmortem survival. Of course, we might also treat the ET hypothesis as another puzzle case where it's unclear what to say. In fact, Hales's hypothesis sounds suspiciously like many of the sci-fi transplant cases littering the philosophical literature on personal identity, merely substituting aliens for future scientists.

So to deal with Hales's ET hypothesis, we simply need to note again what we first observed in chapter 1. Whether the best explanation for a survival case ultimately turns out to be persistence of an immaterial spirit or something else, the basis for asserting survival will be the same as what we rely on in many everyday, unproblematic cases: continuity of character and memory. In the everyday unproblematic cases, we can justifiably and profitably assert identity without having a scientific or metaphysical theory to ground that practice. We don't need it here either.

So ironically, Hales might need to agree with Almeder that the evidence (strongly?) suggests postmortem survival. They would disagree only over the underlying explanation of the phenomenon. Perhaps Hales would still protest that, from his materialist perspective, he finds no reason to believe that immaterial *spirits* survive. But as we've seen, a belief in spirits is not something to which survivalists are committed. In fact, as Merricks and Corcoran illustrate, survivalists needn't even renounce materialism.

Arguably, the debate between Almeder and Hales was misconceived from the beginning, as the pitting of one fledging scientific view (reincarnation) against an established (or at least entrenched) scientific view (mechanistic materialism). But reincarnation isn't a scientific theory, and survival research isn't traditionally empirical scientific research, no matter how investigators like Stevenson, and philosophers like Almeder, try to make it look otherwise. The individuals whose identity and survival are at issue aren't natural kinds, whose essential features science can or will uncover. Whether we call them persons, souls, or minds, they are identified by means of considerations that are ineliminably normative. And to acknowledge this is not to venerate data over theory, as Hales suggests. It's merely to recognize, first, the limitations of any naturalistic theory in the face of normative considerations, and second, the dispensability of metaphysical theories when it comes to justifying our practices about identifying persons.

6. Summing Up

Nevertheless, evidence matters when we try to evaluate the rival survival and super-psi hypotheses, just as it does when we consider hypotheses in terms of the Unusual Suspects. It's what helps us decide whether our normative considerations about persons are appropriate. So it's time now to see where our inquiry has led, and to see if we can take a reasonably confident stand on the issue of survival. First, I think we must agree with Almeder and Griffin that the totality of survival evidence has a kind of cumulative force, even if individual strands of evidence are less than convincing when considered on their own merits (Almeder, 1992; Griffin, 1997). Griffin offers several arguments in defense of that position, some of which seem more persuasive than others. But they all raise important issues and merit our scrutiny now.

(1) According to Griffin, when we look at the totality of evidence, the survival hypothesis is more parsimonious than any rival. He writes,

> Whereas the non-survivalist interpreter must come up with a variety of hypotheses to handle the various kinds of data…,the survivalist can use one hypothesis—survival with (limited) agency—to explain the basic features of all the phenomena. (Griffin, 1997, p. 266)

Now first of all, although I also feel the tug of theoretical or explanatory simplicity, we should probably be wary of leaning too heavily on our intuitions concerning parsimony. This issue is too big to be addressed here, but I can refer interested readers to several papers discussing problems with the concept of simplicity in science: Ackermann, 1961; Barker, 1961; Bunge, 1961; Quine, 1963 (all reprinted in Foster & Martin, 1966). Moreover, we can hardly be confident that nature will conform to our preferred standard of theoretical simplicity. As C. S. Peirce noted, "Certain it is that most hypotheses which at first seemed to unite great simplicity with entire sufficiency have had to be greatly complicated in the further progress of science" (Hartshorne, Weiss, & Burks, 1931-1958, vol. 5, para. 26). Besides, we typically pay a price for theoretical simplicity—usually, theoretical complexity somewhere else. So although survivalists may require only one hypothesis to cover a wide range of phenomena, they also enlarge and complicate our ontological inventory. And it's doubtful that one form of simplicity is inherently preferable to the other.

But quite apart from the interesting abstract matters of justifying and clarifying appeals to parsimony, it's also unclear that the super-psi hypothesis is at a great disadvantage here. Griffin may be correct that one hypothesis—postmortem survival with limited agency—handles the basic features of all types of survival cases. But nonsurvivalists seem to be in a similar position. Analogously, they require only antemortem existence and a modest level of agency.

Granted, hypothesized super-psi scenarios will differ somewhat from one case (or type of case) to another. For example, in cases of mediumship we might sometimes appeal to mediumistic psi, and in other cases to sitter psi. Similarly, in reincarnation cases we might sometimes appeal to the subject's receptive psi and in others to telepathic influence from one or more parents. But survivalists likewise need to propose various scenarios and types of psychic activity to accommodate the evidence. Although Griffin clearly has an admirably full grasp of the issues, his phrase "limited agency" obscures the complex array of stories survivalists must tell. For example, some mediumistic cases suggest that the subject more or less passively receives messages or impressions from the deceased, whereas others seem to indicate PK (or telepathic influence, or temporary possession) on the part of the communicator. Again, reincarnation cases suggest a different sort of relationship between the previous personality and a living agent than those suggested by the various forms of possession. And it's unclear what sort of hypothesis (presumably, a type of PK) survivalists will propose to account for the clothing and accessories of apparitions. So in the end, both the survival and super-psi hypotheses require only one type of existence and a variety of explanation forms. And (as we noted in chapter 1) both require the same array of psi-abilities. They differ primarily with respect to the ontological status of the (ostensible) communicators.

(2) Griffin claims, next, that the survival

> evidence taken collectively is stronger...because each of the kinds of evidence increases the antecedent probability of a survivalist interpretation of the others....the appropriate "background" on the basis of which to estimate the antecedent probabilities of the competing hypotheses...should be...*all* the evidence other than that directly relevant to the issue at hand. (Griffin, 1997, p. 266)

But just as we should be wary of our intuitions concerning parsimony, we should also be wary (especially in this subject matter) of how we assess antecedent probability. In fact, the history of science suggests strongly that subjective probability assessments of anomalous phenomena carry very little weight. Moreover, we know how to judge antecedent probability in connection with phenomena that are already reasonably well understood. That's why we can make informed judgments about the likelihood of (say) fraud or misperception in cases of ostensible psychic functioning. We know what sorts of situations might motivate fraud or facilitate misperception, and we have a clear and substantial background of information to which we can appeal when making those judgments. But when it comes to phenomena that at least appear to violate fundamental scientific laws or metaphysical assumptions, although we can still argue reasonably for their existence, we have virtually no basis for making judgments about their antecedent probability.

But in any case, if we heed Griffin's admonition to consider all the evidence, we'll also need to consider the totality of evidence for psychic functioning among the living. And as we've noted (and as Griffin also realizes), that includes extensive and impressive bodies of data indicating, if not super psi, then at least very dandy psi. In short, the relevant background includes material that also seems to increase the antecedent probability of super-psi interpretations of the survival evidence. In fact, the background material includes cases that clearly only *appear* to be evidence of survival—for example, the Cagliostro case (chapter 2) and that of Patience Worth (chapter 5). As we've seen, these cases point most forcibly to the existence of wide-ranging psi and hidden latent capacities. Moreover, the background includes the entire body of evidence for ostensible precognition, which—if we reject backwards causation—can only be understood in terms of intimidating and extensive clockwise psychic influence and information gathering (Braude, 1997). So when we consider the antecedent probability of the super-psi and survival hypotheses relative to the total background of relevant evidence, it begins to look very much like a draw.

We should also recall that survivalist explanations posit individual psychic interactions just (or nearly) as impressive as those required by super-psi explanations. So survivalists can't argue for the antecedent probability of the survival hypothesis on the grounds that, unlike the super-psi hypothesis, it avoids positing controversially complex or refined instances of psychic functioning.

(3) Griffin's third claim may be his most persuasive. Both he and Almeder argue that the various strands of survival evidence mutually reinforce one another. And it's certainly true, as many have noted, that individual arguments and threads of evidence may not be strong enough to support one's belief in a given position (in this case, for some form of personal survival). However, when bound together, those individual threads may form a strong cord capable of sustaining reasonable belief. Griffin also claims, less convincingly in my view, that the relation of mutual reinforcement is clearest or strongest between OBEs and other kinds of survival evidence (Griffin, 1997, p. 267). But that claim may rest on what seemed in the previous chapter to be a serious overestimation of the OBE evidence, right from the start. At any rate, it's true that the various lines of survival evidence point, in different ways, to the same conclusion: that we, or some essential, purposeful, and distinctive chunk of our personal psychology can survive physical death. And it's true that, taken together, they point more strongly toward that conclusion than they do separately.

Moreover, when we look at the totality of cases, we find diverse types of evidence, exhibiting numerous internal connections and similarities. The different forms of mediumship and other ostensible manifestations of possession share many features, and they likewise bear internal similarities to the reincarnation data. The haunting evidence tends to stand apart from these cases, but it blends by degrees into the evidence for apparitions, which in turn connects closely to cases of OBEs and NDEs. And some of those latter cases share common features with cases of mediumship and possession. As a whole, the types of survival evidence form a reasonably coherent, if motley, body of material. In fact, so long as we're willing initially to entertain the existence of a community of purposeful surviving personalities, it seems reasonable to suppose that their interests and modes of interaction with the living would be as diverse after bodily death as they were beforehand. So at the very least, it's not surprising that the survival evidence is as varied and complex as it is. It might even be pretty much what we could reasonably have anticipated.

We might also make a similar point by considering the presumably unique perspective of each particular surviving personality. As I've noted throughout this book, we should be very careful not to rely on assumptions about what forms postmortem communications and interactions are likely to take. We simply have too little to go on. Nevertheless, if we grant for the sake of argument that one's personality (or an essential part of it) may survive bodily death and then exhibit some of the characteristics and purposes it exhibited during life, we could again reasonably expect the evidence to exhibit a variety of forms—in fact, many (if not all) of the forms that we actually encounter. Moreover, we should probably be open to the possibility that some individuals will be transformed psychologically by the passage to postmortem existence, so that they lose or profoundly alter their earlier psychological regularities.

Analogously (I suppose), if I were to survive a horrendous and normally fatal accident and then try to contact my friends and loved ones, I'd undoubtedly do so in various ways, depending on my state of mind and my access to lines of communication. Some people I'd contact in person, others by phone, email, etc.; some I'd simply say hello to and others I would engage more thoroughly; some I might even need to convince that I in fact survived. It's also possible that I might prefer to remain presumed dead. More generally, which methods of interaction (if any) I adopt will depend on numerous constraints, both physical and psychological. For example, my actions will be constrained by the availability of phones, an internet connection, or a means of travel to bring me into close contact with others; the physical impairments resulting from my accident; the emotional impact or trauma of the accident; and how eager I am to let others know I've survived.

So, as far as the survival evidence is concerned, if we extrapolate from my case to the presumably idiosyncratic situations of every potentially surviving postmortem individual, we'd expect to find a hodgepodge of types of evidence, and in some cases we'd expect to find none at all. And in fact that's what we do observe.

So perhaps at this point the scales are tilting slightly toward the survivalist and away from the super-psi hypothesis. But (to me at least) it's the issue of crippling complexity (first raised in chapter 3) that tips the balance even more convincingly in that direction. We've seen that the survival hypothesis posits one primary source of information about an apparently communicating, reincarnated, or possessing entity: namely, that particular postmortem individual. By contrast, the super-psi hypothesis *requires* multiple sources of information, at least for the best cases. Of course, that fact alone makes the survival hypothesis seem more parsimonious than its super-psi rival. But as we just noted, parsimony (or explanatory simplicity) can be interpreted and evaluated in different ways, and while it may be aesthetically pleasing, it's no guarantee of the truth.

However, we've also noted that the best cases are challenging, not simply because of the *amount* of veridical information they provide, or because the information presented required confirmation from multiple sources, but also because of the *consistency* with which subjects provide the information. Moreover (for reasons already discussed), success at a psi task apparently requires avoiding a potentially huge array of deliberate and adventitious obstacles. And if that's right, then the psychic consistency required by the super-psi hypothesis seems more mysterious than that required by the survivalist. Here is where the problem of multiple sources emerges most critically. If, in fact, psychic efforts face countless obstacles from within the surrounding causal nexus, then the multiple causal chains required by the super-psi hypothesis may be more vulnerable to those obstacles than the single causal link posited by survivalists.

Let's consider again why that is. As we've noted, super-psi explanations require, at least for the best cases, multiple sources of information—hence, several distinct causal connections between the psychic subject and the world. So it would seem that if any one of those causal chains is undermined, crucial bits of data would be lost. But the survivalist scenario requires no more than the integrity of a single causal connection between the psychic subject and a postmortem individual. And although it, too, is vulnerable to interference within the surrounding causal nexus, it might be relatively immune from *ongoing* interference. Analogies can be misleading in this subject matter, and I usually shun mechanistic analogies generally and radio analogies in particular (especially when discussing ESP). But perhaps a radio analogy will best convey what I have in mind.

The difference between the causal scenarios posited by the survival and super-psi hypotheses seems akin to the following. The psychic achievement required by the super-psi hypothesis resembles tuning a radio to several different stations, in order to get distinctive collections of information available only from those stations. Each attempt to dial a station and get the needed information can be hampered by drifting signal frequency, multipath distortion, fluctuations in signal strength, or simply making a connection at the wrong time (i.e., when the station is broadcasting something other than the desired information). By contrast, the survivalist scenario resembles an attempt to dial in a single station. Despite inevitable fluctuations in signal strength or frequency, the dialer needs only to make that one connection and try to hang onto it. Once made, the connection needs only to be maintained. So in a nutshell, undermining the survivalist's single causal connection requires *ongoing* interference. Undermining the multiple connections in super-psi scenarios requires only sporadic interference.

So, we've now weighed the evidence, taken an unusually thorough look at the Unusual Suspects, seriously entertained motivated super-psi interpretations of the data, and waded through the murky problems of crippling complexity. And I think we can say, with little assurance but with some justification, that the evidence provides a reasonable basis for believing in personal postmortem survival. It doesn't clearly support the belief that everyone survives death; it more clearly supports the belief that some do. And it doesn't support the belief that we survive eternally; at best it justifies the belief that some individuals survive for a limited time.

Obviously, this leaves plenty of room for further research and speculation. For example, we haven't even addressed the issue of whether nonhumans might survive, or whether there's any justification for positing a survival cutoff point somewhere on the ontological scale. And of course we haven't considered fully how to frame a metaphysics that adequately accommodates survival. We might need to adopt something like a Cartesian dualism. Or we might find that we need to follow Griffin and adopt a kind of Whiteheadean or process metaphysics. But at least we can now proceed to those topics knowing, hopefully more clearly than at the beginning of this book, that they aren't mere intellectual exercises.

NOTES

1. For the purpose of this example, we can waive the additional benefits of supposing that Mrs. B speaks in fluent Finnish that later requires translation. That would clearly strengthen the case even further, but it would complicate its exposition here. Moreover, we've already considered ideal cases with that sort of feature.

2. In addition to Braude, 1979 and 1997, see, e.g., Bursen, 1978; Goldberg, 1982; Heil, 1978, 1979, 1981, 1983; Malcolm, 1977, 1980.

Bibliography

Ackermann, R. (1961). "Inductive Simplicity." *Philosophy of Science* 28: 152–160.

Akolkar, V. V. (1992). "Search for Sharada: Report of a Case and Its Investigation." *Journal of the American Society for Psychical Research* 86: 209–247.

Allison, L. W. (1934). "Proxy Sittings with Mrs. Leonard." *Proceedings of the Society for Psychical Research* 42: 104–146.

———. (1941). "Further Proxy Sittings with Mrs. Leonard." *Journal of the American Society for Psychical Research* 35: 196–225.

Almeder, R. (1992). *Death and Personal Survival*. Lanham, MD: Rowman & Littlefield.

———. (1996a). "Almeder's Reply to Wheatley and Braude." *Journal of Scientific Exploration* 10: 529–533.

———. (1996b). "Recent Responses to Survival Research." *Journal of Scientific Exploration* 10: 495–517.

———. (2001). "On Reincarnation: A Reply to Hales." *Philosophia* 28: 347–358.

Alvarado, C. S. (1997). "Mapping the Characteristics of Out-of-Body Experiences." *Journal of the American Society for Psychical Research* 91: 15–32.

———. (2000). "Out-of-Body Experiences." In E. Cardeña, S. J. Lynn, and S. Krippner (eds.), *Varieties of Anomalous Experiences*. Washington, DC: American Psychological Association: 183–218.

Anderson, R. I. (1992). "Commentary on the Akolkar and Stevenson Reports." *Journal of the American Society for Psychical Research* 86: 249–256.

Astrain, A. (1912-1925). *Historia de la Compañia de Jesús en la Asistencia de España* (*4 vols.*). Madrid: Razon y Fe.

Aune, B. (1985). *Metaphysics: The Elements*. Minneapolis: University of Minnesota Press.

Ayer, A. J. (1973). *The Central Questions of Philosophy*. London: Weidenfeld and Nicolson.

Barker, S. F. (1961). "On Simplicity in Empirical Hypotheses." *Philosophy of Science* 28: 162–171.

Barrett, W. F. (1917). *On the Threshold of the Unseen*. London: Kegan Paul, Trench, Trubner & Co.

———. (1918). "Note on Telepathy and Telergy." *Proceedings of the Society for Psychical Research* 30: 251–260.

Basmajian, J. (1963). "Control and Training of Individual Motor Units." *Science* 141: 440–441.

———. (1972). "Electromyography Comes of Age." *Science* 176: 603–609.

Baumgarten, F. (1930). *Wunderkinder psychologische Untersuchungen*. Leipzig: Johann Ambrosius Barth.

Beach, F. A., *et al.* (eds.). (1960). *The Neuropsychology of Lashley: Selected Papers of K. S. Lashley*. New York: McGraw-Hill.

Berger, D., *et al.* (1994). "Dissociative Symptoms in Japan." *American Journal of Psychiatry* 151: 148–149.

Berger, R. E., and Persinger, M. A. (1991). "Geophysical Variables and Behavior: LXVII. Quieter Annual Geomagnetic Activity and Larger Effect Size for Experimental Psi (ESP) Studies over Six Decades." *Perceptual & Motor Skills* 73: 1219–1223.

Besterman, T. (1931-32). "Further Inquiries into the Element of Chance in Book-tests." *Proceedings of the Society for Psychical Research* 40: 59–98.

———. (1933). "An Experiment in 'Clairvoyance' with M. Stefan Ossowiecki." *Proceedings of the Society for Psychical Research* 41: 345–352.

Bialystok, E., and Hakuta, K. (1994). *In Other Words: The Science and Psychology of Second-Language Acquisition.* New York: Basic Books.

Bishai, D. (2000). "Can Population Growth Rule Out Reincarnation? A Model of Circular Migration." *Journal of Scientific Exploration* 14: 411–420.

Braude, S. E. (1979). *ESP and Psychokinesis: A Philosophical Examination.* Philadelphia: Temple University Press.

———. (1980). "Selected Poems of Patience Worth." In J. Laughlin (ed.), *New Directions in Prose and Poetry 40.* New York: New Directions Press: 155–166.

———. (1987). "Psi and Our Picture of the World." *Inquiry* 30: 277–294.

———. (1992a). "Reply to Stevenson." *Journal of Scientific Exploration* 6: 151–156. Reply to Stevenson, 1992.

———. (1992b). "Review of S. Pasricha, Claims of Reincarnation: An Empirical Study of Cases in India." *Journal of Parapsychology* 56: 380–384.

———. (1993). "Dissociation and Survival: A Reappraisal of the Evidence." In L. Coly and J. D. S. McMahon (eds.), *Parapsychology and Thanatology.* New York: Parapsychology Foundation, Inc.: 208–237.

———. (1995). *First Person Plural: Multiple Personality and the Philosophy of Mind.* (Rev. ed.) Lanham, MD : Rowman & Littlefield.

———. (1996). "Postmortem Survival: The State of the Debate." In M. Stoeber and H. Meynell (eds.), *Critical Reflections on the Paranormal.* Albany: State University of New York Press: 177–196.

———. (1997). *The Limits of Influence: Psychokinesis and the Philosophy of Science.* (Rev. ed.) Lanham, MD: University Press of America.

———. (2000). "Dissociation and Latent Abilities: The Strange Case of Patience Worth." *Journal of Trauma and Dissociation* 1 (2): 13–48.

———. (2001a). "Out-of-Body Experiences and Survival of Death." *International Journal of Parapsychology* 12: 83–129.

———. (2001b). "The Problem of Super Psi." In F. Steinkamp (ed.), *Parapsychology, Philosophy, and the Mind: A Festschrift in Honor of John Beloff's 80th Birthday.* Jefferson, NC: McFarland.

———. (2002). *ESP and Psychokinesis: A Philosophical Examination (rev. ed.).* Parkland, FL: Brown Walker Press.

Broad, C. D. (1953). *Religion, Philosophy and Psychical Research.* London: Routledge & Kegan Paul.

———. (1958/1976). "Personal Identity and Survival." In J. M. O. Wheatley and H. L. Edge (eds.), *Philosophical Dimensions of Parapsychology.* Springfield, IL: Charles C. Thomas: 348–365.

———. (1962). *Lectures on Psychical Research.* London: Routledge & Kegan Paul.

Broughton, R. S. (1991). *Parapsychology: The Controversial Science.* New York: Ballantine Books.

Brown, D. (1970). "Knowing How and Knowing That, What." In O. P. Wood and G. Pitcher (eds.), *Ryle.* London: Macmillan: 213–248.

Brown, R. (1971). *Unfinished Symphonies: Voices from the Beyond.* New York: Bantam.

Bryant, R. A., and McConkey, K. M. (1989a). "Hypnotic Blindness: A Behavioral and Experiential Analysis." *Journal of Abnormal Psychology* 98: 71–77.

———. (1989b). "Hypnotic Blindness: Awareness and Attribution." *Journal of Abnormal Psychology* 98: 443–447.

———. (1989c). "Visual Conversion Disorder: A Case Analysis of the Influence of Visual Information." *Journal of Abnormal Psychology* 98: 326–329.

Bunge, M. (1961). "The Weight of Simplicity in the Construction and Assaying of Scientific Theories." *Philosophy of Science* 28: 120–149.

Bursen, H. A. (1978). *Dismantling the Memory Machine.* Dordrecht: D. Reidel.

Clowe, C. W. (1949). "The Case of Patience Worth: A Theory." *Journal of the American Society for Psychical Research* 43: 70–81.

Cook, E. (1997). "Dr. Cook's Reply to Comments on Her Review of *Parapsychology and Thanatology.*" *Journal of Parapsychology* 61: 159–167.

Cook, E. W., Greyson, B., and Stevenson, I. (1998). "Do Any Near-Death Experiences Provide Evidence for the Survival of Human Personality after Death? Relevant Features and Illustrative Case Reports." *Journal of Scientific Exploration* 12: 377–406.

Corcoran, K. (2001a). "Physical Persons and Postmortem Survival without Temporal Gaps." In K. Corcoran (ed.), *Soul, Body, and Survival.* Ithaca, NY: Cornell University Press: 201–217.

———. (ed.). (2001b). *Soul, Body, and Survival.* Ithaca, NY: Cornell University Press.

Cory, C. E. (1919). "Patience Worth." *Psychological Review* 26: 397–407.

Crabtree, A. (1985). *Multiple Man: Explorations in Possession and Multiple Personality.* London: Holt, Reinhart & Winston.

———. (1993). *From Mesmer to Freud: Magnetic Sleep and the Roots of Psychological Healing.* New Haven, CT: Yale University Press.

———. (March 17, 1998). "Life after Death: Conviction and Doubt." Paper presented at the First Edith Bruce Lecture on Immortality, Hart House, University of Toronto.

Crapanzano, V., and Garrison, V. (eds.). (1977). *Case Studies in Spirit Possession.* New York: John Wiley & Sons.

Crookall, R. (1966). *The Next World—and the Next. Ghostly Garments.* London: Theosophical Publishing House.

Dale, L. A., White, R., and Murphy, G. (1962). "A Selection of Cases from a Recent Survey of Spontaneous ESP Phenomena." *Journal of the American Society for Psychical Research* 56: 3–47.

Dickinson, G. L. (1911). "A Case of Emergence of a Latent Memory under Hypnosis." *Proceedings of the Society for Psychical Research* 25: 455–467.

Dingwall, E. J. (1924). "An Experiment with the Polish Medium Stefan Ossowiecki." *Journal of the Society for Psychical Research* 21: 259–263.

Dodds, E. R. (1934). "Why I Do Not Believe in Survival." *Proceedings of the Society for Psychical Research* 42: 147–172.

Downs, J., Dahmer, S. K., and Battle, A. O. (1990). "Letter to the Editor: Multiple Personality Disorder in India." *American Journal of Psychiatry* 147: 1260.

Dreifuss, F. E. (1961). "Observations on Aphasia in a Polyglot Poet." *Acta Psychiatrica et Neurologica Scandinavica* 36: 91–97.

Ducasse, C. J. (1961). *A Critical Examination of the Belief in a Life after Death.* Springfield, IL: Charles C. Thomas.

———. (1962). "What Would Constitute Conclusive Evidence of Survival After Death?" *Journal of the Society for Psychical Research* 41: 401–406.

Edwards, P. (1996). *Reincarnation: A Critical Examination.* Amherst, NY: Prometheus Books.

Eich, E., *et al.* (1997). "Memory, Amnesia, and Dissociative Identity Disorder." *Psychological Science* 8: 417–422.

Eisenbud, J. (1992). *Parapsychology and the Unconscious.* Berkeley, CA: North Atlantic Books.

Escobar, J. I. (1995). "Transcultural Aspects of Dissociative and Somatoform Disorders." *Psychiatric Clinics of North America* 18: 555–569.

Feldman, F. (1992). *Confrontations with the Reaper: A Philosophical Study of the Nature and Value of Death.* New York: Oxford University Press.

Flew, A. (1976). *The Presumption of Atheism.* London: Elek/Pemberton.

———. (1987). *The Logic of Mortality.* Oxford: Blackwell.

Flournoy, T. (1900/1994). *From India to the Planet Mars: A Case of Multple Personality with Imaginary Languages.* Princeton, NJ: Princeton University Press.

———. (1902). "Nouvelles observations sur un Cas de Somnambullisme avec Glossolalie." *Archives de Psychologie* 1: 101–255.

Foster, M. H., and Martin, M. L. (eds.). (1966). *Probability, Confirmation, and Simplicity: Readings in the Philosophy of Inductive Logic.* New York: Odyssey Press.

Frank, J. D., and Frank, J. B. (1991). *Persuasion and Healing: A Comparative Study of Psychotherapy.* Baltimore: Johns Hopkins University Press.

Gangdev, P. S., and Matjane, M. (1996). "Dissociative Disorders in Black South Africans: A Report on Five Cases." *Dissociation* 9: 176–181.

Gauld, A. (1971). "A Series of 'Drop-In' Communicators." *Proceedings of the Society for Psychical Research* 55: 273–340.

———. (1977). "Discarnate Survival." In B. Wolman (ed.), *Handbook of Parapsychology.* New York: Van Nostrand Reinhold: 577–630.

———. (1982). *Mediumship and Survival.* London: Heinemann.

———. (1992). *A History of Hypnotism.* Cambridge: Cambridge University Press.

———. (1993). "A Series of 'Drop in' Communicators: Supplementary Information." *Proceedings of the Society for Psychical Research* 57: 311–316.

Gauld, A., and Cornell, A. D. (1979). *Poltergeists.* London: Routledge & Kegan Paul.

Geach, P. (1969). *God and the Soul.* New York: Schocken.

Gearhart, L., and Persinger, M. A. (1986). "Geophysical Variables and Behavior: XXXIII. Onsets of Historical and Contemporary Poltergeist Episodes Occurred with Sudden Increases in Geomagnetic Activity." *Perceptual & Motor Skills* 62: 463–466.

Gibbes, E. B. (1937). "Have We Indisputable Evidence of Survival?" *Journal of the American Society for Psychical Research* 31: 65–79.

Ginet, C. (1975). *Knowledge, Perception, and Memory.* Boston: Reidel.

Goldberg, B. (1977). "A Problem with Anomalous Monism." *Philosophical Studies* 32: 175–180.

———. (1982). "Mechanism and Meaning." In C. Ginet and S. Shoemaker (eds.), *Knowledge and Mind.* Oxford: Oxford University Press: 191–210.

Gregory, A. (1985). *The Strange Case of Rudi Schneider.* Metuchen, NJ: Scarecrow Press.

Griffin, D. R. (1997). *Parapsychology, Philosophy, and Spirituality: A Postmodern Exploration.* Albany: State University of New York Press.

Grim, P. (1994). "Notes on Evidence and Externalism: A Response to Woodhouse." *New Ideas in Psychology* 12: 23–26.

Grinspoon, L., and Bakalar, J. (1979). *Psychedelic Drugs Reconsidered.* New York: Basic Books.

Grosso, M. (1981). "Toward an Explanation of Near-Death Phenomena." *Journal of the American Society for Psychical Research* 75: 37–60.

Gurney, E., Myers, F. W. H., and Podmore, F. (1886). *Phantasms of the Living*. London: Society for Psychical Research.

Hales, S. D. (2001a). "Evidence and the Afterlife." *Philosophia* 28: 335–346.

———. (2001b). "Reincarnation Redux." *Philosophia* 28: 359–367.

Haraldsson, E. (1991). "Children Claiming Past-Life Memories: Four Cases in Sri Lanka." *Journal of Scientific Exploration* 5: 233–261.

———. (1995). "Personality and Abilities of Children Claiming Previous-Life Memories." *Journal of Nervous and Mental Disease* 183: 445–451.

———. (1997). "A Psychological Comparison between Ordinary Children and Those Who Claim Previous-Life Memories." *Journal of Scientific Exploration* 11: 323–335.

———. (2000a). "Birthmarks and Claims of Previous-Life Memories. I. The Case of Purnima Ekanayake." *Journal of the Society for Psychical Research* 64: 16–25.

———. (2000b). "Birthmarks and Claims of Previous-Life Memories. II. The Case of Chatura Karunaratne." *Journal of the Society for Psychical Research* 64: 82–92.

Haraldsson, E., Pratt, J. G., and Kristjansson, M. (1978). "Further Experiments with the Icelandic Medium Hafsteinn Björnsson." *Journal of the American Society for Psychical Research* 72: 339–347.

Haraldsson, E., and Samararatne, G. (1999). "Children Who Speak of Memories of a Previous Life as a Buddhist Monk: Three New Cases." *Journal of the Society for Psychical Research* 63: 268–291.

Haraldsson, E., and Stevenson, I. (1974). "An Experiment with the Icelandic Medium Hafsteinn Björnsson." *Journal of the American Society for Psychical Research* 68: 192–202.

———. (1975a). "A Communicator of the 'Drop in' Type in Iceland: The Case of Gudni Magnusson." *Journal of the American Society for Psychical Research* 69: 245–261.

———. (1975b). "A Communicator of the 'Drop in' Type in Iceland: The Case of Runolfur Runolfsson." *Journal of the American Society for Psychical Research* 69: 33–59.

Harris, M. (1986). *Investigating the Unexplained*. New York: Prometheus Books.

Harrison, J. (1976). "Religion and Psychical Research." In S. C. Thakur (ed.), *Philosophy and Psychical Research*. New York: Humanities Press: 97–121.

Hart, H. (1956). "Six Theories about Apparitions." *Proceedings of the Society for Psychical Research* 50: 153–239.

Hartshorne, C., Weiss, P., and Burks, A. (eds.). (1931-1958). *Collected Papers of Charles Sanders Peirce*, 8 vols. Cambridge, MA: Belknap Press.

Hastings, A. (1991). *With the Tongues of Men and Angels: A Study of Channeling*. Fort Worth: Holt, Rinehart & Winston.

Heil, J. (1978). "Traces of Things Past." *Philosophy of Science* 45: 60–67.

———. (1979). "Making Things Simple." *Critica* 11: 3–33.

———. (1981). "Does Cognitive Psychology Rest on a Mistake?" *Mind* 90: 321–342.

———. (1983). *Perception and Cognition*. Berkeley: University of California Press.

Hermelin, B., O'Connor, N., and Lee, S. (1987). "Musical Inventiveness of Five Idiot Savants." *Psychological Medicine* 17: 685–694.

Hick, J. (1976). *Death and Eternal Life*. London: Collins.

Hilgard, E. R. (1986). *Divided Consciousness: Multiple Controls in Human Thought and Action* (expanded edition). New York: Wiley-Interscience.

Hodgson, R. (1892). "A Record of Observations of Certain Phenomena of Trance." *Proceedings of the Society for Psychical Research* 8: 1–167.

———. (1898). "A Further Record of Observations of Certain Phenomena of Trance." *Proceedings of the Society for Psychical Research* 13: 284–582.

———. (1901). "Report of Meeting of S.P.R." *Journal of the Society for Psychical Research* 10: 98–104.

Huby, P. M. (1976). "Some Aspects of the Problem of Survival." In S. C. Thakur (ed.), *Philosophy and Psychical Research*. New York: Humanities Press: 122–141.

Hughes, D. J. (1992). "Differences between Trance Channeling and Multiple Personality Disorder on Structured Interview." *Journal of Transpersonal Psychology* 24: 181–192.

Hyslop, J. H. (1909). "A Case of Veridical Hallucinations." *Proceedings of the American Society for Psychical Research* 3: 1–469.

———. (1917). "The Doris Fischer Case of Multiple Personality: Part III." *Proceedings of the American Society for Psychical Research* 11: 5–866.

Irwin, H. J. (1985). *Flight of Mind: A Psychological Study of the Out-of-Body Experience*. Metuchen, NJ: Scarecrow Press.

———. (2000). "The Disembodied Self: An Empirical Study of Dissociation and the Out-of-Body Experience." *Journal of Parapsychology* 64: 261–277.

James, W. (1886/1986). "Report of the Committee on Mediumistic Phenomena." In F. Burkhardt and F. Bowers (eds.), *The Works of William James, Vol 16: Essays in Psychical Research*. Cambridge, MA: Harvard University Press: 14–18.

———. (1890/1986). "A Record of Observation of Certain Phenomena of Trance." In F. Burkhardt and F. Bowers (eds.), *The Works of William James, Vol 16: Essays in Psychical Research*. Cambridge, MA: Harvard University Press: 79–88. Originally published in *Proceedings of the Society for Psychical Research* 6 (1909): 651–659.

———. (1896). "A Case of Psychic Automatism, Including 'Speaking with Tongues', by Albert Le Baron." *Proceedings of the Society for Psychical Research* 12: 277–297.

———. (1909/1986). "Report on Mrs. Piper's Hodgson-Control." In F. Burkhardt and F. Bowers (eds.), *The Works of William James, Vol. 16: Essays in Psychical Research*. Cambridge, MA: Harvard University Press: 253–360. Originally published in *Proceedings of the Society for Psychical Research* 23 (1909): 2–121.

———. (1978). *Pragmatism and the Meaning of Truth*. Cambridge, MA: Harvard University Press.

Johnson, A. (1914-15). "A Reconstruction of Some 'Concordant Automatisms'." *Proceedings of the Society for Psychical Research* 27: 1–156.

Johnston, M. (1992). "Reasons and Reductionism." *The Philosophical Review* 101: 589–618.

Kampman, R. (1976). "Hypnotically Induced Multiple Personality: An Experimental Study." *International Journal of Clinical and Experimental Hypnosis* 24: 215–227.

Kampman, R., and Hirvenoja, R. (1976). "Dynamic Relation of the Secondary Personality Induced by Hypnosis to the Present Personality." In F. H. Frankel and H. S. Zamansky (eds.), *Hypnosis at Its Bicentennial: Selected Papers*. New York: Plenum: 183–188.

Keen, M. (1999). "For and against the Survival Hypothesis." Paper presented at the Gwen Tate Lecture, The Society for Psychical Research, London, October 14, 1999.

Keil, J. (1991). "New Cases in Burma, Thailand, and Turkey: A Limited Field Study Replication of Some Aspects of Ian Stevenson's Research." *Journal of Scientific Exploration* 5: 27–59.

———. (1996). "Cases of the Reincarnation Type: An Evaluation of Some Indirect Evidence with Examples of 'Silent' Cases." *Journal of Scientific Exploration* 10: 467–485.

Kellehear, A. (1995). *Experiences near Death: Beyond Medicine and Religion*. Oxford: Oxford University Press.

Kenneson, C. (1998). *Musical Prodigies: Perilous Journeys, Remarkable Lives.* Portland, OR: Amadeus Press.

Kim, J. (1993). *Supervenience and Mind.* Cambridge: Cambridge University Press.

Krippner, S. (1987). "Cross-Cultural Approaches to Multiple Personality Disorder: Therapeutic Practices in Brazilian Spiritism." *Ethos* 15: 273–295.

Lashley, K. S. (1929). *Brain Mechanisms and Intelligence.* Chicago: University of Chicago Press.

———. (1950). "In Search of the Engram." *Symposia of the Society for Experimental Biology* 4: 454–482.

Lawrence, M. M. (1993). "Paranormal Experiences of Previously Unconscious Patients." In L. Coly and J. D. S. McMahon (eds.), *Parapsychology and Thanatology.* New York: Parapsychology Foundation, Inc.: 122–148.

Lewicki, D. R., Schaut, G. H., and Persinger, M. A. (1987). "Geophysical Variables and Behavior: XLIV. Days of Subjective Precognitive Experiences and the Days before the Actual Events Display Correlated Geomagnetic Activity." *Perceptual & Motor Skills* 65: 173–174.

Lewis-Fernández, R. (1994). "Culture and Dissociation: A Comparison of *Ataque de Nervios* among Puerto Ricans and Possession Syndrome in India." In D. Spiegel (ed.), *Dissociation: Culture, Mind, and Body.* Washington, DC: American Psychiatric Press, Inc.

Litvag, I. (1972). *Singer in the Shadows.* New York: Macmillan.

Lodge, O. (1916). *Raymond, or Life and Death.* London: Methuen.

MacKenzie, A. (1982). *Hauntings and Apparitions.* London: Heinemann.

Mackie, J. L. (1982). *The Miracle of Theism.* Oxford: Oxford University Press.

Maher, M. C. (2000). "Quantitative Investigation of the General Wayne Inn." *Journal of Parapsychology* 64: 365–390.

Maher, M. C., and Hansen, G. P. (1995). "Quantitative Investigation of a 'Haunted Castle' in New Jersey." *Journal of the American Society for Psychical Research* 89: 19–50.

Malcolm, N. (1977). *Memory and Mind.* Ithaca, NY: Cornell University Press.

———. (1980). "'Functionalism' in the Philosophy of Psychology." *Proceedings of the Aristotelian Society* 80: 211–229.

Markwick, B. (1978). "The Soal-Goldney Experiments with Basil Shackleton: New Evidence of Data Manipulation." *Proceedings of the Society for Psychical Research* 56: 250–277.

Martin, R., and Barresi, J. (eds.). (2003). *Personal Identity.* Oxford: Blackwell.

Martínez-Taboas, A. (1995). "The Use of the Dissociative Experiences Scales in Puerto Rico." *Dissociation* 8: 14–23.

May, E. C. (1995). "AC Technical Trials: Inspiration for the Target Entropy Concept." Paper presented at the 38th Annual Convention of the Parapsychological Association, August 5-8, Durham, NC.

———. (1996). "The American Institutes for Research Review of the Department of Defense's STAR GATE Program: A Commentary." *Journal of Scientific Exploration* 10: 89–107.

McDougall, W. (1906). "The Case of Sally Beauchamp." *Proceedings of the Society for Psychical Research* 19: 410–431.

McTaggart, J. M. E. (1930/1997). *Some Dogmas of Religion.* Bristol: Thoemmes Press.

Merricks, T. (1998). "There Are No Criteria of Identity over Time." *Noûs* 32: 106–124.

———. (2001). "How to Live Forever without Saving Your Soul: Physicalism and Immortality." In K. Corcoran (ed.), *Soul, Body, and Survival.* Ithaca, NY: Cornell

University Press: 183–200.

Messerschmidt, R. A. (1927-28). "Quantitative Investigation of the Alleged Independent Operation of Conscious and Subconscious Processes." *Journal of Abnormal and Social Psychology* 22: 325–340.

Middleton, W., and Butler, J. (1998). "Dissociative Identity Disorder: An Australian Series." *Australian and New Zealand Journal of Psychiatry* 32: 794–804.

Mills, A. (1989). "A Replication Study: Three Cases of Children in Northern India Who Are Said to Remember a Previous Life." *Journal of Scientific Exploration* 3: 133–184.

————. (1990a). "Moslem Cases of the Reincarnation Type in Northern India: A Test of the Hypothesis of Imposed Identification Part I: Analysis of 26 Cases." *Journal of Scientific Exploration* 4: 171–188.

————. (1990b). "Moslem Cases of the Reincarnation Type in Northern India: A Test of the Hypothesis of Imposed Identification Part II: Reports of Three Cases." *Journal of Scientific Exploration* 4: 189–202.

————. (1994). "Nightmares in Western Children: An Alternative Interpretation Suggested by Data in Three Cases." *Journal of the American Society for Psychical Research* 88: 309–325.

Mills, A., Haraldsson, E., and Keil, H. H. J. (1994). "Replication Studies of Cases Suggestive of Reincarnation by Three Independent Investigators." *Journal of the American Society for Psychical Research* 88: 207–219.

Moody, R. A. (1976). *Life after Life*. Harrisburg, PA: Stackpole Books.

Morelock, M. J., and Feldman, D. H. (1991). "Extreme Precocity." In N. Colangelo and G. A. Davis (eds.), *Handbook of Gifted Education*. Boston: Allyn and Bacon: 347–364.

Myers, F. W. H. (1889). "On Recognized Apparitions Occurring More Than a Year after Death." *Proceedings of the Society for Psychical Research* 6: 13–65.

————. (1890). "A Defence of Phantasms of the Dead." *Proceedings of the Society for Psychical Research* 6: 314–357.

————. (1900). "Pseudo-Possession." *Proceedings of the Society for Psychical Research* 15: 384–415.

————. (1903). *Human Personality and Its Survival of Bodily Death*. London: Longmans, Green, & Co.

Myers, F. W. H., *et al.* (1889-90). "A Record of Observations of Certain Phenomena of Trance." *Proceedings of the Society for Psychical Research* 6: 436–659.

Oakley, D. (1999). "Hypnosis and Conversion Hysteria: A Unifying Model." *Cognitive Neuropsychiatry* 4: 243–265.

O'Connell, D. N., Shor, R. E., and Orne, M. T. (1970). "Hypnotic Age Regression: An Empirical and Methodological Analysis." *Journal of Abnormal Psychology* 76 (Monograph Supplement No. 3): 1–32.

Orne, M. T. (1951). "The Mechanisms of Hypnotic Age Regression: An Experimental Study." *Journal of Abnormal and Social Psychology* 46: 213–225.

————. (1959). "The Nature of Hypnosis: Artifact and Essence." *Journal of Abnormal and Social Psychology* 58: 277–299.

————. (1962). "Hypnotically Induced Hallucinations." In L. J. West (ed.), *Hallucinations*. New York: Grune & Stratton: 211–219.

————. (1972). "On the Simulating Subject as a Quasi-control Group in Hypnosis Research: What, Why, and How." In E. Fromm and R. E. Shor (eds.), *Hypnosis: Developments in Research and New Perspectives*. Chicago: Aldine-Atherton: 399–443.

Osborne, L. (2001). "Regional Disturbances." The New York Times on the Web.: www.nytimes.com/2001/05/06/magazine/06LATAH.html

Osis, K., and Haraldsson, E. (1976). "OOBEs in Indian Swamis: Sathya Sai Baba and Dadaji." In J. D. Morris, W. G. Roll, and R. L. Morris (eds.), *Research in Parapsychology 1975*. Metuchen, NJ: Scarecrow Press: 147–150.

Osis, K., and McCormick, D. (1980). "Kinetic Effects at the Ostensible Location of an Out-of-Body Projection during Perceptual Testing." *Journal of the American Society for Psychical Research* 74: 319–329.

Osty, E. (1923). *Supernormal Faculties in Man*. London: Methuen.

Owen, I. M., and Sparrow, M. (1976). *Conjuring Up Philip: An Adventure in Psychokinesis*. New York: Harper & Row.

Pagenstecher, G. (1922). "Past Events Seership: A Study in Psychometry." *Proceedings of the American Society for Psychical Research* 16: 1–136.

Palmer, J. (1978). "Extrasensory Perception: Research Findings." In S. Krippner (ed.), *Advances in Parapsychological Research, Vol. 2: Extrasensory Perception*. New York: Plenum Press: 59–243.

Parrott, I. (1978). *The Music of Rosemary Brown*. London: Regency Press.

Pasricha, S. (1990a). *Claims of Reincarnation: An Empirical Study of Cases in India*. New Delhi: Harman.

———. (1990b). "Three Conjectured Features of Reincarnation-Type Cases in Northern India." *Journal of the American Society for Psychical Research* 84: 227–233.

———. (1992). "Are Reincarnation Type Cases Shaped by Parental Guidance? An Empirical Study Concerning the Limits of Parents' Influence on Children." *Journal of Scientific Exploration* 6: 167–180.

———. (1998). "Cases of the Reincarnation Type in Northern India with Birthmarks and Birth Defects." *Journal of Scientific Exploration* 12: 259–293.

Paterson, R. W. K. (1995). *Philosophy and the Belief in a Life after Death*. New York: St. Martin's Press, Inc.

Pearsall, P., Schwartz, G. E. R., and Russek, L. G. S. (1999). "Changes in Heart Transplant Recipients that Parallel the Personalities of Their Donors." *Integrative Medicine* 2 (2/3): 65–72.

Penelhum, T. (1970). *Survival and Disembodied Existence*. London: Routledge & Kegan Paul.

Perry, J. (ed.). (1975). *Personal Identity*. Berkeley: University of California Press.

———. (1978). *A Dialogue on Personal Identity and Immortality*. Indianapolis: Hackett Publishing Co.

Persinger, M. A. (1985). "Geophysical Variables and Behavior: XXX. Intense Paranormal Experiences Occur during Days of Quiet, Global, Geomagnetic Activity." *Perceptual & Motor Skills* 61: 320–322.

Persinger, M. A., and Cameron, R. A. (1986). "Are Earth Faults at Fault in Some Poltergeist-Like Episodes?" *Journal of the American Society for Psychical Research* 80: 49–73.

Persinger, M. A., Tiller, S. G., and Koren, S. A. (2000). "Experimental Simulation of a Haunt Experience and Elicitation of Paroxysmal Electroencephalographic Activity by Transcerebral Complex Magnetic Fields: Induction of a Synthetic Ghost?" *Perceptual & Motor Skills* 90: 659–674.

Pessoa, F. (1998). *The Book of Disquiet* (A. MacAdam, trans.). Boston: Exact Change.

Piddington, J. G. (1908). "A Series of Concordant Automatisms." *Proceedings of the Society for Psychical Research* 22: 19–440.

Piper, A. L. (1929). *The Life and Work of Mrs. Piper*. London: Kegan Paul, Trench, Trubner & Co.

Podmore, F. (1890). "Phantasms of the Dead from Another Point of View." *Proceedings of the Society for Psychical Research* 6: 229–313.

———. (1910/1975). *The Newer Spiritualism*. New York: Arno Press.

Pollack, J. H. (1964). *Croiset the Clairvoyant.* New York: Doubleday.

Pribram, K. (1971). *Languages of the Brain.* Englewood Cliffs, N.J.: Prentice Hall.

———. (1977). "Holonomy and Structure in the Organization of Perception." In U. M. Nicholas (ed.), *Images, Perception and Knowledge.* Dordrecht: Reidel:

Pribram, K., Nuwer, M., and Baron, R. U. (1974). "The Holographic Hypothesis of Memory Structure in Brain Function and Perception." In R. C. Atkinson, D. H. Krantz, R. C. Luce, and P. Suppes (eds.), *Contemporary Development in Mathematical Psychology.* San Francisco: Freeman:

Prince, W. F. (1915/16). "The Doris Case of Multiple Personality Parts I & II." *Proceedings of the American Society for Psychical Research* 9 & 10: 23–700; 701–1419.

———. (1921). "Psychometric Experiments with Señora Maria Reyes de Z." *Proceedings of the American Society for Psychical Research* 15: 189–314.

———. (1927/1964). *The Case of Patience Worth.* New Hyde Park, NY: University Books.

Puthoff, H. E. (1996). "CIA-Initiated Remote Viewing Program at Stanford Research Institute." *Journal of Scientific Exploration* 10: 63–76.

Putnam, F. W. (1989). *Diagnosis and Treatment of Multiple Personality Disorder.* New York: Guilford.

———. (1997). *Dissociation in Children and Adolescents: A Developmental Perspective.* New York: The Guilford Press.

Quine, W. V. O. (1963). "On Simple Theories of a Complex World." *Synthese* 15: 103–106.

Quinton, A. (1975). "The Soul." In J. Perry (ed.), *Personal Identity.* Berkeley: University of California Press: 53–72. Originally published in *The Journal of Philosophy* 59 (15) (1962): 393–409.

Radclyffe-Hall, M., and Troubridge, U. (1920). "On a Series of Sittings with Mrs. Osborne Leonard." *Proceedings of the Society for Psychical Research* 30: 339–554.

Radin, D. (1997). *The Conscious Universe: The Scientific Truth of Psychic Phenomena.* New York: Harper Edge.

Raikov, V. L. (1976). "The Possibility of Creativity in the Active Stage of Hypnosis." *International Journal of Clinical and Experimental Hypnosis* 24: 258–268.

Rhine, L. E. (1981). *The Invisible Picture: A Study of Psychic Experiences.* Jefferson, N.C.: McFarland & Co.

Richet, C. (1923/1975). *Thirty Years of Psychical Research.* New York: Macmillan/Arno Press.

———. (1924). "The Difficulty of Survival from the Scientific Point of View." *Proceedings of the Society for Psychical Research* 34: 107–113.

Richmond, K. (1936). "Preliminary Studies of the Recorded Leonard Material." *Proceedings of the Society for Psychical Research* 44: 17–52.

Rogo, D. S. (1987). *The Infinite Boundary: A Psychic Look at Spirit Possession, Madness, and Multiple Personality.* New York: Dodd, Mead & Co.

Rorty, A. O. (ed.). (1976). *The Identities of Persons.* Berkeley: University of California Press.

Ross, C. A. (1997). *Dissociative Identity Disorder: Diagnosis, Clinical Features, and Treatment of Multiple Personality.* New York: John Wiley & Sons.

Rossi, E. R., and Cheek, D. B. (1988). *Mind-body Therapy: Methods of Ideodynamic Healing in Hypnosis.* New York: W.W. Norton.

Roy, A. E. (1996). *The Archives of the Mind.* Essex: SNU Publications.

Saavedra-Aguilar, J. C., and Gomez-Jeria, J. S. (1989). "A Neurological Model for Near-Death Experiences." *Journal of Near-Death Studies* 7 (4): 205–222.

Sabom, M. (1998). *Light and Death.* Grand Rapids: Zondervan.

Sacks, O. (1985). *The Man Who Mistook His Wife for a Hat.* New York: Summit.

Sahay, K. K. N. (1927). *Reincarnation: Verified Cases of Rebirth after Death.* Bareilly, India: N.L. Gupta.

Salter, M. W. H. (1921). "A Further Report on Sittings with Mrs. Leonard." *Proceedings of the Society for Psychical Research* 32: 1–143.

———. (1926). "A Report on Some Recent Sittings with Mrs. Leonard." *Proceedings of the Society for Psychical Research* 36: 187–332.

———. (1930). "Some Incidents Occurring at Sittings with Mrs. Leonard Which May Throw Light on Their Modus Operandi." *Proceedings of the Society for Psychical Research* 39: 306–332.

Saltmarsh, H. F. (1929). "Report on the Investigation of Some Sittings with Mrs. Warren Elliott." *Proceedings of the Society for Psychical Research* 39: 47–184.

Sar, V., Yargic, L. I., and Tutkun, H. (1995). "Current Status of Dissociative Identity Disorder in Turkey." Paper presented at the Fifth International Spring Conference of the International Society for the Study of Dissociation, May, Amsterdam.

———. (1996). "Structured Interview Data on 35 Cases of Dissociative Identity Disorder in Turkey." *American Journal of Psychiatry* 153: 1329–1333.

Schiller, F. C. S. (1902). "Professor Flournoy's 'Nouvelles observations sur un Cas de Somnambullisme avec Glossolalie'." *Proceedings of the Society for Psychical Research* 17: 245–251.

———. (1928). "*The Case of Patience Worth: A Critical Study of Certain Unusual Phenomena*, by Walter Franklin Prince." *Proceedings of the Society for Psychical Research* 36: 573–576.

Schlick, M. (1936). "Meaning and Verification." *Philosophical Review* 45.

Schmeidler, G. R. (1994). "ESP Experiments 1978-1992: The Glass Is Half Full." In S. Krippner (ed.), *Advances in Parapsychological Research, Vol. 7.* Jefferson, NC: McFarland & Co.: 104–197.

Schmidt, H. (1975). "Toward a Mathematical Theory of Psi." *Journal of the American Society for Psychical Research* 69: 301–319.

———. (1976). "PK Effect on Pre-Recorded Targets." *Journal of the American Society for Psychical Research* 70: 267–291.

Schonberg, H. C. (1970). *The Lives of the Great Composers.* New York: W.W. Norton & Co.

Schouten, S., and Stevenson, I. (1998). "Does the Socio-Psychological Hypothesis Explain Cases of the Reincarnation Type?" *Journal of Nervous and Mental Disease* 186: 504–506.

Sidgwick, E. M. (1885). "Notes on the Evidence, Collected by the Society, for Phantasms of the Dead." *Proceedings of the Society for Psychical Research* 3: 69–150.

———. (1891). "On the Evidence for Clairvoyance." *Proceedings of the Society for Psychical Research* 7: 30–99.

———. (1911). "Review of Dr. Tanner's *Studies in Spiritism.*" *Proceedings of the Society for Psychical Research* 25: 102–108.

———. (1915). "A Contribution to the Study of the Psychology of Mrs. Piper's Trance Phenomena." *Proceedings of the Society for Psychical Research* 28: 1–657.

———. (1921). "An Examination of Book-Tests Obtained in Sittings with Mrs. Leonard." *Proceedings of the Society for Psychical Research* 31: 241–400.

———. (1922). "Phantasms of the Living. An Examination and Analysis of Cases of Telepathy between Living Persons Printed in the *Journal* of the Society since the Publication of the Book *Phantasms of the Living* by Gurney, Myers, and Podmore, in 1886." *Proceedings of the Society for Psychical Research* 33: 23–429.

Siegel, R. K. (1980). "The Psychology of Life after Death." *American Psychologist* 35: 911–931.

―――. (1981). "Accounting for "After Life" Experiences." *Psychology Today* 15 (1): 65–75.

Sinclair, U. (1930/1962). *Mental Radio*. Springfield, IL: Charles C. Thomas.

Smith, S. (1974). *The Book of James: Conversations from Beyond*. New York: G.P. Putnam's Sons.

Soal, S. G. (1925). "A Report on Some Communications through Mrs. Blanche Cooper." *Proceedings of the Society for Psychical Research* 35: 471–594.

Society for Psychical Research (1894). "Report on the Census of Hallucinations." *Proceedings of the Society for Psychical Research* 10: 25–422.

―――. (1923). "On the Element of Chance in Book-Tests." *Proceedings of the Society for Psychical Research* 33: 606–620.

Somer, E. (1997). "Paranormal and Dissociative Experiences in Middle-Eastern Jews in Israel: Diagnostic and Treatment Dilemmas." *Dissociation* 10: 174–181.

Spiegel, H., and Spiegel, D. (1978). *Trance and Treatment: Clinical Uses of Hypnosis*. New York: Basic Books.

Spottiswoode, S. J. P. (1997). "Apparent Association between Effect Size in Free Response Anomalous Cognition Experiments and Local Sidereal Time." *Journal of Scientific Exploration* 11: 109–122.

Stanley, J., and Williamson, T. (2001). "Knowing How." *Journal of Philosophy* 98 (8): 411–444.

Steinberg, M. (1990). "Transcultural Issues in Psychiatry: The Ataque and Multiple Personality Disorder." *Dissociation* 3: 31–33.

Stevens, E. W. (1887). *The Watseka Wonder: A Narrative of Startling Phenomena Occurring in the Case of Mary Lurancy Vennum*. Chicago: Religio-Philosophical Publishing House.

Stevenson, I. (1970). "A Communicator Unknown to Medium and Sitters: The Case of Robert Passanah." *Journal of the American Society for Psychical Research* 64: 53–65.

Stevenson, I. (1972). "Some New Cases Suggestive of Reincarnation II. The Case of Bishen Chand." *Journal of the American Society for Psychical Research* 66: 375–400.

―――. (1973). "A Communicator of the 'Drop In' Type in France: The Case of Robert Marie." *Journal of the American Society for Psychical Research* 67: 47–76.

―――. (1974a). *Twenty Cases Suggestive of Reincarnation*, 2nd ed. rev. Charlottesville: University Press of Virginia.

―――. (1974b). *Xenoglossy: A Review and Report of a Case*. Charlottesville: University Press of Virginia.

―――. (1975). *Cases of the Reincarnation Type Vol. 1: Ten Cases in India*. Charlottesville: University Press of Virginia.

―――. (1977). *Cases of the Reincarnation Type Vol. 2: Ten Cases in Sri Lanka*. Charlottesville: University Press of Virginia.

―――. (1980). *Cases of the Reincarnation Type Vol. 3: Twelve Cases in Lebanon and Turkey*. Charlottesville: University Press of Virginia.

―――. (1983). *Cases of the Reincarnation Type Vol. 4: Twelve Cases in Thailand and Burma*. Charlottesville: University Press of Virginia.

―――. (1984). *Unlearned Language: New Studies in Xenoglossy*. Charlottesville: University Press of Virginia.

―――. (1990). "Phobias in Children Who Claim to Remember Previous Lives." *Journal of Scientific Exploration* 4: 243–254.

―――. (1997a). *Reincarnation and Biology: A Contribution to the Etiology of Birthmarks and Birth Defects*. Westport, CT: Praeger.

———. (1997b). *Where Reincarnation and Biology Intersect.* Westport, CT: Praeger.
———. (2000a). "The Phenomenon of Claimed Memories of Previous Lives: Possible Interpretations and Importance." *Medical Hypotheses* 54: 652–659.
———. (2000b). "Unusual Play in Young Children Who Claim to Remember Previous Lives." *Journal of Scientific Exploration* 14: 557–570.
Stevenson, I., and Keil, J. (2000). "The Stability of Assessments of Paranormal Connections in Reincarnation-Type Cases." *Journal of Scientific Exploration* 14: 365–382.
Stevenson, I., and Pasricha, S. (1979). "A Case of Secondary Personality with Xenoglossy." *American Journal of Psychiatry* 136: 1591–1592.
———. (1980). "A Preliminary Report on an Unusual Case of the Reincarnation Type with Xenoglossy." *Journal of the American Society for Psychical Research* 74: 331–348.
Stevenson, I., Pasricha, S., and McLean-Rice, N. (1989). "A Case of the Possession Type in India With Evidence of Paranormal Knowledge." *Journal of Scientific Exploration* 3: 81–101.
Stevenson, I., and G. Samararatne. (1988). "Three New Cases of the Reincarnation Type in Sri Lanka with Written Records Made before Verifications." *Journal of Scientific Exploration* 2: 217–238.
Suryani, L. K., and Jensen, G. D. (1993). *Trance and Possession in Bali.* Oxford: Oxford University Press.
Sylvia, C. (1997). *A Change of Heart: A Memoir.* New York: Warner Books.
Takahashi, Y. (1990). "Is Multiple Personality Disorder Really Rare in Japan?" *Dissociation* 3: 57–59. Commentaries and response: 60–69.
Tandy, V. (2000). "Something in the Cellar." *Journal of the Society for Psychical Research* 64: 129–140.
Tandy, V., and Lawrence, T. R. (1998). "The Ghost in the Machine." *Journal of the Society for Psychical Research* 62: 360–364.
Tanner, A. E. (1910). *Studies in Spiritism.* New York: Appleton.
Tarazi, L. (1990). "An Unusual Case of Hypnotic Regression with Some Unexplained Contents." *Journal of the American Society for Psychical Research* 84: 309–344.
———. (1997). *Under the Inquisition: An Experience Relived.* Charlottesville, VA: Hampton Roads.
Targ, R. (1996). "Remote Viewing at Stanford Research Institute in the 1970s: A Memoir." *Journal of Scientific Exploration* 10: 77–88.
Targ, R., and Puthoff, H. E. (1977). *Mind-Reach: Scientists Look at Psychic Ability.* New York: Delacorte.
Targ, R., Puthoff, H. E., and May, E. C. (1979). "Direct Perception of Remote Geographical Locations." In C. T. Tart, H. E. Puthoff, and R. Targ (eds.), *Mind at Large.* New York: Praeger: 77–106.
Tart, C. T. (1983). "Initial Integrations of Some Psychedelic Understandings into Everyday Life." In L. Grinspoon and J. Bakalar (eds.), *Psychedelic Reflections.* New York: Human Sciences Press: 223–233.
Thomas, C. D. (1932-33). "A Consideration of a Series of Proxy Sittings." *Proceedings of the Society for Psychical Research* 41: 139–185.
———. (1935). "A Proxy Case Extending over Eleven Sittings with Mrs. Osborne Leonard." *Proceedings of the Society for Psychical Research* 43: 439–519.
———. (1938-39). "A Proxy Experiment of Significant Success." *Proceedings of the Society for Psychical Research* 45: 257–306.
———. (1939). "A New Type of Proxy Case." *Journal of the Society for Psychical Research* 31: 103–106, 120–123.
Thomas, J. F. (1937). *Beyond Normal Cognition: An Evaluative and Methodological*

Study of the Mental Content of Certain Trance Phenomena. Boston: Boston Society for Psychical Research.

Thouless, R. H. (1959). "Review of R. Heywood, *The Sixth Sense: An Enquiry into Extra-sensory Perception*." *Journal of the Society for Psychical Research* 40: 140–142.

Treffert, D. A. (1989). *Extraordinary People: Understanding "Idiot Savants."* New York: Harper & Row.

Tucker, J. B. (2000). "A Scale to Measure the Strength of Childrens' Claims of Previous Lives: Methodology and Initial Findings." *Journal of Scientific Exploration* 14: 571–581.

Tutkun, H., *et al.* (1998). "Frequency of Dissociative Disorders among Psychiatric Inpatients in a Turkish University Clinic." *American Journal of Psychiatry* 155: 800–805.

Tutkun, H., Yargic, L. I., and Sar, V. (1995). "Dissociative Identity Disorder: A Clinical Investigation of 20 Cases in Turkey." *Dissociation* 8: 3–9.

Tyrrell, G. N. M. (1938/1961). *Science and Psychical Phenomena*. New Hyde Park, NY: University Books. Published with Tyrrell, 1942/1961.

———. (1939). "A Communicator Introduced in Automatic Script." *Journal of the Society for Psychical Research* 31: 91–95.

———. (1942/1961). *Apparitions*. New Hyde Park, NY: University Books. Published with Tyrrell, 1938/1961.

Ullman, M., Krippner, S., and Vaughan, A. (1989). *Dream Telepathy: Experiments in Nocturnal ESP*. (second ed.). Jefferson, NC: McFarland & Co.

Varma, V. K., Bouri, M., and Wig, N. N. (1981). "Multiple Personality in India: Comparison with Hysterical Possession State." *American Journal of Psychotherapy* 35: 113–120.

Venn, J. (1986). "Hypnosis and the Reincarnation Hypothesis: A Critical Review and Intensive Case Study." *Journal of the American Society for Psychical Research* 80: 409–425.

Verrall, H. d. G. M. W. H. S. (1910). "Report on the Junot Sittings with Mrs. Piper." *Proceedings of the Society for Psychical Research* 24: 351–664.

———. (1911). "The Element of Chance in Cross-Correspondences." *Journal of the Society for Psychical Research* 15: 153–172.

Viscott, D. S. (1969). "A Musical Idiot Savant." *Psychiatry* 32: 494–515.

Walters, J., and Gardner, H. (1986). "The Crystallizing Experience: Discovering an Intellectual Gift." In R. J. Sternberg and J. E. Davidson (eds.), *Conceptions of Giftedness*. Cambridge: Cambridge University Press: 306–331.

Warcollier, R. (1938/1975). *Experimental Telepathy*. New York: Arno Press.

West, D. (2000). "Correspondence: The Gordon Davis Precognitive 'Communications'." *Journal of the Society for Psychical Research* 64: 252–254.

West, D. J. (1948). "Investigation of a Case of Xenoglossy." *Journal of the Society for Psychical Research* 34: 267–269.

Wheatley, J. M. O. (1998). "Review of *The Limits of Influence* (rev. ed.) by Stephen E. Braude." *Journal of the American Society for Psychical Research* 92: 291-297.

White, L., Tursky, B., and Schwartz, G. E. (eds.). (1985). *Placebo: Theory, Research, and Mechanisms*. New York: The Guilford Press.

Winkelman, M. (1980). "The Effects of Schooling and Formal Education upon Extrasensory Abilities." In W. G. Roll and J. Beloff (eds.), *Research in Parapsychology 1980*. Metuchen, NJ: Scarecrow Press: 26–29.

Winkelman, M. (1981). "The Effects of Formal Education on Extrasensory Abilities: The Ozolco Study." *Journal of Parapsychology* 45: 321–336.

Wisdom, J. (1952). *Other Minds*. Oxford: Blackwell.

Woodhouse, M. B. (1994a). "Discussion of Out-of-Body Experiences and the Mind-

Body Problem: A Reply to Braude, Grim, and Blackmore." *New Ideas in Psychology* 12: 31–37.

———. (1994b). "Out-of-Body Experiences and the Mind-Body Problem." *New Ideas in Psychology* 12: 1–16.

Worth, P. (1917). *The Sorry Tale*. New York: Henry Holt & Co.

———. (1918). *Hope Trueblood*. New York: Henry Holt & Co.

Yargic, L. I., Tutkun, H., and Sar, V. (1995). "Reliability and Validity of the Turkish Version of the Dissociative Experiences Scale." *Dissociation* 8: 10–13.

Zaleski, C. G. (1988). *Otherworld Journeys: Accounts of Near-Death Experience in Medieval and Modern Times*. Oxford: Oxford University Press.

Zenith, R. (ed.). (1998). *Fernando Pessoa & Co.: Selected Poems*. New York: Grove Press.

Zorab, G. (1940). "A Case for Survival." *Journal of the Society for Psychical Research* 31: 142–152.

———. (1962). "Cases of the Chaffin Will Type and the Problem of Survival." *Journal of the Society for Psychical Research* 41: 407–417.

Zorab, G., and MacKenzie, A. (1980). "A Modern Haunting." *Journal of the Society for Psychical Research* 50: 284–293.

Zoroglu, S., *et al.* (1996). "Dissociative Identity Disorder in Childhood: Five Turkish Cases." *Dissociation* 9: 253–260.

Index

abilities, 9, 30, 85, 81, 86–87, 90,
  114–132, 179
  athletic, 81, 87, 89, 118, 206, 279
  childrens', inhibition of, 126–127
  domain-specificity, 152–156
  improvisational, 134, 145, 151, 159,
    163, 171
  latent, 11, 24, 102, 117–118, 122,
    124, 131, 151–152, 154, 159–161,
    165–166, 171–174, 190–191, 205,
    207, 302
  linguistic, 9, 17, 24, 103–132,
    161–166, 186, 200, 204–205
  literary, 117, 133–175
  mathematical, 25, 120, 117, 126,
    152–154, 179
  musical, 9, 24, 87, 89, 114, 117–120,
    152, 154, 156, 159, 166–168, 179,
    186, 198, 206
  nature of, 17, 23–25, 81, 87,
    118–119, 126–127, 151–155
  need for practice, 24–25, 115–119,
    122, 159, 168
  situation-sensitivity, 80, 205–206
  visual arts, in, 117, 152–153,
    168–169, 179, 207–216
Ackermann, R., 301
Akolkar, V.V., 102, 104–113, 132
Allison, L.W., 78–79
Almeder, R., 3, 14–20, 231, 246–247,
  250, 257–260, 271, 281, 287,
  298–301, 303
alter personalities, 110, 112–113, 117,
  131, 158–162, 170, 173, 205, 277
Alvarado, C., 247, 279
American Society for Psychical Research
  (ASPR), 41
Anderson, R.I., 104
animism, 247–248, 257–258, 260, 264,
  266, 282
antecedent probability, 314, 315
"Antonia" case, 190–198, 207, 222–224
apparitions, 22, 226–235, 251, 260–269,
  276, 281–282, 302, 304

clothing of, 261–262, 266–269, 281
collective, 227–228, 234, 264, 266
reciprocal, 245, 248, 259–269, 276,
  281–282;
  See also Ghosts, Haunting
apports, 235
astral body, 245, 248, 258, 266–269,
  291, 293, 299
Aune, B., 6
automatic writing, 53, 57–58, 97, 112,
  124, 139, 145, 151–152, 161–166
Ayer, A.J., 30

Bacon, Kevin, 100
Bakalar, J., 279
Balfour, G.W., 95
Barker, S.F., 301
Baron, R.U., 292
Barresi, J., 4
Barrett, W.F., 19, 67, 100
Barrington, M.R., 206, 224
Basmajian, J., 11, 52
Battle, A.O. 132
Baumgarten, F., 153
Beach, F. A., 291
Bennie Junot, case of, 61–62
Berger, D., 132, 244
Berger, R.E., 75–76
Besterman, T., 80, 213
Bialystok, E., 120–122
bilocation, 282
Bishen Chand, case of, 183–187, 222
biofeedback, 11, 38, 52
birthmarks, 179, 181, 187, 221
Bishai, D., 292
Bjornsson, H., 44–51, 83, 125, 222
Blanche Poynings, case of, 195
book–tests, 72–78
Bouri, M., 132, 244
Broad, C.D., 14, 20, 30, 33, 53–54, 110,
  246–249, 252, 263, 265, 282,
  294–295, 297
Broughton, R.S., 29
Brown, D., 10

323

About the Author

Stephen E. Braude is professor of philosophy and chairman of the philosophy department at the University of Maryland Baltimore County. He studied philosophy and English at Oberlin College and the University of London, and in 1971 he received his Ph.D. in philosophy from the University of Massachusetts at Amherst.

After publishing a number of articles in the philosophy of language, temporal logic, and the philosophy of time, he turned his attention to several related problems in the philosophy of science and the philosophy of mind—in particular, questions concerning causality, scientific explanation generally, and psychological explanation specifically. One of his overriding concerns was to demonstrate the inadequacy of mechanistic theories in psychology and cognitive science. He also examined the evidence of parapsychology to see whether it would provide new insights into these and other traditional philosophical issues. After that, he shifted his focus to problems in philosophical psychopathology, writing extensively on the connections between dissociation and classic philosophical problems as well as central issues in parapsychology—for example, the unity of consciousness, multiple personality and moral responsibility, and the nature of mental mediumship.

Prof. Braude is past president of the Parapsychological Association and the recipient of several grants and fellowships, including research fellowships from the National Endowment for the Humanities and the BIAL Foundation in Portugal. He has published more than fifty philosophical essays in such journals as *Noûs; The Philosophical Review; Philosophical Studies; Analysis; Inquiry; Philosophia; Philosophy, Psychiatry and Psychology; The Journal of Scientific Exploration;* and *The Journal of Trauma and Dissociation.* His three previous books are *ESP and Psychokinesis: A Philosophical Examination; The Limits of Influence: Psychokinesis and the Philosophy of Science;* and *First Person Plural: Multiple Personality and the Philosophy of Mind.* He is also a professional pianist and composer and a prize-winning stereo photographer.